2018 U.S. INDUSTRY & MARKET OUTLOOK

NATIONAL EDITION

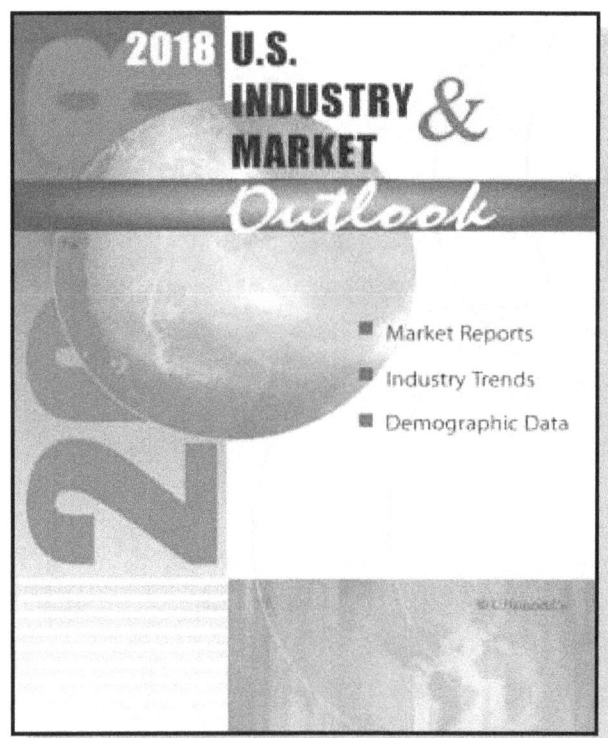

The 2018 U.S. Industry & Market Outlook report is the leading annual publication that describes over 100 major U.S. industries and 500+ minor industries. Published each year in October, the Outlook report provides the most current and accurate estimates of the size of the largest manufacutring, retail, wholesale and services industries in the United States.

With over 250 pages, the National edition of the 2018 U.S. Industry & Market Outlook features:

- 2018 establishments, employment and sales totals for each industry
- 2019 forecast establishments, employment and sales totals
- 5-year trend establishments and sales totals
- Industry financial ratios such as sales per employees, sales per establishment and employees per establishment
- 2018 establishments and sales totals for 500+ minor industries
- Industry definitions and descriptions

The 2018 U.S. Industry & Market Outlook report is available in the Barnes Reports' online subscription service.

The Outlook report is available for purchase in either PDF, spreadsheet (Excel) or print format edition.

The 2018 U.S. Industry & Market Outlook report is an essential reference tool for industry researchers, market analysts, CEOs and leading industry executives.

Copyright © 2017 By C. Barnes & Co.

Printed in USA

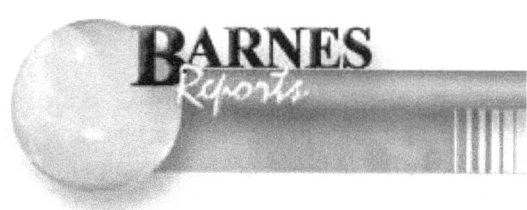

2018 U.S. Industry & Market Outlook

Copyright © 2017 By C. Barnes & Co.
Printed in USA

All rights reserved. This publication may not be reproduced, stored in any information or retrieval system or transmitted in whole or in part, in any form or by any means - electronic, mechanical, photocopying, recording or otherwise - without the express written permission of C. Barnes & Co.

Note: Every effort has been made to verify and ensure the accuracy of the information within this publication. However, if any errors exist in this publication C. Barnes & Co. disclaims any liability for any loss or damage to any party as a result of the information or errors in this publication.

2018 U.S. INDUSTRY & MARKET OUTLOOK

TABLE OF CONTENTS

INDUSTRY	PAGE NUMBER
Construction	
Single-Family Housing Construction Industry	7
Electrical Contractors Industry	9
Plumbing & Heating & A/C Contractors	11
Carpentry Contractors Industry	13
Manufacturing	
Breakfast Cereal Manufacturing Industry	15
Frozen Food Manufacturing Industry	17
Cookie Cracker & Pasta Mfg. Industry	19
Snack Food Manufacturing Industry	21
Soft-Drink Manufacturing Industry	23
Breweries & Beer-Making Industry	25
Wineries & Wine-Making Industry	27
Distilleries & Alcohol-Making Industry	29
Men's & Boys' Apparel Mfg. Industry	31
Women's & Girls' Apparel Mfg. Industry	33
Paper Mills Industry	35
Printing Industry	37
Petroleum Refineries Industry	39
Petrochemical Manufacturing Industry	41
Pharmaceutical Preparation Mfg. Industry	43
Electronic Computer Manufacturing Industry	45
Telephone Equipment Mfg. Industry	47
Radio/TV Broadcast Equipment Industry	49
Audio & Visual Equipment Mfg. Industry	51
Semi-Conductor & Electronic Components Mfg.	53
Software Reproducing Industry	55
Major Appliance Manufacturing Industry	57
Automobile & Motor Vehicle Mfg. Industry	59
Heavy Duty Truck Mfg.	61
Automobile Gas Engine & Engine Parts Mfg.	63
Aircraft Manufacturing Industry	65
Kitchen Cabinet & Countertop Mfg. Industry	67
Household & Institutional Furniture Mfg.	69
Office Furniture Manufacturing Industry	71
Medical Equipment & Supplies Mfg. Industry	73
Sign Manufacturing	75

TABLE OF CONTENTS

INDUSTRY	PAGE NUMBER
Wholesales	
Automobile & Other Vehicles Wholesale	77
Motor Vehicle Parts & Supplies Wholesales	79
Furniture Wholesale Industry	81
Home Furnishings Wholesale Industry	83
Office Equipment Wholesales Industry	85
Computer & Equipment Wholesale Industry	87
Hardware Wholesale Industry	89
Printing & Writing Paper Wholesales	91
Men's & Boys' Clothing Wholesales Industry	93
Women's & Children's Clothing Wholesale	95
General-Line Grocery Wholesale Industry	97
Beer & Ale Wholesale Industry	99
Wine & Alcoholic Beverages Wholesales	101
Book/Periodical/Newspaper Wholesales	103
Retail	
New Car Dealers Industry	105
Furniture Stores Industry	107
Appliance/TV/Electronics Stores Industry	109
Computer & Software Stores Industry	111
Home Centers Industry	113
Hardware Stores Industry	115
Grocery Stores Industry	117
Beer & Wine & Liquor Stores Industry	119
Pharmacies & Drug Stores Industry	121
Gas Stations with Convenience Stores	123
Men's Clothing Stores Industry	125
Women's Clothing Stores Industry	127
Family Clothing Stores Industry	129
Book Stores Retailing Industry	131
Department Stores Industry	133
Warehouse Clubs & Superstores Industry	135
Office Supplies & Stationery Stores Industry	137
Electronic Shopping & Mail Order Houses	139

TABLE OF CONTENTS

INDUSTRY	PAGE NUMBER

Transportation & Warehouse

Scheduled Air Transportation Industry	141
Local Freight Trucking Industry	143
Freight Trucking Long Distance Industry	145
General Warehousing & Storage Industry	147

Information

Newspaper Publishing Industry	149
Periodical Publishing Industry	151
Book Publishing Industry	153
Database & Directory Publishing Industry	155
Software Publishing Industry	157
Motion Pictures & Video Production Industry	159
Music Publishing Industry	161
Radio Broadcasting Industry	163
Television Broadcasting Services Industry	165
Cable Television Networks Industry	167
Wired Telecommunications Carriers Industry	169
Wireless Telecommunications Carriers	171
Data Processing Services Industry	173

Finance & Insurance

Commercial Banking Industry	175
Mortgage & Non-Mortgage Loan Brokers	177
Investment Banking & Securities Dealing	179
Securities Brokerage Industry	181
Life Insurance Carriers Industry	183
Health & Medical Insurance Carriers	185
Property & Casualty Insurance Carriers	187
Insurance Agencies & Brokerages Industry	189

Real Estate

Offices of Real Estate Agents & Brokers	191
Real Estate Property Managers Industry	193

Professional Services

Offices of Lawyers Industry	195
Offices of Certified Public Accountants	197
Architectural Services Industry	199
Engineering Services Industry	201
Interior Design Services Industry	203
Graphic Designs Services Industry	205
Computer Systems Designs Services Industry	207

TABLE OF CONTENTS

INDUSTRY	PAGE NUMBER

Professional Services

Management Consulting Services Industry	209
Advertising Agencies Industry	211
Public Relations Agencies Industry	213
Direct Mail Advertising Industry	215
Marketing Research & Public Opinion Polling	217
Veterinary Services	219
Telemarketing Services Industry	221
Security Guards & Patrol Services Industry	223

Educational Services

Colleges & Universities Industry	225
Exam Preparation & Tutoring Industry	227
Educational Support Services Industry	229

Health Care Services

Offices of Physicians Industry	231
Offices of Dentists Industry	233
Medical Laboratories Industry	235
Home Health Care Services Industry	237
Medical & Surgical Hospitals Industry	239
Nursing Care Facilities Industry	241
Community Care Facilities for the Elderly	243

Arts & Recreation

Musical Groups & artists Industry	245
Spectator Sports Industry	247
Agents & Managers for Artists & Athletes	249
Golf Courses & Country Clubs Industry	251
Fitness & Recreational Sports Centers	253

Accomodation & Food

Hotels & Motels Industry	255
Full-Service Restaurants Industry	257
Fast Food Restaurants Industry	259
Drinking Places & Bars Industry	261

Appendix: Definitions & Terms	263

SINGLE-FAMILY HOUSING CONSTRUCTION INDUSTRY
(NAICS 236115)

NAICS 236115: Single-Family Housing Construction. This industry comprises establishments primarily responsible for the entire construction (i.e., new work, additions, alterations, and repairs) of single family residential housing units (e.g., single family detached houses, town houses, or row houses where each housing unit is separated by a ground-to-roof wall and where no housing units are constructed above or below). This industry includes establishments responsible for additions and alterations to mobile homes and on-site assembly of modular and prefabricated houses. Establishments identified as single family construction management firms are also included in this industry.

INDUSTRY ESTABLISHMENTS, SALES & EMPLOYMENT TRENDS

	Year					Percent Chg. Year-to-Year			
	2015	2016	2017	2018	2019	15-16	16-17	17-18	18-19
Establishments	100,940	102,838	105,715	106,059	106,139	1.9%	2.8%	0.3%	0.1%
Sales ($Millions)	66,168	68,833	72,635	74,962	77,389	4.0%	5.5%	3.2%	3.2%
Employment	267,055	272,077	279,688	280,597	280,809	1.9%	2.8%	0.3%	0.1%
Sales ($M)/Estab.	0.66	0.67	0.69	0.71	0.73	2.1%	2.7%	2.9%	3.2%
Sales ($)/Emp.	247,769	252,991	259,699	267,151	275,595	2.1%	2.7%	2.9%	3.2%

3-YEAR TREND – ESTIMATED NUMBER OF ESTABLISHMENTS

Year	Employee Size of Establishment									Total Employment
	1-4 Emps.	5-9 Emps.	10-19 Emps.	20-49 Emps.	50-99 Emps.	100-249 Emps.	250-499 Emps.	>500 Emps.	Non-Employer	
2017	41,768	7,163	2,595	927	128	49	8	2	53,075	105,715
2018	41,903	7,186	2,604	930	128	49	8	2	53,248	106,059
2019	41,935	7,191	2,606	931	128	49	8	2	53,288	106,139

3-YEAR TREND – ESTIMATED INDUSTRY SALES ($MILLIONS)

Year	Employee Size of Establishment									Total Employment
	1-4 Emps.	5-9 Emps.	10-19 Emps.	20-49 Emps.	50-99 Emps.	100-249 Emps.	250-499 Emps.	>500 Emps.	Non-Employer	
2017	25,829.5	11,642.0	10,607.9	10,027.8	3,038.7	3,155.1	1,810.1	830.4	5,693.4	72,634.8
2018	26,657.1	12,015.0	10,947.7	10,349.1	3,136.1	3,256.2	1,868.1	857.0	5,875.8	74,962.0
2019	27,520.4	12,404.0	11,302.3	10,684.2	3,237.6	3,361.7	1,928.6	884.7	6,066.1	77,389.5

3-YEAR TREND – ESTIMATED NUMBER OF EMPLOYEES

Year	Employee Size of Establishment									Total Employment
	1-4 Emps.	5-9 Emps.	10-19 Emps.	20-49 Emps.	50-99 Emps.	100-249 Emps.	250-499 Emps.	>500 Emps.	Non-Employer	
2017	104,419	41,543	35,295	27,899	7,590	6,207	2,437	1,224	53,075	279,688
2018	104,758	41,678	35,410	27,989	7,614	6,227	2,445	1,228	53,248	280,597
2019	104,838	41,709	35,437	28,010	7,620	6,232	2,447	1,229	53,288	280,809

Single-Family Housing Construction Industry
(NAICS 236115)

Sub-Industries – 2018 Estimated Industry Sales, Establishments & Employment

Sub-Industries	Category*	Establishments	Sales ($Mill)	Employment
Single-family housing construction	Major1	63,808	37,127.4	154,381
Single-family home remodeling, additions, and repairs	Minor1	3,837	2,913.3	11,692
General remodeling, single-family houses	Minor2	18,325	11,177.3	45,520
Mobile home repair, on site	Minor2	186	137.4	526
Patio and deck construction and repair	Minor2	510	349.0	1,619
Repairing fire damage, single-family houses	Minor2	236	534.1	2,766
New construction, single-family houses	Minor2	19,036	22,495.0	63,343
Prefabricated single-family house erection	Minor2	69	138.1	482
Townhouse construction	Minor2	51	90.4	268

*Category-Major categories (Major1) are more general descriptions for companies that self-selected to capture the many functions they perform in the industry. Minor categories (Minor1, Minor2) are more specific for companies that have more detailed functions (Minor1 is a larger category than Minor2). Minor categories figures (sales, etc.) can be aggregated to larger minor categories (Minor2 sums to Minor1) and major categories overall figures.

Electrical Contractors Industry
NAICS 23821

NAICS 23821: Electrical Contractors . This industry comprises establishments primarily engaged in one or more of the following: (1) performing electrical work at the site (e.g., installing wiring); (2) servicing electrical equipment at the site; and (3) the combined activity of selling and installing electrical equipment. The electrical work performed includes new work, additions, alterations, and maintenance and repairs.

Industry Establishments, Sales & Employment Trends

	Year					Percent Chg. Year-to-Year			
	2015	2016	2017	2018	2019	15-16	16-17	17-18	18-19
Establishments	123,422	126,356	130,634	134,529	136,848	2.4%	3.4%	3.0%	1.7%
Sales ($Millions)	128,014	139,639	153,979	168,892	182,932	9.1%	10.3%	9.7%	8.3%
Employment	791,917	810,743	838,192	863,184	878,063	2.4%	3.4%	3.0%	1.7%
Sales ($M)/Estab.	1.04	1.11	1.18	1.26	1.34	6.5%	6.7%	6.5%	6.5%
Sales ($)/Emp.	161,650	172,235	183,704	195,662	208,336	6.5%	6.7%	6.5%	6.5%

3-Year Trend – Estimated Number of Establishments

Year	Employee Size of Establishment									Total Employment
	1-4 Emps.	5-9 Emps.	10-19 Emps.	20-49 Emps.	50-99 Emps.	100-249 Emps.	250-499 Emps.	>500 Emps.	Non-Employer	
2017	46,357	13,430	8,105	5,373	1,671	844	185	80	54,588	130,634
2018	47,739	13,831	8,347	5,533	1,721	869	191	83	56,215	134,529
2019	48,562	14,069	8,491	5,628	1,751	884	194	84	57,184	136,848

3-Year Trend – Estimated Industry Sales ($Millions)

Year	Employee Size of Establishment									Total Employment
	1-4 Emps.	5-9 Emps.	10-19 Emps.	20-49 Emps.	50-99 Emps.	100-249 Emps.	250-499 Emps.	>500 Emps.	Non-Employer	
2017	13,727.7	10,453.3	15,864.7	27,833.9	19,032.8	25,892.1	19,161.7	17,603.8	4,409.1	153,979.1
2018	15,073.8	11,478.3	17,420.4	30,563.3	20,899.2	28,431.1	21,040.7	19,144.0	4,841.5	168,892.2
2019	16,337.1	12,440.3	18,880.4	33,124.7	22,650.7	30,813.8	22,804.1	20,633.8	5,247.2	182,932.1

3-Year Trend – Estimated Number of Employees

Year	Employee Size of Establishment									Total Employment
	1-4 Emps.	5-9 Emps.	10-19 Emps.	20-49 Emps.	50-99 Emps.	100-249 Emps.	250-499 Emps.	>500 Emps.	Non-Employer	
2017	115,893	77,897	110,235	161,716	99,273	106,374	53,882	58,335	54,588	838,192
2018	119,349	80,219	113,521	166,537	102,233	109,546	55,489	60,074	56,215	863,184
2019	121,406	81,602	115,478	169,408	103,995	111,434	56,445	61,109	57,184	878,063

© Barnes Reports: 2018 U.S. Industry & Market Outlook

Electrical Contractors Industry
NAICS 23821

Sub-Industries – 2018 Estimated Industry Sales, Establishments & Employment

Sub-Industries	Category*	Establishments	Sales ($Mill)	Employment
Electrical work	Major1	80,701	60,238.8	362,668
Electric power systems contractors	Minor1	940	9,038.6	9,201
Cogeneration specialization	Minor2	32	46.7	835
Computer power conditioning	Minor2	32	32.8	142
Standby or emergency power specialization	Minor2	63	74.8	545
Switchgear and related devices installation	Minor2	34	143.1	492
Electronic controls installation	Minor1	1,134	1,664.5	8,626
Computerized controls installation	Minor2	142	800.8	2,253
Energy management controls	Minor2	709	2,365.4	6,934
Environmental system control installation	Minor2	188	1,230.3	2,065
Communications specialization	Minor1	1,972	3,815.9	19,946
Cable television installation	Minor2	711	1,255.0	9,090
Fiber optic cable installation	Minor2	789	1,600.0	8,521
Sound equipment specialization	Minor2	4,471	1,330.0	9,312
Telephone and telephone equipment installation	Minor2	2,334	3,640.9	19,978
Voice, data, and video wiring contractor	Minor2	619	1,143.1	6,343
Safety and security specialization	Minor1	1,560	1,571.6	12,319
Access control systems specialization	Minor2	253	477.3	2,155
Closed circuit television installation	Minor2	120	173.5	1,067
Fire detection and burglar alarm systems specialization	Minor2	3,183	3,819.6	27,713
Banking machine installation and service	Minor2	106	198.6	988
Computer installation	Minor2	777	757.2	4,451
General electrical contractor	Minor2	32,891	72,053.6	341,356
Lighting contractor	Minor2	767	1,420.2	6,184

*Category-Major categories (Major1) are more general descriptions for companies that self-selected to capture the many functions they perform in the industry. Minor categories (Minor1, Minor2) are more specific for companies that have more detailed functions (Minor1 is a larger category than Minor2). Minor categories figures (sales, etc.) can be aggregated to larger minor categories (Minor2 sums to Minor1) and major categories overall figures.

PLUMBING & HEATING & A/C CONTRACTORS
NAICS 23822

NAICS 23822: Plumbing & Heating & A/C Contractors. This industry comprises establishments primarily engaged in one or more of the following: (1) installing plumbing, heating, and air-conditioning equipment; (2) servicing plumbing, heating, and air-conditioning equipment; and (3) the combined activity of selling and installing plumbing, heating, and air-conditioning equipment. The plumbing, heating, and air-conditioning work performed includes new work, additions, alterations, and maintenance and repairs.

INDUSTRY ESTABLISHMENTS, SALES & EMPLOYMENT TRENDS

	Year					Percent Chg. Year-to-Year			
	2015	2016	2017	2018	2019	15-16	16-17	17-18	18-19
Establishments	140,401	145,448	152,273	158,171	162,291	3.6%	4.7%	3.9%	2.6%
Sales ($Millions)	161,262	174,862	192,221	209,747	226,351	8.4%	9.9%	9.1%	7.9%
Employment	962,567	997,167	1,043,959	1,084,395	1,112,639	3.6%	4.7%	3.9%	2.6%
Sales ($M)/Estab.	1.15	1.20	1.26	1.33	1.39	4.7%	5.0%	5.0%	5.2%
Sales ($)/Emp.	167,533	175,358	184,127	193,423	203,436	4.7%	5.0%	5.0%	5.2%

3-YEAR TREND – ESTIMATED NUMBER OF ESTABLISHMENTS

Year	Employee Size of Establishment									Total Employ-ment
	1-4 Emps.	5-9 Emps.	10-19 Emps.	20-49 Emps.	50-99 Emps.	100-249 Emps.	250-499 Emps.	>500 Emps.	Non-Employer	
2017	63,054	19,609	12,161	7,276	2,129	928	179	62	46,875	152,273
2018	65,496	20,368	12,632	7,558	2,211	964	186	64	48,690	158,171
2019	67,202	20,899	12,961	7,755	2,269	989	191	66	49,958	162,291

3-YEAR TREND – ESTIMATED INDUSTRY SALES ($MILLIONS)

Year	Employee Size of Establishment									Total Employ-ment
	1-4 Emps.	5-9 Emps.	10-19 Emps.	20-49 Emps.	50-99 Emps.	100-249 Emps.	250-499 Emps.	>500 Emps.	Non-Employer	
2017	19,446.7	15,895.2	24,790.3	39,260.2	25,251.3	29,677.4	19,280.7	14,159.6	4,459.4	192,220.8
2018	21,240.4	17,361.4	27,077.0	42,881.6	27,580.5	32,414.8	21,059.1	15,261.2	4,870.7	209,746.7
2019	22,936.5	18,747.7	29,239.1	46,305.8	29,782.8	35,003.2	22,740.8	16,335.2	5,259.6	226,350.8

3-YEAR TREND – ESTIMATED NUMBER OF EMPLOYEES

Year	Employee Size of Establishment									Total Employ-ment
	1-4 Emps.	5-9 Emps.	10-19 Emps.	20-49 Emps.	50-99 Emps.	100-249 Emps.	250-499 Emps.	>500 Emps.	Non-Employer	
2017	157,635	113,731	165,392	219,016	126,462	117,069	52,057	45,723	46,875	1,043,959
2018	163,741	118,136	171,798	227,500	131,360	121,603	54,073	47,494	48,690	1,084,395
2019	168,005	121,213	176,272	233,425	134,781	124,771	55,482	48,731	49,958	1,112,639

© Barnes Reports: 2018 U.S. Industry & Market Outlook

Plumbing & Heating & A/C Contractors
NAICS 23822

Sub-Industries – 2018 Estimated Industry Sales, Establishments & Employment

Sub-Industries	Category*	Establishments	Sales ($Mill)	Employment
Plumbing, heating, air-conditioning	Major1	21,426	27,254.4	143,132
Boiler and furnace contractors	Minor1	396	609.2	3,206
Boiler maintenance contractor	Minor2	156	2,714.3	1,964
Boiler setting contractor	Minor2	36	103.8	434
Heating systems repair and maintenance	Minor2	1,993	1,497.8	9,687
Hydronics heating contractor	Minor2	118	123.5	872
Plumbing contractors	Minor1	54,855	53,141.4	314,212
Septic system construction	Minor2	2,897	1,770.3	12,146
Sprinkler contractors	Minor1	1,616	1,618.2	11,726
Fire sprinkler system installation	Minor2	1,795	6,166.7	36,248
Irrigation sprinkler system installation	Minor2	1,605	2,119.8	12,523
Heating and air conditioning contractors	Minor1	27,942	39,534.7	163,366
Mechanical contractor	Minor2	10,873	30,520.1	137,870
Process piping contractor	Minor2	133	690.2	3,095
Solar energy contractor	Minor2	1,407	3,107.1	9,642
Ventilation and duct work contractor	Minor2	789	2,046.9	10,219
Warm air heating and air conditioning contractor	Minor2	26,942	33,281.1	195,084
Refrigeration contractor	Minor2	3,192	3,447.2	18,968

*Category-Major categories (Major1) are more general descriptions for companies that self-selected to capture the many functions they perform in the industry. Minor categories (Minor1, Minor2) are more specific for companies that have more detailed functions (Minor1 is a larger category than Minor2). Minor categories figures (sales, etc.) can be aggregated to larger minor categories (Minor2 sums to Minor1) and major categories overall figures.

CARPENTRY CONTRACTORS INDUSTRY
NAICS 23835

NAICS 23835: Carpentry Contractors. This industry comprises establishments primarily engaged in framing, carpentry, and finishing work. The carpentry work performed includes new work, additions, alterations, and maintenance and repairs. Activities performed by establishments in this industry range from the installation of doors and windows to paneling, steel framing work, and ship joinery.

INDUSTRY ESTABLISHMENTS, SALES & EMPLOYMENT TRENDS

	Year					Percent Chg. Year-to-Year			
	2015	2016	2017	2018	2019	15-16	16-17	17-18	18-19
Establishments	76,157	78,564	81,694	84,711	86,767	3.2%	4.0%	3.7%	2.4%
Sales ($Millions)	23,261	25,425	28,074	30,884	33,557	9.3%	10.4%	10.0%	8.7%
Employment	191,688	197,746	205,623	213,218	218,392	3.2%	4.0%	3.7%	2.4%
Sales ($M)/Estab.	0.31	0.32	0.34	0.36	0.39	6.0%	6.2%	6.1%	6.1%
Sales ($)/Emp.	121,348	128,575	136,530	144,849	153,653	6.0%	6.2%	6.1%	6.1%

3-YEAR TREND – ESTIMATED NUMBER OF ESTABLISHMENTS

Year	Employee Size of Establishment									Total Employment
	1-4 Emps.	5-9 Emps.	10-19 Emps.	20-49 Emps.	50-99 Emps.	100-249 Emps.	250-499 Emps.	>500 Emps.	Non-Employer	
2017	21,582	4,034	1,972	897	188	62	9	0	52,951	81,694
2018	22,379	4,183	2,044	930	195	65	9	0	54,907	84,711
2019	22,922	4,285	2,094	952	199	66	9	0	56,239	86,767

3-YEAR TREND – ESTIMATED INDUSTRY SALES ($MILLIONS)

Year	Employee Size of Establishment									Total Employment
	1-4 Emps.	5-9 Emps.	10-19 Emps.	20-49 Emps.	50-99 Emps.	100-249 Emps.	250-499 Emps.	>500 Emps.	Non-Employer	
2017	6,799.0	3,340.6	4,105.4	4,942.6	2,274.3	2,031.6	944.5	5.8	3,630.1	28,073.7
2018	7,479.7	3,675.0	4,516.5	5,437.4	2,502.0	2,235.0	1,039.0	6.2	3,993.5	30,884.3
2019	8,126.9	3,993.0	4,907.3	5,907.9	2,718.5	2,428.4	1,128.9	6.7	4,339.1	33,556.7

3-YEAR TREND – ESTIMATED NUMBER OF EMPLOYEES

Year	Employee Size of Establishment									Total Employment
	1-4 Emps.	5-9 Emps.	10-19 Emps.	20-49 Emps.	50-99 Emps.	100-249 Emps.	250-499 Emps.	>500 Emps.	Non-Employer	
2017	53,954	23,400	26,814	26,993	11,151	7,845	2,496	19	52,951	205,623
2018	55,947	24,264	27,804	27,990	11,563	8,135	2,589	20	54,907	213,218
2019	57,304	24,853	28,479	28,669	11,843	8,333	2,651	21	56,239	218,392

© Barnes Reports: 2018 U.S. Industry & Market Outlook

CARPENTRY CONTRACTORS INDUSTRY
NAICS 23835

SUB-INDUSTRIES — 2018 ESTIMATED INDUSTRY SALES, ESTABLISHMENTS & EMPLOYMENT

Sub-Industries	Category*	Establishments	Sales ($Mill)	Employment
Carpentry work	Major1	49,252	10,166.0	88,061
Cabinet and finish carpentry	Minor1	9,265	3,199.5	22,749
Cabinet building and installation	Minor2	6,346	2,560.2	18,743
Finish and trim carpentry	Minor2	3,533	1,169.8	9,190
Window and door installation and erection	Minor1	2,447	1,241.5	8,302
Garage door, installation or erection	Minor2	3,613	1,519.0	10,710
Window and door (prefabricated) installation	Minor2	3,293	2,860.2	14,760
Framing contractor	Minor2	6,415	7,124.3	33,922
Lightweight steel framing (metal stud) installation	Minor2	269	387.6	2,630
Ship joinery	Minor2	46	82.0	199
Store fixture installation	Minor2	233	574.2	3,951

*Category-Major categories (Major1) are more general descriptions for companies that self-selected to capture the many functions they perform in the industry. Minor categories (Minor1, Minor2) are more specific for companies that have more detailed functions (Minor1 is a larger category than Minor2). Minor categories figures (sales, etc.) can be aggregated to larger minor categories (Minor2 sums to Minor1) and major categories overall figures.

BREAKFAST CEREAL MANUFACTURING INDUSTRY
NAICS 31123

NAICS 31123: Breakfast Cereal Manufacturing. This industry comprises establishments primarily responsible for manufacturing cereal breakfast foods and related preparations, except breakfast bars. Establishments primarily engaged in manufacturing granola bars and other types of breakfast bars are classified in 2064.

INDUSTRY ESTABLISHMENTS, SALES & EMPLOYMENT TRENDS

	Year					Percent Chg. Year-to-Year			
	2015	2016	2017	2018	2019	15-16	16-17	17-18	18-19
Establishments	91	92	93	95	98	1.1%	1.7%	2.3%	2.5%
Sales ($Millions)	10,306	10,799	11,435	12,196	13,054	4.8%	5.9%	6.7%	7.0%
Employment	10,875	10,992	11,177	11,437	11,723	1.1%	1.7%	2.3%	2.5%
Sales ($M)/Estab.	113.73	117.92	122.78	127.98	133.64	3.7%	4.1%	4.2%	4.4%
Sales ($)/Emp.	947,643	982,492	1,023,020	1,066,383	1,113,534	3.7%	4.1%	4.2%	4.4%

3-YEAR TREND – ESTIMATED NUMBER OF ESTABLISHMENTS

Year	Employee Size of Establishment									Total Employment
	1-4 Emps.	5-9 Emps.	10-19 Emps.	20-49 Emps.	50-99 Emps.	100-249 Emps.	250-499 Emps.	>500 Emps.	Non-Employer	
2017	20	9	5	3	5	15	11	9	15	93
2018	20	9	5	3	5	16	12	9	15	95
2019	20	10	5	3	5	16	12	10	16	98

3-YEAR TREND – ESTIMATED INDUSTRY SALES ($MILLIONS)

Year	Employee Size of Establishment									Total Employment
	1-4 Emps.	5-9 Emps.	10-19 Emps.	20-49 Emps.	50-99 Emps.	100-249 Emps.	250-499 Emps.	>500 Emps.	Non-Employer	
2017	19.0	23.6	33.0	52.4	192.0	1,552.5	3,837.4	5,722.7	1.9	11,434.6
2018	20.2	25.2	35.2	55.9	204.8	1,656.0	4,093.1	6,103.9	2.0	12,196.4
2019	21.7	27.0	37.7	59.8	219.2	1,772.5	4,381.1	6,533.0	2.2	13,054.2

3-YEAR TREND – ESTIMATED NUMBER OF EMPLOYEES

Year	Employee Size of Establishment									Total Employment
	1-4 Emps.	5-9 Emps.	10-19 Emps.	20-49 Emps.	50-99 Emps.	100-249 Emps.	250-499 Emps.	>500 Emps.	Non-Employer	
2017	49	54	70	93	305	1,944	3,289	5,359	15	11,177
2018	50	55	72	95	312	1,989	3,365	5,484	15	11,437
2019	51	56	73	97	320	2,039	3,449	5,621	16	11,723

© Barnes Reports: 2018 U.S. Industry & Market Outlook

BREAKFAST CEREAL MANUFACTURING INDUSTRY
NAICS 31123

Sub-Industries – 2018 Estimated Industry Sales, Establishments & Employment

Sub-Industries	Category*	Establishments	Sales ($Mill)	Employment
Cereal breakfast foods	Major1	64	6,602.3	9,122
Coffee substitutes, made from grain	Minor2	4	0.7	29
Corn flakes: prepared as cereal breakfast food	Minor2	2	0.2	41
Corn, hulled: prepared as cereal breakfast food	Minor2	0	0.0	1
Granola and muesli, except bars and clusters	Minor2	5	1.0	146
Hominy grits: prepared as cereal breakfast food	Minor2	0	0.0	4
Infants' foods, cereal type	Minor2	6	2.1	90
Oatmeal: prepared as cereal breakfast food	Minor2	1	0.4	8
Rice: prepared as cereal breakfast food	Minor2	7	0.3	696
Soy: prepared as cereal breakfast food	Minor2	0	0.1	3
Wheat flakes: prepared as cereal breakfast food	Minor2	4	5,589.3	1,297

*Category-Major categories (Major1) are more general descriptions for companies that self-selected to capture the many functions they perform in the industry. Minor categories (Minor1, Minor2) are more specific for companies that have more detailed functions (Minor1 is a larger category than Minor2). Minor categories figures (sales, etc.) can be aggregated to larger minor categories (Minor2 sums to Minor1) and major categories overall figures.

Frozen Food Manufacturing Industry
NAICS 31141

NAICS 31141: Frozen Food Manufacturing. This industry comprises establishments primarily manufacturing frozen bakery products, except bread and bread-type rolls. Establishments primarily engaged in manufacturing frozen bread and bread-type rolls are classified in 2051.

Industry Establishments, Sales & Employment Trends

	Year					Percent Chg. Year-to-Year			
	2015	2016	2017	2018	2019	15-16	16-17	17-18	18-19
Establishments	1,374	1,401	1,437	1,451	1,467	2.0%	2.6%	0.9%	1.1%
Sales ($Millions)	28,947	30,220	31,860	33,208	34,748	4.4%	5.4%	4.2%	4.6%
Employment	75,108	76,586	78,546	79,285	80,168	2.0%	2.6%	0.9%	1.1%
Sales ($M)/Estab.	21.06	21.57	22.17	22.89	23.69	2.4%	2.8%	3.3%	3.5%
Sales ($)/Emp.	385,404	394,587	405,621	418,848	433,439	2.4%	2.8%	3.3%	3.5%

3-Year Trend – Estimated Number of Establishments

Year	Employee Size of Establishment									Total Employment
	1-4 Emps.	5-9 Emps.	10-19 Emps.	20-49 Emps.	50-99 Emps.	100-249 Emps.	250-499 Emps.	>500 Emps.	Non-Employer	
2017	113	78	79	130	91	111	60	48	727	1,437
2018	114	79	80	131	92	112	60	49	734	1,451
2019	115	80	81	132	93	113	61	49	742	1,467

3-Year Trend – Estimated Industry Sales ($Millions)

Year	Employee Size of Establishment									Total Employment
	1-4 Emps.	5-9 Emps.	10-19 Emps.	20-49 Emps.	50-99 Emps.	100-249 Emps.	250-499 Emps.	>500 Emps.	Non-Employer	
2017	47.9	87.5	222.9	962.5	1,484.5	4,874.7	8,834.9	15,293.6	51.5	31,859.9
2018	50.0	91.3	232.7	1,004.8	1,549.8	5,089.1	9,223.5	15,913.5	53.7	33,208.5
2019	52.4	95.7	243.9	1,053.4	1,624.6	5,335.0	9,669.2	16,617.5	56.3	34,748.1

3-Year Trend – Estimated Number of Employees

Year	Employee Size of Establishment									Total Employment
	1-4 Emps.	5-9 Emps.	10-19 Emps.	20-49 Emps.	50-99 Emps.	100-249 Emps.	250-499 Emps.	>500 Emps.	Non-Employer	
2017	282	455	1,081	3,903	5,404	13,978	17,340	35,374	727	78,546
2018	285	459	1,091	3,940	5,455	14,110	17,503	35,707	734	79,285
2019	288	464	1,103	3,984	5,516	14,267	17,698	36,105	742	80,168

© Barnes Reports: 2018 U.S. Industry & Market Outlook

FROZEN FOOD MANUFACTURING INDUSTRY
NAICS 31141

SUB-INDUSTRIES – 2018 ESTIMATED INDUSTRY SALES, ESTABLISHMENTS & EMPLOYMENT

Sub-Industries	Category*	Establishments	Sales ($Mill)	Employment
Frozen fruits and vegetables	Major1	217	2,695.1	5,237
Frozen fruits and vegetables	Minor1	42	1,053.2	4,402
Citrus pulp, dried	Minor2	15	31.0	44
Fruits, quick frozen and cold pack (frozen)	Minor2	89	3,211.4	6,911
Potato products, quick frozen and cold pack	Minor2	57	456.6	5,244
Vegetables, quick frozen & cold pack, excl. potato produc	Minor2	96	5,296.1	10,773
Fruit juices	Minor1	167	3,873.4	4,361
Fruit juices, frozen	Minor2	20	82.6	1,017
Frozen specialties, nec	Major1	376	7,110.1	21,919
Breakfasts, frozen and packaged	Minor2	24	2,183.9	799
Dinners, frozen and packaged	Minor2	41	2,538.5	5,231
Ethnic foods, nec, frozen	Minor2	104	1,248.1	4,712
Lunches, frozen and packaged	Minor2	6	111.2	141
Pizza, frozen	Minor2	131	2,668.6	6,771
Snacks, incl. onion rings, cheese sticks, etc.	Minor2	45	228.1	900
Spaghetti and meatballs, frozen	Minor2	1	2.8	6
Waffles, frozen	Minor2	19	417.2	339
Whipped topping, frozen	Minor2	1	0.7	478

*Category-Major categories (Major1) are more general descriptions for companies that self-selected to capture the many functions they perform in the industry. Minor categories (Minor1, Minor2) are more specific for companies that have more detailed functions (Minor1 is a larger category than Minor2). Minor categories figures (sales, etc.) can be aggregated to larger minor categories (Minor2 sums to Minor1) and major categories overall figures.

COOKIE CRACKER & PASTA MFG. INDUSTRY
NAICS 31182

NAICS 31182: Cookie Cracker & Pasta Mfg. This industry comprises establishments primarily manufacturing fresh cookies, crackers, pretzels, and similar `dry' bakery products. Establishments primarily engaged in producing other fresh bakery products are classified in 2051.

INDUSTRY ESTABLISHMENTS, SALES & EMPLOYMENT TRENDS

	Year					Percent Chg. Year-to-Year			
	2015	2016	2017	2018	2019	15-16	16-17	17-18	18-19
Establishments	1,581	1,592	1,613	1,634	1,658	0.7%	1.3%	1.3%	1.5%
Sales ($Millions)	22,600	23,696	25,087	26,572	28,228	4.9%	5.9%	5.9%	6.2%
Employment	49,097	49,441	50,097	50,748	51,496	0.7%	1.3%	1.3%	1.5%
Sales ($M)/Estab.	14.30	14.89	15.55	16.26	17.03	4.1%	4.5%	4.6%	4.7%
Sales ($)/Emp.	460,309	479,285	500,765	523,596	548,154	4.1%	4.5%	4.6%	4.7%

3-YEAR TREND – ESTIMATED NUMBER OF ESTABLISHMENTS

Year	Employee Size of Establishment									Total Employment
	1-4 Emps.	5-9 Emps.	10-19 Emps.	20-49 Emps.	50-99 Emps.	100-249 Emps.	250-499 Emps.	>500 Emps.	Non-Employer	
2017	251	132	126	149	71	78	44	22	740	1,613
2018	254	133	127	151	72	79	44	23	750	1,634
2019	258	135	129	153	73	80	45	23	761	1,658

3-YEAR TREND – ESTIMATED INDUSTRY SALES ($MILLIONS)

Year	Employee Size of Establishment									Total Employment
	1-4 Emps.	5-9 Emps.	10-19 Emps.	20-49 Emps.	50-99 Emps.	100-249 Emps.	250-499 Emps.	>500 Emps.	Non-Employer	
2017	136.7	188.5	451.9	1,419.9	1,496.5	4,378.9	8,350.5	8,611.9	52.2	25,087.0
2018	145.0	199.8	479.1	1,505.4	1,586.6	4,642.6	8,853.2	9,104.6	55.3	26,571.6
2019	154.2	212.5	509.6	1,600.9	1,687.3	4,937.3	9,415.2	9,651.8	58.8	28,227.5

3-YEAR TREND – ESTIMATED NUMBER OF EMPLOYEES

Year	Employee Size of Establishment									Total Employment
	1-4 Emps.	5-9 Emps.	10-19 Emps.	20-49 Emps.	50-99 Emps.	100-249 Emps.	250-499 Emps.	>500 Emps.	Non-Employer	
2017	628	763	1,707	4,484	4,243	9,779	12,764	14,989	740	50,097
2018	636	773	1,729	4,542	4,298	9,906	12,930	15,184	750	50,748
2019	645	785	1,755	4,609	4,361	10,052	13,120	15,408	761	51,496

© Barnes Reports: 2018 U.S. Industry & Market Outlook

COOKIE CRACKER & PASTA MFG. INDUSTRY
NAICS 31182

SUB-INDUSTRIES – 2018 ESTIMATED INDUSTRY SALES, ESTABLISHMENTS & EMPLOYMENT

Sub-Industries	Category*	Establishments	Sales ($Mill)	Employment
Cookies and crackers	Major1	259	1,400.6	7,236
Bakery products, dry	Minor2	190	1,996.2	2,841
Biscuits, dry	Minor2	19	6.7	3,916
Communion wafers	Minor2	3	43.1	71
Cones, ice cream	Minor2	54	106.3	1,302
Cookies	Minor2	507	15,906.7	19,524
Cracker meal and crumbs	Minor2	4	75.4	145
Crackers, dry, nec	Minor2	25	372.9	839
Matzoths	Minor2	4	0.7	102
Pretzels	Minor2	227	1,231.7	4,406
Rice cakes	Minor2	16	12.1	35
Rusk, machine made	Minor2	1	0.7	3
Soda crackers	Minor2	1	101.0	170
Sugar wafers	Minor2	1	6.7	16
Prepared flour mixes and doughs	Major1	114	1,451.6	4,467
Flours and flour mixes, from purchased flour	Minor1	18	270.1	1,133
Biscuit mixes, prepared: from purchased flour	Minor2	2	73.7	47
Blended flour: from purchased flour	Minor2	7	160.3	114
Bread and bread type roll mixes: from purchased flour	Minor2	26	20.2	836
Cake mixes, prepared: from purchased flour	Minor2	22	232.5	334
Doughnut mixes, prepared: from purchased flour	Minor2	20	226.8	551
Farina, except cereal breakfast food: from purchased flour	Minor2	4	8.7	30
Pancake mixes, prepared: from purchased flour	Minor2	22	59.2	90
Pizza mixes: from purchased flour	Minor2	7	121.3	103
Doughs and batters, from purchased flour	Minor1	9	221.0	424
Biscuit dough, prepared: from purchased flour	Minor2	13	1,713.0	489
Doughs, frozen or refrigerated: from purchased flour	Minor2	26	306.2	943
Pancake batter, frozen or refrigerated: from purchased flour	Minor2	4	24.6	32
Pizza doughs, prepared: from purchased flour	Minor2	28	421.7	551

*Category-Major categories (Major1) are more general descriptions for companies that self-selected to capture the many functions they perform in the industry. Minor categories (Minor1, Minor2) are more specific for companies that have more detailed functions (Minor1 is a larger category than Minor2). Minor categories figures (sales, etc.) can be aggregated to larger minor categories (Minor2 sums to Minor1) and major categories overall figures.

Snack Food Manufacturing Industry
NAICS 31191

NAICS 31191: Snack Food Manufacturing. This industry comprises establishments primarily responsible for manufacturing potato chips, corn chips, and similar snacks. Pretzels and crackers are classified in 2052; candy covered popcorn is classified in 2064; salted, roasted, cooked or canned nuts and seeds are classified in 2068; and packaged unpopped popcorn is classified in 2099.

Industry Establishments, Sales & Employment Trends

	Year					Percent Chg. Year-to-Year			
	2015	2016	2017	2018	2019	15-16	16-17	17-18	18-19
Establishments	6,590	6,617	6,686	6,803	6,934	0.4%	1.0%	1.8%	1.9%
Sales ($Millions)	34,752	36,379	38,442	40,906	43,651	4.7%	5.7%	6.4%	6.7%
Employment	52,297	52,511	53,058	53,988	55,030	0.4%	1.0%	1.8%	1.9%
Sales ($M)/Estab.	5.27	5.50	5.75	6.01	6.29	4.3%	4.6%	4.6%	4.7%
Sales ($)/Emp.	664,510	692,777	724,535	757,677	793,230	4.3%	4.6%	4.6%	4.7%

3-Year Trend – Estimated Number of Establishments

Year	Employee Size of Establishment									Total Employ-ment
	1-4 Emps.	5-9 Emps.	10-19 Emps.	20-49 Emps.	50-99 Emps.	100-249 Emps.	250-499 Emps.	>500 Emps.	Non-Employer	
2017	179	95	90	97	67	81	44	21	6,011	6,686
2018	182	97	92	99	68	83	44	22	6,117	6,803
2019	185	99	94	101	69	84	45	22	6,235	6,934

3-Year Trend – Estimated Industry Sales ($Millions)

Year	Employee Size of Establishment									Total Employ-ment
	1-4 Emps.	5-9 Emps.	10-19 Emps.	20-49 Emps.	50-99 Emps.	100-249 Emps.	250-499 Emps.	>500 Emps.	Non-Employer	
2017	152.1	213.5	508.3	1,451.3	2,193.3	7,165.2	12,980.5	13,295.7	482.2	38,442.0
2018	162.1	227.6	541.9	1,547.0	2,338.0	7,637.9	13,837.0	14,100.2	514.0	40,905.7
2019	173.3	243.3	579.3	1,654.0	2,499.7	8,166.2	14,794.1	14,991.6	549.5	43,651.1

3-Year Trend – Estimated Number of Employees

Year	Employee Size of Establishment									Total Employ-ment
	1-4 Emps.	5-9 Emps.	10-19 Emps.	20-49 Emps.	50-99 Emps.	100-249 Emps.	250-499 Emps.	>500 Emps.	Non-Employer	
2017	446	553	1,228	2,932	3,977	10,235	12,691	14,985	6,011	53,058
2018	454	563	1,250	2,983	4,047	10,414	12,913	15,248	6,117	53,988
2019	463	574	1,274	3,041	4,125	10,615	13,162	15,542	6,235	55,030

© Barnes Reports: 2018 U.S. Industry & Market Outlook

SNACK FOOD MANUFACTURING INDUSTRY
NAICS 31191

Sub-Industries – 2018 Estimated Industry Sales, Establishments & Employment

Sub-Industries	Category*	Establishments	Sales ($Mill)	Employment
Potato chips and similar snacks	Major1	3,296	40,351.2	32,447
Potato chips and other potato-based snacks	Minor1	1,088	371.4	8,126
Potato sticks	Minor2	30	1.8	45
Corn chips and other corn-based snacks	Minor1	408	21.8	5,021
Popcorn, already popped (except candy covered)	Minor2	484	14.8	537
Tortilla chips	Minor2	1,028	134.6	5,875
Cheese curls and puffs	Minor2	91	1.2	1,009
Onion fries	Minor2	45	0.4	13
Pork rinds	Minor2	333	8.4	915

*Category-Major categories (Major1) are more general descriptions for companies that self-selected to capture the many functions they perform in the industry. Minor categories (Minor1, Minor2) are more specific for companies that have more detailed functions (Minor1 is a larger category than Minor2). Minor categories figures (sales, etc.) can be aggregated to larger minor categories (Minor2 sums to Minor1) and major categories overall figures.

Soft Drink Mfg. (NAICS 312111)

NAICS 312111: Soft Drink Manufacturing
This U.S. industry comprises establishments primarily engaged in establishments primarily engaged in manufacturing soft drinks and carbonated waters. Fruit and vegetable juices are classified in 2032-2038; fruit syrups for flavoring are classified in 2087; and nonalcoholic cider is classified in 2099. Bottling natural spring waters is classified in 5149.

Industry Establishments, Sales & Employment Trends

	Year					Percent Chg. Year-to-Year			
	2015	2016	2017	2018	2019	15-16	16-17	17-18	18-19
Establishments	568	558	549	530	508	-1.7%	-1.6%	-3.5%	-4.0%
Sales ($Millions)	33,566	35,643	37,877	39,384	40,652	6.2%	6.3%	4.0%	3.2%
Employment	44,318	43,551	42,846	41,348	39,685	-1.7%	-1.6%	-3.5%	-4.0%
Sales ($M)/Estab.	59.13	63.89	69.01	74.36	79.97	8.1%	8.0%	7.7%	7.5%
Sales ($)/Emp.	757,398	818,414	884,018	952,503	1,024,378	8.1%	8.0%	7.7%	7.5%

3-Year Trend – Estimated Number of Establishments

Year	Employee Size of Establishment									Total Employ-ment
	1-4 Emps.	5-9 Emps.	10-19 Emps.	20-49 Emps.	50-99 Emps.	100-249 Emps.	250-499 Emps.	>500 Emps.	Non-Employer	
2017	89	36	42	49	63	133	50	8	79	549
2018	86	35	40	48	61	129	49	7	76	530
2019	82	33	39	46	58	124	47	7	73	508

3-Year Trend – Estimated Industry Sales ($Millions)

Year	Employee Size of Establishment									Total Employ-ment
	1-4 Emps.	5-9 Emps.	10-19 Emps.	20-49 Emps.	50-99 Emps.	100-249 Emps.	250-499 Emps.	>500 Emps.	Non-Employer	
2017	83.0	87.7	256.3	804.7	2,254.4	12,900.0	16,383.3	5,096.4	10.7	37,876.5
2018	86.2	91.1	266.3	835.8	2,341.7	13,399.6	17,017.8	5,334.5	11.1	39,384.1
2019	88.8	93.9	274.5	861.7	2,414.1	13,813.8	17,543.9	5,549.9	11.4	40,652.0

3-Year Trend – Estimated Number of Employees

Year	Employee Size of Establishment									Total Employ-ment
	1-4 Emps.	5-9 Emps.	10-19 Emps.	20-49 Emps.	50-99 Emps.	100-249 Emps.	250-499 Emps.	>500 Emps.	Non-Employer	
2017	222	207	565	1,484	3,733	16,824	14,624	5,107	79	42,846
2018	215	200	546	1,432	3,602	16,236	14,113	4,928	76	41,348
2019	206	192	524	1,375	3,457	15,583	13,545	4,730	73	39,685

SOFT DRINK MFG.
(NAICS 312111)

SUB-INDUSTRIES — 2018 ESTIMATED INDUSTRY SALES, ESTABLISHMENTS & EMPLOYMENT

Sub-Industries	Category*	Establishments	Sales ($Mill)	Employment
Bottled and canned soft drinks	Major1	208	28,675.3	14,233
Iced tea and fruit drinks, bottled and canned	Minor1	7	283.8	317
Fruit drinks (less than 100% juice): packaged in cans, etc	Minor2	10	110.0	245
Lemonade: packaged in cans, bottles, etc.	Minor2	2	34.4	17
Tea, iced: packaged in cans, bottles, etc.	Minor2	3	103.5	47
Pasteurized and mineral waters, bottled and canned	Minor1	14	46.0	366
Mineral water, carbonated: packaged in cans, bottles, etc	Minor2	21	278.7	605
Water, natural: packaged in cans, bottles, etc.	Minor2	48	278.0	1,043
Carbonated soft drinks, bottled and canned	Minor1	40	290.1	5,448
Carbonated beverages, nonalcoholic: pkged. in cans, bot	Minor2	56	4,422.5	4,861
Soft drinks: packaged in cans, bottles, etc.	Minor2	121	4,861.9	14,168

*Category-Major categories (Major1) are more general descriptions for companies that self-selected to capture the many functions they perform in the industry. Minor categories (Minor1, Minor2) are more specific for companies that have more detailed functions (Minor1 is a larger category than Minor2). Minor categories figures (sales, etc.) can be aggregated to larger minor categories (Minor2 sums to Minor1) and major categories overall figures.

Breweries & Beer-Making Industry
NAICS 31212

NAICS 31212: Breweries. This industry comprises establishments primarily engaged in brewing beer, ale, malt liquors, and nonalcoholic beer.

Industry Establishments, Sales & Employment Trends

	Year					Percent Chg. Year-to-Year			
	2015	2016	2017	2018	2019	15-16	16-17	17-18	18-19
Establishments	2,736	2,934	3,090	3,270	3,441	7.3%	5.3%	5.8%	5.3%
Sales ($Millions)	29,743	32,260	34,588	37,352	40,265	8.5%	7.2%	8.0%	7.8%
Employment	43,217	46,357	48,813	51,653	54,366	7.3%	5.3%	5.8%	5.3%
Sales ($M)/Estab.	10.87	10.99	11.19	11.42	11.70	1.1%	1.8%	2.1%	2.4%
Sales ($)/Emp.	688,229	695,890	708,585	723,130	740,635	1.1%	1.8%	2.1%	2.4%

3-Year Trend – Estimated Number of Establishments

Year	Employee Size of Establishment									Total Employ-ment
	1-4 Emps.	5-9 Emps.	10-19 Emps.	20-49 Emps.	50-99 Emps.	100-249 Emps.	250-499 Emps.	>500 Emps.	Non-Employer	
2017	1,300	516	390	264	94	49	11	21	445	3,090
2018	1,376	546	412	280	99	51	12	23	470	3,270
2019	1,448	575	434	294	104	54	13	24	495	3,441

3-Year Trend – Estimated Industry Sales ($Millions)

Year	Employee Size of Establishment									Total Employ-ment
	1-4 Emps.	5-9 Emps.	10-19 Emps.	20-49 Emps.	50-99 Emps.	100-249 Emps.	250-499 Emps.	>500 Emps.	Non-Employer	
2017	1,214.5	1,267.4	2,406.0	4,319.5	3,367.9	4,702.6	3,686.0	13,570.9	53.5	34,588.3
2018	1,316.0	1,373.4	2,607.2	4,680.7	3,649.6	5,095.9	3,994.3	14,576.5	58.0	37,351.6
2019	1,422.9	1,484.9	2,819.0	5,060.9	3,946.0	5,509.8	4,318.7	15,640.4	62.7	40,265.3

3-Year Trend – Estimated Number of Employees

Year	Employee Size of Establishment									Total Employ-ment
	1-4 Emps.	5-9 Emps.	10-19 Emps.	20-49 Emps.	50-99 Emps.	100-249 Emps.	250-499 Emps.	>500 Emps.	Non-Employer	
2017	3,250	2,994	5,300	7,956	5,569	6,124	3,286	13,891	445	48,813
2018	3,439	3,168	5,608	8,418	5,893	6,481	3,477	14,699	470	51,653
2019	3,620	3,334	5,902	8,860	6,202	6,821	3,659	15,471	495	54,366

BREWERIES & BEER-MAKING INDUSTRY
NAICS 31212

SUB-INDUSTRIES – 2018 ESTIMATED INDUSTRY SALES, ESTABLISHMENTS & EMPLOYMENT

Sub-Industries	Category*	Establishments	Sales ($Mill)	Employment
Malt beverages	Major1	1,693	3,092.6	16,908
Malt beverage products	Minor1	45	2,275.2	1,154
Brewers' grain	Minor2	93	182.7	579
Extract, malt	Minor2	9	17.0	81
Syrups, malt	Minor2	9	13.5	58
Ale (alcoholic beverage)	Minor2	105	1,527.2	1,256
Beer (alcoholic beverage)	Minor2	1,213	30,138.7	31,222
Liquors, malt	Minor2	90	89.2	351
Near beer	Minor2	12	15.6	44

*Category-Major categories (Major1) are more general descriptions for companies that self-selected to capture the many functions they perform in the industry. Minor categories (Minor1, Minor2) are more specific for companies that have more detailed functions (Minor1 is a larger category than Minor2). Minor categories figures (sales, etc.) can be aggregated to larger minor categories (Minor2 sums to Minor1) and major categories overall figures.

WINERIES & WINE-MAKING INDUSTRY
NAICS 31213

NAICS 31213: Wineries. This industry comprises establishments primarily engaged in one or more of the following: (1) growing grapes and manufacturing wine and brandies; (2) manufacturing wine and brandies from grapes and other fruits grown elsewhere; and (3) blending wines and brandies.

INDUSTRY ESTABLISHMENTS, SALES & EMPLOYMENT TRENDS

	Year					Percent Chg. Year-to-Year			
	2015	2016	2017	2018	2019	15-16	16-17	17-18	18-19
Establishments	4,167	4,315	4,468	4,580	4,671	3.6%	3.5%	2.5%	2.0%
Sales ($Millions)	13,501	13,858	14,306	14,675	15,037	2.6%	3.2%	2.6%	2.5%
Employment	46,778	48,447	50,158	51,423	52,440	3.6%	3.5%	2.5%	2.0%
Sales ($M)/Estab.	3.24	3.21	3.20	3.20	3.22	-0.9%	-0.3%	0.1%	0.5%
Sales ($)/Emp.	288,615	286,045	285,225	285,379	286,741	-0.9%	-0.3%	0.1%	0.5%

3-YEAR TREND – ESTIMATED NUMBER OF ESTABLISHMENTS

Year	Employee Size of Establishment									Total Employ-ment
	1-4 Emps.	5-9 Emps.	10-19 Emps.	20-49 Emps.	50-99 Emps.	100-249 Emps.	250-499 Emps.	>500 Emps.	Non-Employer	
2017	1,855	790	555	450	112	47	10	5	643	4,468
2018	1,902	810	569	462	114	48	10	5	659	4,580
2019	1,939	826	581	471	117	49	10	6	672	4,671

3-YEAR TREND – ESTIMATED INDUSTRY SALES ($MILLIONS)

Year	Employee Size of Establishment									Total Employ-ment
	1-4 Emps.	5-9 Emps.	10-19 Emps.	20-49 Emps.	50-99 Emps.	100-249 Emps.	250-499 Emps.	>500 Emps.	Non-Employer	
2017	827.1	926.1	1,636.9	3,512.9	1,912.1	2,180.4	1,503.2	1,733.6	73.9	14,306.2
2018	849.2	950.8	1,680.6	3,606.7	1,963.2	2,238.6	1,543.3	1,766.8	75.8	14,675.1
2019	870.7	974.9	1,723.2	3,698.1	2,013.0	2,295.3	1,582.4	1,801.3	77.8	15,036.7

3-YEAR TREND – ESTIMATED NUMBER OF EMPLOYEES

Year	Employee Size of Establishment									Total Employ-ment
	1-4 Emps.	5-9 Emps.	10-19 Emps.	20-49 Emps.	50-99 Emps.	100-249 Emps.	250-499 Emps.	>500 Emps.	Non-Employer	
2017	4,637	4,583	7,554	13,555	6,624	5,949	2,807	3,804	643	50,158
2018	4,754	4,699	7,744	13,897	6,791	6,099	2,878	3,900	659	51,423
2019	4,848	4,792	7,897	14,172	6,925	6,220	2,935	3,977	672	52,440

© Barnes Reports: 2018 U.S. Industry & Market Outlook

WINERIES & WINE-MAKING INDUSTRY
NAICS 31213

SUB-INDUSTRIES — 2018 ESTIMATED INDUSTRY SALES, ESTABLISHMENTS & EMPLOYMENT

Sub-Industries	Category*	Establishments	Sales ($Mill)	Employment
Wines, brandy, and brandy spirits	Major1	933	10,011.7	13,414
Wines	Minor1	3,301	4,106.6	35,149
Wine coolers (beverages)	Minor2	19	13.4	88
Brandy	Minor2	16	158.2	213
Brandy spirits	Minor2	4	5.2	30
Neutral spirits, fruit	Minor2	4	1.6	11
Wine cellars, bonded: engaged in blending wines	Minor2	303	378.4	2,517

*Category-Major categories (Major1) are more general descriptions for companies that self-selected to capture the many functions they perform in the industry. Minor categories (Minor1, Minor2) are more specific for companies that have more detailed functions (Minor1 is a larger category than Minor2). Minor categories figures (sales, etc.) can be aggregated to larger minor categories (Minor2 sums to Minor1) and major categories overall figures.

DISTILLERIES & ALCOHOL-MAKING INDUSTRY
NAICS 31214

NAICS 31214: Distilleries. This industry comprises establishments primarily engaged in one or more of the following: (1) distilling potable liquors (except brandies); (2) distilling and blending liquors; and (3) blending and mixing liquors and other ingredients.

INDUSTRY ESTABLISHMENTS, SALES & EMPLOYMENT TRENDS

	Year					Percent Chg. Year-to-Year			
	2015	2016	2017	2018	2019	15-16	16-17	17-18	18-19
Establishments	863	907	943	1,015	1,087	5.1%	4.0%	7.6%	7.0%
Sales ($Millions)	10,180	11,381	12,622	14,459	16,464	11.8%	10.9%	14.5%	13.9%
Employment	10,227	10,743	11,178	12,028	12,873	5.1%	4.0%	7.6%	7.0%
Sales ($M)/Estab.	11.79	12.55	13.38	14.24	15.15	6.4%	6.6%	6.5%	6.4%
Sales ($)/Emp.	995,409	1,059,345	1,129,263	1,202,110	1,278,939	6.4%	6.6%	6.5%	6.4%

3-YEAR TREND – ESTIMATED NUMBER OF ESTABLISHMENTS

Year	Employee Size of Establishment									Total Employment
	1-4 Emps.	5-9 Emps.	10-19 Emps.	20-49 Emps.	50-99 Emps.	100-249 Emps.	250-499 Emps.	>500 Emps.	Non-Employer	
2017	526	125	68	45	20	16	5	3	136	943
2018	566	134	73	48	21	18	6	4	146	1,015
2019	605	144	78	52	23	19	6	4	156	1,087

3-YEAR TREND – ESTIMATED INDUSTRY SALES ($MILLIONS)

Year	Employee Size of Establishment									Total Employment
	1-4 Emps.	5-9 Emps.	10-19 Emps.	20-49 Emps.	50-99 Emps.	100-249 Emps.	250-499 Emps.	>500 Emps.	Non-Employer	
2017	775.4	483.0	660.6	1,156.4	1,116.0	2,506.5	2,816.0	3,090.7	17.9	12,622.4
2018	888.3	553.4	756.8	1,324.7	1,278.4	2,871.3	3,225.9	3,539.3	20.5	14,458.6
2019	1,011.6	630.2	861.9	1,508.6	1,455.9	3,269.9	3,673.7	4,029.2	23.3	16,464.3

3-YEAR TREND – ESTIMATED NUMBER OF EMPLOYEES

Year	Employee Size of Establishment									Total Employment
	1-4 Emps.	5-9 Emps.	10-19 Emps.	20-49 Emps.	50-99 Emps.	100-249 Emps.	250-499 Emps.	>500 Emps.	Non-Employer	
2017	1,314	723	922	1,349	1,169	2,067	1,590	1,909	136	11,178
2018	1,414	778	992	1,451	1,257	2,225	1,711	2,054	146	12,028
2019	1,514	832	1,061	1,553	1,346	2,381	1,831	2,198	156	12,873

© Barnes Reports: 2018 U.S. Industry & Market Outlook

Distilleries & Alcohol-Making Industry
NAICS 31214

Sub-Industries — 2018 Estimated Industry Sales, Establishments & Employment

Sub-Industries	Category*	Establishments	Sales ($Mill)	Employment
Distilled and blended liquors	Major1	622	468.1	6,095
Distiller's dried grains and solubles, and alcohol	Minor1	45	62.8	259
Ethyl alcohol for beverage purposes	Minor2	8	1.2	14
Grain alcohol for beverage purposes	Minor2	25	371.1	229
Grain alcohol for medicinal purposes	Minor2	4	132.1	313
Neutral spirits, except fruit	Minor2	20	74.6	43
Cordials and premixed alcoholic cocktails	Minor1	8	6.1	36
Cocktails, alcoholic	Minor2	86	21.2	135
Cordials, alcoholic	Minor2	4	6.9	52
Applejack (alcoholic beverage)	Minor2	12	8.2	49
Bourbon whiskey	Minor2	45	13,162.3	3,231
Corn whiskey	Minor2	12	3.3	23
Gin (alcoholic beverage)	Minor2	4	0.8	5
Rum (alcoholic beverage)	Minor2	57	99.1	1,441
Scotch whiskey	Minor2	4	0.4	3
Vodka (alcoholic beverage)	Minor2	57	40.4	99

*Category-Major categories (Major1) are more general descriptions for companies that self-selected to capture the many functions they perform in the industry. Minor categories (Minor1, Minor2) are more specific for companies that have more detailed functions (Minor1 is a larger category than Minor2). Minor categories figures (sales, etc.) can be aggregated to larger minor categories (Minor2 sums to Minor1) and major categories overall figures.

MEN'S & BOYS' APPAREL MFG. INDUSTRY
NAICS 31522

NAICS 31522: Men's & Boys' Apparel Manufacturing. This industry comprises establishments primarily engaged in manufacturing men's and boys' cut and sew apparel from purchased fabric. Men's and boys' clothing jobbers, who perform entrepreneurial functions involved in apparel manufacture, including buying raw materials, designing and preparing samples, arranging for apparel to be made from their materials, and marketing finished apparel, are included.

INDUSTRY ESTABLISHMENTS, SALES & EMPLOYMENT TRENDS

	Year					Percent Chg. Year-to-Year			
	2015	2016	2017	2018	2019	15-16	16-17	17-18	18-19
Establishments	1,346	1,287	1,222	1,161	1,097	-4.4%	-5.0%	-5.0%	-5.5%
Sales ($Millions)	3,937	3,536	3,163	2,831	2,523	-10.2%	-10.5%	-10.5%	-10.9%
Employment	11,021	10,534	10,005	9,505	8,981	-4.4%	-5.0%	-5.0%	-5.5%
Sales ($M)/Estab.	2.92	2.75	2.59	2.44	2.30	-6.0%	-5.8%	-5.8%	-5.7%
Sales ($)/Emp.	357,225	335,639	316,197	297,826	280,885	-6.0%	-5.8%	-5.8%	-5.7%

3-YEAR TREND – ESTIMATED NUMBER OF ESTABLISHMENTS

Year	Employee Size of Establishment									Total Employment
	1-4 Emps.	5-9 Emps.	10-19 Emps.	20-49 Emps.	50-99 Emps.	100-249 Emps.	250-499 Emps.	>500 Emps.	Non-Employer	
2017	214	74	44	51	22	24	5	1	788	1,222
2018	204	71	41	48	21	22	4	1	749	1,161
2019	192	67	39	46	20	21	4	1	707	1,097

3-YEAR TREND – ESTIMATED NUMBER OF ESTABLISHMENTS

Year	Employee Size of Establishment									Total Employment
	1-4 Emps.	5-9 Emps.	10-19 Emps.	20-49 Emps.	50-99 Emps.	100-249 Emps.	250-499 Emps.	>500 Emps.	Non-Employer	
2017	94.8	86.6	127.4	393.5	370.8	1,082.5	701.6	260.4	45.7	3,163.4
2018	84.8	77.5	114.0	352.1	331.7	968.6	627.8	233.3	40.9	2,830.7
2019	75.6	69.0	101.6	313.8	295.6	863.1	559.4	208.1	36.4	2,522.8

3-YEAR TREND – ESTIMATED NUMBER OF ESTABLISHMENTS

Year	Employee Size of Establishment									Total Employment
	1-4 Emps.	5-9 Emps.	10-19 Emps.	20-49 Emps.	50-99 Emps.	100-249 Emps.	250-499 Emps.	>500 Emps.	Non-Employer	
2017	536	432	593	1,530	1,294	2,976	1,320	536	788	10,005
2018	509	410	563	1,454	1,229	2,827	1,254	509	749	9,505
2019	481	388	532	1,374	1,162	2,672	1,185	481	707	8,981

© Barnes Reports: 2018 U.S. Industry & Market Outlook

Men's & Boys' Apparel Mfg. Industry
NAICS 31522

Sub-Industries — 2018 Estimated Industry Sales, Establishments & Employment

Sub-Industries	Category*	Establishments	Sales ($Mill)	Employment
Men's and boy's trousers and slacks	Major1	446	17.1	3,947
Men's and boys' jeans and dungarees	Minor1	74	344.6	478
Dungarees: men's, youths', and boys'	Minor2	27	0.1	592
Jeans: men's, youths', and boys'	Minor2	244	1,651.0	1,890
Men's and boys' dress slacks and shorts	Minor1	5	0.0	0
Shorts (outerwear): men's, youths', and boys'	Minor2	32	249.3	186
Slacks, dress: men's, youths', and boys'	Minor2	101	2.6	510
Men's and boy's suits and coats	Major1	65	63.3	330
Tailored suits and formal jackets	Minor1	16	12.3	16
Formal jackets, men's and youths': from purchased mater	Minor2	3	10.5	4
Jackets, tailored suit-type: men's and boys'	Minor2	5	13.5	8
Suits, men's and boys': made from purchased materials	Minor2	22	199.9	349
Tailored dress and sport coats: men's and boys'	Minor2	4	2.0	5
Tuxedos: made from purchased materials	Minor2	15	3.4	10
Coats, overcoats and vests	Minor1	9	4.7	15
Coats, tailored: men's and boys': from purchased material	Minor2	4	65.1	93
Overcoats and topcoats: men's, youths' and boys'	Minor2	1	0.2	1
Vests: made from purchased materials	Minor2	5	4.3	16
Men's and boys' uniforms	Minor1	26	84.0	235
Firemen's uniforms: made from purchased materials	Minor2	6	8.4	64
Military uniforms, men's and youths': purchased materials	Minor2	41	85.3	713
Policemen's uniforms: made from purchased materials	Minor2	11	9.4	41

*Category-Major categories (Major1) are more general descriptions for companies that self-selected to capture the many functions they perform in the industry. Minor categories (Minor1, Minor2) are more specific for companies that have more detailed functions (Minor1 is a larger category than Minor2). Minor categories figures (sales, etc.) can be aggregated to larger minor categories (Minor2 sums to Minor1) and major categories overall figures.

Women's & Girls' Apparel Mfg. Industry
NAICS 31524

NAICS 31524: Women's & Girls' Apparel Manufacturing Industry. This industry comprises establishments primarily engaged in manufacturing women's and girls' apparel from purchased fabric. Women's and girls' clothing jobbers, who perform entrepreneurial functions involved in apparel manufacture, including buying raw materials, designing and preparing samples, arranging for apparel to be made from their materials, and marketing finished apparel, are included.

Industry Establishments, Sales & Employment Trends

	Year					Percent Chg. Year-to-Year			
	2015	2016	2017	2018	2019	15-16	16-17	17-18	18-19
Establishments	3,114	3,069	3,021	2,936	2,838	-1.5%	-1.6%	-2.8%	-3.3%
Sales ($Millions)	3,537	3,433	3,350	3,241	3,134	-2.9%	-2.4%	-3.3%	-3.3%
Employment	18,959	18,681	18,390	17,871	17,275	-1.5%	-1.6%	-2.8%	-3.3%
Sales ($M)/Estab.	1.14	1.12	1.11	1.10	1.10	-1.5%	-0.9%	-0.4%	0.0%
Sales ($)/Emp.	186,541	183,788	182,171	181,356	181,404	-1.5%	-0.9%	-0.4%	0.0%

3-Year Trend – Estimated Number of Establishments

Year	Employee Size of Establishment									Total Employment
	1-4 Emps.	5-9 Emps.	10-19 Emps.	20-49 Emps.	50-99 Emps.	100-249 Emps.	250-499 Emps.	>500 Emps.	Non-Employer	
2017	501	212	159	130	46	20	3	2	1,948	3,021
2018	486	206	155	126	44	20	3	2	1,893	2,936
2019	470	200	149	122	43	19	3	2	1,830	2,838

3-Year Trend – Estimated Number of Establishments

Year	Employee Size of Establishment									Total Employment
	1-4 Emps.	5-9 Emps.	10-19 Emps.	20-49 Emps.	50-99 Emps.	100-249 Emps.	250-499 Emps.	>500 Emps.	Non-Employer	
2017	146.2	163.1	307.1	664.2	512.1	616.7	296.9	519.6	124.3	3,350.1
2018	141.0	157.3	296.2	640.7	494.0	594.9	286.4	510.7	119.9	3,241.1
2019	135.9	151.6	285.4	617.3	475.9	573.1	275.9	503.2	115.5	3,133.8

3-Year Trend – Estimated Number of Establishments

Year	Employee Size of Establishment									Total Employment
	1-4 Emps.	5-9 Emps.	10-19 Emps.	20-49 Emps.	50-99 Emps.	100-249 Emps.	250-499 Emps.	>500 Emps.	Non-Employer	
2017	1,251	1,232	2,163	3,912	2,708	2,569	846	1,760	1,948	18,390
2018	1,216	1,197	2,102	3,802	2,632	2,496	823	1,710	1,893	17,871
2019	1,175	1,157	2,032	3,675	2,544	2,413	795	1,653	1,830	17,275

© Barnes Reports: 2018 U.S. Industry & Market Outlook

WOMEN'S & GIRLS' APPAREL MFG. INDUSTRY
NAICS 31524

SUB-INDUSTRIES – 2018 ESTIMATED INDUSTRY SALES, ESTABLISHMENTS & EMPLOYMENT

Sub-Industries	Category*	Establishments	Sales ($Mill)	Employment
Women's, junior's, and misses' dresses	Major1	965	2,406.5	9,703
Bridal and formal gowns	Minor1	350	34.7	1,133
Gowns, formal	Minor2	114	16.0	488
Wedding gowns and dresses	Minor2	724	45.0	1,805
Dresses, paper, cut and sewn	Minor2	141	76.2	911
Ensemble dresses: women's, misses', and juniors'	Minor2	38	10.4	199
Housedresses	Minor2	17	4.1	58
Women's and misses' blouses and shirts	Major1	394	432.0	1,529
Blouses, women's and juniors': made from purchased mat	Minor2	107	170.9	1,655
Shirts, women's and juniors': made from purchased mater	Minor2	14	4.5	57
T-shirts and tops, women's: made from purchased materi	Minor2	73	40.8	334

*Category-Major categories (Major1) are more general descriptions for companies that self-selected to capture the many functions they perform in the industry. Minor categories (Minor1, Minor2) are more specific for companies that have more detailed functions (Minor1 is a larger category than Minor2). Minor categories figures (sales, etc.) can be aggregated to larger minor categories (Minor2 sums to Minor1) and major categories overall figures.

PAPER MILLS INDUSTRY
NAICS 32212

NAICS 32212: Paper Mills Industry. This industry comprises establishments primarily engaged in manufacturing paper from pulp. These establishments may manufacture or purchase pulp. In addition, the establishments may convert the paper they make. The activity of making paper classifies an establishment into this industry regardless of the output.

INDUSTRY ESTABLISHMENTS, SALES & EMPLOYMENT TRENDS

	Year					Percent Chg. Year-to-Year			
	2015	2016	2017	2018	2019	15-16	16-17	17-18	18-19
Establishments	270	259	247	239	231	-4.0%	-4.8%	-3.0%	-3.5%
Sales ($Millions)	37,712	38,918	39,924	41,530	42,985	3.2%	2.6%	4.0%	3.5%
Employment	48,204	46,299	44,068	42,732	41,219	-4.0%	-4.8%	-3.0%	-3.5%
Sales ($M)/Estab.	139.66	150.06	161.73	173.50	186.17	7.4%	7.8%	7.3%	7.3%
Sales ($)/Emp.	782,337	840,591	905,972	971,883	1,042,848	7.4%	7.8%	7.3%	7.3%

3-YEAR TREND – ESTIMATED NUMBER OF ESTABLISHMENTS

Year	Employee Size of Establishment									Total Employ-ment
	1-4 Emps.	5-9 Emps.	10-19 Emps.	20-49 Emps.	50-99 Emps.	100-249 Emps.	250-499 Emps.	>500 Emps.	Non-Employer	
2017	32	16	10	17	29	33	41	37	31	247
2018	31	16	10	17	28	32	40	35	30	239
2019	30	15	9	16	27	31	38	34	29	231

3-YEAR TREND – ESTIMATED NUMBER OF ESTABLISHMENTS

Year	Employee Size of Establishment									Total Employ-ment
	1-4 Emps.	5-9 Emps.	10-19 Emps.	20-49 Emps.	50-99 Emps.	100-249 Emps.	250-499 Emps.	>500 Emps.	Non-Employer	
2017	27.4	37.0	56.9	260.0	962.5	2,918.4	12,295.2	23,363.5	3.3	39,924.0
2018	28.3	38.3	58.8	269.0	995.8	3,019.3	12,720.5	24,396.8	3.4	41,530.2
2019	29.1	39.4	60.5	276.6	1,023.9	3,104.7	13,080.3	25,367.1	3.5	42,985.1

3-YEAR TREND – ESTIMATED NUMBER OF ESTABLISHMENTS

Year	Employee Size of Establishment									Total Employ-ment
	1-4 Emps.	5-9 Emps.	10-19 Emps.	20-49 Emps.	50-99 Emps.	100-249 Emps.	250-499 Emps.	>500 Emps.	Non-Employer	
2017	80	95	137	523	1,738	4,150	11,967	25,347	31	44,068
2018	78	93	133	507	1,685	4,024	11,604	24,578	30	42,732
2019	75	89	128	489	1,625	3,882	11,194	23,708	29	41,219

© Barnes Reports: 2018 U.S. Industry & Market Outlook

Paper Mills Industry
NAICS 32212

Sub-Industries – 2018 Estimated Industry Sales, Establishments & Employment

Sub-Industries	Category*	Establishments	Sales ($Mill)	Employment
Paper mills	Major1	51	30,753.4	22,807
Towels, tissues and napkins; paper and stock	Minor1	3	864.4	2,423
Cleansing paper	Minor2	1	3.7	22
Facial tissue stock	Minor2	0	2.4	35
Napkin stock, paper	Minor2	1	7.9	410
Pattern tissue	Minor2	1	0.6	5
Sanitary tissue paper	Minor2	1	0.4	257
Tissue paper	Minor2	3	122.4	1,117
Toilet tissue stock	Minor2	1	0.8	211
Toweling tissue (paper)	Minor2	0	2.5	21
Parchment, securites, and bank note papers	Minor1	2	597.1	1,135
Specialty or chemically treated papers	Minor1	10	132.1	1,511
Book, bond and printing papers	Minor1	13	974.7	2,211
Poster and art papers	Minor1	28	1,053.0	356
Stationary, envelope and tablet papers	Minor1	43	88.0	2,083
Catalog, magazine, and newsprint papers	Minor1	11	339.6	2,847
Wrapping and packaging papers	Minor1	22	101.4	2,596
Building and roofing paper, felts and insulation siding	Minor1	3	1,889.2	505
Pressed and molded pulp and fiber products	Minor2	1	0.2	74
Lath, fiber	Minor2	0	0.1	1
Molded pulp products	Minor2	2	13.3	179
Pressed pulp products	Minor2	0	0.1	256
Tube stock	Minor2	0	1.7	12
Fine paper	Minor2	2	4,508.4	1,009
Kraft paper	Minor2	1	0.4	56
Rope or jute paper	Minor2	0	1.2	9
Uncoated paper	Minor2	0		32
Wallpaper (hanging paper)	Minor2	19	35.0	255
Rope or jute paper	Minor2	0	1.2	9
Uncoated paper	Minor2	0		32
Wallpaper (hanging paper)	Minor2	19	35.0	255

*Category-Major categories (Major1) are more general descriptions for companies that self-selected to capture the many functions they perform in the industry. Minor categories (Minor1, Minor2) are more specific for companies that have more detailed functions (Minor1 is a larger category than Minor2). Minor categories figures (sales, etc.) can be aggregated to larger minor categories (Minor2 sums to Minor1) and major categories overall figures.

PRINTING INDUSTRY
NAICS 32311

NAICS 32311: Printing Industry. This industry comprises establishments primarily engaged in printing on apparel and textile products, paper, metal, glass, plastics, and other materials, except fabric (grey goods). The printing processes employed include, but are not limited to, lithographic, gravure, screen, flexographic, digital, and letterpress. Establishments in this industry do not manufacture the stock that they print but may perform postprinting activities, such as bending, cutting, or laminating the materials they print, and mailing.

INDUSTRY ESTABLISHMENTS, SALES & EMPLOYMENT TRENDS

	Year					Percent Chg. Year-to-Year			
	2015	2016	2017	2018	2019	15-16	16-17	17-18	18-19
Establishments	33,497	33,050	32,475	31,721	30,831	-1.3%	-1.7%	-2.3%	-2.8%
Sales ($Millions)	75,045	76,230	77,496	78,456	79,226	1.6%	1.7%	1.2%	1.0%
Employment	392,503	387,271	380,526	371,692	361,261	-1.3%	-1.7%	-2.3%	-2.8%
Sales ($M)/Estab.	2.24	2.31	2.39	2.47	2.57	3.0%	3.5%	3.6%	3.9%
Sales ($)/Emp.	191,195	196,840	203,655	211,079	219,303	3.0%	3.5%	3.6%	3.9%

3-YEAR TREND – ESTIMATED NUMBER OF ESTABLISHMENTS

Year	Employee Size of Establishment									Total Employ-ment
	1-4 Emps.	5-9 Emps.	10-19 Emps.	20-49 Emps.	50-99 Emps.	100-249 Emps.	250-499 Emps.	>500 Emps.	Non-Employer	
2017	11,045	4,633	3,009	2,359	925	588	144	50	9,120	32,475
2018	11,375	4,526	2,939	2,304	903	575	141	49	8,908	31,721
2019	11,056	4,399	2,857	2,239	878	559	137	48	8,658	30,831

3-YEAR TREND – ESTIMATED NUMBER OF ESTABLISHMENTS

Year	Employee Size of Establishment									Total Employ-ment
	1-4 Emps.	5-9 Emps.	10-19 Emps.	20-49 Emps.	50-99 Emps.	100-249 Emps.	250-499 Emps.	>500 Emps.	Non-Employer	
2017	3,347.0	3,499.9	5,716.6	11,860.2	10,222.7	17,530.6	14,503.7	9,993.0	822.6	77,496.3
2018	3,386.7	3,541.5	5,784.4	12,001.0	10,344.1	17,738.6	14,675.9	10,151.8	832.3	78,456.3
2019	3,417.8	3,573.9	5,837.5	12,110.9	10,438.9	17,901.2	14,810.4	10,295.2	840.0	79,225.7

3-YEAR TREND – ESTIMATED NUMBER OF ESTABLISHMENTS

Year	Employee Size of Establishment									Total Employ-ment
	1-4 Emps.	5-9 Emps.	10-19 Emps.	20-49 Emps.	50-99 Emps.	100-249 Emps.	250-499 Emps.	>500 Emps.	Non-Employer	
2017	29,114	26,872	40,926	70,999	54,938	74,207	42,022	32,328	9,120	380,526
2018	28,438	26,249	39,976	69,350	53,663	72,484	41,046	31,578	8,908	371,692
2019	27,640	25,512	38,854	67,404	52,157	70,450	39,894	30,692	8,658	361,261

© Barnes Reports: 2018 U.S. Industry & Market Outlook

PRINTING INDUSTRY
NAICS 32311

Sub-Industries – 2018 Estimated Industry Sales, Establishments & Employment

Sub-Industries	Category*	Establishments	Sales ($Mill)	Employment
Commercial printing, lithographic	Major1	17,975	37,853.7	169,438
Offset and photolithographic printing	Minor1	456	756.1	5,539
Offset printing	Minor2	11,224	29,959.3	161,919
Photo-offset printing	Minor2	151	197.3	1,250
Photolithographic printing	Minor2	45	84.0	398
Promotional printing, lithographic	Minor1	133	406.1	2,454
Advertising posters, lithographed	Minor2	66	97.1	614
Catalogs, lithographed	Minor2	21	4,428.2	579
Circulars, lithographed	Minor2	4	64.4	552
Coupons, lithographed	Minor2	6	7.3	42
Business form and card printing, lithographic	Minor1	336	404.7	2,823
Billheads, lithographed	Minor2	2	1.0	5
Forms, business: lithographed	Minor2	115	551.4	3,071
Visiting cards, lithographed	Minor2	3	9.7	46
Calendar and card printing, lithographic	Minor1	25	11.1	573
Calendars, lithographed	Minor2	42	181.5	570
Cards, lithographed	Minor2	24	31.7	708
Playing cards, lithographed	Minor2	13	10.4	488
Post cards, picture: lithographed	Minor2	23	27.8	349
Souvenir cards, lithographed	Minor2	11	9.2	542
Atlas and map printing, lithographic	Minor1	3	0.7	6
Maps, lithographed	Minor2	28	55.9	237
Poster and decal printing, lithographic	Minor1	144	400.8	2,980
Tag, ticket, and schedule printing: lithographic	Minor1	43	103.8	1,067
Wrapper and seal printing, lithographic	Minor1	21	33.2	180
Publication printing, lithographic	Minor1	71	92.0	1,172
Newspapers, lithographed only	Minor2	27	74.1	570
Periodicals, lithographed	Minor2	9	14.8	2,158
Color lithography	Minor2	193	1,055.8	4,122
Fashion plates, lithographed	Minor2	15	34.4	153
Letters, circular or form: lithographed	Minor2	45	99.7	572
Lithographing on metal	Minor2	414	1,298.1	6,074
Menus, lithographed	Minor2	24	70.2	311
Trading stamps, lithographed	Minor2	6	31.0	131

*Category-Major categories (Major1) are more general descriptions for companies that self-selected to capture the many functions they perform in the industry. Minor categories (Minor1, Minor2) are more specific for companies that have more detailed functions (Minor1 is a larger category than Minor2). Minor categories figures (sales, etc.) can be aggregated to larger minor categories (Minor2 sums to Minor1) and major categories overall figures.

Petroleum Refineries Industry
NAICS 32411

NAICS 32411: Petroleum Refineries. Establishments primarily engaged in producing gasoline, kerosene, distillate fuel oils, residual fuel oils, and lubricants, through fractionation or straight distillation of crude oil, redistillation of unfinished petroleum derivatives, cracking or other processes. Establishments of this business also produce aliphatic and aromatic chemicals as byproducts. Natural gasoline from natural gas is classified in mining.

Industry Establishments, Sales & Employment Trends

	Year					Percent Chg. Year-to-Year			
	2015	2016	2017	2018	2019	15-16	16-17	17-18	18-19
Establishments	265	272	279	288	300	2.5%	2.6%	3.5%	4.0%
Sales ($Millions)	633,858	687,842	747,830	817,014	894,954	8.5%	8.7%	9.3%	9.5%
Employment	55,693	57,097	58,572	60,638	63,063	2.5%	2.6%	3.5%	4.0%
Sales ($M)/Estab.	2,393.26	2,533.21	2,684.77	2,833.22	2,984.17	5.8%	6.0%	5.5%	5.3%
Sales ($)/Emp.	11,381,370	12,046,910	12,767,687	13,473,676	14,191,532	5.8%	6.0%	5.5%	5.3%

3-Year Trend – Estimated Number of Establishments

Year	Employee Size of Establishment									Total Employment
	1-4 Emps.	5-9 Emps.	10-19 Emps.	20-49 Emps.	50-99 Emps.	100-249 Emps.	250-499 Emps.	>500 Emps.	Non-Employer	
2017	26	9	17	19	12	25	44	52	75	279
2018	27	10	17	20	12	26	46	53	77	288
2019	28	10	18	20	12	27	48	55	80	300

3-Year Trend – Estimated Number of Establishments

Year	Employee Size of Establishment									Total Employment
	1-4 Emps.	5-9 Emps.	10-19 Emps.	20-49 Emps.	50-99 Emps.	100-249 Emps.	250-499 Emps.	>500 Emps.	Non-Employer	
2017	329.7	311.9	1,394.6	4,152.7	5,578.6	32,804.1	193,487.8	509,760.4	10.2	747,830.1
2018	364.0	344.5	1,540.0	4,585.6	6,160.1	36,223.8	213,657.7	554,127.1	11.2	817,014.0
2019	403.5	381.8	1,706.9	5,082.6	6,827.7	40,149.4	236,811.9	603,577.7	12.5	894,953.8

3-Year Trend – Estimated Number of Establishments

Year	Employee Size of Establishment									Total Employment
	1-4 Emps.	5-9 Emps.	10-19 Emps.	20-49 Emps.	50-99 Emps.	100-249 Emps.	250-499 Emps.	>500 Emps.	Non-Employer	
2017	66	55	229	570	687	3,183	12,850	40,859	75	58,572
2018	68	57	237	590	711	3,295	13,303	42,300	77	60,638
2019	71	59	246	613	740	3,427	13,835	43,991	80	63,063

© Barnes Reports: 2018 U.S. Industry & Market Outlook

PETROLEUM REFINERIES INDUSTRY
NAICS 32411

Sub-Industries – 2018 Estimated Industry Sales, Establishments & Employment

Sub-Industries	Category*	Establishments	Sales ($Mill)	Employment
Petroleum refining	Major1	127	800,025.3	47,603
Gases and liquefied petroleum gases	Minor1	12	1,246.1	972
Gas, refinery	Minor2	12	13,448.9	3,015
Liquefied petroleum gases, LPG	Minor2	3	3.2	60
Light distillates	Minor1	1	4.3	334
Alkylates	Minor2	0	1.0	3
Gasoline blending plants	Minor2	4	12.4	542
Jet fuels	Minor2	4	13.2	267
Kerosene	Minor2	0	0.1	1
Solvents	Minor2	6	1,758.7	177
Intermediate distillates	Minor1	0	0.2	2
Acid oil	Minor2	0	0.1	1
Diesel fuels	Minor2	27	122.4	895
Oils, fuel	Minor2	33	96.3	2,560
Oils, illuminating	Minor2	1	1.7	17
Oils, partly refined: sold for rerunning	Minor2	1	4.2	107
Still oil	Minor2	0	0.4	4
Heavy distillates	Minor1	0	0.7	7
Mineral jelly	Minor2	0	0.1	2
Mineral oils, natural	Minor2	2	1.9	711
Mineral waxes, natural	Minor2	1	19.8	125
Oils, lubricating	Minor2	15	29.8	899
Paraffin wax	Minor2	1	56.9	26
Residues	Minor1	4	4.1	47
Asphalt or asphaltic materials, made in refineries	Minor2	6	43.0	370
Coke, petroleum	Minor2	2	1.5	456
Greases, lubricating	Minor2	1	2.0	59
Petrolatums, nonmedicinal	Minor2	1	0.5	173
Road materials, bituminous	Minor2	1	42.4	21
Road oils	Minor2	1	0.9	26
Aromatic chemical products	Minor1	9	4.0	153
Nonaromatic chemical products	Minor1	11	58.8	892
Fractionation products of crude petroleum, hydrocarbons	Minor1	2	9.1	110

*Category-Major categories (Major1) are more general descriptions for companies that self-selected to capture the many functions they perform in the industry. Minor categories (Minor1, Minor2) are more specific for companies that have more detailed functions (Minor1 is a larger category than Minor2). Minor categories figures (sales, etc.) can be aggregated to larger minor categories (Minor2 sums to Minor1) and major categories overall figures.

Petrochemical Manufacturing Industry
NAICS 32511

NAICS 32511: Petrochemical Manufacturing Industry. This industry comprises establishments primarily engaged in (1) manufacturing acyclic (i.e., aliphatic) hydrocarbons such as ethylene, propylene, and butylene made from refined petroleum or liquid hydrocarbon and/or (2) manufacturing cyclic aromatic hydrocarbons such as benzene, toluene, styrene, xylene, ethyl benzene, and cumene made from refined petroleum or liquid hydrocarbons.

Industry Establishments, Sales & Employment Trends

	Year					Percent Chg. Year-to-Year			
	2015	2016	2017	2018	2019	15-16	16-17	17-18	18-19
Establishments	70	71	72	74	76	0.2%	1.7%	2.6%	3.4%
Sales ($Millions)	37,244	40,877	45,411	50,671	56,736	9.8%	11.1%	11.6%	12.0%
Employment	7,229	7,242	7,363	7,557	7,811	0.2%	1.7%	2.6%	3.4%
Sales ($M)/Estab.	528.88	579.39	633.05	688.29	745.64	9.5%	9.3%	8.7%	8.3%
Sales ($)/Emp.	5,152,340	5,644,379	6,167,188	6,705,336	7,263,981	9.5%	9.3%	8.7%	8.3%

3-Year Trend – Estimated Number of Establishments

Year	Employee Size of Establishment									Total Employment
	1-4 Emps.	5-9 Emps.	10-19 Emps.	20-49 Emps.	50-99 Emps.	100-249 Emps.	250-499 Emps.	>500 Emps.	Non-Employer	
2017	13	6	7	7	6	10	8	5	9	72
2018	14	6	7	7	6	10	8	5	9	74
2019	14	6	8	8	6	11	9	5	9	76

3-Year Trend – Estimated Number of Establishments

Year	Employee Size of Establishment									Total Employment
	1-4 Emps.	5-9 Emps.	10-19 Emps.	20-49 Emps.	50-99 Emps.	100-249 Emps.	250-499 Emps.	>500 Emps.	Non-Employer	
2017	79.3	96.1	282.1	746.6	1,406.7	6,319.0	17,038.3	19,441.4	1.1	45,410.7
2018	88.4	107.3	314.8	833.1	1,569.8	7,051.4	19,012.9	21,692.6	1.2	50,671.5
2019	99.0	120.1	352.4	932.9	1,757.7	7,895.7	21,289.6	24,287.3	1.4	56,736.2

3-Year Trend – Estimated Number of Establishments

Year	Employee Size of Establishment									Total Employment
	1-4 Emps.	5-9 Emps.	10-19 Emps.	20-49 Emps.	50-99 Emps.	100-249 Emps.	250-499 Emps.	>500 Emps.	Non-Employer	
2017	33	35	97	215	363	1,284	2,371	2,956	9	7,363
2018	34	36	100	220	373	1,318	2,433	3,034	9	7,557
2019	35	38	103	228	385	1,363	2,515	3,136	9	7,811

© Barnes Reports: 2018 U.S. Industry & Market Outlook

Petrochemical Manufacturing Industry
NAICS 32511

Sub-Industries – 2018 Estimated Industry Sales, Establishments & Employment

Sub-Industries	Category*	Establishments	Sales ($Mill)	Employment
Alcohols, non beverage	Minor1	1	391.1	189
Alcohols, industrial: denatured (non-beverage)	Minor2	1	116.5	224
Amyl alcohol	Minor2	0	0.3	50
Ethyl alcohol, ethanol	Minor2	17	13,325.3	2,669
Ethylene glycols	Minor2	1	3.2	56
Grain alcohol, industrial	Minor2	0	0.3	8
Methyl alcohol, synthetic, methanol	Minor2	0	483.6	189
Olefins	Minor1	1	25,146.3	595
Ethylene	Minor2	0	60.4	86
Propylene, butylene	Minor2	0	33.8	67
Coke, calcined petroleum: made from purchased material	Minor2	8	16.8	479
Fuel briquettes and waxes	Minor1	6	70.1	72
Fuel briquettes or boulets: made with petroleum binder	Minor2	13	16.8	1,648
Waxes, petroleum: not produced in petroleum refineries	Minor2	24	6,168.9	1,013
Phenol, alkylated and cumene	Minor2	0	40.7	27
Styrene	Minor2	0	100.3	23
Toluene	Minor2	0	0.4	0
Cyclic organic intermediates	Minor1	0	861.9	94
Tar, coal tar, and related chemicals	Minor1	0	1,661.7	18
Coal tar: crudes, intermediates, and distillates	Minor2	0	2,136.1	35
Tar	Minor2	1	20.7	8
Chemical indicators	Minor2	0	16.2	7

*Category-Major categories (Major1) are more general descriptions for companies that self-selected to capture the many functions they perform in the industry. Minor categories (Minor1, Minor2) are more specific for companies that have more detailed functions (Minor1 is a larger category than Minor2). Minor categories figures (sales, etc.) can be aggregated to larger minor categories (Minor2 sums to Minor1) and major categories overall figures.

PHARMACEUTICAL PREPARATION MFG. INDUSTRY
(NAICS 325412)

NAICS 325412: Pharmaceutical Preparation Manufacturing. This U.S. industry comprises establishments primarily engaged in manufacturing in-vivo diagnostic substances and pharmaceutical preparations (except biological) intended for internal and external consumption in dose forms, such as ampoules, tablets, capsules, vials, ointments, powders, solutions, and suspensions.

INDUSTRY ESTABLISHMENTS, SALES & EMPLOYMENT TRENDS

	Year					Percent Chg. Year-to-Year			
	2015	2016	2017	2018	2019	15-16	16-17	17-18	18-19
Establishments	1,659	1,673	1,713	1,780	1,863	0.9%	2.4%	3.9%	4.7%
Sales ($Millions)	157,226	161,653	169,096	179,523	192,256	2.8%	4.6%	6.2%	7.1%
Employment	108,022	108,967	111,537	115,937	121,332	0.9%	2.4%	3.9%	4.7%
Sales ($M)/Estab.	94.78	96.60	98.72	100.83	103.18	1.9%	2.2%	2.1%	2.3%
Sales ($)/Emp.	1,455,497	1,483,508	1,516,049	1,548,461	1,584,550	1.9%	2.2%	2.1%	2.3%

3-YEAR TREND – ESTIMATED NUMBER OF ESTABLISHMENTS

Year	Employee Size of Establishment									Total Employ-ment
	1-4 Emps.	5-9 Emps.	10-19 Emps.	20-49 Emps.	50-99 Emps.	100-249 Emps.	250-499 Emps.	>500 Emps.	Non-Employer	
2017	388	205	129	184	145	118	96	67	381	1,713
2018	404	214	134	191	150	122	100	70	396	1,780
2019	422	224	140	200	157	128	104	73	414	1,863

3-YEAR TREND – ESTIMATED NUMBER OF ESTABLISHMENTS

Year	Employee Size of Establishment									Total Employ-ment
	1-4 Emps.	5-9 Emps.	10-19 Emps.	20-49 Emps.	50-99 Emps.	100-249 Emps.	250-499 Emps.	>500 Emps.	Non-Employer	
2017	610.2	848.8	1,340.8	5,053.8	8,737.7	19,176.1	52,726.1	80,564.1	38.2	169,095.9
2018	652.4	907.5	1,433.5	5,403.1	9,341.6	20,501.5	56,370.4	84,872.4	40.8	179,523.2
2019	704.2	979.6	1,547.4	5,832.5	10,083.9	22,130.7	60,849.9	90,083.6	44.1	192,255.9

3-YEAR TREND – ESTIMATED NUMBER OF ESTABLISHMENTS

Year	Employee Size of Establishment									Total Employ-ment
	1-4 Emps.	5-9 Emps.	10-19 Emps.	20-49 Emps.	50-99 Emps.	100-249 Emps.	250-499 Emps.	>500 Emps.	Non-Employer	
2017	971	1,192	1,755	5,532	8,587	14,843	27,934	50,343	381	111,537
2018	1,009	1,239	1,825	5,750	8,925	15,429	29,036	52,328	396	115,937
2019	1,056	1,296	1,909	6,018	9,341	16,147	30,387	54,763	414	121,332

Pharmaceutical Preparation Mfg. Industry (NAICS 325412)

Sub-Industries – 2018 Estimated Industry Sales, Establishments & Employment

Sub-Industries	Category*	Establishments	Sales ($Mill)	Employment
Pharmaceutical preparations	Major1	1,119	164,961.1	84,415
Drugs affecting neoplasms and endrocrine systems	Minor1	3	284.6	216
Adrenal pharmaceutical preparations	Minor2	10	32.8	100
Hormone preparations	Minor2	2	1.6	37
Insulin preparations	Minor2	1	0.2	2
Pituitary gland pharmaceutical preparations	Minor2	0	0.1	1
Thyroid preparations	Minor2	1	0.4	53
Drugs acting on the central nervous system & sense organ	Minor1	5	78.7	938
Analgesics	Minor2	3	8.3	41
Barbituric acid pharmaceutical preparations	Minor2	1	5.4	37
Procaine pharmaceutical preparations	Minor2	1	0.5	0
Sodium salicylate tablets	Minor2	0	0.4	3
Tranquilizers or mental drug preparations	Minor2	1	0.1	4
Drugs acting on the cardiovascular system, except diagnc	Minor1	5	7.1	1,176
Digitalis pharmaceutical preparations	Minor2	2	4.4	35
Drugs acting on the respiratory system	Minor1	3	77.0	575
Antihistamine preparations	Minor2	0	0.3	138
Cold remedies	Minor2	1	0.9	7
Cough medicines	Minor2	5	2.0	204
Lozenges, pharmaceutical	Minor2	1	7.2	14
Syrups, pharmaceutical	Minor2	1	80.6	34
Drugs acting on the gastrointestinal or genitourinary syste	Minor1	4	195.1	69
Antacids	Minor2	1	0.5	5
Diuretics	Minor2	0	10.0	3
Effervescent salts	Minor2	1	22.4	79
Laxatives	Minor2	1	0.3	53
Dermatologicals	Minor1	55	428.8	1,099
Vitamin, nutrient, and hematinic preparations for human u	Minor1	185	2,009.7	8,828
Drugs affecting parasitic and infective diseases	Minor1	14	330.6	801
Chlorination tablets and kits (water purification)	Minor2	13	41.7	136
Druggists' preparations (pharmaceuticals)	Minor2	75	3,477.8	3,013
Emulsions, pharmaceutical	Minor2	0	0.4	3
Extracts of botanicals: powdered, pilular, solid, or fluid	Minor2	6	20.1	230
Misc. pharmaceutical preparations	Minor2	258	7,432.2	13,590

*Category-Major categories (Major1) are more general descriptions for companies that self-selected to capture the many functions they perform in the industry. Minor categories (Minor1, Minor2) are more specific for companies that have more detailed functions (Minor1 is a larger category than Minor2). Minor categories figures (sales, etc.) can be aggregated to larger minor categories (Minor2 sums to Minor1) and major categories overall figures.

ELECTRONIC COMPUTER MANUFACTURING INDUSTRY (NAICS 334111)

NAICS 334111: Electronic Computer Manufacturing . This U.S. industry comprises establishments primarily engaged in manufacturing and/or assembling electronic computers, such as mainframes, personal computers, workstations, laptops, and computer servers. Computers can be analog, digital, or hybrid. Digital computers, the most common type, are devices that do all of the following: (1) store the processing program or programs and the data immediately necessary for the execution of the program; (2) can be freely programmed in accordance with the requirements of the user; (3) perform arithmetical computations specified by the user.

INDUSTRY ESTABLISHMENTS, SALES & EMPLOYMENT TRENDS

	Year					Percent Chg. Year-to-Year			
	2015	2016	2017	2018	2019	15-16	16-17	17-18	18-19
Establishments	520	489	464	451	446	-5.8%	-5.2%	-2.7%	-1.0%
Sales ($Millions)	22,826	21,926	21,297	21,148	21,347	-3.9%	-2.9%	-0.7%	0.9%
Employment	11,250	10,594	10,038	9,763	9,665	-5.8%	-5.2%	-2.7%	-1.0%
Sales ($M)/Estab.	43.94	44.82	45.94	46.90	47.83	2.0%	2.5%	2.1%	2.0%
Sales ($)/Emp.	2,029,029	2,069,738	2,121,634	2,166,017	2,208,659	2.0%	2.5%	2.1%	2.0%

3-YEAR TREND – ESTIMATED NUMBER OF ESTABLISHMENTS

Year	Employee Size of Establishment									Total Employment
	1-4 Emps.	5-9 Emps.	10-19 Emps.	20-49 Emps.	50-99 Emps.	100-249 Emps.	250-499 Emps.	>500 Emps.	Non-Employer	
2017	182	42	46	35	21	18	6	2	111	464
2018	177	41	45	34	21	17	6	2	108	451
2019	175	40	45	34	21	17	6	2	107	446

3-YEAR TREND – ESTIMATED NUMBER OF ESTABLISHMENTS

Year	Employee Size of Establishment									Total Employment
	1-4 Emps.	5-9 Emps.	10-19 Emps.	20-49 Emps.	50-99 Emps.	100-249 Emps.	250-499 Emps.	>500 Emps.	Non-Employer	
2017	461.6	279.5	777.8	1,544.0	2,088.6	4,690.9	5,533.7	5,910.4	10.1	21,296.5
2018	454.9	275.4	766.3	1,521.3	2,058.0	4,622.2	5,452.6	5,987.1	9.9	21,147.7
2019	457.8	277.2	771.3	1,531.2	2,071.4	4,652.2	5,488.0	6,087.3	10.0	21,346.5

3-YEAR TREND – ESTIMATED NUMBER OF ESTABLISHMENTS

Year	Employee Size of Establishment									Total Employment
	1-4 Emps.	5-9 Emps.	10-19 Emps.	20-49 Emps.	50-99 Emps.	100-249 Emps.	250-499 Emps.	>500 Emps.	Non-Employer	
2017	455	243	631	1,047	1,272	2,250	1,817	2,211	111	10,038
2018	443	237	614	1,019	1,237	2,189	1,767	2,150	108	9,763
2019	438	234	608	1,009	1,225	2,167	1,749	2,129	107	9,665

© Barnes Reports: 2018 U.S. Industry & Market Outlook

ELECTRONIC COMPUTER MANUFACTURING INDUSTRY (NAICS 334111)

Sub-Industries – 2018 Estimated Industry Sales, Establishments & Employment

Sub-Industries	Category*	Establishments	Sales ($Mill)	Employment
Electronic computers	Major1	311	5,431.4	5,324
Computers, digital, analog or hybrid	Minor2	38	9.7	699
Mainframe computers	Minor2	14	2.5	455
Minicomputers	Minor2	21	12.9	1,997
Personal computers (microcomputers)	Minor2	68	15,691.2	1,288

*Category-Major categories (Major1) are more general descriptions for companies that self-selected to capture the many functions they perform in the industry. Minor categories (Minor1, Minor2) are more specific for companies that have more detailed functions (Minor1 is a larger category than Minor2). Minor categories figures (sales, etc.) can be aggregated to larger minor categories (Minor2 sums to Minor1) and major categories overall figures.

Telephone Equipment Mfg. Industry
NAICS 33421

NAICS 33421: Telephone Apparatus Manufacturing This industry comprises establishments primarily engaged in manufacturing wire telephone and data communications equipment. These products may be standalone or board-level components of a larger system. Examples of products made by these establishments are central office switching equipment, cordless telephones (except cellular), PBX equipment, telephones, telephone answering machines, and data communications equipment, such as bridges, routers, and gateways.

Industry Establishments, Sales & Employment Trends

	Year					Percent Chg. Year-to-Year			
	2015	2016	2017	2018	2019	15-16	16-17	17-18	18-19
Establishments	335	319	305	298	295	-4.8%	-4.4%	-2.6%	-0.8%
Sales ($Millions)	7,980	7,540	7,191	6,974	6,878	-5.5%	-4.6%	-3.0%	-1.4%
Employment	10,834	10,315	9,863	9,611	9,532	-4.8%	-4.4%	-2.6%	-0.8%
Sales ($M)/Estab.	23.79	23.61	23.55	23.44	23.31	-0.8%	-0.3%	-0.5%	-0.6%
Sales ($)/Emp.	736,563	730,943	729,048	725,632	721,606	-0.8%	-0.3%	-0.5%	-0.6%

3-Year Trend – Estimated Number of Establishments

Year	Employee Size of Establishment									Total Employment
	1-4 Emps.	5-9 Emps.	10-19 Emps.	20-49 Emps.	50-99 Emps.	100-249 Emps.	250-499 Emps.	>500 Emps.	Non-Employer	
2017	70	33	40	38	28	15	5	3	73	305
2018	68	32	39	37	28	15	4	3	71	298
2019	68	32	39	37	27	15	4	3	71	295

3-Year Trend – Estimated Number of Establishments

Year	Employee Size of Establishment									Total Employment
	1-4 Emps.	5-9 Emps.	10-19 Emps.	20-49 Emps.	50-99 Emps.	100-249 Emps.	250-499 Emps.	>500 Emps.	Non-Employer	
2017	60.9	74.8	229.9	580.9	942.6	1,393.1	1,381.0	2,521.4	6.3	7,190.9
2018	58.6	72.0	221.4	559.3	907.5	1,341.2	1,329.6	2,478.5	6.1	6,974.2
2019	57.7	70.9	217.8	550.3	892.8	1,319.6	1,308.1	2,454.9	6.0	6,878.1

3-Year Trend – Estimated Number of Establishments

Year	Employee Size of Establishment									Total Employment
	1-4 Emps.	5-9 Emps.	10-19 Emps.	20-49 Emps.	50-99 Emps.	100-249 Emps.	250-499 Emps.	>500 Emps.	Non-Employer	
2017	175	190	545	1,151	1,676	1,952	1,324	2,777	73	9,863
2018	171	185	531	1,122	1,634	1,902	1,290	2,706	71	9,611
2019	169	184	526	1,112	1,620	1,886	1,280	2,683	71	9,532

© Barnes Reports: 2018 U.S. Industry & Market Outlook

Telephone Equipment Mfg. Industry
NAICS 33421

Sub-Industries — 2018 Estimated Industry Sales, Establishments & Employment

Sub-Industries	Category*	Establishments	Sales ($Mill)	Employment
Telephone and telegraph apparatus	Major1	115	3,977.4	5,214
Telephones and telephone apparatus	Minor1	48	1,172.4	1,241
Autotransformers for telephone switchboards	Minor2	1	0.9	4
Communication headgear, telephone	Minor2	8	18.7	117
Facsimile equipment	Minor2	2	1.9	11
Headsets, telephone	Minor2	10	11.7	160
Modems	Minor2	11	556.0	121
Switching equipment, telephone	Minor2	5	9.8	506
Telephone answering machines	Minor2	2	0.8	8
Telephone central office equipment, dial or manual	Minor2	3	3.2	61
Telephone dialing devices, automatic	Minor2	3	2.1	40
Telephone sets, all types except cellular radio	Minor2	10	31.1	162
Telephone station equipment and parts, wire	Minor2	5	2.7	47
Telephones, sound powered (no battery)	Minor2	1	0.4	3
Toll switching equipment, telephone	Minor2	1	0.3	8
Telegraph and related apparatus	Minor1	1	0.3	5
PBX equipment, manual or automatic	Minor2	3	3.5	32
Telegraph or telephone carrier and repeater equipment	Minor2	2	1.1	15
Telegraph station equipment and parts, wire	Minor2	0	0.1	0
Carrier equipment, telephone or telegraph	Minor2	5	80.6	43
Data sets, telephone or telegraph	Minor2	2	0.7	59
Electronic secretary	Minor2	2	1.7	11
Message concentrators	Minor2	9	119.6	56
Multiplex equipment, telephone and telegraph	Minor2	1	2.4	52
Switchboards, telephone or telegraph	Minor2	0	0.1	0
Telephone cords, jacks, adapters, etc.	Minor2	5	7.5	38
Fiber optics communications equipment	Minor2	45	967.3	1,598

*Category-Major categories (Major1) are more general descriptions for companies that self-selected to capture the many functions they perform in the industry. Minor categories (Minor1, Minor2) are more specific for companies that have more detailed functions (Minor1 is a larger category than Minor2). Minor categories figures (sales, etc.) can be aggregated to larger minor categories (Minor2 sums to Minor1) and major categories overall figures.

Radio/TV Broadcast Equipment Industry
NAICS 33422

NAICS 33422: Radio/TV Broadcast Equipment. Establishments primarily engaged in manufacturing radio and television broadcasting and communications equipment. Includes closed-circuit and cable television equipment; studio equipment; light communications equipment; transmitters, transceivers and receivers (except household and automotive); cellular radio telephones; communication antennas; receivers; RF power amplifiers; and fixed and mobile radio systems.

Industry Establishments, Sales & Employment Trends

	Year					Percent Chg. Year-to-Year			
	2015	2016	2017	2018	2019	15-16	16-17	17-18	18-19
Establishments	1,000	954	917	893	885	-4.5%	-3.9%	-2.6%	-0.9%
Sales ($Millions)	32,195	30,603	29,394	28,555	28,165	-4.9%	-4.0%	-2.9%	-1.4%
Employment	45,426	43,375	41,687	40,582	40,208	-4.5%	-3.9%	-2.6%	-0.9%
Sales ($M)/Estab.	32.21	32.06	32.05	31.98	31.83	-0.4%	-0.1%	-0.2%	-0.4%
Sales ($)/Emp.	708,735	705,551	705,128	703,636	700,484	-0.4%	-0.1%	-0.2%	-0.4%

3-Year Trend – Estimated Number of Establishments

Year	Employee Size of Establishment									Total Employment
	1-4 Emps.	5-9 Emps.	10-19 Emps.	20-49 Emps.	50-99 Emps.	100-249 Emps.	250-499 Emps.	>500 Emps.	Non-Employer	
2017	201	110	106	117	70	53	23	18	220	917
2018	196	107	103	113	68	52	22	18	214	893
2019	194	106	102	112	67	51	22	18	212	885

3-Year Trend – Estimated Number of Establishments

Year	Employee Size of Establishment									Total Employment
	1-4 Emps.	5-9 Emps.	10-19 Emps.	20-49 Emps.	50-99 Emps.	100-249 Emps.	250-499 Emps.	>500 Emps.	Non-Employer	
2017	155.1	223.4	538.4	1,573.9	2,070.4	4,258.5	6,186.6	14,368.9	19.0	29,394.3
2018	149.2	214.9	517.9	1,513.9	1,991.4	4,096.0	5,950.6	14,102.7	18.2	28,554.9
2019	146.7	211.2	509.1	1,488.0	1,957.5	4,026.2	5,849.1	13,959.4	17.9	28,165.1

3-Year Trend – Estimated Number of Establishments

Year	Employee Size of Establishment									Total Employment
	1-4 Emps.	5-9 Emps.	10-19 Emps.	20-49 Emps.	50-99 Emps.	100-249 Emps.	250-499 Emps.	>500 Emps.	Non-Employer	
2017	502	639	1,435	3,508	4,143	6,712	6,674	17,854	220	41,687
2018	489	622	1,397	3,415	4,033	6,534	6,497	17,381	214	40,582
2019	485	616	1,384	3,384	3,996	6,474	6,437	17,221	212	40,208

© Barnes Reports: 2018 U.S. Industry & Market Outlook

Radio/TV Broadcast Equipment Industry
NAICS 33422

Sub-Industries – 2018 Estimated Industry Sales, Establishments & Employment

Sub-Industries	Category*	Establishments	Sales ($Mill)	Employment
Radio and t.v. communications equipment	Major1	267	18,768.5	14,492
Radio broadcasting and communications equipment	Minor1	73	1,370.6	2,906
Airborne radio communications equipment	Minor2	9	24.5	589
Amplifiers, RF power and IF	Minor2	16	593.5	823
Carrier equipment, radio communications	Minor2	7	34.6	48
Cellular radio telephone	Minor2	25	106.3	1,031
Citizens' band (CB) radio	Minor2	1	5.3	19
Marine radio communications equipment	Minor2	5	18.0	56
Multiplex equipment	Minor2	1	6.1	11
Pagers (one-way)	Minor2	8	7.0	408
Radio receiver networks	Minor2	11	13.4	732
Receivers, radio communications	Minor2	8	25.5	125
Transmitter-receivers, radio	Minor2	9	135.4	279
Television broadcasting and communications equipment	Minor1	33	1,270.7	1,450
Cable television equipment	Minor2	19	62.0	1,109
Cameras, television	Minor2	8	9.7	456
Television antennas (transmitting) and ground equipment	Minor2	4	0.3	117
Television closed circuit equipment	Minor2	16	346.2	249
Television monitors	Minor2	7	36.8	109
Radio and t.v. communications equipment, nec	Minor2	14	42.4	109
Antennas, transmitting and communications	Minor2	35	180.2	2,127
Digital encoders	Minor2	16	80.8	157
Encryption devices	Minor2	3	49.3	106
Light communications equipment	Minor2	4	17.0	83
Microwave communication equipment	Minor2	24	1,045.9	2,061
Mobile communication equipment	Minor2	46	1,021.5	1,055
Radio and television switching equipment	Minor2	1	19.7	157
Receiver-transmitter units (transceiver)	Minor2	6	141.4	249
Satellites, communications	Minor2	142	444.7	3,177
Space satellite communications equipment	Minor2	28	2,571.9	3,560
Studio equipment, radio and television broadcasting	Minor2	24	49.7	520
Telemetering equipment, electronic	Minor2	15	39.4	2,068
Transmitting apparatus, radio or television	Minor2	8	16.3	147

*Category-Major categories (Major1) are more general descriptions for companies that self-selected to capture the many functions they perform in the industry. Minor categories (Minor1, Minor2) are more specific for companies that have more detailed functions (Minor1 is a larger category than Minor2). Minor categories figures (sales, etc.) can be aggregated to larger minor categories (Minor2 sums to Minor1) and major categories overall figures.

AUDIO & VISUAL EQUIPMENT MFG. INDUSTRY
NAICS 33431

NAICS 33431: Audio & Video Equipment Manufacturing Industry.
This industry comprises establishments primarily engaged in manufacturing electronic audio and video equipment for home entertainment, motor vehicle, public address and musical instrument amplifications. Examples of products made by these establishments are video cassette recorders, televisions, stereo equipment, speaker systems, household-type video cameras, jukeboxes, and amplifiers for musical instruments and public address systems.

Industry Establishments, Sales & Employment Trends

	Year					Percent Chg. Year-to-Year			
	2015	2016	2017	2018	2019	15-16	16-17	17-18	18-19
Establishments	639	608	582	573	574	-4.9%	-4.3%	-1.5%	0.2%
Sales ($Millions)	2,677	2,525	2,410	2,376	2,393	-5.7%	-4.5%	-1.4%	0.7%
Employment	8,551	8,131	7,780	7,663	7,682	-4.9%	-4.3%	-1.5%	0.2%
Sales ($M)/Estab.	4.19	4.15	4.14	4.15	4.17	-0.8%	-0.2%	0.1%	0.5%
Sales ($)/Emp.	313,108	310,521	309,809	310,019	311,469	-0.8%	-0.2%	0.1%	0.5%

3-Year Trend – Estimated Number of Establishments

Year	Employee Size of Establishment									Total Employment
	1-4 Emps.	5-9 Emps.	10-19 Emps.	20-49 Emps.	50-99 Emps.	100-249 Emps.	250-499 Emps.	>500 Emps.	Non-Employer	
2017	208	78	65	47	26	14	4	0	139	582
2018	205	77	64	47	26	13	4	0	137	573
2019	206	77	64	47	26	13	4	0	138	574

3-Year Trend – Estimated Number of Establishments

Year	Employee Size of Establishment									Total Employment
	1-4 Emps.	5-9 Emps.	10-19 Emps.	20-49 Emps.	50-99 Emps.	100-249 Emps.	250-499 Emps.	>500 Emps.	Non-Employer	
2017	92.7	91.5	190.1	368.5	451.7	629.7	566.0	7.7	12.3	2,410.3
2018	91.4	90.2	187.3	363.2	445.2	620.6	557.8	7.7	12.1	2,375.7
2019	92.1	90.9	188.7	365.8	448.4	625.1	561.8	7.8	12.2	2,392.7

3-Year Trend – Estimated Number of Establishments

Year	Employee Size of Establishment									Total Employment
	1-4 Emps.	5-9 Emps.	10-19 Emps.	20-49 Emps.	50-99 Emps.	100-249 Emps.	250-499 Emps.	>500 Emps.	Non-Employer	
2017	521	454	879	1,424	1,567	1,721	1,059	17	139	7,780
2018	513	447	865	1,403	1,544	1,695	1,043	16	137	7,663
2019	514	448	867	1,406	1,548	1,699	1,045	16	138	7,682

© Barnes Reports: 2018 U.S. Industry & Market Outlook

Audio & Visual Equipment Mfg. Industry
NAICS 33431

Sub-Industries – 2018 Estimated Industry Sales, Establishments & Employment

Sub-Industries	Category*	Establishments	Sales ($Mill)	Employment
Household audio and video equipment	Major1	153	1,504.2	2,117
Household audio equipment	Minor1	33	66.5	707
Amplifiers: radio, public address, or musical instrument	Minor2	30	59.3	592
Audio electronic systems	Minor2	134	270.9	944
Coin-operated phonographs, juke boxes	Minor2	1	5.0	52
Compact disk players	Minor2	6	2.7	20
FM and AM radio tuners	Minor2	3	0.9	10
Loudspeakers, electrodynamic or magnetic	Minor2	12	27.1	279
Microphones	Minor2	9	23.5	189
Music distribution apparatus	Minor2	19	26.2	125
Phonograph and radio combinations	Minor2	0	0.0	0
Phonographs	Minor2	0	0.1	0
Pillows, stereo	Minor2	1	0.5	4
Public address systems	Minor2	2	5.5	29
Radio receiving sets	Minor2	2	1.4	49
Recording machines, except dictation and telephone answ	Minor2	4	4.6	29
Sound reproducing equipment	Minor2	12	11.6	65
Speaker monitors	Minor2	5	8.6	40
Speaker systems	Minor2	35	88.4	745
Tape players, household use	Minor2	0	0.2	1
Tape recorders: cassette, cartridge or reel: household use	Minor2	3	2.7	19
Household video equipment	Minor2	8	6.7	499
Television receiving sets	Minor2	6	6.1	637
Video camera-audio recorders, household use	Minor2	10	11.1	49
Video cassette recorders/players and accessories	Minor2	9	8.5	56
Video triggers (remote control TV devices)	Minor2	3	131.6	40
Electronic kits for home assembly: radio, TV, phonograph	Minor2	16	12.3	98
Home entertainment equipment, electronic, nec	Minor2	54	89.7	269
Pickup heads, phonograph	Minor2	0	0.0	0

*Category-Major categories (Major1) are more general descriptions for companies that self-selected to capture the many functions they perform in the industry. Minor categories (Minor1, Minor2) are more specific for companies that have more detailed functions (Minor1 is a larger category than Minor2). Minor categories figures (sales, etc.) can be aggregated to larger minor categories (Minor2 sums to Minor1) and major categories overall figures.

Semi-Conductor & Electronic Components Mfg.
NAICS 33441

NAICS 33441: Semiconductor and Other Electronic Component Manufacturing This industry comprises establishments primarily engaged in manufacturing semiconductors and other components for electronic applications. Examples of products made by these establishments are capacitors, resistors, microprocessors, bare and loaded printed circuit boards, electron tubes, electronic connectors, and computer modems.

Industry Establishments, Sales & Employment Trends

	Year					Percent Chg. Year-to-Year			
	2015	2016	2017	2018	2019	15-16	16-17	17-18	18-19
Establishments	5,233	5,044	4,896	4,765	4,719	-3.6%	-2.9%	-2.7%	-1.0%
Sales ($Millions)	145,966	146,771	149,121	152,019	157,593	0.6%	1.6%	1.9%	3.7%
Employment	209,729	202,149	196,210	190,949	189,129	-3.6%	-2.9%	-2.7%	-1.0%
Sales ($M)/Estab.	27.89	29.10	30.46	31.91	33.39	4.3%	4.7%	4.8%	4.7%
Sales ($)/Emp.	695,973	726,055	760,006	796,126	833,260	4.3%	4.7%	4.8%	4.7%

3-Year Trend – Estimated Number of Establishments

Year	Employee Size of Establishment									Total
	1-4 Emps.	5-9 Emps.	10-19 Emps.	20-49 Emps.	50-99 Emps.	100-249 Emps.	250-499 Emps.	>500 Emps.	Non-Employer	Employment
2017	968	493	543	736	429	359	123	70	1,173	4,896
2018	942	480	528	717	418	350	120	68	1,142	4,765
2019	933	475	523	710	414	346	119	68	1,131	4,719

3-Year Trend – Estimated Number of Establishments

Year	Employee Size of Establishment									Total
	1-4 Emps.	5-9 Emps.	10-19 Emps.	20-49 Emps.	50-99 Emps.	100-249 Emps.	250-499 Emps.	>500 Emps.	Non-Employer	Employment
2017	838.2	1,121.7	3,104.5	11,150.1	14,295.0	32,232.3	37,344.0	48,921.5	113.5	149,120.7
2018	851.1	1,139.1	3,152.6	11,322.6	14,516.2	32,731.0	37,921.8	50,269.7	115.2	152,019.2
2019	881.1	1,179.2	3,263.6	11,721.4	15,027.5	33,883.8	39,257.5	52,259.9	119.3	157,593.3

3-Year Trend – Estimated Number of Establishments

Year	Employee Size of Establishment									Total
	1-4 Emps.	5-9 Emps.	10-19 Emps.	20-49 Emps.	50-99 Emps.	100-249 Emps.	250-499 Emps.	>500 Emps.	Non-Employer	Employment
2017	2,421	2,860	7,380	22,162	25,507	45,301	35,924	53,483	1,173	196,210
2018	2,356	2,783	7,182	21,567	24,823	44,086	34,960	52,049	1,142	190,949
2019	2,333	2,756	7,113	21,362	24,587	43,666	34,627	51,553	1,131	189,129

© Barnes Reports: 2018 U.S. Industry & Market Outlook

Semi-Conductor & Electronic Components Mfg.
NAICS 33441

Sub-Industries – 2018 Estimated Industry Sales, Establishments & Employment

Sub-Industries	Category*	Establishments	Sales ($Mill)	Employment
Semiconductors and related devices	Major1	1,863	33,910.2	61,052
Semiconductor diodes and rectifiers	Minor1	13	16.9	272
Controlled rectifiers, solid state	Minor2	1	1.6	0
Diodes, solid state (germanium, silicon, etc.)	Minor2	7	8.6	224
Light emitting diodes	Minor2	56	102.6	721
Thrystors	Minor2	1	1.3	16
Zener diodes	Minor2	1	0.3	5
Integrated circuits, semiconductor networks, etc.	Minor1	297	17,223.4	12,544
Computer logic modules	Minor2	56	186.1	458
Hybrid integrated circuits	Minor2	46	113.1	850
Magnetic bubble memory device	Minor2	4	11.1	68
Memories, solid state	Minor2	18	253.7	1,516
Metal oxide silicon (MOS) devices	Minor2	5	0.4	498
Microcircuits, integrated (semiconductor)	Minor2	104	7,648.5	8,422
Microprocessors	Minor2	43	37,058.6	14,692
Monolithic integrated circuits (solid state)	Minor2	5	0.5	4,264
Random access memory (RAM)	Minor2	20	39.4	681
Read-only memory (ROM)	Minor2	10	0.4	7
Semiconductor circuit networks	Minor2	56	445.6	3,832
Thin film circuits	Minor2	12	13.5	318
Wafers (semiconductor devices)	Minor2	40	150.8	3,691
Light sensitive devices	Minor1	233	4,604.0	4,677
Radiation sensors	Minor1	88	40.9	5,418
Misc. semiconductor devices	Minor1	251	2,505.1	7,059
Electronic components, nec	Major1	500	1,801.3	4,440
Electronic circuits	Minor1	815	40,476.5	42,091
Attenuators	Minor2	7	170.5	2,135
Commutators, electronic	Minor2	17	161.7	398
Delay lines	Minor2	5	20.9	71
Impedance conversion units, high frequency	Minor2	2	2.0	6
Microwave components	Minor2	134	4,237.5	7,026
Passive repeaters	Minor2	1	19.5	26
Pulse forming networks	Minor2	3	4.7	9
Misc. electronic components	Minor2	50	787.8	3,464

*Category-Major categories (Major1) are more general descriptions for companies that self-selected to capture the many functions they perform in the industry. Minor categories (Minor1, Minor2) are more specific for companies that have more detailed functions (Minor1 is a larger category than Minor2). Minor categories figures (sales, etc.) can be aggregated to larger minor categories (Minor2 sums to Minor1) and major categories overall figures.

Software Reproducing Industry
(NAICS 334611)

NAICS 334611 Software Reproducing This U.S. industry comprises establishments primarily engaged in mass reproducing computer software. These establishments do not generally develop any software, they mass reproduce data and programs on magnetic media, such as diskettes, tapes, or cartridges. Establishments in this industry mass reproduce products, such as CD-ROMs and game cartridges.

Industry Establishments, Sales & Employment Trends

	Year					Percent Chg. Year-to-Year			
	2015	2016	2017	2018	2019	15-16	16-17	17-18	18-19
Establishments	580	556	536	521	515	-4.2%	-3.6%	-2.8%	-1.0%
Sales ($Millions)	1,626	1,538	1,472	1,426	1,412	-5.4%	-4.3%	-3.1%	-1.0%
Employment	7,856	7,528	7,254	7,054	6,982	-4.2%	-3.6%	-2.8%	-1.0%
Sales ($M)/Estab.	2.80	2.77	2.75	2.74	2.74	-1.3%	-0.7%	-0.4%	0.0%
Sales ($)/Emp.	206,954	204,321	202,928	202,152	202,197	-1.3%	-0.7%	-0.4%	0.0%

3-Year Trend – Estimated Number of Establishments

Year	Employee Size of Establishment									Total
	1-4 Emps.	5-9 Emps.	10-19 Emps.	20-49 Emps.	50-99 Emps.	100-249 Emps.	250-499 Emps.	>500 Emps.	Non-Employer	Employment
2017	241	54	41	42	12	12	2	3	128	536
2018	234	53	40	41	12	12	2	3	125	521
2019	232	52	39	41	12	12	2	3	124	515

3-Year Trend – Estimated Number of Establishments

Year	Employee Size of Establishment									Total
	1-4 Emps.	5-9 Emps.	10-19 Emps.	20-49 Emps.	50-99 Emps.	100-249 Emps.	250-499 Emps.	>500 Emps.	Non-Employer	Employment
2017	63.8	37.9	71.1	196.7	122.2	329.3	170.8	469.1	11.2	1,472.1
2018	61.8	36.7	68.9	190.5	118.4	319.0	165.4	454.5	10.9	1,426.1
2019	61.2	36.3	68.2	188.6	117.2	315.8	163.8	449.9	10.8	1,411.7

3-Year Trend – Estimated Number of Establishments

Year	Employee Size of Establishment									Total
	1-4 Emps.	5-9 Emps.	10-19 Emps.	20-49 Emps.	50-99 Emps.	100-249 Emps.	250-499 Emps.	>500 Emps.	Non-Employer	Employment
2017	602	316	553	1,278	713	1,514	537	1,613	128	7,254
2018	586	307	537	1,243	693	1,472	522	1,568	125	7,054
2019	580	304	532	1,230	686	1,457	517	1,552	124	6,982

SOFTWARE REPRODUCING INDUSTRY
(NAICS 334611)

SUB-INDUSTRIES – 2018 ESTIMATED INDUSTRY SALES, ESTABLISHMENTS & EMPLOYMENT

Sub-Industries	Category*	Establishments	Sales ($Mill)	Employment
Computer related services, nec	Major1	114	77.4	627
Computer related maintenance services	Minor1	26	74.0	609
Disk and diskette conversion service	Minor2	1	1.9	12
Disk and diskette recertification service	Minor2	0	0.1	1
Tape recertification service	Minor2	0	0.1	0
Word processing equipment maintenance	Minor2	0	0.1	1
Computer data escrow service	Minor2	1	3.1	17
Computer related consulting services	Minor1	321	1,054.7	4,775
Computer hardware requirements analysis	Minor2	2	6.2	25
Data processing consultant	Minor2	11	35.7	196
Online services technology consultants	Minor2	45	172.7	792

*Category-Major categories (Major1) are more general descriptions for companies that self-selected to capture the many functions they perform in the industry. Minor categories (Minor1, Minor2) are more specific for companies that have more detailed functions (Minor1 is a larger category than Minor2). Minor categories figures (sales, etc.) can be aggregated to larger minor categories (Minor2 sums to Minor1) and major categories overall figures.

MAJOR APPLIANCE MANUFACTURING INDUSTRY
NAICS 33522

NAICS 33522: Appliance Manufacturing Industry. This industry comprises establishments primarily engaged in manufacturing household-type cooking appliances, household-type laundry equipment, household-type refrigerators, upright and chest freezers, and other electrical and nonelectrical major household-type appliances, such as dishwashers, water heaters, and garbage disposal units.

INDUSTRY ESTABLISHMENTS, SALES & EMPLOYMENT TRENDS

	Year					Percent Chg. Year-to-Year			
	2015	2016	2017	2018	2019	15-16	16-17	17-18	18-19
Establishments	229	215	203	196	189	-5.9%	-5.7%	-3.7%	-3.4%
Sales ($Millions)	13,997	13,506	13,128	12,887	12,719	-3.5%	-2.8%	-1.8%	-1.3%
Employment	29,493	27,764	26,190	25,213	24,356	-5.9%	-5.7%	-3.7%	-3.4%
Sales ($M)/Estab.	61.19	62.72	64.63	65.91	67.34	2.5%	3.0%	2.0%	2.2%
Sales ($)/Emp.	474,584	486,454	501,269	511,135	522,214	2.5%	3.0%	2.0%	2.2%

3-YEAR TREND – ESTIMATED NUMBER OF ESTABLISHMENTS

Year	Employee Size of Establishment									Total Employ-ment
	1-4 Emps.	5-9 Emps.	10-19 Emps.	20-49 Emps.	50-99 Emps.	100-249 Emps.	250-499 Emps.	>500 Emps.	Non-Employer	
2017	41	14	16	19	11	12	6	20	64	203
2018	39	14	15	18	10	12	6	20	61	196
2019	38	13	15	17	10	12	6	19	59	189

3-YEAR TREND – ESTIMATED NUMBER OF ESTABLISHMENTS

Year	Employee Size of Establishment									Total Employ-ment
	1-4 Emps.	5-9 Emps.	10-19 Emps.	20-49 Emps.	50-99 Emps.	100-249 Emps.	250-499 Emps.	>500 Emps.	Non-Employer	
2017	19.9	18.2	51.5	159.0	199.7	627.9	1,058.2	10,987.7	6.1	13,128.2
2018	19.0	17.4	49.2	152.0	190.9	600.3	1,011.6	10,840.6	5.9	12,887.0
2019	18.3	16.8	47.4	146.4	183.9	578.3	974.5	10,747.9	5.7	12,719.2

3-YEAR TREND – ESTIMATED NUMBER OF ESTABLISHMENTS

Year	Employee Size of Establishment									Total Employ-ment
	1-4 Emps.	5-9 Emps.	10-19 Emps.	20-49 Emps.	50-99 Emps.	100-249 Emps.	250-499 Emps.	>500 Emps.	Non-Employer	
2017	102	82	217	561	633	1,568	1,808	21,154	64	26,190
2018	98	79	209	540	609	1,509	1,741	20,365	61	25,213
2019	95	77	202	522	589	1,458	1,682	19,673	59	24,356

© Barnes Reports: 2018 U.S. Industry & Market Outlook

MAJOR APPLIANCE MANUFACTURING INDUSTRY
NAICS 33522

SUB-INDUSTRIES – 2018 ESTIMATED INDUSTRY SALES, ESTABLISHMENTS & EMPLOYMENT

Sub-Industries	Category*	Establishments	Sales ($Mill)	Employment
Household cooking equipment	Major1	40	138.1	9,535
Indoor cooking equipment	Minor1	3	1.1	2,168
Convection ovens, including portable: household	Minor2	3	12.2	424
Electric ranges, domestic	Minor2	2	8,258.8	66
Gas ranges, domestic	Minor2	4	0.3	1,694
Microwave ovens, including portable: household	Minor2	4	2.9	21
Stoves, disk	Minor2	4	16.2	18
Barbecues, grills, and braziers (outdoor cooking)	Minor2	72	161.8	2,882
Household refrigerators and freezers	Major1	34	1,299.5	1,471
Freezers, home and farm	Minor2	12	1,493.8	195
Ice boxes, household: metal or wood	Minor2	1	17.3	9
Refrigerator cabinets, household: metal and wood	Minor2	4	185.6	248
Refrigerators, mechanical and absorption: household	Minor2	15	1,299.5	6,480

*Category-Major categories (Major1) are more general descriptions for companies that self-selected to capture the many functions they perform in the industry. Minor categories (Minor1, Minor2) are more specific for companies that have more detailed functions (Minor1 is a larger category than Minor2). Minor categories figures (sales, etc.) can be aggregated to larger minor categories (Minor2 sums to Minor1) and major categories overall figures.

Automobile & Motor Vehicle Mfg. Industry
NAICS 33611

NAICS 33611: Automobile & Light Motor Vehicle Manufacturing. This industry comprises establishments primarily engaged in (1) manufacturing complete automobile and light duty motor vehicles (i.e., body and chassis or unibody) or (2) manufacturing chassis only.

Industry Establishments, Sales & Employment Trends

	Year					Percent Chg. Year-to-Year			
	2015	2016	2017	2018	2019	15-16	16-17	17-18	18-19
Establishments	312	308	300	295	293	-1.1%	-2.9%	-1.4%	-0.8%
Sales ($Millions)	201,027	200,574	200,963	202,262	204,482	-0.2%	0.2%	0.6%	1.1%
Employment	60,069	59,388	57,682	56,867	56,406	-1.1%	-2.9%	-1.4%	-0.8%
Sales ($M)/Estab.	644.27	650.19	670.72	684.73	697.91	0.9%	3.2%	2.1%	1.9%
Sales ($)/Emp.	3,346,586	3,377,345	3,483,963	3,556,724	3,625,182	0.9%	3.2%	2.1%	1.9%

3-Year Trend – Estimated Number of Establishments

Year	Employee Size of Establishment									Total Employment
	1-4 Emps.	5-9 Emps.	10-19 Emps.	20-49 Emps.	50-99 Emps.	100-249 Emps.	250-499 Emps.	>500 Emps.	Non-Employer	
2017	85	38	28	29	12	12	2	45	50	300
2018	83	38	27	28	11	11	2	44	49	295
2019	83	38	27	28	11	11	2	44	49	293

3-Year Trend – Estimated Number of Establishments

Year	Employee Size of Establishment									Total Employment
	1-4 Emps.	5-9 Emps.	10-19 Emps.	20-49 Emps.	50-99 Emps.	100-249 Emps.	250-499 Emps.	>500 Emps.	Non-Employer	
2017	305.4	364.8	665.2	1,821.4	1,601.5	4,316.4	2,424.7	189,459.0	4.8	200,963.2
2018	303.5	362.5	661.0	1,809.8	1,591.4	4,289.0	2,409.3	190,830.7	4.7	202,262.0
2019	304.5	363.8	663.3	1,816.3	1,597.1	4,304.4	2,417.9	193,009.5	4.7	204,481.7

3-Year Trend – Estimated Number of Establishments

Year	Employee Size of Establishment									Total Employment
	1-4 Emps.	5-9 Emps.	10-19 Emps.	20-49 Emps.	50-99 Emps.	100-249 Emps.	250-499 Emps.	>500 Emps.	Non-Employer	
2017	211	223	379	867	684	1,453	559	53,256	50	57,682
2018	208	220	373	855	675	1,433	551	52,504	49	56,867
2019	207	218	370	848	669	1,421	546	52,078	49	56,406

© Barnes Reports: 2018 U.S. Industry & Market Outlook

Automobile & Motor Vehicle Mfg. Industry
NAICS 33611

Sub-Industries — 2018 Estimated Industry Sales, Establishments & Employment

Sub-Industries	Category*	Establishments	Sales ($Mill)	Employment
Motor vehicles and car bodies	Major1	112	106,651.7	27,690
Automobile assembly, including specialty automobiles	Minor1	104	93,745.1	25,198
Ambulances (motor vehicles), assembly of	Minor2	7	312.5	621
Automobile bodies, passenger car, not including engine, e	Minor2	32	120.5	948
Cars, armored, assembly of	Minor2	9	141.5	345
Cars, electric, assembly of	Minor2	7	15.6	83
Chassis, motor vehicle	Minor2	21	1,267.5	1,661
Hearses (motor vehicles), assembly of	Minor2	1	6.3	150
Patrol wagons (motor vehicles), assembly of	Minor2	1	0.6	164
Station wagons (motor vehicles), assembly of	Minor2	0	0.1	0
Taxicabs, assembly of	Minor2	1	0.7	6

*Category-Major categories (Major1) are more general descriptions for companies that self-selected to capture the many functions they perform in the industry. Minor categories (Minor1, Minor2) are more specific for companies that have more detailed functions (Minor1 is a larger category than Minor2). Minor categories figures (sales, etc.) can be aggregated to larger minor categories (Minor2 sums to Minor1) and major categories overall figures.

Heavy Duty Truck Manufacturing Industry
NAICS 33612

NAICS 33612: Heavy Duty Truck Manufacturing Industry
This industry comprises establishments primarily engaged in (1) manufacturing heavy duty truck chassis and assembling complete heavy duty trucks, buses, heavy duty motor homes, and other special purpose heavy duty motor vehicles for highway use or (2) manufacturing heavy duty truck chassis only.

Industry Establishments, Sales & Employment Trends

	Year					Percent Chg. Year-to-Year			
	2015	2016	2017	2018	2019	15-16	16-17	17-18	18-19
Establishments	96	95	92	90	88	-1.1%	-2.8%	-2.8%	-2.2%
Sales ($Millions)	20,345	20,263	20,152	20,106	20,191	-0.4%	-0.5%	-0.2%	0.4%
Employment	20,873	20,643	20,057	19,495	19,063	-1.1%	-2.8%	-2.8%	-2.2%
Sales ($M)/Estab.	211.91	213.41	218.44	224.24	230.28	0.7%	2.4%	2.7%	2.7%
Sales ($)/Emp.	974,671	981,556	1,004,692	1,031,377	1,059,176	0.7%	2.4%	2.7%	2.7%

3-Year Trend – Estimated Number of Establishments

Year	Employee Size of Establishment								Non-Employer	Total Employment
	1-4 Emps.	5-9 Emps.	10-19 Emps.	20-49 Emps.	50-99 Emps.	100-249 Emps.	250-499 Emps.	>500 Emps.		
2017	13	6	8	12	5	10	6	17	15	92
2018	13	6	7	12	5	9	6	17	15	90
2019	13	5	7	12	5	9	5	16	15	88

3-Year Trend – Estimated Number of Establishments

Year	Employee Size of Establishment								Non-Employer	Total Employment
	1-4 Emps.	5-9 Emps.	10-19 Emps.	20-49 Emps.	50-99 Emps.	100-249 Emps.	250-499 Emps.	>500 Emps.		
2017	13.6	15.3	51.2	220.2	186.1	1,003.3	2,029.0	16,631.4	1.5	20,151.6
2018	13.3	15.0	50.2	216.0	182.7	984.6	1,991.1	16,652.1	1.4	20,106.4
2019	13.2	14.8	49.8	214.1	181.0	975.7	1,973.2	16,768.0	1.4	20,191.3

3-Year Trend – Estimated Number of Establishments

Year	Employee Size of Establishment								Non-Employer	Total Employment
	1-4 Emps.	5-9 Emps.	10-19 Emps.	20-49 Emps.	50-99 Emps.	100-249 Emps.	250-499 Emps.	>500 Emps.		
2017	34	33	105	376	285	1,212	1,677	16,320	15	20,057
2018	33	33	102	365	277	1,178	1,630	15,862	15	19,495
2019	32	32	99	357	271	1,152	1,594	15,511	15	19,063

© Barnes Reports: 2018 U.S. Industry & Market Outlook

Heavy Duty Truck Manufacturing Industry
NAICS 33612

Sub-Industries – 2018 Estimated Industry Sales, Establishments & Employment

Sub-Industries	Category*	Establishments	Sales ($Mill)	Employment
Truck and tractor truck assembly	Minor1	12	14,430.1	5,018
Motor trucks, except off-highway, assembly of	Minor2	1	0.4	2,987
Truck tractors for highway use, assembly of	Minor2	3	1.1	2,563
Trucks, pickup, assembly of	Minor2	5	4.5	1,308
Military motor vehicle assembly	Minor1	5	522.9	2,174
Amphibian motor vehicles, assembly of	Minor2	0	0.1	3
Personnel carriers (motor vehicles), assembly of	Minor2	3	6.2	49
Reconnaissance cars, assembly of	Minor2	1	2.1	16
Scout cars (motor vehicles), assembly of	Minor2	1	0.4	25
Universal carriers, military, assembly of	Minor2	0	0.3	3
Bus and other large specialty vehicle assembly	Minor1	5	26.1	457
Brooms, powered (motor vehicles), assembly of	Minor2	0	0.1	2
Buses, all types, assembly of	Minor2	8	48.6	817
Fire department vehicles (motor vehicles), assembly of	Minor2	19	4,970.0	2,593
Mobile lounges (motor vehicle), assembly of	Minor2	1	0.7	8
Motor buses, except trackless trollies, assembly of	Minor2	1	12.3	219
Motor homes, self contained, assembly of	Minor2	2	7.7	296
Road oilers (motor vehicles), assembly of	Minor2	1	1.2	14
Snow plows (motor vehicles), assembly of	Minor2	6	22.9	224
Street sprinklers and sweepers (motor vehicles), assembly	Minor2	2	13.1	481
Wreckers (tow truck), assembly of	Minor2	13	35.4	239

*Category-Major categories (Major1) are more general descriptions for companies that self-selected to capture the many functions they perform in the industry. Minor categories (Minor1, Minor2) are more specific for companies that have more detailed functions (Minor1 is a larger category than Minor2). Minor categories figures (sales, etc.) can be aggregated to larger minor categories (Minor2 sums to Minor1) and major categories overall figures.

AUTOMOBILE GAS ENGINE & ENGINE PARTS MFG.
NAICS 33631

NAICS 33631: Motor Vehicle Gas Engine & Engine Parts Manufacturing Industry. This industry comprises establishments primarily engaged in manufacturing and/or rebuilding motor vehicle gasoline engines, and engine parts, whether or not for vehicular use.

INDUSTRY ESTABLISHMENTS, SALES & EMPLOYMENT TRENDS

	Year					Percent Chg. Year-to-Year			
	2015	2016	2017	2018	2019	15-16	16-17	17-18	18-19
Establishments	1,030	1,007	967	946	931	-2.2%	-4.0%	-2.1%	-1.6%
Sales ($Millions)	24,528	23,190	21,732	20,704	19,884	-5.5%	-6.3%	-4.7%	-4.0%
Employment	49,317	48,233	46,306	45,311	44,607	-2.2%	-4.0%	-2.1%	-1.6%
Sales ($M)/Estab.	23.82	23.03	22.48	21.89	21.35	-3.3%	-2.4%	-2.6%	-2.4%
Sales ($)/Emp.	497,351	480,792	469,322	456,932	445,749	-3.3%	-2.4%	-2.6%	-2.4%

3-YEAR TREND – ESTIMATED NUMBER OF ESTABLISHMENTS

Year	Employee Size of Establishment									Total Employ-ment
	1-4 Emps.	5-9 Emps.	10-19 Emps.	20-49 Emps.	50-99 Emps.	100-249 Emps.	250-499 Emps.	>500 Emps.	Non-Employer	
2017	370	136	75	80	32	50	34	29	161	967
2018	362	133	74	78	31	49	33	28	158	946
2019	356	131	72	77	31	48	33	28	155	931

3-YEAR TREND – ESTIMATED NUMBER OF ESTABLISHMENTS

Year	Employee Size of Establishment									Total Employ-ment
	1-4 Emps.	5-9 Emps.	10-19 Emps.	20-49 Emps.	50-99 Emps.	100-249 Emps.	250-499 Emps.	>500 Emps.	Non-Employer	
2017	178.7	172.8	239.8	674.3	592.9	2,491.1	5,702.9	11,665.6	14.2	21,732.4
2018	169.2	163.7	227.1	638.8	561.7	2,359.8	5,402.4	11,167.7	13.5	20,703.9
2019	161.9	156.6	217.2	611.0	537.2	2,257.0	5,167.0	10,763.0	12.9	19,883.6

3-YEAR TREND – ESTIMATED NUMBER OF ESTABLISHMENTS

Year	Employee Size of Establishment									Total Employ-ment
	1-4 Emps.	5-9 Emps.	10-19 Emps.	20-49 Emps.	50-99 Emps.	100-249 Emps.	250-499 Emps.	>500 Emps.	Non-Employer	
2017	925	790	1,022	2,402	1,896	6,275	9,833	23,002	161	46,306
2018	905	773	1,000	2,351	1,856	6,140	9,622	22,508	158	45,311
2019	891	761	984	2,314	1,827	6,045	9,472	22,158	155	44,607

© Barnes Reports: 2018 U.S. Industry & Market Outlook

Automobile Gas Engine & Engine Parts Mfg.
NAICS 33631

Sub-Industries – 2018 Estimated Industry Sales, Establishments & Employment

Sub-Industries	Category*	Establishments	Sales ($Mill)	Employment
Motor vehicle parts and accessories	Major1	610	17,772.8	35,353
Motor vehicle engines and parts	Minor1	77	1,364.8	2,580
Acceleration equipment, motor vehicle	Minor2	5	3.6	131
Camshafts, motor vehicle	Minor2	6	11.3	257
Choker rods, motor vehicle	Minor2	0	0.0	0
Cleaners, air, motor vehicle	Minor2	7	1.2	159
Connecting rods, motor vehicle engine	Minor2	4	3.0	190
Crankshaft assemblies, motor vehicle	Minor2	3	19.0	99
Cylinder heads, motor vehicle	Minor2	15	20.1	204
Differentials and parts, motor vehicle	Minor2	4	6.4	48
Exhaust systems and parts, motor vehicle	Minor2	36	109.1	1,517
Filters: oil, fuel, and air, motor vehicle	Minor2	21	655.3	991
Fuel pipes, motor vehicle	Minor2	0	0.0	0
Fuel pumps, motor vehicle	Minor2	5	62.8	278
Fuel systems and parts, motor vehicle	Minor2	23	356.1	669
Gas tanks, motor vehicle	Minor2	4	0.9	79
Governors, motor vehicle	Minor2	1	0.7	5
Lubrication systems and parts, motor vehicle	Minor2	4	2.3	259
Manifolds, motor vehicle	Minor2	5	7.1	211
Mufflers (exhaust), motor vehicle	Minor2	18	27.5	681
Oil pump, motor vehicle	Minor2	3	0.5	14
Oil strainers, motor vehicle	Minor2	1	0.2	4
Propane conversion equipment, motor vehicle	Minor2	40	5.4	80
Radiators and radiator shells and cores, motor vehicle	Minor2	23	156.6	820
Rebuilding engines and transmissions, factory basis	Minor2	25	111.6	526
Tie rods, motor vehicle	Minor2	1	0.1	71
Water pump, motor vehicle	Minor2	7	5.8	85

*Category-Major categories (Major1) are more general descriptions for companies that self-selected to capture the many functions they perform in the industry. Minor categories (Minor1, Minor2) are more specific for companies that have more detailed functions (Minor1 is a larger category than Minor2). Minor categories figures (sales, etc.) can be aggregated to larger minor categories (Minor2 sums to Minor1) and major categories overall figures.

Aircraft Manufacturing Industry
(NAICS 336411)

NAICS 336411: Aircraft Manufacturing. This U.S. industry comprises establishments primarily engaged in one or more of the following: (1) manufacturing or assembling complete aircraft; (2) developing and making aircraft prototypes; (3) aircraft conversion (i.e., major modifications to systems); and (4) complete aircraft overhaul and rebuilding (i.e., periodic restoration of aircraft to original design specifications).

Industry Establishments, Sales & Employment Trends

	Year					Percent Chg. Year-to-Year			
	2015	2016	2017	2018	2019	15-16	16-17	17-18	18-19
Establishments	385	388	384	385	388	0.6%	-1.1%	0.3%	0.9%
Sales ($Millions)	99,369	102,090	104,736	108,209	112,350	2.7%	2.6%	3.3%	3.8%
Employment	49,576	49,892	49,368	49,503	49,940	0.6%	-1.1%	0.3%	0.9%
Sales ($M)/Estab.	257.95	263.33	273.03	281.31	289.52	2.1%	3.7%	3.0%	2.9%
Sales ($)/Emp.	2,004,390	2,046,209	2,121,545	2,185,920	2,249,706	2.1%	3.7%	3.0%	2.9%

3-Year Trend – Estimated Number of Establishments

Year	Employee Size of Establishment									Total Employment
	1-4 Emps.	5-9 Emps.	10-19 Emps.	20-49 Emps.	50-99 Emps.	100-249 Emps.	250-499 Emps.	>500 Emps.	Non-Employer	
2017	102	42	37	41	22	23	16	38	64	384
2018	102	42	37	41	22	23	16	38	64	385
2019	103	42	37	41	22	23	16	38	65	388

3-Year Trend – Estimated Number of Establishments

Year	Employee Size of Establishment									Total Employment
	1-4 Emps.	5-9 Emps.	10-19 Emps.	20-49 Emps.	50-99 Emps.	100-249 Emps.	250-499 Emps.	>500 Emps.	Non-Employer	
2017	225.2	243.7	539.9	1,583.6	1,867.9	5,263.1	12,340.1	82,666.3	6.4	104,736.1
2018	233.0	252.2	558.7	1,638.8	1,933.0	5,446.7	12,770.7	85,369.1	6.6	108,209.0
2019	243.3	263.3	583.3	1,710.8	2,017.9	5,685.8	13,331.1	88,508.0	6.9	112,350.3

3-Year Trend – Estimated Number of Establishments

Year	Employee Size of Establishment									Total Employment
	1-4 Emps.	5-9 Emps.	10-19 Emps.	20-49 Emps.	50-99 Emps.	100-249 Emps.	250-499 Emps.	>500 Emps.	Non-Employer	
2017	254	243	501	1,229	1,301	2,888	4,635	38,253	64	49,368
2018	255	243	502	1,232	1,305	2,896	4,648	38,358	64	49,503
2019	257	245	507	1,243	1,316	2,922	4,689	38,696	65	49,940

© Barnes Reports: 2018 U.S. Industry & Market Outlook

AIRCRAFT MANUFACTURING INDUSTRY
(NAICS 336411)

SUB-INDUSTRIES – 2018 ESTIMATED INDUSTRY SALES, ESTABLISHMENTS & EMPLOYMENT

Sub-Industries	Category*	Establishments	Sales ($Mill)	Employment
Aircraft	Major1	293	47,664.8	31,725
Motorized aircraft	Minor1	4	5.3	114
Airplanes, fixed or rotary wing	Minor2	33	60,369.8	11,359
Helicopters	Minor2	33	133.3	6,115
Nonmotorized and lighter-than-air aircraft	Minor1	1	0.6	5
Airships	Minor2	4	17.0	68
Balloons, hot air (aircraft)	Minor2	7	6.5	35
Blimps	Minor2	2	5.8	44
Dirigibles	Minor2	1	0.3	2
Gliders (aircraft)	Minor2	2	0.9	6
Hang gliders	Minor2	6	4.5	27
Autogiros	Minor2	1	0.2	3

*Category-Major categories (Major1) are more general descriptions for companies that self-selected to capture the many functions they perform in the industry. Minor categories (Minor1, Minor2) are more specific for companies that have more detailed functions (Minor1 is a larger category than Minor2). Minor categories figures (sales, etc.) can be aggregated to larger minor categories (Minor2 sums to Minor1) and major categories overall figures.

Kitchen Cabinet & Countertop Mfg. Industry
NAICS 33711

NAICS 33711: Kitchen Cabinet & Countertop Mfg Industry. This industry comprises establishments primarily engaged in manufacturing wood or plastics laminated on wood kitchen cabinets, bathroom vanities, and countertops (except freestanding). The cabinets and counters may be made on a stock or custom basis.

Industry Establishments, Sales & Employment Trends

	Year					Percent Chg. Year-to-Year			
	2015	2016	2017	2018	2019	15-16	16-17	17-18	18-19
Establishments	8,866	8,413	8,017	7,690	7,412	-5.1%	-4.7%	-4.1%	-3.6%
Sales ($Millions)	12,661	12,712	12,852	13,069	13,355	0.4%	1.1%	1.7%	2.2%
Employment	84,663	80,342	76,564	73,440	70,783	-5.1%	-4.7%	-4.1%	-3.6%
Sales ($M)/Estab.	1.43	1.51	1.60	1.70	1.80	5.8%	6.1%	6.0%	6.0%
Sales ($)/Emp.	149,543	158,230	167,865	177,959	188,674	5.8%	6.1%	6.0%	6.0%

3-Year Trend – Estimated Number of Establishments

Year	Employee Size of Establishment									Total Employment
	1-4 Emps.	5-9 Emps.	10-19 Emps.	20-49 Emps.	50-99 Emps.	100-249 Emps.	250-499 Emps.	>500 Emps.	Non-Employer	
2017	3,125	1,188	739	434	112	70	35	14	2,299	8,017
2018	2,998	1,140	709	416	108	67	34	14	2,205	7,690
2019	2,889	1,099	683	401	104	64	33	13	2,126	7,412

3-Year Trend – Estimated Number of Establishments

Year	Employee Size of Establishment									Total Employment
	1-4 Emps.	5-9 Emps.	10-19 Emps.	20-49 Emps.	50-99 Emps.	100-249 Emps.	250-499 Emps.	>500 Emps.	Non-Employer	
2017	730.8	730.3	1,141.9	1,775.7	1,008.4	1,687.6	2,880.9	2,699.7	197.2	12,852.4
2018	740.5	739.9	1,157.0	1,799.2	1,021.7	1,709.9	2,919.1	2,782.3	199.8	13,069.4
2019	754.2	753.6	1,178.4	1,832.5	1,040.6	1,741.6	2,973.1	2,877.7	203.5	13,355.0

3-Year Trend – Estimated Number of Establishments

Year	Employee Size of Establishment									Total Employment
	1-4 Emps.	5-9 Emps.	10-19 Emps.	20-49 Emps.	50-99 Emps.	100-249 Emps.	250-499 Emps.	>500 Emps.	Non-Employer	
2017	7,813	6,892	10,048	13,066	6,661	8,781	10,260	10,743	2,299	76,564
2018	7,495	6,611	9,638	12,533	6,389	8,423	9,841	10,305	2,205	73,440
2019	7,224	6,372	9,290	12,079	6,158	8,118	9,485	9,932	2,126	70,783

© Barnes Reports: 2018 U.S. Industry & Market Outlook

Kitchen Cabinet & Countertop Mfg. Industry
NAICS 33711

Sub-Industries — 2018 Estimated Industry Sales, Establishments & Employment

Sub-Industries	Category*	Establishments	Sales ($Mill)	Employment
Wood kitchen cabinets	Major1	6,373	8,954.8	52,406
Vanities, bathroom: wood	Minor2	53	135.4	791
Counter and sink tops	Minor1	601	1,689.0	10,421
Counters or counter display cases, wood	Minor2	329	1,127.6	5,380
Drainboards, plastic laminated	Minor2	18	205.9	120
Sink tops, plastic laminated	Minor2	307	917.8	4,211
Table or counter tops, plastic laminated	Minor2	10	39.0	112

*Category-Major categories (Major1) are more general descriptions for companies that self-selected to capture the many functions they perform in the industry. Minor categories (Minor1, Minor2) are more specific for companies that have more detailed functions (Minor1 is a larger category than Minor2). Minor categories figures (sales, etc.) can be aggregated to larger minor categories (Minor2 sums to Minor1) and major categories overall figures.

HOUSEHOLD & INSTITUTIONAL FURNITURE MFG.
NAICS 33712

NAICS 33712: Household and Institutional Furniture Manufacturing
This industry comprises establishments primarily engaged in manufacturing household-type and public building furniture (i.e., library, school, theater, and church furniture). The furniture may be made on a stock or custom basis and may be assembled or unassembled (i.e., knockdown).

INDUSTRY ESTABLISHMENTS, SALES & EMPLOYMENT TRENDS

	Year					Percent Chg. Year-to-Year			
	2015	2016	2017	2018	2019	15-16	16-17	17-18	18-19
Establishments	6,220	5,899	5,618	5,396	5,208	-5.2%	-4.8%	-4.0%	-3.5%
Sales ($Millions)	20,737	20,000	19,475	19,153	18,982	-3.6%	-2.6%	-1.7%	-0.9%
Employment	111,872	106,105	101,054	97,060	93,673	-5.2%	-4.8%	-4.0%	-3.5%
Sales ($M)/Estab.	3.33	3.39	3.47	3.55	3.64	1.7%	2.2%	2.4%	2.7%
Sales ($)/Emp.	185,368	188,491	192,721	197,336	202,637	1.7%	2.2%	2.4%	2.7%

3-YEAR TREND – ESTIMATED NUMBER OF ESTABLISHMENTS

Year	Employee Size of Establishment									Total
	1-4 Emps.	5-9 Emps.	10-19 Emps.	20-49 Emps.	50-99 Emps.	100-249 Emps.	250-499 Emps.	>500 Emps.	Non-Employer	Employ-ment
2017	1,924	730	517	421	179	160	42	34	1,611	5,618
2018	1,848	701	496	404	172	154	41	33	1,548	5,396
2019	1,783	677	479	390	166	148	39	32	1,494	5,208

3-YEAR TREND – ESTIMATED NUMBER OF ESTABLISHMENTS

Year	Employee Size of Establishment									Total
	1-4 Emps.	5-9 Emps.	10-19 Emps.	20-49 Emps.	50-99 Emps.	100-249 Emps.	250-499 Emps.	>500 Emps.	Non-Employer	Employ-ment
2017	452.0	450.6	802.2	1,729.9	1,615.8	3,892.9	3,484.0	6,921.0	126.7	19,475.3
2018	441.2	439.9	783.1	1,688.7	1,577.2	3,800.1	3,401.0	6,898.6	123.7	19,153.4
2019	434.3	433.0	770.8	1,662.2	1,552.5	3,740.5	3,347.6	6,918.9	121.8	18,981.6

3-YEAR TREND – ESTIMATED NUMBER OF ESTABLISHMENTS

Year	Employee Size of Establishment									Total
	1-4 Emps.	5-9 Emps.	10-19 Emps.	20-49 Emps.	50-99 Emps.	100-249 Emps.	250-499 Emps.	>500 Emps.	Non-Employer	Employ-ment
2017	4,810	4,233	7,027	12,670	10,624	20,161	12,350	27,567	1,611	101,054
2018	4,620	4,066	6,749	12,169	10,204	19,365	11,862	26,477	1,548	97,060
2019	4,459	3,924	6,514	11,745	9,848	18,689	11,448	25,553	1,494	93,673

© Barnes Reports: 2018 U.S. Industry & Market Outlook

Household & Institutional Furniture Mfg.
NAICS 33712

Sub-Industries – 2018 Estimated Industry Sales, Establishments & Employment

Sub-Industries	Category*	Establishments	Sales ($Mill)	Employment
Wood household furniture	Major1	1,073	4,103.1	18,684
Wood bedroom furniture	Minor1	36	1,439.8	2,484
Bed frames, except water bed frames: wood	Minor2	21	129.0	1,163
Chiffoniers and chifforobes	Minor2	0	0.1	1
Commodes	Minor2	1	3.9	25
Dressers, household: wood	Minor2	3	1.8	100
Dressing tables: wood	Minor2	0	0.1	1
Headboards: wood	Minor2	3	21.0	95
Vanity dressers: wood	Minor2	1	0.4	7
Wardrobes, household: wood	Minor2	1	1.0	10
Waterbed frames: wood	Minor2	4	14.3	79
Kitchen and dining room furniture	Minor1	35	58.5	446
Buffets (furniture)	Minor2	1	1.2	6
Chairs, household, except upholstered: wood	Minor2	31	43.7	412
Chairs, Bentwood	Minor2	3	2.2	18
China closets	Minor2	8	7.2	60
Dining room furniture: wood	Minor2	13	56.4	1,042
Silverware chests: wood	Minor2	1	0.1	15
Stools, household: wood	Minor2	4	3.9	29
Tables, household: wood	Minor2	30	81.9	776
Children's wood furniture	Minor1	45	76.7	622
Wood game room furniture	Minor1	8	8.6	63
Wood desks, bookcases, and magazine racks	Minor1	18	38.3	220
Wood stands and chests, except bedside stands	Minor1	71	63.6	1,018
Wood lawn and garden furniture	Minor1	79	81.1	659
Misc. wood household furniture	Minor2	64	81.3	812
Upholstered household furniture	Major1	1,554	6,319.3	28,846
Public building and related furniture	Major1	734	195.6	10,522
Furniture and fixtures, nec	Major1	1,554	6,319.3	28,846

*Category-Major categories (Major1) are more general descriptions for companies that self-selected to capture the many functions they perform in the industry. Minor categories (Minor1, Minor2) are more specific for companies that have more detailed functions (Minor1 is a larger category than Minor2). Minor categories figures (sales, etc.) can be aggregated to larger minor categories (Minor2 sums to Minor1) and major categories overall figures.

Office Furniture Manufacturing Industry
NAICS 33721

NAICS 33721: Office Furniture Manufacturing Industry. This industry comprises establishments primarily engaged in manufacturing office furniture and/or office and store fixtures. The furniture may be made on a stock or custom basis and may be assembled or unassembled (i.e., knockdown).

Industry Establishments, Sales & Employment Trends

	Year					Percent Chg. Year-to-Year			
	2015	2016	2017	2018	2019	15-16	16-17	17-18	18-19
Establishments	5,010	4,888	4,800	4,711	4,647	-2.4%	-1.8%	-1.8%	-1.4%
Sales ($Millions)	22,164	22,152	22,391	22,669	23,118	-0.1%	1.1%	1.2%	2.0%
Employment	98,836	96,435	94,699	92,951	91,675	-2.4%	-1.8%	-1.8%	-1.4%
Sales ($M)/Estab.	4.42	4.53	4.66	4.81	4.98	2.4%	2.9%	3.1%	3.4%
Sales ($)/Emp.	224,245	229,707	236,445	243,886	252,170	2.4%	2.9%	3.1%	3.4%

3-Year Trend – Estimated Number of Establishments

Year	Employee Size of Establishment									Total Employment
	1-4 Emps.	5-9 Emps.	10-19 Emps.	20-49 Emps.	50-99 Emps.	100-249 Emps.	250-499 Emps.	>500 Emps.	Non-Employer	
2017	1,040	628	621	642	282	159	36	16	1,377	4,800
2018	1,020	616	609	630	276	156	36	16	1,351	4,711
2019	1,006	608	601	621	273	154	35	16	1,333	4,647

3-Year Trend – Estimated Number of Establishments

Year	Employee Size of Establishment									Total Employment
	1-4 Emps.	5-9 Emps.	10-19 Emps.	20-49 Emps.	50-99 Emps.	100-249 Emps.	250-499 Emps.	>500 Emps.	Non-Employer	
2017	327.9	520.3	1,294.5	3,542.8	3,417.4	5,200.5	4,012.4	3,963.8	111.5	22,391.2
2018	331.6	526.2	1,309.0	3,582.5	3,455.6	5,258.6	4,057.3	4,036.0	112.7	22,669.5
2019	337.9	536.1	1,333.7	3,649.9	3,520.6	5,357.6	4,133.6	4,133.4	114.9	23,117.7

3-Year Trend – Estimated Number of Establishments

Year	Employee Size of Establishment									Total Employment
	1-4 Emps.	5-9 Emps.	10-19 Emps.	20-49 Emps.	50-99 Emps.	100-249 Emps.	250-499 Emps.	>500 Emps.	Non-Employer	
2017	2,599	3,640	8,444	19,323	16,733	20,056	10,591	11,937	1,377	94,699
2018	2,551	3,573	8,288	18,966	16,424	19,686	10,396	11,716	1,351	92,951
2019	2,516	3,524	8,174	18,706	16,198	19,416	10,253	11,555	1,333	91,675

Office Furniture Manufacturing Industry
NAICS 33721

Sub-Industries – 2018 Estimated Industry Sales, Establishments & Employment

Sub-Industries	Category*	Establishments	Sales ($Mill)	Employment
Wood office furniture	Major1	519	2,722.5	13,485
Wood office chairs, benches and stools	Minor1	17	16.8	371
Benches, office: wood	Minor2	8	14.4	26
Chairs, office: padded, upholstered, or plain: wood	Minor2	30	162.8	1,223
Stools, office: wood	Minor2	2	6.1	37
Wood office filing cabinets and bookcases	Minor1	33	72.4	454
Bookcases, office: wood	Minor2	6	15.1	22
Cabinets, office: wood	Minor2	282	357.4	2,210
Filing cabinets (boxes), office: wood	Minor2	9	20.1	99
Wood office desks and tables	Minor1	10	37.8	258
Desks, office: wood	Minor2	20	55.2	375
Tables, office: wood	Minor2	16	90.6	97
Panel systems and partitions (free-standing), office: wood	Minor2	15	987.7	207
Office furniture, except wood	Major1	2,442	13,813.3	52,906
Office chairs, benches, and stools, except wood	Minor1	113	73.5	1,073
Benches, office: except wood	Minor2	30	13.7	107
Chairs, office: padded or plain: except wood	Minor2	196	485.9	7,047
Stools, office: except wood	Minor2	6	2.9	35
Office bookcases, wallcases and partitions, except wood	Minor1	30	7.1	61
Panel systems and partitions, office: except wood	Minor2	154	115.5	3,763
Wallcases, office: except wood	Minor2	18	1.4	15
Office cabinets and filing drawers, except wood	Minor1	148	127.3	1,166
Cabinets, office: except wood	Minor2	362	201.9	3,496
File drawer frames: except wood	Minor2	6	0.6	6
Filing boxes, cabinets, and cases: except wood	Minor2	101	20.9	2,034
Office desks and tables, except wood	Minor1	142	3,246.5	2,379

*Category-Major categories (Major1) are more general descriptions for companies that self-selected to capture the many functions they perform in the industry. Minor categories (Minor1, Minor2) are more specific for companies that have more detailed functions (Minor1 is a larger category than Minor2). Minor categories figures (sales, etc.) can be aggregated to larger minor categories (Minor2 sums to Minor1) and major categories overall figures.

Medical Equipment & Supplies Mfg. Industry
NAICS 33911

NAICS 33911: Medical Equipment and Supplies Manufacturing This industry comprises establishments primarily engaged in manufacturing medical equipment and supplies. Examples of products made by these establishments are laboratory apparatus and furniture, surgical and medical instruments, surgical appliances and supplies, dental equipment and supplies, orthodontic goods, dentures, and orthodontic appliances.

Industry Establishments, Sales & Employment Trends

	Year					Percent Chg. Year-to-Year			
	2015	2016	2017	2018	2019	15-16	16-17	17-18	18-19
Establishments	12,841	12,934	12,990	12,815	12,593	0.7%	0.4%	-1.3%	-1.7%
Sales ($Millions)	75,241	80,275	85,616	89,860	93,983	6.7%	6.7%	5.0%	4.6%
Employment	239,624	241,362	242,409	239,146	234,994	0.7%	0.4%	-1.3%	-1.7%
Sales ($M)/Estab.	5.86	6.21	6.59	7.01	7.46	5.9%	6.2%	6.4%	6.4%
Sales ($)/Emp.	313,999	332,594	353,189	375,753	399,937	5.9%	6.2%	6.4%	6.4%

3-Year Trend – Estimated Number of Establishments

Year	Employee Size of Establishment									Total Employment
	1-4 Emps.	5-9 Emps.	10-19 Emps.	20-49 Emps.	50-99 Emps.	100-249 Emps.	250-499 Emps.	>500 Emps.	Non-Employer	
2017	6,149	1,776	1,104	886	423	330	145	80	2,098	12,990
2018	6,066	1,753	1,089	874	417	325	143	79	2,070	12,815
2019	5,961	1,722	1,070	859	410	320	140	77	2,034	12,593

3-Year Trend – Estimated Number of Establishments

Year	Employee Size of Establishment									Total Employment
	1-4 Emps.	5-9 Emps.	10-19 Emps.	20-49 Emps.	50-99 Emps.	100-249 Emps.	250-499 Emps.	>500 Emps.	Non-Employer	
2017	2,632.9	1,999.3	3,123.7	6,638.8	6,963.5	14,637.2	21,640.3	27,754.5	225.9	85,616.1
2018	2,757.5	2,093.9	3,271.6	6,953.0	7,293.1	15,329.9	22,664.5	29,260.0	236.5	89,860.0
2019	2,875.9	2,183.9	3,412.1	7,251.6	7,606.3	15,988.4	23,638.0	30,779.8	246.7	93,982.7

3-Year Trend – Estimated Number of Establishments

Year	Employee Size of Establishment									Total Employment
	1-4 Emps.	5-9 Emps.	10-19 Emps.	20-49 Emps.	50-99 Emps.	100-249 Emps.	250-499 Emps.	>500 Emps.	Non-Employer	
2017	15,372	10,303	15,010	26,674	25,118	41,586	42,082	64,165	2,098	242,409
2018	15,165	10,165	14,808	26,315	24,780	41,027	41,516	63,302	2,070	239,146
2019	14,901	9,988	14,551	25,858	24,349	40,314	40,795	62,203	2,034	234,994

© Barnes Reports: 2018 U.S. Industry & Market Outlook

MEDICAL EQUIPMENT & SUPPLIES MFG. INDUSTRY
NAICS 33911

Sub-Industries — 2018 Estimated Industry Sales, Establishments & Employment

Sub-Industries	Category*	Establishments	Sales ($Mill)	Employment
Surgical and medical instruments	Major1	2,782	11,797.3	43,921
Ophthalmic instruments and apparatus	Minor1	42	70.7	2,592
Muscle exercise apparatus, ophthalmic	Minor2	20	3.4	149
Ophthalmic lasers	Minor2	22	4.9	78
Diagnostic apparatus, medical	Minor1	388	957.6	9,111
Biopsy instruments and equipment	Minor2	12	1.9	43
Blood pressure apparatus	Minor2	20	13.4	268
Corneal microscopes	Minor2	2	0.3	3
Eye examining instruments and apparatus	Minor2	61	14.0	368
Gastroscopes, except electromedical	Minor2	3	2.0	24
Optometers	Minor2	31	7.1	106
Otoscopes, except electromedical	Minor2	2	0.3	6
Retinoscopes	Minor2	1	0.2	2
Tonometers, medical	Minor2	3	0.3	62
Veterinarians' instruments and apparatus	Minor1	67	28.0	320
Rifles, for propelling hypodermics into animals	Minor2	1	0.1	2
Surgical instruments and apparatus	Minor1	581	17,961.7	20,927
Medical instruments and equipment, blood and bone work	Minor1	319	644.6	5,881
Inhalation therapy equipment	Minor1	29	15.4	195
Operating tables	Minor1	4	2.9	30
Oxygen tents	Minor1	1	0.0	1
Physiotherapy equipment, electrical	Minor1	27	10.8	2,412
Skin grafting equipment	Minor1	34	5.6	70
Stethoscopes and stethographs	Minor1	2	1.1	13
Ultrasonic medical cleaning equipment	Minor1	13	15.7	71
Surgical appliances and supplies	Major1	1,669	30,397.8	59,986
Personal safety equipment	Minor1	922	5,212.6	25,048
Cotton and cotton applicators	Minor1	41	743.0	1,596
Prosthetic appliances	Minor1	2,005	10,149.8	21,380
Orthopedic appliances	Minor1	3,613	11,616.8	41,364
Bandages and dressings	Minor1	56	125.3	1,471
Bandages: plastic, muslin, plaster of paris, etc.	Minor2	17	10.5	535
Dressings, surgical	Minor2	19	35.5	1,069
Gauze, surgical	Minor2	3	9.2	43

*Category-Major categories (Major1) are more general descriptions for companies that self-selected to capture the many functions they perform in the industry. Minor categories (Minor1, Minor2) are more specific for companies that have more detailed functions (Minor1 is a larger category than Minor2). Minor categories figures (sales, etc.) can be aggregated to larger minor categories (Minor2 sums to Minor1) and major categories overall figures.

Sign Manufacturing
NAICS 33995

NAICS 33995: Sign Manufacturing Industry. This industry comprises establishments primarily engaged in manufacturing signs and related displays of all materials (except printing paper and paperboard signs, notices, displays).

Industry Establishments, Sales & Employment Trends

	Year					Percent Chg. Year-to-Year			
	2015	2016	2017	2018	2019	15-16	16-17	17-18	18-19
Establishments	16,116	15,734	15,295	14,955	14,564	-2.4%	-2.8%	-2.2%	-2.6%
Sales ($Millions)	12,666	13,020	13,369	13,801	14,203	2.8%	2.7%	3.2%	2.9%
Employment	81,188	79,267	77,056	75,341	73,372	-2.4%	-2.8%	-2.2%	-2.6%
Sales ($M)/Estab.	0.79	0.83	0.87	0.92	0.98	5.3%	5.6%	5.6%	5.7%
Sales ($)/Emp.	156,002	164,249	173,494	183,187	193,572	5.3%	5.6%	5.6%	5.7%

3-Year Trend – Estimated Number of Establishments

Year	Employee Size of Establishment								Non-Employer	Total Employ-ment
	1-4 Emps.	5-9 Emps.	10-19 Emps.	20-49 Emps.	50-99 Emps.	100-249 Emps.	250-499 Emps.	>500 Emps.		
2017	2,765	1,003	657	519	153	84	23	4	10,089	15,295
2018	2,703	981	642	508	149	82	22	4	9,864	14,955
2019	2,633	955	625	494	145	80	22	4	9,606	14,564

3-Year Trend – Estimated Number of Establishments

Year	Employee Size of Establishment								Non-Employer	Total Employ-ment
	1-4 Emps.	5-9 Emps.	10-19 Emps.	20-49 Emps.	50-99 Emps.	100-249 Emps.	250-499 Emps.	>500 Emps.		
2017	766.8	731.3	1,204.0	2,519.1	1,629.8	2,401.0	2,207.0	979.4	930.4	13,368.8
2018	790.7	754.1	1,241.6	2,597.7	1,680.7	2,476.0	2,275.9	1,025.1	959.5	13,801.4
2019	812.7	775.0	1,276.0	2,669.7	1,727.3	2,544.6	2,339.0	1,072.3	986.1	14,202.7

3-Year Trend – Estimated Number of Establishments

Year	Employee Size of Establishment								Non-Employer	Total Employ-ment
	1-4 Emps.	5-9 Emps.	10-19 Emps.	20-49 Emps.	50-99 Emps.	100-249 Emps.	250-499 Emps.	>500 Emps.		
2017	6,912	5,819	8,932	15,627	9,077	10,532	6,626	3,443	10,089	77,056
2018	6,758	5,689	8,733	15,279	8,875	10,298	6,479	3,367	9,864	75,341
2019	6,581	5,540	8,505	14,879	8,643	10,028	6,309	3,279	9,606	73,372

© Barnes Reports: 2018 U.S. Industry & Market Outlook

SIGN MANUFACTURING
NAICS 33995

SUB-INDUSTRIES — 2018 ESTIMATED INDUSTRY SALES, ESTABLISHMENTS & EMPLOYMENT

Sub-Industries	Category*	Establishments	Sales ($Mill)	Employment
Signs and advertising specialties	Major1	12,913	9,195.4	50,698
Electric signs	Minor1	428	1,286.0	7,145
Neon signs	Minor2	422	588.8	2,757
Scoreboards, electric	Minor2	28	603.8	432
Advertising artwork	Minor2	166	111.3	622
Advertising novelties	Minor2	173	443.3	3,260
Displays and cutouts, window and lobby	Minor2	164	711.2	4,603
Displays, paint process	Minor2	27	45.5	255
Letters for signs, metal	Minor2	24	26.9	145
Name plates: except engraved, etched, etc.: metal	Minor2	43	65.7	708
Signs, not made in custom sign painting shops	Minor2	566	723.5	4,715

*Category-Major categories (Major1) are more general descriptions for companies that self-selected to capture the many functions they perform in the industry. Minor categories (Minor1, Minor2) are more specific for companies that have more detailed functions (Minor1 is a larger category than Minor2). Minor categories figures (sales, etc.) can be aggregated to larger minor categories (Minor2 sums to Minor1) and major categories overall figures.

AUTOMOBILE & OTHER VEHICLES WHOLESALE (NAICS 42311)

NAICS 42311: Automobile & Other Vehicle Wholesale. This industry comprises establishments primarily engaged in wholesaling new and used passenger automobiles, trucks, trailers, and other motor vehicles, such as motorcycles, motor homes, and snowmobiles.

INDUSTRY ESTABLISHMENTS, SALES & EMPLOYMENT TRENDS

	Year					Percent Chg. Year-to-Year			
	2015	2016	2017	2018	2019	15-16	16-17	17-18	18-19
Establishments	7,408	7,415	7,441	7,478	7,549	0.1%	0.3%	0.5%	1.0%
Sales ($Millions)	419,362	409,199	402,489	397,526	395,970	-2.4%	-1.6%	-1.2%	-0.4%
Employment	115,366	115,482	115,885	116,452	117,570	0.1%	0.3%	0.5%	1.0%
Sales ($M)/Estab.	56.61	55.18	54.09	53.16	52.45	-2.5%	-2.0%	-1.7%	-1.3%
Sales ($)/Emp.	3,635,063	3,543,402	3,473,166	3,413,639	3,367,965	-2.5%	-2.0%	-1.7%	-1.3%

3-YEAR TREND – ESTIMATED NUMBER OF ESTABLISHMENTS

Year	Employee Size of Establishment									Total Employment
	1-4 Emps.	5-9 Emps.	10-19 Emps.	20-49 Emps.	50-99 Emps.	100-249 Emps.	250-499 Emps.	>500 Emps.	Non-Employer	
2017	3,068	836	813	1,006	456	184	18	6	1,055	7,441
2018	3,083	840	817	1,010	458	185	18	6	1,061	7,478
2019	3,112	848	824	1,020	463	186	18	6	1,071	7,549

3-YEAR TREND – ESTIMATED INDUSTRY SALES ($MILLIONS)

Year	Employee Size of Establishment									Total Employment
	1-4 Emps.	5-9 Emps.	10-19 Emps.	20-49 Emps.	50-99 Emps.	100-249 Emps.	250-499 Emps.	>500 Emps.	Non-Employer	
2017	16,124.5	11,545.8	28,231.9	92,461.4	92,183.0	100,146.2	33,200.4	28,395.3	200.7	402,489.2
2018	15,929.2	11,405.9	27,890.0	91,341.4	91,066.4	98,933.1	32,798.2	27,963.2	198.3	397,525.7
2019	15,873.7	11,366.2	27,792.8	91,023.2	90,749.1	98,588.4	32,683.9	27,695.2	197.6	395,970.0

3-YEAR TREND – ESTIMATED NUMBER OF EMPLOYEES

Year	Employee Size of Establishment									Total Employment
	1-4 Emps.	5-9 Emps.	10-19 Emps.	20-49 Emps.	50-99 Emps.	100-249 Emps.	250-499 Emps.	>500 Emps.	Non-Employer	
2017	7,669	4,847	11,052	30,266	27,089	23,180	5,260	5,467	1,055	115,885
2018	7,707	4,871	11,106	30,414	27,222	23,294	5,286	5,493	1,061	116,452
2019	7,781	4,918	11,213	30,706	27,483	23,517	5,336	5,546	1,071	117,570

© Barnes Reports: 2018 U.S. Industry & Market Outlook

AUTOMOBILE & OTHER VEHICLES WHOLESALE (NAICS 42311)

SUB-INDUSTRIES – 2018 ESTIMATED INDUSTRY SALES, ESTABLISHMENTS & EMPLOYMENT

Sub-Industries	Category*	Establishments	Sales ($Mill)	Employment
Automobiles and other motor vehicles	Major1	1,651	95,949.1	27,565
Automotive brokers	Minor1	663	13,492.9	4,421
Automobile auction	Minor2	527	97,358.2	28,922
Automobiles	Minor2	1,526	41,809.7	14,056
Trucks, noncommercial	Minor2	121	3,463.7	724
Vans, noncommercial	Minor2	9	728.2	92
Commercial vehicles	Minor1	107	5,404.7	4,443
Ambulances	Minor2	278	4,948.4	1,920
Busses	Minor2	152	13,242.3	2,310
Fire trucks	Minor2	97	5,064.3	924
Taxicabs	Minor2	84	1,009.5	414
Trailers for trucks, new and used	Minor2	229	15,053.3	4,100
Truck bodies	Minor2	96	6,423.7	1,959
Truck tractors	Minor2	117	8,797.4	2,826
Trucks, commercial	Minor2	599	64,241.9	15,015
Vans, commercial	Minor2	29	383.0	503
Recreational vehicles, motor homes, and trailers	Minor1	110	4,953.1	1,367
Campers (pickup coaches) for mounting on trucks	Minor2	14	451.6	109
Motor homes	Minor2	15	659.6	155
Motor vehicles, kit form	Minor2	7	92.2	23
Pop-up campers	Minor2	2	23.6	10
Recreation vehicles, all-terrain	Minor2	38	654.9	230
Snowmobiles	Minor2	67	347.5	271
Trailers for passenger vehicles	Minor2	36	990.6	491
Motorized cycles	Minor1	35	614.7	164
Mopeds	Minor2	20	189.1	76
Motor scooters	Minor2	72	1,331.1	342
Motorcycles	Minor2	778	9,847.2	3,021

*Category-Major categories (Major1) are more general descriptions for companies that self-selected to capture the many functions they perform in the industry. Minor categories (Minor1, Minor2) are more specific for companies that have more detailed functions (Minor1 is a larger category than Minor2). Minor categories figures (sales, etc.) can be aggregated to larger minor categories (Minor2 sums to Minor1) and major categories overall figures.

MOTOR VEHICLE PARTS & SUPPLIES WHOLESALES (NAICS 42312)

NAICS 42312: Motor Vehicle Parts & Supplies Wholesale. Establishments primarily engaged in the wholesale distribution of new and used passenger automobiles, trucks, trailers, and other motor vehicles, including motorcycles, motor homes, and snowmobiles. Automotive distributors primarily engaged in selling at retail to individual consumers for personal use, and also selling a limited amount of new and used passenger automobiles and trucks at wholesale, are classified in SIC 5511.

INDUSTRY ESTABLISHMENTS, SALES & EMPLOYMENT TRENDS

	Year					Percent Chg. Year-to-Year			
	2015	2016	2017	2018	2019	15-16	16-17	17-18	18-19
Establishments	15,641	15,783	15,878	15,959	16,116	0.9%	0.6%	0.5%	1.0%
Sales ($Millions)	181,430	193,510	206,297	219,590	234,788	6.7%	6.6%	6.4%	6.9%
Employment	201,034	202,861	204,084	205,127	207,141	0.9%	0.6%	0.5%	1.0%
Sales ($M)/Estab.	11.60	12.26	12.99	13.76	14.57	5.7%	6.0%	5.9%	5.9%
Sales ($)/Emp.	902,486	953,902	1,010,845	1,070,509	1,133,470	5.7%	6.0%	5.9%	5.9%

3-YEAR TREND – ESTIMATED NUMBER OF ESTABLISHMENTS

Year	Employee Size of Establishment									Total
	1-4 Emps.	5-9 Emps.	10-19 Emps.	20-49 Emps.	50-99 Emps.	100-249 Emps.	250-499 Emps.	>500 Emps.	Non-Employer	Employment
2017	5,487	3,097	2,561	1,662	541	219	42	16	2,252	15,878
2018	5,515	3,113	2,574	1,670	544	220	42	16	2,264	15,959
2019	5,569	3,144	2,600	1,687	549	223	42	16	2,286	16,116

3-YEAR TREND – ESTIMATED INDUSTRY SALES ($MILLIONS)

Year	Employee Size of Establishment									Total
	1-4 Emps.	5-9 Emps.	10-19 Emps.	20-49 Emps.	50-99 Emps.	100-249 Emps.	250-499 Emps.	>500 Emps.	Non-Employer	Employment
2017	8,611.0	12,775.7	26,567.6	45,626.7	32,656.2	35,668.2	22,819.1	21,070.1	502.3	206,297.0
2018	9,168.4	13,602.6	28,287.2	48,579.9	34,769.9	37,976.8	24,296.0	22,374.5	534.8	219,590.3
2019	9,808.0	14,551.5	30,260.5	51,968.7	37,195.4	40,626.0	25,990.9	23,814.8	572.1	234,787.9

3-YEAR TREND – ESTIMATED NUMBER OF EMPLOYEES

Year	Employee Size of Establishment									Total
	1-4 Emps.	5-9 Emps.	10-19 Emps.	20-49 Emps.	50-99 Emps.	100-249 Emps.	250-499 Emps.	>500 Emps.	Non-Employer	Employment
2017	13,717	17,964	34,833	50,021	32,140	27,651	12,108	13,396	2,252	204,084
2018	13,788	18,056	35,011	50,277	32,305	27,792	12,170	13,465	2,264	205,127
2019	13,923	18,233	35,355	50,770	32,622	28,065	12,289	13,597	2,286	207,141

© Barnes Reports: 2018 U.S. Industry & Market Outlook

Motor Vehicle Parts & Supplies Wholesales (NAICS 42312)

Sub-Industries – 2018 Estimated Industry Sales, Establishments & Employment

Sub-Industries	Category*	Establishments	Sales ($Mill)	Employment
Automobiles and other motor vehicles	Major1	3,523	53,001.6	48,554
Automotive brokers	Minor1	1,415	7,453.4	7,787
Automobile auction	Minor2	1,125	53,780.0	50,944
Automobiles	Minor2	3,256	23,095.4	24,759
Trucks, noncommercial	Minor2	259	1,913.3	1,276
Vans, noncommercial	Minor2	19	402.2	162
Commercial vehicles	Minor1	228	2,985.5	7,826
Ambulances	Minor2	593	2,733.5	3,383
Busses	Minor2	325	7,314.9	4,069
Fire trucks	Minor2	207	2,797.5	1,628
Taxicabs	Minor2	178	557.7	729
Trailers for trucks, new and used	Minor2	488	8,315.3	7,221
Truck bodies	Minor2	206	3,548.4	3,451
Truck tractors	Minor2	251	4,859.6	4,978
Trucks, commercial	Minor2	1,279	35,486.8	26,448
Vans, commercial	Minor2	63	211.6	887
Recreational vehicles, motor homes, and trailers	Minor1	235	2,736.1	2,409
Campers (pickup coaches) for mounting on trucks	Minor2	29	249.4	191
Motor homes	Minor2	32	364.4	273
Motor vehicles, kit form	Minor2	14	50.9	41
Pop-up campers	Minor2	3	13.1	17
Recreation vehicles, all-terrain	Minor2	82	361.8	405
Snowmobiles	Minor2	143	192.0	477
Trailers for passenger vehicles	Minor2	77	547.2	864
Motorized cycles	Minor1	74	339.6	289
Mopeds	Minor2	42	104.5	133
Motor scooters	Minor2	154	735.3	603
Motorcycles	Minor2	1,660	5,439.5	5,321

*Category-Major categories (Major1) are more general descriptions for companies that self-selected to capture the many functions they perform in the industry. Minor categories (Minor1, Minor2) are more specific for companies that have more detailed functions (Minor1 is a larger category than Minor2). Minor categories figures (sales, etc.) can be aggregated to larger minor categories (Minor2 sums to Minor1) and major categories overall figures.

Furniture Wholesale Industry
(NAICS 42321)

NAICS 42321: Furniture Wholesale. Establishments primarily engaged in the wholesale distribution of furniture, including bedsprings, mattresses, and other household furniture; office furniture; and furniture for public parks and buildings. Establishments primarily engaged in the wholesale distribution of partitions, shelving, lockers, and store fixtures are classified in SIC 5046.

Industry Establishments, Sales & Employment Trends

	Year					Percent Chg. Year-to-Year			
	2015	2016	2017	2018	2019	15-16	16-17	17-18	18-19
Establishments	7,218	7,291	7,345	7,396	7,484	1.0%	0.7%	0.7%	1.2%
Sales ($Millions)	42,965	45,245	47,698	50,303	53,367	5.3%	5.4%	5.5%	6.1%
Employment	65,420	66,082	66,568	67,037	67,827	1.0%	0.7%	0.7%	1.2%
Sales ($M)/Estab.	5.95	6.21	6.49	6.80	7.13	4.3%	4.7%	4.7%	4.9%
Sales ($)/Emp.	656,758	684,677	716,536	750,365	786,821	4.3%	4.7%	4.7%	4.9%

3-Year Trend – Estimated Number of Establishments

Year	Employee Size of Establishment									Total Employ-ment
	1-4 Emps.	5-9 Emps.	10-19 Emps.	20-49 Emps.	50-99 Emps.	100-249 Emps.	250-499 Emps.	>500 Emps.	Non-Employer	
2017	2,958	1,011	800	573	185	68	7	3	1,739	7,345
2018	2,979	1,019	805	577	187	69	7	3	1,751	7,396
2019	3,014	1,031	815	584	189	69	7	3	1,772	7,484

3-Year Trend – Estimated Industry Sales ($Millions)

Year	Employee Size of Establishment									Total Employ-ment
	1-4 Emps.	5-9 Emps.	10-19 Emps.	20-49 Emps.	50-99 Emps.	100-249 Emps.	250-499 Emps.	>500 Emps.	Non-Employer	
2017	3,550.0	3,190.4	6,344.2	12,028.2	8,547.3	8,480.5	2,986.3	2,342.2	228.9	47,698.0
2018	3,743.8	3,364.7	6,690.7	12,685.0	9,014.1	8,943.6	3,149.4	2,469.9	241.4	50,302.6
2019	3,972.0	3,569.7	7,098.4	13,457.9	9,563.3	9,488.6	3,341.3	2,620.3	256.1	53,367.5

3-Year Trend – Estimated Number of Employees

Year	Employee Size of Establishment									Total Employ-ment
	1-4 Emps.	5-9 Emps.	10-19 Emps.	20-49 Emps.	50-99 Emps.	100-249 Emps.	250-499 Emps.	>500 Emps.	Non-Employer	
2017	7,395	5,866	10,877	17,244	11,000	8,597	2,072	1,777	1,739	66,568
2018	7,447	5,908	10,954	17,365	11,078	8,658	2,087	1,790	1,751	67,037
2019	7,535	5,977	11,083	17,570	11,209	8,760	2,111	1,811	1,772	67,827

© Barnes Reports: 2018 U.S. Industry & Market Outlook

Furniture Wholesale Industry (NAICS 42321)

Sub-Industries – 2018 Estimated Industry Sales, Establishments & Employment

Sub-Industries	Category*	Establishments	Sales ($Mill)	Employment
Furniture	Major1	3,427	20,494.9	26,915
Office and public building furniture	Minor1	376	4,133.0	4,280
Bar furniture	Minor2	16	157.5	152
Cafeteria furniture	Minor2	4	31.1	9
Church pews	Minor2	36	88.7	135
Filing units	Minor2	73	602.8	646
Lockers	Minor2	143	368.6	741
Office furniture, nec	Minor2	810	13,107.7	14,670
Public building furniture, nec	Minor2	36	391.2	469
Restaurant furniture, nec	Minor2	16	262.6	244
School desks	Minor2	38	444.5	391
Theater seats	Minor2	5	30.2	56
Household furniture	Minor1	454	4,797.9	6,418
Dining room furniture	Minor2	12	109.1	200
Dressers	Minor2	259	239.1	1,009
Juvenile furniture	Minor2	28	263.1	330
Sofas and couches	Minor2	15	71.4	108
Tables, occasional	Minor2	21	153.0	165
Beds and bedding	Minor1	64	601.5	642
Beds	Minor2	626	690.2	2,706
Bedsprings	Minor2	2	2.2	24
Mattresses	Minor2	174	621.9	1,596
Waterbeds	Minor2	16	26.6	214
Bookcases	Minor2	22	43.5	132
Chairs	Minor2	297	782.9	1,544
Desks, nec	Minor2	8	21.7	67
Outdoor and lawn furniture, nec	Minor2	115	971.9	1,064
Racks	Minor2	218	354.4	1,480
Shelving	Minor2	77	388.6	545
Unfinished furniture	Minor2	10	50.6	84

*Category-Major categories (Major1) are more general descriptions for companies that self-selected to capture the many functions they perform in the industry. Minor categories (Minor1, Minor2) are more specific for companies that have more detailed functions (Minor1 is a larger category than Minor2). Minor categories figures (sales, etc.) can be aggregated to larger minor categories (Minor2 sums to Minor1) and major categories overall figures.

HOME FURNISHINGS WHOLESALE INDUSTRY (NAICS 42322)

NAICS 42322: Home Furnishings Wholesales. Establishments primarily engaged in the wholesale distribution of homefurnishings and housewares, including antiques; china; glassware and earthenware; lamps (including electric); curtains and draperies; linens and towels; and carpets, linoleum, and all other types of hard and soft surface floor coverings. Wholesale distribution of other electrical household goods is classified in SIC 5064; precious metal flatware in SIC 5094.

INDUSTRY ESTABLISHMENTS, SALES & EMPLOYMENT TRENDS

	Year					Percent Chg. Year-to-Year			
	2015	2016	2017	2018	2019	15-16	16-17	17-18	18-19
Establishments	8,595	8,508	8,420	8,401	8,421	-1.0%	-1.0%	-0.2%	0.2%
Sales ($Millions)	45,835	47,674	49,729	52,295	55,285	4.0%	4.3%	5.2%	5.7%
Employment	82,332	81,498	80,653	80,471	80,666	-1.0%	-1.0%	-0.2%	0.2%
Sales ($M)/Estab.	5.33	5.60	5.91	6.23	6.57	5.1%	5.4%	5.4%	5.5%
Sales ($)/Emp.	556,701	584,969	616,579	649,857	685,361	5.1%	5.4%	5.4%	5.5%

3-YEAR TREND – ESTIMATED NUMBER OF ESTABLISHMENTS

Year	Employee Size of Establishment									Total Employment
	1-4 Emps.	5-9 Emps.	10-19 Emps.	20-49 Emps.	50-99 Emps.	100-249 Emps.	250-499 Emps.	>500 Emps.	Non-Employer	
2017	3,174	1,297	984	656	206	87	20	2	1,994	8,420
2018	3,167	1,294	982	655	205	87	20	2	1,989	8,401
2019	3,174	1,297	985	656	206	87	20	2	1,994	8,421

3-YEAR TREND – ESTIMATED INDUSTRY SALES ($MILLIONS)

Year	Employee Size of Establishment									Total Employment
	1-4 Emps.	5-9 Emps.	10-19 Emps.	20-49 Emps.	50-99 Emps.	100-249 Emps.	250-499 Emps.	>500 Emps.	Non-Employer	
2017	3,163.7	3,398.0	6,486.3	11,445.7	7,885.9	9,007.7	6,822.4	1,252.7	266.4	49,728.8
2018	3,327.0	3,573.4	6,821.0	12,036.2	8,292.8	9,472.5	7,174.5	1,317.3	280.1	52,294.8
2019	3,517.2	3,777.7	7,211.1	12,724.5	8,767.1	10,014.1	7,584.7	1,392.6	296.1	55,285.3

3-YEAR TREND – ESTIMATED NUMBER OF EMPLOYEES

Year	Employee Size of Establishment									Total Employment
	1-4 Emps.	5-9 Emps.	10-19 Emps.	20-49 Emps.	50-99 Emps.	100-249 Emps.	250-499 Emps.	>500 Emps.	Non-Employer	
2017	7,935	7,523	13,389	19,756	12,220	10,994	5,699	1,145	1,994	80,653
2018	7,917	7,506	13,359	19,711	12,192	10,969	5,686	1,142	1,989	80,471
2019	7,936	7,524	13,391	19,759	12,221	10,996	5,700	1,145	1,994	80,666

© Barnes Reports: 2018 U.S. Industry & Market Outlook

Home Furnishings Wholesale Industry
(NAICS 42322)

Sub-Industries – 2018 Estimated Industry Sales, Establishments & Employment

Sub-Industries	Category*	Establishments	Sales ($Mill)	Employment
Homefurnishings	Major1	989	7,696.2	13,739
Kitchenware	Minor1	220	3,058.9	3,846
Aluminumware	Minor2	11	149.3	255
China	Minor2	40	719.5	773
Crockery	Minor2	4	51.7	45
Glassware	Minor2	97	676.3	942
Kitchen tools and utensils, nec	Minor2	79	538.6	985
Stainless steel flatware	Minor2	21	215.7	366
Tupperware	Minor2	348	308.6	785
Grills, barbecue	Minor2	57	320.2	645
Linens and towels	Minor1	117	2,540.8	2,112
Bedspreads	Minor2	26	567.1	479
Blankets	Minor2	135	332.6	532
Linens, table	Minor2	31	167.0	223
Pillowcases	Minor2	9	67.9	91
Sheets, textile	Minor2	64	1,473.0	1,194
Slip covers (furniture)	Minor2	6	251.5	32
Towels	Minor2	70	566.0	391
Window furnishings	Minor1	111	897.4	1,697
Curtains	Minor2	27	150.8	356
Draperies	Minor2	160	762.7	1,500
Venetian blinds	Minor2	24	152.4	334
Vertical blinds	Minor2	57	254.2	392
Window covering parts and accessories	Minor2	193	746.5	1,387
Window shades	Minor2	33	197.5	304
Floor coverings	Minor1	1,295	11,172.5	16,059
Carpets	Minor2	1,714	5,560.4	9,316
Floor cushion and padding	Minor2	21	183.3	227
Resilient floor coverings: tile or sheet	Minor2	40	781.6	855
Rugs	Minor2	332	1,642.3	2,665
Wood flooring	Minor2	122	1,523.9	1,663
Decorative home furnishings and supplies	Minor1	1,804	7,543.0	14,188
Fireplace equipment and accessories	Minor2	59	535.1	792
Misc. home furnishings wholesales	Minor2	84	490.3	1,302

*Category-Major categories (Major1) are more general descriptions for companies that self-selected to capture the many functions they perform in the industry. Minor categories (Minor1, Minor2) are more specific for companies that have more detailed functions (Minor1 is a larger category than Minor2). Minor categories figures (sales, etc.) can be aggregated to larger minor categories (Minor2 sums to Minor1) and major categories overall figures.

OFFICE EQUIPMENT WHOLESALES INDUSTRY
(NAICS 42342)

NAICS 42342: Office Equipment Wholesales. Establishments primarily engaged in the wholesale distribution of office machines and related equipment, including photocopy and microfilm equipment and safes and vaults. These establishments frequently also sell office supplies, but wholesaling most office supplies is classified in SIC 5111-5113. Wholesaling office furniture is classified in SIC 5021, and wholesaling computers and peripheral equipment is classified in SIC 5045.

INDUSTRY ESTABLISHMENTS, SALES & EMPLOYMENT TRENDS

	Year					Percent Chg. Year-to-Year			
	2015	2016	2017	2018	2019	15-16	16-17	17-18	18-19
Establishments	7,839	7,765	7,824	8,012	8,242	-0.9%	0.8%	2.4%	2.9%
Sales ($Millions)	33,554	32,812	32,822	33,460	34,408	-2.2%	0.0%	1.9%	2.8%
Employment	108,394	107,376	108,188	110,780	113,965	-0.9%	0.8%	2.4%	2.9%
Sales ($M)/Estab.	4.28	4.23	4.19	4.18	4.17	-1.3%	-0.7%	-0.4%	0.0%
Sales ($)/Emp.	309,556	305,581	303,382	302,038	301,913	-1.3%	-0.7%	-0.4%	0.0%

3-YEAR TREND – ESTIMATED NUMBER OF ESTABLISHMENTS

Year	Employee Size of Establishment									Total Employment
	1-4 Emps.	5-9 Emps.	10-19 Emps.	20-49 Emps.	50-99 Emps.	100-249 Emps.	250-499 Emps.	>500 Emps.	Non-Employer	
2017	3,880	1,132	885	752	318	177	35	8	638	7,824
2018	3,973	1,159	907	770	326	181	36	8	653	8,012
2019	4,087	1,192	933	792	335	186	37	8	672	8,242

3-YEAR TREND – ESTIMATED INDUSTRY SALES ($MILLIONS)

Year	Employee Size of Establishment									Total Employment
	1-4 Emps.	5-9 Emps.	10-19 Emps.	20-49 Emps.	50-99 Emps.	100-249 Emps.	250-499 Emps.	>500 Emps.	Non-Employer	
2017	1,711.0	1,312.0	2,580.6	5,798.7	5,400.0	8,075.4	5,382.1	2,470.8	91.9	32,822.4
2018	1,744.8	1,337.9	2,631.7	5,913.5	5,506.9	8,235.3	5,488.6	2,507.4	93.7	33,459.8
2019	1,795.0	1,376.4	2,707.4	6,083.6	5,665.3	8,472.1	5,646.4	2,564.9	96.4	34,407.6

3-YEAR TREND – ESTIMATED NUMBER OF EMPLOYEES

Year	Employee Size of Establishment									Total Employment
	1-4 Emps.	5-9 Emps.	10-19 Emps.	20-49 Emps.	50-99 Emps.	100-249 Emps.	250-499 Emps.	>500 Emps.	Non-Employer	
2017	9,699	6,565	12,040	22,622	18,913	22,277	10,162	5,272	638	108,188
2018	9,931	6,722	12,329	23,164	19,366	22,811	10,406	5,398	653	110,780
2019	10,217	6,915	12,683	23,830	19,922	23,467	10,705	5,553	672	113,965

© Barnes Reports: 2018 U.S. Industry & Market Outlook

Office Equipment Wholesales Industry (NAICS 42342)

Sub-Industries – 2018 Estimated Industry Sales, Establishments & Employment

Sub-Industries	Category*	Establishments	Sales ($Mill)	Employment
Office equipment	Major1	4,620	9,291.4	66,494
Calculating machines	Minor1	70	78.0	437
Accounting machines, excluding machine program readable	Minor2	63	55.2	585
Adding machines	Minor2	10	21.7	267
Cash registers	Minor2	656	638.7	4,019
Calculators, electronic	Minor2	15	29.2	100
Copying equipment	Minor1	784	1,240.5	9,496
Blueprinting equipment	Minor2	41	32.5	216
Duplicating machines	Minor2	162	295.6	3,103
Microfilm equipment	Minor2	82	106.8	914
Micrographic equipment	Minor2	31	59.7	534
Mimeograph machines	Minor2	3	1.8	68
Photocopy machines	Minor2	658	20,718.2	18,726
Whiteprinting equipment	Minor2	5	6.1	8
Typewriter and dictation equipment	Minor1	15	8.9	60
Dictating machines	Minor2	88	94.0	852
Typewriters	Minor2	69	58.3	400
Addressing and mailing machines	Minor1	38	39.4	260
Addressing machines	Minor2	8	3.9	40
Mailing machines	Minor2	164	191.3	1,663
Bank automatic teller machines	Minor2	126	218.9	1,059
Check writing, signing, and endorsing machines	Minor2	69	67.0	339
Vaults and safes	Minor2	235	202.6	1,140

*Category-Major categories (Major1) are more general descriptions for companies that self-selected to capture the many functions they perform in the industry. Minor categories (Minor1, Minor2) are more specific for companies that have more detailed functions (Minor1 is a larger category than Minor2). Minor categories figures (sales, etc.) can be aggregated to larger minor categories (Minor2 sums to Minor1) and major categories overall figures.

Computer & Equipment Wholesale Industry
(NAICS 42343)

NAICS 42343: Computer & Peripheral Equipment and Software Wholesalers. This U.S. industry comprises establishments primarily engaged in wholesaling computers, computer peripheral equipment, loaded computer boards, and/or computer software.

Industry Establishments, Sales & Employment Trends

	Year					Percent Chg. Year-to-Year			
	2015	2016	2017	2018	2019	15-16	16-17	17-18	18-19
Establishments	9,651	9,366	8,874	8,653	8,477	-2.9%	-5.3%	-2.5%	-2.0%
Sales ($Millions)	178,108	179,840	178,885	182,418	187,094	1.0%	-0.5%	2.0%	2.6%
Employment	168,720	163,744	155,146	151,283	148,207	-2.9%	-5.3%	-2.5%	-2.0%
Sales ($M)/Estab.	18.46	19.20	20.16	21.08	22.07	4.0%	5.0%	4.6%	4.7%
Sales ($)/Emp.	1,055,640	1,098,296	1,153,009	1,205,805	1,262,388	4.0%	5.0%	4.6%	4.7%

3-Year Trend – Estimated Number of Establishments

Year	Employee Size of Establishment									Total Employment
	1-4 Emps.	5-9 Emps.	10-19 Emps.	20-49 Emps.	50-99 Emps.	100-249 Emps.	250-499 Emps.	>500 Emps.	Non-Employer	
2017	4,257	1,334	1,046	895	317	210	52	40	723	8,874
2018	4,151	1,301	1,020	872	309	204	51	39	705	8,653
2019	4,066	1,275	1,000	855	303	200	50	38	691	8,477

3-Year Trend – Estimated Industry Sales ($Millions)

Year	Employee Size of Establishment									Total Employment
	1-4 Emps.	5-9 Emps.	10-19 Emps.	20-49 Emps.	50-99 Emps.	100-249 Emps.	250-499 Emps.	>500 Emps.	Non-Employer	
2017	6,411.5	5,282.3	10,418.1	23,577.3	18,376.8	32,732.1	27,580.4	54,392.1	114.4	178,885.1
2018	6,507.2	5,361.2	10,573.7	23,929.4	18,651.2	33,220.8	27,992.2	56,066.4	116.1	182,418.0
2019	6,647.8	5,477.0	10,802.2	24,446.5	19,054.2	33,938.7	28,597.1	58,012.2	118.6	187,094.4

3-Year Trend – Estimated Number of Employees

Year	Employee Size of Establishment									Total Employment
	1-4 Emps.	5-9 Emps.	10-19 Emps.	20-49 Emps.	50-99 Emps.	100-249 Emps.	250-499 Emps.	>500 Emps.	Non-Employer	
2017	10,641	7,739	14,232	26,931	18,844	26,438	15,247	34,351	723	155,146
2018	10,376	7,546	13,877	26,260	18,375	25,779	14,868	33,495	705	151,283
2019	10,165	7,393	13,595	25,726	18,001	25,255	14,565	32,814	691	148,207

© Barnes Reports: 2018 U.S. Industry & Market Outlook

Computer & Equipment Wholesale Industry (NAICS 42343)

Sub-Industries – 2018 Estimated Industry Sales, Establishments & Employment

Sub-Industries	Category*	Establishments	Sales ($Mill)	Employment
Computers, peripherals, and software	Major1	4,235	138,213.1	72,038
Computer peripheral equipment	Minor1	773	8,480.2	16,782
Disk drives	Minor2	17	37.4	493
Keying equipment	Minor2	8	10.7	89
Printers, computer	Minor2	127	721.8	5,679
Terminals, computer	Minor2	22	120.1	343
Accounting machines using machine readable programs	Minor2	11	15.7	92
Anti-static equipment and devices	Minor2	7	14.9	92
Computer software	Minor2	2,035	9,308.5	29,241
Computers and accessories, personal and home entertain	Minor2	318	5,254.0	4,080
Computers, nec	Minor2	1,064	19,726.1	20,829
Mainframe computers	Minor2	33	503.3	1,416
Word processing equipment	Minor2	4	12.3	107

*Category-Major categories (Major1) are more general descriptions for companies that self-selected to capture the many functions they perform in the industry. Minor categories (Minor1, Minor2) are more specific for companies that have more detailed functions (Minor1 is a larger category than Minor2). Minor categories figures (sales, etc.) can be aggregated to larger minor categories (Minor2 sums to Minor1) and major categories overall figures.

HARDWARE WHOLESALE INDUSTRY
(NAICS 42371)

NAICS 42371: Hardware Wholesales. Establishments primarily engaged in the wholesale distribution of cutlery and general hardware, including handsaws; saw blades; brads, staples, and tacks; and bolts, nuts, rivets, and screws. Establishments primarily engaged in the wholesale distribution of nails, noninsulated wire, and screening are classified in SIC 5051.

INDUSTRY ESTABLISHMENTS, SALES & EMPLOYMENT TRENDS

	Year					Percent Chg. Year-to-Year			
	2015	2016	2017	2018	2019	15-16	16-17	17-18	18-19
Establishments	6,598	6,486	6,373	6,341	6,338	-1.7%	-1.8%	-0.5%	0.0%
Sales ($Millions)	52,005	53,183	54,579	56,732	59,322	2.3%	2.6%	3.9%	4.6%
Employment	86,485	85,027	83,538	83,118	83,088	-1.7%	-1.8%	-0.5%	0.0%
Sales ($M)/Estab.	7.88	8.20	8.56	8.95	9.36	4.0%	4.5%	4.5%	4.6%
Sales ($)/Emp.	601,318	625,479	653,344	682,547	713,973	4.0%	4.5%	4.5%	4.6%

3-YEAR TREND – ESTIMATED NUMBER OF ESTABLISHMENTS

Year	Employee Size of Establishment									Total Employment
	1-4 Emps.	5-9 Emps.	10-19 Emps.	20-49 Emps.	50-99 Emps.	100-249 Emps.	250-499 Emps.	>500 Emps.	Non-Employer	
2017	2,053	1,228	970	654	190	81	24	10	363	6,373
2018	2,839	1,222	965	651	189	81	24	10	361	6,341
2019	2,838	1,221	965	650	189	81	24	10	361	6,338

3-YEAR TREND – ESTIMATED INDUSTRY SALES ($MILLIONS)

Year	Employee Size of Establishment									Total Employment
	1-4 Emps.	5-9 Emps.	10-19 Emps.	20-49 Emps.	50-99 Emps.	100-249 Emps.	250-499 Emps.	>500 Emps.	Non-Employer	
2017	2,784.2	3,148.7	6,254.7	11,163.4	7,140.7	8,206.2	8,231.7	7,595.7	53.5	54,578.9
2018	2,893.2	3,271.9	6,499.4	11,600.2	7,420.1	8,527.3	8,553.8	7,910.7	55.6	56,732.1
2019	3,025.2	3,421.2	6,796.0	12,129.5	7,758.7	8,916.4	8,944.2	8,273.1	58.1	59,322.5

3-YEAR TREND – ESTIMATED NUMBER OF EMPLOYEES

Year	Employee Size of Establishment									Total Employment
	1-4 Emps.	5-9 Emps.	10-19 Emps.	20-49 Emps.	50-99 Emps.	100-249 Emps.	250-499 Emps.	>500 Emps.	Non-Employer	
2017	7,133	7,121	13,189	19,683	11,303	10,231	7,025	7,490	363	83,538
2018	7,097	7,085	13,123	19,584	11,246	10,180	6,989	7,452	361	83,118
2019	7,095	7,082	13,118	19,577	11,242	10,176	6,987	7,449	361	83,088

© Barnes Reports: 2018 U.S. Industry & Market Outlook

Hardware Wholesale Industry (NAICS 42371)

Sub-Industries – 2018 Estimated Industry Sales, Establishments & Employment

Sub-Industries	Category*	Establishments	Sales ($Mill)	Employment
Hardware	Major1	1,955	32,493.9	37,304
Bolts, nuts, and screws	Minor1	140	1,396.4	2,584
Bolts	Minor2	184	1,022.8	2,553
Nuts (hardware)	Minor2	74	1,178.5	2,259
Rivets	Minor2	15	120.1	165
Screws	Minor2	46	2,253.4	1,644
Hand tools	Minor1	245	2,042.4	4,566
Cutlery	Minor2	55	2,240.1	894
Garden tools, hand	Minor2	17	230.0	192
Power tools and accessories	Minor1	123	1,529.8	1,942
Power handtools	Minor2	44	689.7	913
Saw blades	Minor2	29	223.6	402
Miscellaneous fasteners	Minor1	374	2,154.0	5,254
Brads	Minor2	2,194	2,271.2	8,673
Staples	Minor2	101	173.8	1,886
Tacks	Minor2	114	120.1	488
Builders' hardware, nec	Minor2	283	4,048.8	7,044
Casters and glides	Minor2	53	330.7	554
Chains	Minor2	139	542.1	743
Furniture hardware, nec	Minor2	45	566.0	1,366
Nozzles	Minor2	11	29.5	84
Padlocks	Minor2	5	46.5	90
Security devices, locks	Minor2	77	568.8	1,018
Shelf or light hardware	Minor2	19	460.1	502

*Category-Major categories (Major1) are more general descriptions for companies that self-selected to capture the many functions they perform in the industry. Minor categories (Minor1, Minor2) are more specific for companies that have more detailed functions (Minor1 is a larger category than Minor2). Minor categories figures (sales, etc.) can be aggregated to larger minor categories (Minor2 sums to Minor1) and major categories overall figures.

Printing & Writing Paper Wholesales
(NAICS 42411)

NAICS 42411: Printing & Writing Paper Wholesales. Establishments primarily engaged in the wholesale distribution of printing and writing paper, including envelope paper; fine paper; and groundwood paper.

Industry Establishments, Sales & Employment Trends

	Year					Percent Chg. Year-to-Year			
	2015	2016	2017	2018	2019	15-16	16-17	17-18	18-19
Establishments	1,184	1,145	1,124	1,111	1,103	-3.3%	-1.8%	-1.2%	-0.7%
Sales ($Millions)	18,270	18,580	19,241	20,061	21,026	1.7%	3.6%	4.3%	4.8%
Employment	12,242	11,836	11,618	11,484	11,405	-3.3%	-1.8%	-1.2%	-0.7%
Sales ($M)/Estab.	15.43	16.23	17.12	18.06	19.06	5.2%	5.5%	5.5%	5.5%
Sales ($)/Emp.	1,492,447	1,569,809	1,656,097	1,746,849	1,843,562	5.2%	5.5%	5.5%	5.5%

3-Year Trend – Estimated Number of Establishments

Year	Employee Size of Establishment									Total Employment
	1-4 Emps.	5-9 Emps.	10-19 Emps.	20-49 Emps.	50-99 Emps.	100-249 Emps.	250-499 Emps.	>500 Emps.	Non-Employer	
2017	518	172	110	110	23	17	1	1	172	1,124
2018	512	170	109	109	23	17	1	1	170	1,111
2019	509	169	108	108	22	17	1	1	169	1,103

3-Year Trend – Estimated Industry Sales ($Millions)

Year	Employee Size of Establishment									Total Employment
	1-4 Emps.	5-9 Emps.	10-19 Emps.	20-49 Emps.	50-99 Emps.	100-249 Emps.	250-499 Emps.	>500 Emps.	Non-Employer	
2017	1,379.9	1,202.3	1,937.7	5,128.8	2,332.6	4,715.1	882.9	1,637.0	24.4	19,240.8
2018	1,438.7	1,253.6	2,020.3	5,347.5	2,432.1	4,916.1	920.5	1,707.2	25.5	20,061.5
2019	1,507.9	1,313.8	2,117.5	5,604.6	2,549.0	5,152.5	964.8	1,789.5	26.7	21,026.4

3-Year Trend – Estimated Number of Employees

Year	Employee Size of Establishment									Total Employment
	1-4 Emps.	5-9 Emps.	10-19 Emps.	20-49 Emps.	50-99 Emps.	100-249 Emps.	250-499 Emps.	>500 Emps.	Non-Employer	
2017	1,295	996	1,497	3,314	1,353	2,154	276	560	172	11,618
2018	1,281	985	1,480	3,276	1,337	2,129	273	554	170	11,484
2019	1,272	978	1,470	3,253	1,328	2,115	271	550	169	11,405

© Barnes Reports: 2018 U.S. Industry & Market Outlook

PRINTING & WRITING PAPER WHOLESALES
(NAICS 42411)

SUB-INDUSTRIES — 2018 ESTIMATED INDUSTRY SALES, ESTABLISHMENTS & EMPLOYMENT

Sub-Industries	Category*	Establishments	Sales ($Mill)	Employment
Printing and writing paper	Major1	691	8,066.2	6,831
Fine paper	Minor2	130	3,150.4	1,895
Printing paper	Minor2	262	8,010.4	2,497
Writing paper	Minor2	28	834.4	261

*Category-Major categories (Major1) are more general descriptions for companies that self-selected to capture the many functions they perform in the industry. Minor categories (Minor1, Minor2) are more specific for companies that have more detailed functions (Minor1 is a larger category than Minor2). Minor categories figures (sales, etc.) can be aggregated to larger minor categories (Minor2 sums to Minor1) and major categories overall figures.

Men's & Boys' Clothing Wholesales Industry (NAICS 42432)

NAICS 42432: Men's & Boys' Clothing Wholesales. Establishments primarily engaged in the wholesale distribution of men's and boys' apparel and furnishings, sportswear, hosiery, underwear, nightwear, and work clothing.

Industry Establishments, Sales & Employment Trends

	Year					Percent Chg. Year-to-Year			
	2015	2016	2017	2018	2019	15-16	16-17	17-18	18-19
Establishments	5,679	5,774	5,789	5,812	5,863	1.7%	0.3%	0.4%	0.9%
Sales ($Millions)	47,260	50,366	53,118	56,108	59,584	6.6%	5.5%	5.6%	6.2%
Employment	55,838	56,778	56,921	57,149	57,646	1.7%	0.3%	0.4%	0.9%
Sales ($M)/Estab.	8.32	8.72	9.18	9.65	10.16	4.8%	5.2%	5.2%	5.3%
Sales ($)/Emp.	846,381	887,073	933,186	981,789	1,033,625	4.8%	5.2%	5.2%	5.3%

3-Year Trend – Estimated Number of Establishments

Year	Employee Size of Establishment									Total Employment
	1-4 Emps.	5-9 Emps.	10-19 Emps.	20-49 Emps.	50-99 Emps.	100-249 Emps.	250-499 Emps.	>500 Emps.	Non-Employer	
2017	1,986	644	446	310	129	88	31	4	2,151	5,789
2018	1,994	647	448	311	130	88	31	4	2,159	5,812
2019	2,011	652	452	314	131	89	31	4	2,178	5,863

3-Year Trend – Estimated Industry Sales ($Millions)

Year	Employee Size of Establishment									Total Employment
	1-4 Emps.	5-9 Emps.	10-19 Emps.	20-49 Emps.	50-99 Emps.	100-249 Emps.	250-499 Emps.	>500 Emps.	Non-Employer	
2017	2,628.8	2,241.7	3,906.8	7,177.2	6,591.0	12,029.2	14,143.2	4,111.7	288.4	53,118.0
2018	2,777.1	2,368.1	4,127.2	7,582.1	6,962.9	12,707.8	14,941.0	4,337.1	304.7	56,108.0
2019	2,949.9	2,515.5	4,384.0	8,053.8	7,396.1	13,498.5	15,870.7	4,592.1	323.7	59,584.3

3-Year Trend – Estimated Number of Employees

Year	Employee Size of Establishment									Total Employment
	1-4 Emps.	5-9 Emps.	10-19 Emps.	20-49 Emps.	50-99 Emps.	100-249 Emps.	250-499 Emps.	>500 Emps.	Non-Employer	
2017	4,964	3,737	6,072	9,328	7,690	11,055	8,896	3,028	2,151	56,921
2018	4,984	3,752	6,097	9,365	7,721	11,099	8,932	3,040	2,159	57,149
2019	5,028	3,784	6,150	9,447	7,788	11,196	9,010	3,066	2,178	57,646

Men's & Boys' Clothing Wholesales Industry (NAICS 42432)

Sub-Industries – 2018 Estimated Industry Sales, Establishments & Employment

Sub-Industries	Category*	Establishments	Sales ($Mill)	Employment
Men's and boy's clothing	Major1	2,898	25,165.7	27,249
Men's and boys' hats, scarves, and gloves	Minor1	30	172.5	168
Caps, men's and boys'	Minor2	91	626.2	1,317
Gloves, men's and boys'	Minor2	131	1,060.3	1,219
Hats, men's and boys'	Minor2	120	664.1	677
Mittens, men's and boys'	Minor2	2	15.4	82
Mufflers, men's and boys'	Minor2	1	2.1	2
Scarves, men's and boys'	Minor2	6	17.5	115
Men's and boys' robes, nightwear, and undergarments	Minor1	18	58.2	118
Nightwear, men's and boys'	Minor2	5	58.9	167
Robes, men's and boys'	Minor2	3	21.0	20
Underwear, men's and boys'	Minor2	52	359.7	343
Men's and boys' outerwear	Minor1	82	869.5	1,071
Coats, men's and boys'	Minor2	29	137.4	237
Leather and sheep lined clothing, men's and boys'	Minor2	38	169.7	391
Fur clothing, men's and boys'	Minor2	7	23.8	31
Men's and boys' furnishings	Minor1	29	263.7	213
Apparel belts, men's and boys'	Minor2	169	1,206.8	1,182
Handkerchiefs, men's and boys'	Minor2	1	7.0	7
Hosiery, men's and boys'	Minor2	59	324.0	343
Neckwear, men's and boys'	Minor2	54	511.9	273
Umbrellas, men's and boys'	Minor2	32	355.5	187
Men's and boys' suits and trousers	Minor1	37	264.4	346
Suits, men's and boys'	Minor2	20	172.5	314
Trousers, men's and boys'	Minor2	19	276.3	281
Men's and boys' sportswear and work clothing	Minor1	195	1,198.4	1,502
Beachwear, men's and boys'	Minor2	33	190.7	195
Sportswear, men's and boys'	Minor2	848	14,108.0	10,702
Uniforms, men's and boys'	Minor2	297	2,761.4	3,508
Work clothing, men's and boys'	Minor2	114	649.3	1,071
Shirts, men's and boys'	Minor2	356	3,301.4	3,526
Sweaters, men's and boys'	Minor2	36	1,094.6	290

*Category-Major categories (Major1) are more general descriptions for companies that self-selected to capture the many functions they perform in the industry. Minor categories (Minor1, Minor2) are more specific for companies that have more detailed functions (Minor1 is a larger category than Minor2). Minor categories figures (sales, etc.) can be aggregated to larger minor categories (Minor2 sums to Minor1) and major categories overall figures.

Women's & Children's Clothing Wholesale
(NAICS 42433)

NAICS 42433: Women's & Children's Clothing Wholesales. Establishments primarily engaged in the wholesale distribution of women's, children's, and infants' clothing and accessories, including hosiery, lingerie, millinery, and furs.

Industry Establishments, Sales & Employment Trends

	Year					Percent Chg. Year-to-Year			
	2015	2016	2017	2018	2019	15-16	16-17	17-18	18-19
Establishments	12,576	12,753	13,059	13,379	13,772	1.4%	2.4%	2.5%	2.9%
Sales ($Millions)	67,653	70,209	73,950	78,079	83,039	3.8%	5.3%	5.6%	6.4%
Employment	90,737	92,010	94,222	96,532	99,362	1.4%	2.4%	2.5%	2.9%
Sales ($M)/Estab.	5.38	5.51	5.66	5.84	6.03	2.3%	2.9%	3.1%	3.3%
Sales ($)/Emp.	745,592	763,063	784,843	808,838	835,723	2.3%	2.9%	3.1%	3.3%

3-Year Trend – Estimated Number of Establishments

Year	Employee Size of Establishment									Total Employment
	1-4 Emps.	5-9 Emps.	10-19 Emps.	20-49 Emps.	50-99 Emps.	100-249 Emps.	250-499 Emps.	>500 Emps.	Non-Employer	
2017	5,024	1,285	908	617	240	103	28	4	4,852	13,059
2018	5,147	1,316	930	632	246	105	29	4	4,971	13,379
2019	5,298	1,355	957	650	253	108	30	4	5,116	13,772

3-Year Trend – Estimated Industry Sales ($Millions)

Year	Employee Size of Establishment									Total Employment
	1-4 Emps.	5-9 Emps.	10-19 Emps.	20-49 Emps.	50-99 Emps.	100-249 Emps.	250-499 Emps.	>500 Emps.	Non-Employer	
2017	6,350.8	4,267.9	7,583.1	13,641.4	11,661.4	13,469.9	12,381.7	3,972.1	621.4	73,949.7
2018	6,708.6	4,508.4	8,010.4	14,410.0	12,318.5	14,228.8	13,079.3	4,158.8	656.4	78,079.1
2019	7,138.7	4,797.4	8,524.0	15,333.9	13,108.3	15,141.1	13,917.9	4,379.5	698.5	83,039.2

3-Year Trend – Estimated Number of Employees

Year	Employee Size of Establishment									Total Employment
	1-4 Emps.	5-9 Emps.	10-19 Emps.	20-49 Emps.	50-99 Emps.	100-249 Emps.	250-499 Emps.	>500 Emps.	Non-Employer	
2017	12,560	7,450	12,343	18,566	14,248	12,963	8,156	3,084	4,852	94,222
2018	12,867	7,633	12,646	19,021	14,598	13,281	8,356	3,160	4,971	96,532
2019	13,245	7,857	13,016	19,579	15,026	13,671	8,601	3,252	5,116	99,362

Women's & Children's Clothing Wholesale (NAICS 42433)

Sub-Industries – 2018 Estimated Industry Sales, Establishments & Employment

Sub-Industries	Category*	Establishments	Sales ($Mill)	Employment
Women's and children's clothing	Major1	6,001	39,652.1	46,786
Women's and children's outerwear	Minor1	123	1,937.1	1,495
Coats: women's, children's, and infants'	Minor2	29	51.9	204
Fur clothing, women's and children's	Minor2	98	250.0	489
Leather and sheep lined clothing, women's and children's	Minor2	23	47.2	99
Women's and children's lingerie and undergarments	Minor1	126	2,005.2	1,230
Corsets	Minor2	31	31.7	89
Lingerie	Minor2	929	1,632.9	4,920
Nightwear: women's, children's, and infants'	Minor2	25	154.0	437
Underwear: women's, children's, and infants'	Minor2	56	213.6	304
Women's and children's sportswear and swimsuits	Minor1	182	831.9	1,289
Sportswear, women's and children's	Minor2	655	6,264.7	10,169
Swimsuits: women's, children's, and infants'	Minor2	123	417.9	670
Women's and children's accessories	Minor1	559	3,735.6	5,719
Apparel belts, women's and children's	Minor2	370	2,840.2	2,427
Caps and gowns	Minor2	22	63.5	118
Gloves, women's and children's	Minor2	26	88.2	126
Handbags	Minor2	584	5,931.1	4,300
Handkerchiefs, women's and children's	Minor2	1	2.3	3
Hats: women's, children's, and infants'	Minor2	95	275.5	480
Hosiery: women's, children's, and infants'	Minor2	233	2,768.2	1,830
Millinery	Minor2	43	48.0	146
Mittens: women's, children's, and infants'	Minor2	3	1.5	5
Purses	Minor2	985	704.2	2,360
Scarves, women's and children's	Minor2	32	41.8	97
Children's goods	Minor1	434	1,570.2	1,979
Baby goods	Minor2	644	2,033.0	2,767
Diapers	Minor2	314	905.5	790
Infants' wear	Minor2	148	745.3	1,031
Women's and children's dresses, suits, skirts, and blouses	Minor1	129	1,300.1	1,115
Blouses	Minor2	38	192.7	471
Dresses	Minor2	216	1,076.5	1,631
Skirts	Minor2	62	87.5	149
Suits: women's, children's, and infants'	Minor2	6	2.3	23
Coordinate sets: women's, children's, and infants'	Minor2	31	175.7	783

*Category-Major categories (Major1) are more general descriptions for companies that self-selected to capture the many functions they perform in the industry. Minor categories (Minor1, Minor2) are more specific for companies that have more detailed functions (Minor1 is a larger category than Minor2). Minor categories figures (sales, etc.) can be aggregated to larger minor categories (Minor2 sums to Minor1) and major categories overall figures.

GENERAL-LINE GROCERY WHOLESALE INDUSTRY
(NAICS 42441)

NAICS 42441: General-Line Grocery Wholesale. Establishments primarily engaged in the wholesale distribution of a general line of groceries. Establishments primarily engaged in roasting coffee, blending tea, or grinding and packaging spices are classified under food processing.

INDUSTRY ESTABLISHMENTS, SALES & EMPLOYMENT TRENDS

	Year					Percent Chg. Year-to-Year			
	2015	2016	2017	2018	2019	15-16	16-17	17-18	18-19
Establishments	3,373	3,301	3,285	3,301	3,333	-2.1%	-0.5%	0.5%	1.0%
Sales ($Millions)	134,359	136,292	141,000	147,416	155,087	1.4%	3.5%	4.5%	5.2%
Employment	120,224	117,674	117,083	117,670	118,813	-2.1%	-0.5%	0.5%	1.0%
Sales ($M)/Estab.	39.84	41.28	42.93	44.66	46.53	3.6%	4.0%	4.0%	4.2%
Sales ($)/Emp.	1,117,573	1,158,221	1,204,277	1,252,792	1,305,301	3.6%	4.0%	4.0%	4.2%

3-YEAR TREND – ESTIMATED NUMBER OF ESTABLISHMENTS

Year	Employee Size of Establishment									Total Employ-ment
	1-4 Emps.	5-9 Emps.	10-19 Emps.	20-49 Emps.	50-99 Emps.	100-249 Emps.	250-499 Emps.	>500 Emps.	Non-Employer	
2017	1,271	432	299	288	189	166	129	42	469	3,285
2018	1,277	435	300	290	190	166	129	42	472	3,301
2019	1,290	439	303	293	192	168	130	42	476	3,333

3-YEAR TREND – ESTIMATED INDUSTRY SALES ($MILLIONS)

Year	Employee Size of Establishment									Total Employ-ment
	1-4 Emps.	5-9 Emps.	10-19 Emps.	20-49 Emps.	50-99 Emps.	100-249 Emps.	250-499 Emps.	>500 Emps.	Non-Employer	
2017	1,640.2	1,466.7	2,550.4	6,508.7	9,377.1	22,146.5	57,958.6	39,256.1	96.0	141,000.3
2018	1,715.5	1,534.1	2,667.4	6,807.3	9,807.4	23,162.8	60,618.1	41,002.7	100.4	147,415.7
2019	1,806.0	1,615.0	2,808.2	7,166.7	10,325.1	24,385.5	63,818.0	43,056.4	105.7	155,086.6

3-YEAR TREND – ESTIMATED NUMBER OF EMPLOYEES

Year	Employee Size of Establishment									Total Employ-ment
	1-4 Emps.	5-9 Emps.	10-19 Emps.	20-49 Emps.	50-99 Emps.	100-249 Emps.	250-499 Emps.	>500 Emps.	Non-Employer	
2017	3,177	2,508	4,066	8,677	11,223	20,877	37,396	28,690	469	117,083
2018	3,193	2,520	4,087	8,720	11,279	20,982	37,583	28,834	472	117,670
2019	3,224	2,545	4,126	8,805	11,388	21,185	37,948	29,114	476	118,813

GENERAL-LINE GROCERY WHOLESALE INDUSTRY
(NAICS 42441)

SUB-INDUSTRIES — 2018 ESTIMATED INDUSTRY SALES, ESTABLISHMENTS & EMPLOYMENT

Sub-Industries	Category*	Establishments	Sales ($Mill)	Employment
Groceries, general line	Major1	1,846	138,160.3	82,716
Food brokers	Minor2	1,455	9,255.4	34,953

*Category-Major categories (Major1) are more general descriptions for companies that self-selected to capture the many functions they perform in the industry. Minor categories (Minor1, Minor2) are more specific for companies that have more detailed functions (Minor1 is a larger category than Minor2). Minor categories figures (sales, etc.) can be aggregated to larger minor categories (Minor2 sums to Minor1) and major categories overall figures.

Beer & Ale Wholesale Industry
(NAICS 42481)

NAICS 42481: Beer & Ale Wholesale. Establishments primarily engaged in the wholesale distribution of beer, ale, porter, and other fermented malt beverages.

Industry Establishments, Sales & Employment Trends

	Year					Percent Chg. Year-to-Year			
	2015	2016	2017	2018	2019	15-16	16-17	17-18	18-19
Establishments	2,667	2,557	2,504	2,484	2,476	-4.1%	-2.1%	-0.8%	-0.3%
Sales ($Millions)	60,522	60,753	62,468	65,094	68,212	0.4%	2.8%	4.2%	4.8%
Employment	97,652	93,640	91,681	90,955	90,657	-4.1%	-2.1%	-0.8%	-0.3%
Sales ($M)/Estab.	22.69	23.76	24.95	26.20	27.55	4.7%	5.0%	5.0%	5.1%
Sales ($)/Emp.	619,776	648,791	681,363	715,675	752,424	4.7%	5.0%	5.0%	5.1%

3-Year Trend – Estimated Number of Establishments

Year	Employee Size of Establishment									Total Employment
	1-4 Emps.	5-9 Emps.	10-19 Emps.	20-49 Emps.	50-99 Emps.	100-249 Emps.	250-499 Emps.	>500 Emps.	Non-Employer	
2017	444	167	214	382	279	275	69	5	669	2,504
2018	441	166	212	379	277	273	68	5	664	2,484
2019	439	165	212	378	276	272	68	5	662	2,476

3-Year Trend – Estimated Industry Sales ($Millions)

Year	Employee Size of Establishment									Total Employment
	1-4 Emps.	5-9 Emps.	10-19 Emps.	20-49 Emps.	50-99 Emps.	100-249 Emps.	250-499 Emps.	>500 Emps.	Non-Employer	
2017	365.8	361.8	1,165.5	5,506.8	8,833.5	23,487.2	19,723.0	2,923.5	101.1	62,468.2
2018	381.1	377.0	1,214.3	5,737.6	9,203.7	24,471.5	20,549.6	3,054.0	105.4	65,094.1
2019	399.4	395.0	1,272.4	6,012.1	9,644.0	25,642.4	21,532.8	3,203.6	110.4	68,212.2

3-Year Trend – Estimated Number of Employees

Year	Employee Size of Establishment									Total Employment
	1-4 Emps.	5-9 Emps.	10-19 Emps.	20-49 Emps.	50-99 Emps.	100-249 Emps.	250-499 Emps.	>500 Emps.	Non-Employer	
2017	1,110	969	2,911	11,502	16,563	34,688	19,937	3,331	669	91,681
2018	1,101	962	2,888	11,411	16,432	34,413	19,779	3,305	664	90,955
2019	1,098	958	2,879	11,373	16,378	34,300	19,714	3,294	662	90,657

© Barnes Reports: 2018 U.S. Industry & Market Outlook

BEER & ALE WHOLESALE INDUSTRY
(NAICS 42481)

Sub-Industries – 2018 Estimated Industry Sales, Establishments & Employment

Sub-Industries	Category*	Establishments	Sales ($Mill)	Employment
Beer and ale	Major1	568	8,500.8	20,336
Ale	Minor2	94	677.1	1,134
Beer and other fermented malt liquors	Minor2	1,143	55,792.1	68,961
Porter	Minor2	679	124.1	524

*Category-Major categories (Major1) are more general descriptions for companies that self-selected to capture the many functions they perform in the industry. Minor categories (Minor1, Minor2) are more specific for companies that have more detailed functions (Minor1 is a larger category than Minor2). Minor categories figures (sales, etc.) can be aggregated to larger minor categories (Minor2 sums to Minor1) and major categories overall figures.

WINE & ALCOHOLIC BEVERAGES WHOLESALES
(NAICS 42482)

NAICS 42482: Wine & Alcoholic Beverages Wholesales. Establishments primarily engaged in the wholesale distribution of distilled spirits, including neutral spirits and ethyl alcohol used in blended wines and distilled liquors.

INDUSTRY ESTABLISHMENTS, SALES & EMPLOYMENT TRENDS

	Year					Percent Chg. Year-to-Year			
	2015	2016	2017	2018	2019	15-16	16-17	17-18	18-19
Establishments	3,449	3,630	3,852	4,021	4,216	5.2%	6.1%	4.4%	4.9%
Sales ($Millions)	74,919	81,675	90,104	98,000	107,223	9.0%	10.3%	8.8%	9.4%
Employment	77,092	81,133	86,098	89,870	94,246	5.2%	6.1%	4.4%	4.9%
Sales ($M)/Estab.	21.72	22.50	23.39	24.37	25.43	3.6%	4.0%	4.2%	4.3%
Sales ($)/Emp.	971,815	1,006,677	1,046,522	1,090,465	1,137,695	3.6%	4.0%	4.2%	4.3%

3-YEAR TREND – ESTIMATED NUMBER OF ESTABLISHMENTS

Year	Employee Size of Establishment									Total Employ-ment
	1-4 Emps.	5-9 Emps.	10-19 Emps.	20-49 Emps.	50-99 Emps.	100-249 Emps.	250-499 Emps.	>500 Emps.	Non-Employer	
2017	1,398	471	319	256	138	145	61	32	1,030	3,852
2018	1,460	492	333	267	145	152	64	34	1,075	4,021
2019	1,531	516	350	280	152	159	67	35	1,127	4,216

3-YEAR TREND – ESTIMATED INDUSTRY SALES ($MILLIONS)

Year	Employee Size of Establishment									Total Employ-ment
	1-4 Emps.	5-9 Emps.	10-19 Emps.	20-49 Emps.	50-99 Emps.	100-249 Emps.	250-499 Emps.	>500 Emps.	Non-Employer	
2017	1,701.9	1,507.7	2,569.7	5,446.0	6,482.4	18,316.5	26,118.6	27,807.2	153.9	90,103.9
2018	1,857.2	1,645.3	2,804.1	5,942.8	7,073.7	19,987.5	28,501.3	30,020.1	168.0	98,000.0
2019	2,039.1	1,806.5	3,078.8	6,525.0	7,766.7	21,945.5	31,293.3	32,583.8	184.4	107,223.0

3-YEAR TREND – ESTIMATED NUMBER OF EMPLOYEES

Year	Employee Size of Establishment									Total Employ-ment
	1-4 Emps.	5-9 Emps.	10-19 Emps.	20-49 Emps.	50-99 Emps.	100-249 Emps.	250-499 Emps.	>500 Emps.	Non-Employer	
2017	3,496	2,734	4,344	7,698	8,226	18,308	17,869	22,395	1,030	86,098
2018	3,649	2,853	4,534	8,035	8,586	19,110	18,651	23,376	1,075	89,870
2019	3,826	2,992	4,755	8,427	9,004	20,041	19,560	24,514	1,127	94,246

© Barnes Reports: 2018 U.S. Industry & Market Outlook

WINE & ALCOHOLIC BEVERAGES WHOLESALES (NAICS 42482)

SUB-INDUSTRIES – 2018 ESTIMATED INDUSTRY SALES, ESTABLISHMENTS & EMPLOYMENT

Sub-Industries	Category*	Establishments	Sales ($Mill)	Employment
Wine and distilled beverages	Major1	396	19,920.5	19,059
Wine	Minor1	2,405	46,723.3	38,870
Brandy and brandy spirits	Minor2	9	292.6	100
Wine coolers, alcoholic	Minor2	14	532.4	447
Liquor	Minor1	1,104	27,405.7	27,960
Cocktails, alcoholic: premixed	Minor2	9	89.4	178
Neutral spirits	Minor2	9	120.6	231
Bottling wines and liquors	Minor2	76	2,915.5	3,025

*Category-Major categories (Major1) are more general descriptions for companies that self-selected to capture the many functions they perform in the industry. Minor categories (Minor1, Minor2) are more specific for companies that have more detailed functions (Minor1 is a larger category than Minor2). Minor categories figures (sales, etc.) can be aggregated to larger minor categories (Minor2 sums to Minor1) and major categories overall figures.

Book/Periodical/Newspaper Wholesales (NAICS 42492)

NAICS 42492: Book & Periodical & Newspaper Wholesales. Establishments primarily engaged in the wholesale distribution of books, periodicals, and newspapers.

Industry Establishments, Sales & Employment Trends

	Year					Percent Chg. Year-to-Year			
	2015	2016	2017	2018	2019	15-16	16-17	17-18	18-19
Establishments	6,934	6,645	6,456	6,386	6,346	-4.2%	-2.8%	-1.1%	-0.6%
Sales ($Millions)	18,005	17,811	17,931	18,379	18,962	-1.1%	0.7%	2.5%	3.2%
Employment	39,814	38,154	37,072	36,667	36,436	-4.2%	-2.8%	-1.1%	-0.6%
Sales ($M)/Estab.	2.60	2.68	2.78	2.88	2.99	3.2%	3.6%	3.6%	3.8%
Sales ($)/Emp.	452,236	466,810	483,686	501,232	520,421	3.2%	3.6%	3.6%	3.8%

3-Year Trend – Estimated Number of Establishments

Year	Employee Size of Establishment									Total Employment
	1-4 Emps.	5-9 Emps.	10-19 Emps.	20-49 Emps.	50-99 Emps.	100-249 Emps.	250-499 Emps.	>500 Emps.	Non-Employer	
2017	980	264	193	144	79	46	15	9	4,725	6,456
2018	970	262	191	143	78	45	15	9	4,674	6,386
2019	964	260	189	142	78	45	15	9	4,644	6,346

3-Year Trend – Estimated Industry Sales ($Millions)

Year	Employee Size of Establishment									Total Employment
	1-4 Emps.	5-9 Emps.	10-19 Emps.	20-49 Emps.	50-99 Emps.	100-249 Emps.	250-499 Emps.	>500 Emps.	Non-Employer	
2017	677.4	480.2	880.2	1,744.5	2,103.0	3,267.4	3,595.9	4,877.0	305.5	17,931.1
2018	693.6	491.7	901.3	1,786.3	2,153.3	3,345.6	3,682.0	5,011.9	312.8	18,378.6
2019	715.3	507.0	929.4	1,841.9	2,220.4	3,449.8	3,796.7	5,178.9	322.6	18,962.0

3-Year Trend – Estimated Number of Employees

Year	Employee Size of Establishment									Total Employment
	1-4 Emps.	5-9 Emps.	10-19 Emps.	20-49 Emps.	50-99 Emps.	100-249 Emps.	250-499 Emps.	>500 Emps.	Non-Employer	
2017	2,451	1,534	2,621	4,344	4,701	5,753	4,334	6,607	4,725	37,072
2018	2,424	1,517	2,593	4,297	4,650	5,691	4,287	6,535	4,674	36,667
2019	2,409	1,507	2,576	4,270	4,621	5,655	4,260	6,494	4,644	36,436

© Barnes Reports: 2018 U.S. Industry & Market Outlook

BOOK/PERIODICAL/NEWSPAPER WHOLESALES (NAICS 42492)

SUB-INDUSTRIES – 2018 ESTIMATED INDUSTRY SALES, ESTABLISHMENTS & EMPLOYMENT

Sub-Industries	Category*	Establishments	Sales ($Mill)	Employment
Books, periodicals, and newspapers	Major1	341	2,420.5	7,277
Books	Minor2	4,537	10,616.4	19,384
Magazines	Minor2	1,119	3,723.9	7,107
Newspapers	Minor2	288	1,323.9	2,228
Periodicals	Minor2	32	215.5	511
Comic books	Minor2	68	78.4	161

*Category-Major categories (Major1) are more general descriptions for companies that self-selected to capture the many functions they perform in the industry. Minor categories (Minor1, Minor2) are more specific for companies that have more detailed functions (Minor1 is a larger category than Minor2). Minor categories figures (sales, etc.) can be aggregated to larger minor categories (Minor2 sums to Minor1) and major categories overall figures.

New Car Dealers Industry
(NAICS 44111)

NAICS 44111: New Car Dealers. Establishments primarily engaged in the retail sale of new automobiles or new and used automobiles. These establishments frequently maintain repair departments and carry stocks of replacement parts, tires, batteries, and automotive accessories. These establishments also frequently sell pickups and vans at retail.

Industry Establishments, Sales & Employment Trends

	Year					Percent Chg. Year-to-Year			
	2015	2016	2017	2018	2019	15-16	16-17	17-18	18-19
Establishments	36,541	35,766	34,954	34,375	34,341	-2.1%	-2.3%	-1.7%	-0.1%
Sales ($Millions)	724,798	735,492	748,435	767,228	800,349	1.5%	1.8%	2.5%	4.3%
Employment	994,406	973,316	951,227	935,471	934,541	-2.1%	-2.3%	-1.7%	-0.1%
Sales ($M)/Estab.	19.84	20.56	21.41	22.32	23.31	3.7%	4.1%	4.2%	4.4%
Sales ($)/Emp.	728,875	755,656	786,810	820,151	856,408	3.7%	4.1%	4.2%	4.4%

3-Year Trend – Estimated Number of Establishments

Year	Employee Size of Establishment									Total Employment
	1-4 Emps.	5-9 Emps.	10-19 Emps.	20-49 Emps.	50-99 Emps.	100-249 Emps.	250-499 Emps.	>500 Emps.	Non-Employer	
2017	2,988	1,240	1,984	6,115	5,296	2,699	176	9	14,441	34,954
2018	2,939	1,226	1,951	6,014	5,208	2,654	173	8	14,202	34,375
2019	2,936	1,225	1,949	6,008	5,203	2,651	173	8	14,188	34,341

3-Year Trend – Estimated Industry Sales ($Millions)

Year	Employee Size of Establishment									Total Employment
	1-4 Emps.	5-9 Emps.	10-19 Emps.	20-49 Emps.	50-99 Emps.	100-249 Emps.	250-499 Emps.	>500 Emps.	Non-Employer	
2017	3,290.4	3,607.2	14,438.5	117,801.9	224,239.6	307,969.3	67,703.2	6,037.0	3,348.5	748,435.5
2018	3,373.0	3,697.7	14,801.0	120,759.7	229,870.0	315,702.1	69,403.1	6,188.8	3,432.6	767,228.0
2019	3,518.6	3,857.4	15,440.0	125,972.8	239,793.2	329,330.6	72,399.2	6,456.0	3,580.8	800,348.6

3-Year Trend – Estimated Number of Employees

Year	Employee Size of Establishment									Total Employment
	1-4 Emps.	5-9 Emps.	10-19 Emps.	20-49 Emps.	50-99 Emps.	100-249 Emps.	250-499 Emps.	>500 Emps.	Non-Employer	
2017	7,471	7,229	26,982	184,074	314,560	340,282	51,201	4,988	14,441	951,227
2018	7,347	7,109	26,535	181,025	309,349	334,645	50,353	4,905	14,202	935,471
2019	7,340	7,102	26,508	180,845	309,042	334,313	50,303	4,900	14,188	934,541

New Car Dealers Industry (NAICS 44111)

Sub-Industries – 2018 Estimated Industry Sales, Establishments & Employment

Sub-Industries	Category*	Establishments	Sales ($Mill)	Employment
New and used car dealers	Major1	9,919	146,002.7	89,896
Automobiles, new and used	Minor2	21,949	596,679.7	813,166
Pickups, new and used	Minor2	525	2,358.5	5,016
Trucks, tractors, and trailers: new and used	Minor2	1,943	21,720.2	26,958
Vans, new and used	Minor2	39	466.9	435

*Category-Major categories (Major1) are more general descriptions for companies that self-selected to capture the many functions they perform in the industry. Minor categories (Minor1, Minor2) are more specific for companies that have more detailed functions (Minor1 is a larger category than Minor2). Minor categories figures (sales, etc.) can be aggregated to larger minor categories (Minor2 sums to Minor1) and major categories overall figures.

Furniture Stores Industry (NAICS 44211)

NAICS 44211: Furniture Stores. Establishments primarily engaged in the retail sale of household furniture. These stores may also sell homefurnishings, major appliances, and floor coverings.

Industry Establishments, Sales & Employment Trends

	Year					Percent Chg. Year-to-Year			
	2015	2016	2017	2018	2019	15-16	16-17	17-18	18-19
Establishments	28,799	27,241	26,234	25,883	25,690	-5.4%	-3.7%	-1.3%	-0.7%
Sales ($Millions)	47,355	45,740	45,207	45,850	46,913	-3.4%	-1.2%	1.4%	2.3%
Employment	207,250	196,041	188,794	186,262	184,879	-5.4%	-3.7%	-1.3%	-0.7%
Sales ($M)/Estab.	1.64	1.68	1.72	1.77	1.83	2.1%	2.6%	2.8%	3.1%
Sales ($)/Emp.	228,491	233,318	239,451	246,157	253,750	2.1%	2.6%	2.8%	3.1%

3-Year Trend – Estimated Number of Establishments

Year	Employee Size of Establishment									Total Employment
	1-4 Emps.	5-9 Emps.	10-19 Emps.	20-49 Emps.	50-99 Emps.	100-249 Emps.	250-499 Emps.	>500 Emps.	Non-Employer	
2017	11,580	4,690	3,053	1,626	220	54	43	6	4,962	26,234
2018	11,425	4,627	3,013	1,604	217	53	42	6	4,895	25,883
2019	11,340	4,592	2,990	1,592	216	53	42	6	4,859	25,690

3-Year Trend – Estimated Industry Sales ($Millions)

Year	Employee Size of Establishment									Total Employment
	1-4 Emps.	5-9 Emps.	10-19 Emps.	20-49 Emps.	50-99 Emps.	100-249 Emps.	250-499 Emps.	>500 Emps.	Non-Employer	
2017	4,844.9	5,156.9	8,444.0	11,901.9	3,547.0	2,330.7	6,257.8	2,183.7	540.1	45,206.8
2018	4,912.3	5,228.7	8,561.5	12,067.6	3,596.4	2,363.1	6,344.9	2,227.5	547.6	45,849.6
2019	5,025.4	5,349.1	8,758.7	12,345.4	3,679.2	2,417.6	6,491.0	2,286.4	560.2	46,913.0

3-Year Trend – Estimated Number of Employees

Year	Employee Size of Establishment									Total Employment
	1-4 Emps.	5-9 Emps.	10-19 Emps.	20-49 Emps.	50-99 Emps.	100-249 Emps.	250-499 Emps.	>500 Emps.	Non-Employer	
2017	28,950	27,199	41,528	48,944	13,095	6,777	12,455	4,884	4,962	188,794
2018	28,562	26,835	40,971	48,287	12,919	6,686	12,288	4,819	4,895	186,262
2019	28,350	26,635	40,666	47,929	12,823	6,637	12,196	4,783	4,859	184,879

© Barnes Reports: 2018 U.S. Industry & Market Outlook

FURNITURE STORES INDUSTRY
(NAICS 44211)

SUB-INDUSTRIES – 2018 ESTIMATED INDUSTRY SALES, ESTABLISHMENTS & EMPLOYMENT

Sub-Industries	Category*	Establishments	Sales ($Mill)	Employment
Furniture stores	Major1	18,146	35,090.6	136,080
Beds and accessories	Minor1	962	800.4	5,056
Bedding and bedsprings	Minor2	350	137.3	1,433
Mattresses	Minor2	1,628	1,090.5	7,880
Waterbeds and accessories	Minor2	117	82.7	1,023
Customized furniture and cabinets	Minor1	527	636.2	3,156
Cabinet work, custom	Minor2	1,510	2,075.3	7,971
Custom made furniture, except cabinets	Minor2	397	392.5	1,753
Bar fixtures, equipment and supplies	Minor2	44	50.8	197
Cabinets, except custom made: kitchen	Minor2	365	423.3	1,703
Juvenile furniture	Minor2	204	285.0	4,290
Office furniture	Minor2	1,089	4,073.7	12,472
Outdoor and garden furniture	Minor2	410	535.6	2,279
Unfinished furniture	Minor2	133	176.0	970

*Category-Major categories (Major1) are more general descriptions for companies that self-selected to capture the many functions they perform in the industry. Minor categories (Minor1, Minor2) are more specific for companies that have more detailed functions (Minor1 is a larger category than Minor2). Minor categories figures (sales, etc.) can be aggregated to larger minor categories (Minor2 sums to Minor1) and major categories overall figures.

APPLIANCE/TV/ELECTRONICS STORES INDUSTRY
(NAICS 44311)

NAICS 44311: Appliance/TV/Electronics Stores. Establishments primarily engaged in the retail sale of electric and gas refrigerators, stoves, and other household appliances, such as electric irons, percolators, hot plates, and vacuum cleaners. Many such stores also sell radio and television sets. Retail stores operated by public utility companies and primarily engaged in the sale of electric and gas appliances for household use are classified in this business.

INDUSTRY ESTABLISHMENTS, SALES & EMPLOYMENT TRENDS

	Year					Percent Chg. Year-to-Year			
	2015	2016	2017	2018	2019	15-16	16-17	17-18	18-19
Establishments	56,748	57,568	59,569	62,312	65,577	1.4%	3.5%	4.6%	5.2%
Sales ($Millions)	94,623	98,968	106,065	115,073	125,872	4.6%	7.2%	8.5%	9.4%
Employment	412,792	418,754	433,309	453,264	477,014	1.4%	3.5%	4.6%	5.2%
Sales ($M)/Estab.	1.67	1.72	1.78	1.85	1.92	3.1%	3.6%	3.7%	3.9%
Sales ($)/Emp.	229,226	236,339	244,778	253,877	263,876	3.1%	3.6%	3.7%	3.9%

3-YEAR TREND – ESTIMATED NUMBER OF ESTABLISHMENTS

Year	Employee Size of Establishment									Total Employment
	1-4 Emps.	5-9 Emps.	10-19 Emps.	20-49 Emps.	50-99 Emps.	100-249 Emps.	250-499 Emps.	>500 Emps.	Non-Employer	
2017	23,967	17,443	4,169	1,717	1,173	544	35	6	10,515	59,569
2018	25,071	18,246	4,361	1,796	1,227	569	36	7	10,999	62,312
2019	26,384	19,202	4,590	1,891	1,291	599	38	7	11,575	65,577

3-YEAR TREND – ESTIMATED INDUSTRY SALES ($MILLIONS)

Year	Employee Size of Establishment									Total Employment
	1-4 Emps.	5-9 Emps.	10-19 Emps.	20-49 Emps.	50-99 Emps.	100-249 Emps.	250-499 Emps.	>500 Emps.	Non-Employer	
2017	10,241.9	19,591.7	11,776.6	12,839.0	19,269.4	24,084.3	5,171.4	2,133.8	956.5	106,064.5
2018	11,116.4	21,264.6	12,782.2	13,935.2	20,914.8	26,140.7	5,612.9	2,268.5	1,038.2	115,073.5
2019	12,165.1	23,270.5	13,988.0	15,249.8	22,887.7	28,606.6	6,142.4	2,426.3	1,136.1	125,872.4

3-YEAR TREND – ESTIMATED NUMBER OF EMPLOYEES

Year	Employee Size of Establishment									Total Employment
	1-4 Emps.	5-9 Emps.	10-19 Emps.	20-49 Emps.	50-99 Emps.	100-249 Emps.	250-499 Emps.	>500 Emps.	Non-Employer	
2017	59,917	101,169	56,704	51,691	69,648	68,566	10,077	5,022	10,515	433,309
2018	62,676	105,828	59,316	54,072	72,855	71,724	10,541	5,253	10,999	453,264
2019	65,960	111,373	62,423	56,905	76,672	75,482	11,093	5,528	11,575	477,014

© Barnes Reports: 2018 U.S. Industry & Market Outlook

Appliance/TV/Electronics Stores Industry (NAICS 44311)

Sub-Industries – 2018 Estimated Industry Sales, Establishments & Employment

Sub-Industries	Category*	Establishments	Sales ($Mill)	Employment
Household appliance stores	Major1	7,367	20,853.8	97,232
Gas household appliances	Minor1	314	532.6	1,553
Gas ranges	Minor2	28	17.5	62
Electric household appliances	Minor1	2,048	3,398.9	11,130
Air conditioning room units, self-contained	Minor2	605	814.2	3,762
Electric household appliances, major	Minor2	2,063	4,557.7	12,251
Electric household appliances, small	Minor2	160	536.2	581
Electric ranges	Minor2	40	85.0	239
Fans, electric	Minor2	148	239.0	574
Garbage disposals	Minor2	136	193.8	611
Microwave ovens	Minor2	31	43.9	107
Vacuum cleaners	Minor2	4,336	3,294.7	11,514
Appliance parts	Minor2	549	534.0	2,112
Kitchens, complete (sinks, cabinets, etc.)	Minor2	609	1,209.8	2,773
Sewing machines	Minor2	2,163	1,853.0	6,046
Stoves, household, nec	Minor2	137	138.8	375
Suntanning equipment and supplies	Minor2	22	37.6	112
Kerosene heaters	Minor2	15	17.5	52
Radio, television, and electronic stores	Major1	20,229	70,958.4	181,511
Antennas	Minor1	508	169.3	1,800
Antennas, satellite dish	Minor2	3,985	679.1	22,484
Video cameras, recorders, and accessories	Minor1	574	351.8	4,124
Video cameras and accessories	Minor2	186	91.7	1,175
Video recorders, players, disc players, and accessories	Minor2	973	227.3	7,070
Video tapes, blank	Minor2	62	11.9	304
Automotive sound equipment	Minor2	3,636	625.4	15,738
Consumer electronic equipment, nec	Minor2	2,650	1,488.7	21,764
High fidelity stereo equipment	Minor2	3,475	748.0	19,480
Marine radios and radar equipment	Minor2	213	46.8	773
Phonographs	Minor2	2	0.1	2
Radios, receiver type	Minor2	198	57.6	975
Radios, two-way, citizens band, weather, short-wave, etc.	Minor2	1,983	554.7	10,181
Tape recorders and players	Minor2	27	3.1	87
Misc. household appliance stores	Minor2	2,840	701.7	14,705

*Category-Major categories (Major1) are more general descriptions for companies that self-selected to capture the many functions they perform in the industry. Minor categories (Minor1, Minor2) are more specific for companies that have more detailed functions (Minor1 is a larger category than Minor2). Minor categories figures (sales, etc.) can be aggregated to larger minor categories (Minor2 sums to Minor1) and major categories overall figures.

Home Centers Industry
(NAICS 44411)

NAICS 44411: Home Centers. This industry comprises establishments known as home centers primarily engaged in retailing a general line of new home repair and improvement materials and supplies, such as lumber, plumbing goods, electrical goods, tools, housewares, hardware, and lawn and garden supplies, with no one merchandise line predominating. The merchandise lines are normally arranged in separate departments.

Industry Establishments, Sales & Employment Trends

	Year					Percent Chg. Year-to-Year			
	2015	2016	2017	2018	2019	15-16	16-17	17-18	18-19
Establishments	7,650	7,512	7,527	7,569	7,658	-1.8%	0.2%	0.6%	1.2%
Sales ($Millions)	157,621	158,488	163,454	169,522	177,351	0.5%	3.1%	3.7%	4.6%
Employment	548,367	538,468	539,540	542,592	548,971	-1.8%	0.2%	0.6%	1.2%
Sales ($M)/Estab.	20.60	21.10	21.72	22.40	23.16	2.4%	2.9%	3.1%	3.4%
Sales ($)/Emp.	287,438	294,332	302,950	312,430	323,061	2.4%	2.9%	3.1%	3.4%

3-Year Trend – Estimated Number of Establishments

Year	Employee Size of Establishment									Total Employment
	1-4 Emps.	5-9 Emps.	10-19 Emps.	20-49 Emps.	50-99 Emps.	100-249 Emps.	250-499 Emps.	>500 Emps.	Non-Employer	
2017	776	675	580	448	154	3,779	88	1	1,127	7,527
2018	781	578	583	450	155	3,801	88	1	1,133	7,569
2019	790	585	590	456	157	3,845	89	1	1,146	7,658

3-Year Trend – Estimated Industry Sales ($Millions)

Year	Employee Size of Establishment									Total Employment
	1-4 Emps.	5-9 Emps.	10-19 Emps.	20-49 Emps.	50-99 Emps.	100-249 Emps.	250-499 Emps.	>500 Emps.	Non-Employer	
2017	286.4	557.1	1,413.0	2,889.1	2,191.4	144,496.9	11,284.7	234.9	100.0	163,453.6
2018	297.0	577.8	1,465.4	2,996.4	2,272.8	149,861.7	11,703.7	243.6	103.8	169,522.3
2019	310.7	604.5	1,533.1	3,134.8	2,377.7	156,782.3	12,244.2	254.8	108.6	177,350.8

3-Year Trend – Estimated Number of Employees

Year	Employee Size of Establishment									Total Employment
	1-4 Emps.	5-9 Emps.	10-19 Emps.	20-49 Emps.	50-99 Emps.	100-249 Emps.	250-499 Emps.	>500 Emps.	Non-Employer	
2017	1,941	3,333	7,881	13,475	9,176	476,554	25,473	581	1,127	539,540
2018	1,952	3,352	7,926	13,551	9,228	479,249	25,617	584	1,133	542,592
2019	1,975	3,391	8,019	13,711	9,336	484,883	25,919	591	1,146	548,971

HOME CENTERS INDUSTRY
(NAICS 44411)

SUB-INDUSTRIES – 2018 ESTIMATED INDUSTRY SALES, ESTABLISHMENTS & EMPLOYMENT

Sub-Industries	Category*	Establishments	Sales ($Mill)	Employment
Lumber and other building materials	Major1	2,485	151,581.5	330,961
Lumber products	Minor1	279	1,276.2	8,831
Flooring, wood	Minor2	84	470.7	1,504
Millwork and lumber	Minor2	180	1,425.8	8,251
Paneling	Minor2	7	21.8	171
Planing mill products and lumber	Minor2	274	709.5	5,973
Siding	Minor2	266	351.0	2,775
Wallboard (composition) and paneling	Minor2	5	23.0	152
Door and window products	Minor1	534	1,786.5	10,153
Doors, storm: wood or metal	Minor2	70	297.4	1,926
Doors, wood or metal, except storm	Minor2	59	222.4	1,038
Garage doors, sale and installation	Minor2	409	1,371.6	8,008
Jalousies	Minor2	1	3.7	14
Sash, wood or metal	Minor2	4	19.8	131
Screens, door and window	Minor2	80	145.7	908
Windows, storm: wood or metal	Minor2	77	292.4	1,925
Insulation and energy conservation products	Minor1	22	88.2	461
Energy conservation products	Minor2	70	267.2	1,225
Insulation material, building	Minor2	33	185.9	940
Solar heating equipment	Minor2	71	217.5	1,085
Prefabricated buildings	Minor1	96	334.9	1,579
Greenhouse kits, prefabricated	Minor2	8	24.3	155
Modular homes	Minor2	85	442.4	1,682
Masonry materials and supplies	Minor1	882	2,872.5	18,859
Bathroom fixtures, equipment and supplies	Minor2	88	331.2	1,774
Cabinets, kitchen	Minor2	319	1,179.5	5,847
Closets, interiors and accessories	Minor2	62	169.4	1,049
Counter tops	Minor2	138	1,439.5	2,470
Eavestroughing parts and supplies	Minor2	1	2.1	10
Electrical construction materials	Minor2	58	219.1	1,173
Fencing	Minor2	366	760.8	5,095
Home centers	Minor2	394	760.7	114,868
Roofing material	Minor2	57	217.6	1,549
Structural clay products	Minor2	5	10.4	54

*Category-Major categories (Major1) are more general descriptions for companies that self-selected to capture the many functions they perform in the industry. Minor categories (Minor1, Minor2) are more specific for companies that have more detailed functions (Minor1 is a larger category than Minor2). Minor categories figures (sales, etc.) can be aggregated to larger minor categories (Minor2 sums to Minor1) and major categories overall figures.

HARDWARE STORES INDUSTRY
(NAICS 44413)

NAICS 44413: Hardware Stores. Establishments primarily engaged in the retail sale of a number of basic hardware lines, such as tools, builders' hardware, paint and glass, housewares and household appliances, and cutlery.

INDUSTRY ESTABLISHMENTS, SALES & EMPLOYMENT TRENDS

	Year					Percent Chg. Year-to-Year			
	2015	2016	2017	2018	2019	15-16	16-17	17-18	18-19
Establishments	16,756	16,886	17,361	17,726	18,208	0.8%	2.8%	2.1%	2.7%
Sales ($Millions)	21,660	22,042	23,018	23,933	25,121	1.8%	4.4%	4.0%	5.0%
Employment	148,316	149,462	153,672	156,901	161,169	0.8%	2.8%	2.1%	2.7%
Sales ($M)/Estab.	1.29	1.31	1.33	1.35	1.38	1.0%	1.6%	1.8%	2.2%
Sales ($)/Emp.	146,043	147,478	149,788	152,536	155,869	1.0%	1.6%	1.8%	2.2%

3-YEAR TREND – ESTIMATED NUMBER OF ESTABLISHMENTS

Year	Employee Size of Establishment									Total
	1-4 Emps.	5-9 Emps.	10-19 Emps.	20-49 Emps.	50-99 Emps.	100-249 Emps.	250-499 Emps.	>500 Emps.	Non-Employer	Employ-ment
2017	6,456	4,164	3,332	1,800	163	20	1	0	1,426	17,361
2018	6,592	4,252	3,402	1,838	166	20	1	0	1,456	17,726
2019	6,771	4,367	3,495	1,888	171	21	1	0	1,495	18,208

3-YEAR TREND – ESTIMATED INDUSTRY SALES ($MILLIONS)

Year	Employee Size of Establishment									Total
	1-4 Emps.	5-9 Emps.	10-19 Emps.	20-49 Emps.	50-99 Emps.	100-249 Emps.	250-499 Emps.	>500 Emps.	Non-Employer	Employ-ment
2017	1,854.0	3,143.1	6,324.9	9,042.2	1,796.6	586.0	103.9	5.2	162.2	23,018.2
2018	1,927.7	3,268.1	6,576.3	9,401.6	1,868.0	609.3	108.1	5.4	168.6	23,933.0
2019	2,023.5	3,430.3	6,902.8	9,868.4	1,960.7	639.5	113.4	5.5	177.0	25,121.2

3-YEAR TREND – ESTIMATED NUMBER OF EMPLOYEES

Year	Employee Size of Establishment									Total
	1-4 Emps.	5-9 Emps.	10-19 Emps.	20-49 Emps.	50-99 Emps.	100-249 Emps.	250-499 Emps.	>500 Emps.	Non-Employer	Employ-ment
2017	16,140	24,152	45,317	54,172	9,663	2,482	301	19	1,426	153,672
2018	16,479	24,659	46,269	55,310	9,866	2,535	308	19	1,456	156,901
2019	16,927	25,330	47,528	56,815	10,134	2,604	316	20	1,495	161,169

© Barnes Reports: 2018 U.S. Industry & Market Outlook

Hardware Stores Industry
(NAICS 44413)

Sub-Industries – 2018 Estimated Industry Sales, Establishments & Employment

Sub-Industries	Category*	Establishments	Sales ($Mill)	Employment
Hardware stores	Major1	12,211	20,053.2	127,907
Tools	Minor1	3,235	1,443.2	13,113
Chainsaws	Minor2	323	206.5	1,159
Snowblowers	Minor2	58	71.2	328
Tools, hand	Minor2	313	240.0	1,737
Tools, power	Minor2	274	340.3	2,638
Builders' hardware	Minor2	750	908.7	6,416
Door locks and lock sets	Minor2	188	271.6	1,138
Pumps and pumping equipment	Minor2	373	398.4	2,465

*Category-Major categories (Major1) are more general descriptions for companies that self-selected to capture the many functions they perform in the industry. Minor categories (Minor1, Minor2) are more specific for companies that have more detailed functions (Minor1 is a larger category than Minor2). Minor categories figures (sales, etc.) can be aggregated to larger minor categories (Minor2 sums to Minor1) and major categories overall figures.

Grocery Stores Industry
(NAICS 44511)

NAICS 44511: Grocery Stores Industry. This industry comprises establishments generally known as supermarkets and grocery stores primarily engaged in retailing a general line of food, such as canned and frozen foods; fresh fruits and vegetables; and fresh and prepared meats, fish, and poultry. Included in this industry are delicatessen-type establishments primarily engaged in retailing a general line of food.

Industry Establishments, Sales & Employment Trends

	Year					Percent Chg. Year-to-Year			
	2015	2016	2017	2018	2019	15-16	16-17	17-18	18-19
Establishments	77,978	77,489	78,584	79,990	81,915	-0.6%	1.4%	1.8%	2.4%
Sales ($Millions)	600,522	592,975	601,136	613,523	632,479	-1.3%	1.4%	2.1%	3.1%
Employment	2,385,971	2,371,019	2,404,507	2,447,536	2,506,445	-0.6%	1.4%	1.8%	2.4%
Sales ($M)/Estab.	7.70	7.65	7.65	7.67	7.72	-0.6%	0.0%	0.3%	0.7%
Sales ($)/Emp.	251,689	250,093	250,004	250,670	252,341	-0.6%	0.0%	0.3%	0.7%

3-Year Trend – Estimated Number of Establishments

Year	Employee Size of Establishment									Total Employment
	1-4 Emps.	5-9 Emps.	10-19 Emps.	20-49 Emps.	50-99 Emps.	100-249 Emps.	250-499 Emps.	>500 Emps.	Non-Employer	
2017	25,027	6,874	7,053	8,782	9,468	8,733	809	52	11,785	78,584
2018	25,475	6,997	7,180	8,939	9,637	8,890	824	53	11,996	79,990
2019	26,088	7,165	7,352	9,154	9,869	9,104	844	55	12,284	81,915

3-Year Trend – Estimated Industry Sales ($Millions)

Year	Employee Size of Establishment									Total Employment
	1-4 Emps.	5-9 Emps.	10-19 Emps.	20-49 Emps.	50-99 Emps.	100-249 Emps.	250-499 Emps.	>500 Emps.	Non-Employer	
2017	8,203.6	5,922.3	15,281.7	50,360.2	119,353.7	296,719.4	92,668.0	11,087.6	1,539.7	601,136.2
2018	8,372.8	6,044.4	15,596.8	51,398.5	121,814.4	302,836.7	94,578.5	11,309.3	1,571.5	613,522.8
2019	8,631.6	6,231.3	16,078.9	52,987.3	125,579.9	312,198.0	97,502.1	11,649.6	1,620.0	632,478.8

3-Year Trend – Estimated Number of Employees

Year	Employee Size of Establishment									Total Employment
	1-4 Emps.	5-9 Emps.	10-19 Emps.	20-49 Emps.	50-99 Emps.	100-249 Emps.	250-499 Emps.	>500 Emps.	Non-Employer	
2017	62,567	39,869	95,926	264,329	562,398	1,101,272	235,407	30,953	11,785	2,404,507
2018	63,687	40,583	97,642	269,059	572,463	1,120,980	239,620	31,507	11,996	2,447,536
2019	65,220	41,559	99,993	275,535	586,241	1,147,960	245,387	32,265	12,284	2,506,445

© Barnes Reports: 2018 U.S. Industry & Market Outlook

Grocery Stores Industry (NAICS 44511)

Sub-Industries – 2018 Estimated Industry Sales, Establishments & Employment

Sub-Industries	Category*	Establishments	Sales ($Mill)	Employment
Grocery stores	Major1	48,441	62,750.7	748,132
Supermarkets	Minor1	6,378	145,202.8	220,052
Supermarkets, chain	Minor2	6,877	327,705.8	977,690
Supermarkets, greater than 100,000 square feet (hyperm	Minor2	52	57.9	12,255
Supermarkets, independent	Minor2	1,731	17,009.1	86,079
Supermarkets, 55,000 - 65,000 square feet (superstore)	Minor2	17	8,859.0	2,528
Supermarkets, 66,000 - 99,000 square feet	Minor2	13	25.5	1,684
Cooperative food stores	Minor2	254	1,020.1	7,992
Delicatessen stores	Minor2	4,886	6,646.6	38,853
Frozen food and freezer plans, except meat	Minor2	123	142.7	2,181
Grocery stores, chain	Minor2	1,377	10,886.6	145,459
Grocery stores, independent	Minor2	9,839	33,216.0	204,630

*Category-Major categories (Major1) are more general descriptions for companies that self-selected to capture the many functions they perform in the industry. Minor categories (Minor1, Minor2) are more specific for companies that have more detailed functions (Minor1 is a larger category than Minor2). Minor categories figures (sales, etc.) can be aggregated to larger minor categories (Minor2 sums to Minor1) and major categories overall figures.

Beer & Wine & Liquor Stores Industry
(NAICS 44531)

NAICS 44531: Beer & Wine & Liquor Stores. Establishments primarily engaged in the retail sale of packaged alcoholic beverages, such as ale, beer, wine, and liquor, for consumption off the premises. Stores selling prepared drinks for consumption on the premises are classified in SIC 5813.

Industry Establishments, Sales & Employment Trends

	Year					Percent Chg. Year-to-Year			
	2015	2016	2017	2018	2019	15-16	16-17	17-18	18-19
Establishments	36,738	36,838	37,693	38,713	40,002	0.3%	2.3%	2.7%	3.3%
Sales ($Millions)	42,082	43,167	45,420	48,068	51,317	2.6%	5.2%	5.8%	6.8%
Employment	172,586	173,058	177,072	181,864	187,918	0.3%	2.3%	2.7%	3.3%
Sales ($M)/Estab.	1.15	1.17	1.21	1.24	1.28	2.3%	2.8%	3.0%	3.3%
Sales ($)/Emp.	243,835	249,440	256,507	264,306	273,080	2.3%	2.8%	3.0%	3.3%

3-Year Trend — Estimated Number of Establishments

Year	Employee Size of Establishment									Total Employment
	1-4 Emps.	5-9 Emps.	10-19 Emps.	20-49 Emps.	50-99 Emps.	100-249 Emps.	250-499 Emps.	>500 Emps.	Non-Employer	
2017	22,262	8,536	2,902	803	52	11	0	1	3,125	37,693
2018	22,864	8,767	2,980	825	54	12	0	1	3,210	38,713
2019	23,626	9,059	3,079	853	56	12	0	1	3,317	40,002

3-Year Trend — Estimated Industry Sales ($Millions)

Year	Employee Size of Establishment									Total Employment
	1-4 Emps.	5-9 Emps.	10-19 Emps.	20-49 Emps.	50-99 Emps.	100-249 Emps.	250-499 Emps.	>500 Emps.	Non-Employer	
2017	12,177.9	12,273.2	10,490.8	7,688.2	1,100.8	639.9	2.0	363.0	684.4	45,420.2
2018	12,887.8	12,988.7	11,102.3	8,136.4	1,165.0	677.2	2.1	384.0	724.3	48,067.7
2019	13,759.0	13,866.7	11,852.8	8,686.4	1,243.7	723.0	2.2	409.7	773.3	51,316.7

3-Year Trend — Estimated Number of Employees

Year	Employee Size of Establishment									Total Employment
	1-4 Emps.	5-9 Emps.	10-19 Emps.	20-49 Emps.	50-99 Emps.	100-249 Emps.	250-499 Emps.	>500 Emps.	Non-Employer	
2017	55,655	49,510	39,460	24,181	3,108	1,423	3	606	3,125	177,072
2018	57,161	50,850	40,528	24,835	3,192	1,462	3	622	3,210	181,864
2019	59,064	52,543	41,878	25,662	3,299	1,510	3	643	3,317	187,918

© Barnes Reports: 2018 U.S. Industry & Market Outlook

Beer & Wine & Liquor Stores Industry (NAICS 44531)

Sub-Industries – 2018 Estimated Industry Sales, Establishments & Employment

Sub-Industries	Category*	Establishments	Sales ($Mill)	Employment
Liquor stores	Major1	23,128	27,634.7	107,132
Wine and beer	Minor1	673	746.0	3,294
Beer (packaged)	Minor2	4,565	7,187.3	23,564
Wine	Minor2	4,399	5,242.6	20,921
Hard liquor	Minor2	5,948	7,257.1	26,953

*Category-Major categories (Major1) are more general descriptions for companies that self-selected to capture the many functions they perform in the industry. Minor categories (Minor1, Minor2) are more specific for companies that have more detailed functions (Minor1 is a larger category than Minor2). Minor categories figures (sales, etc.) can be aggregated to larger minor categories (Minor2 sums to Minor1) and major categories overall figures.

PHARMACIES & DRUG STORES INDUSTRY
(NAICS 44611)

NAICS 44611 Pharmacies and Drug Stores – This industry comprises establishments known as pharmacies and drug stores engaged in retailing prescription or nonprescription drugs and medicines.

INDUSTRY ESTABLISHMENTS, SALES & EMPLOYMENT TRENDS

	Year					Percent Chg. Year-to-Year			
	2015	2016	2017	2018	2019	15-16	16-17	17-18	18-19
Establishments	47,452	47,423	48,364	49,362	50,685	-0.1%	2.0%	2.1%	2.7%
Sales ($Millions)	205,576	211,889	223,917	237,159	253,251	3.1%	5.7%	5.9%	6.8%
Employment	727,028	726,587	741,008	756,284	776,556	-0.1%	2.0%	2.1%	2.7%
Sales ($M)/Estab.	4.33	4.47	4.63	4.80	5.00	3.1%	3.6%	3.8%	4.0%
Sales ($)/Emp.	282,762	291,623	302,179	313,585	326,121	3.1%	3.6%	3.8%	4.0%

3-YEAR TREND – ESTIMATED NUMBER OF ESTABLISHMENTS

Year	Employee Size of Establishment									Total Employment
	1-4 Emps.	5-9 Emps.	10-19 Emps.	20-49 Emps.	50-99 Emps.	100-249 Emps.	250-499 Emps.	>500 Emps.	Non-Employer	
2017	8,598	8,102	13,036	14,465	666	99	11	2	3,386	48,364
2018	8,775	8,269	13,305	14,763	679	101	11	2	3,456	49,362
2019	9,011	8,491	13,661	15,159	697	104	12	2	3,548	50,685

3-YEAR TREND – ESTIMATED INDUSTRY SALES ($MILLIONS)

Year	Employee Size of Establishment									Total Employment
	1-4 Emps.	5-9 Emps.	10-19 Emps.	20-49 Emps.	50-99 Emps.	100-249 Emps.	250-499 Emps.	>500 Emps.	Non-Employer	
2017	4,686.2	11,606.0	46,960.4	137,923.9	13,950.1	5,585.0	2,134.7	712.4	358.7	223,917.4
2018	4,963.3	12,292.3	49,737.5	146,080.3	14,775.1	5,915.3	2,260.9	754.4	379.9	237,159.0
2019	5,300.1	13,126.4	53,112.4	155,992.4	15,777.6	6,316.7	2,414.3	805.4	405.7	253,251.0

3-YEAR TREND – ESTIMATED NUMBER OF EMPLOYEES

Year	Employee Size of Establishment									Total Employment
	1-4 Emps.	5-9 Emps.	10-19 Emps.	20-49 Emps.	50-99 Emps.	100-249 Emps.	250-499 Emps.	>500 Emps.	Non-Employer	
2017	21,496	46,991	177,289	435,394	39,534	12,467	3,261	1,191	3,386	741,008
2018	21,939	47,959	180,944	444,369	40,349	12,724	3,329	1,215	3,456	756,284
2019	22,527	49,245	185,794	456,281	41,431	13,065	3,418	1,248	3,548	776,556

© Barnes Reports: 2018 U.S. Industry & Market Outlook

Pharmacies & Drug Stores Industry (NAICS 44611)

Sub-Industries — 2018 Estimated Industry Sales, Establishments & Employment

Sub-Industries	Category*	Establishments	Sales ($Mill)	Employment
Drug stores and proprietary stores	Major1	22,383	142,869.1	314,249
Drug stores	Minor2	26,055	93,803.2	432,005
Proprietary (non-prescription medicine) stores	Minor2	923	486.7	10,029

*Category-Major categories (Major1) are more general descriptions for companies that self-selected to capture the many functions they perform in the industry. Minor categories (Minor1, Minor2) are more specific for companies that have more detailed functions (Minor1 is a larger category than Minor2). Minor categories figures (sales, etc.) can be aggregated to larger minor categories (Minor2 sums to Minor1) and major categories overall figures.

Gas Stations with Convenience Stores (NAICS 44711)

NAICS 44711: Gas Stations with Convenience Stores. This industry comprises establishments primarily engaged in selling gasoline and lubricating oils. These establishments frequently sell other merchandise, such as tires, batteries, and other automobile parts, or perform minor repair work. Gasoline stations combined with other activities, such as grocery stores, convenience stores, or carwashes, are classified according to the primary activity.

Industry Establishments, Sales & Employment Trends

	Year					Percent Chg. Year-to-Year			
	2015	2016	2017	2018	2019	15-16	16-17	17-18	18-19
Establishments	98,963	98,562	100,175	101,990	104,468	-0.4%	1.6%	1.8%	2.4%
Sales ($Millions)	404,176	419,389	445,836	475,102	510,054	3.8%	6.3%	6.6%	7.4%
Employment	790,505	787,297	800,182	814,681	834,473	-0.4%	1.6%	1.8%	2.4%
Sales ($M)/Estab.	4.08	4.26	4.45	4.66	4.88	4.2%	4.6%	4.7%	4.8%
Sales ($)/Emp.	511,288	532,695	557,168	583,176	611,229	4.2%	4.6%	4.7%	4.8%

3-Year Trend – Estimated Number of Establishments

Year	Employee Size of Establishment									Total Employment
	1-4 Emps.	5-9 Emps.	10-19 Emps.	20-49 Emps.	50-99 Emps.	100-249 Emps.	250-499 Emps.	>500 Emps.	Non-Employer	
2017	34,848	34,253	22,800	5,944	254	52	6	0	2,018	100,175
2018	35,480	34,874	23,213	6,052	259	53	6	0	2,054	101,990
2019	36,342	35,721	23,777	6,199	265	54	6	0	2,104	104,468

3-Year Trend – Estimated Industry Sales ($Millions)

Year	Employee Size of Establishment									Total Employment
	1-4 Emps.	5-9 Emps.	10-19 Emps.	20-49 Emps.	50-99 Emps.	100-249 Emps.	250-499 Emps.	>500 Emps.	Non-Employer	
2017	39,114.8	101,051.5	169,146.7	116,718.2	10,967.2	6,005.9	2,381.5	20.3	430.1	445,836.1
2018	41,682.5	107,684.9	180,250.1	124,380.0	11,687.1	6,400.2	2,537.8	21.4	458.3	475,102.3
2019	44,748.9	115,606.9	193,510.5	133,530.2	12,546.9	6,871.0	2,724.5	22.6	492.0	510,053.6

3-Year Trend – Estimated Number of Employees

Year	Employee Size of Establishment									Total Employment
	1-4 Emps.	5-9 Emps.	10-19 Emps.	20-49 Emps.	50-99 Emps.	100-249 Emps.	250-499 Emps.	>500 Emps.	Non-Employer	
2017	87,121	198,669	310,076	178,911	15,092	6,510	1,767	18	2,018	800,182
2018	88,700	202,269	315,695	182,153	15,365	6,628	1,799	19	2,054	814,681
2019	90,855	207,183	323,364	186,578	15,739	6,789	1,842	19	2,104	834,473

© Barnes Reports: 2018 U.S. Industry & Market Outlook

Gas Stations with Convenience Stores (NAICS 44711)

Sub-Industries — 2018 Estimated Industry Sales, Establishments & Employment

Sub-Industries	Category*	Establishments	Sales ($Mill)	Employment
Gasoline service stations	Major1	46,624	136,282.6	311,513
Gasoline service stations, nec	Minor2	231	288.7	1,954
Filling stations, gasoline	Minor2	52,494	293,151.0	438,587
Marine service station	Minor2	524	849.5	3,596
Truck stops	Minor2	2,117	44,530.5	59,031

*Category-Major categories (Major1) are more general descriptions for companies that self-selected to capture the many functions they perform in the industry. Minor categories (Minor1, Minor2) are more specific for companies that have more detailed functions (Minor1 is a larger category than Minor2). Minor categories figures (sales, etc.) can be aggregated to larger minor categories (Minor2 sums to Minor1) and major categories overall figures.

Men's Clothing Stores Industry
(NAICS 44811)

NAICS 44811: Men's Clothing Stores. This industry comprises establishments primarily engaged in retailing a general line of new men's and boys' clothing. These establishments may provide basic alterations, such as hemming, taking in or letting out seams, or lengthening or shortening sleeves.

Industry Establishments, Sales & Employment Trends

	Year					Percent Chg. Year-to-Year			
	2015	2016	2017	2018	2019	15-16	16-17	17-18	18-19
Establishments	8,663	8,317	8,140	8,052	8,013	-4.0%	-2.1%	-1.1%	-0.5%
Sales ($Millions)	7,540	7,507	7,652	7,891	8,202	-0.4%	1.9%	3.1%	3.9%
Employment	54,451	52,278	51,164	50,609	50,364	-4.0%	-2.1%	-1.1%	-0.5%
Sales ($M)/Estab.	0.87	0.90	0.94	0.98	1.02	3.7%	4.1%	4.3%	4.4%
Sales ($)/Emp.	138,472	143,597	149,552	155,921	162,844	3.7%	4.1%	4.3%	4.4%

3-Year Trend – Estimated Number of Establishments

Year	Employee Size of Establishment									Total
	1-4 Emps.	5-9 Emps.	10-19 Emps.	20-49 Emps.	50-99 Emps.	100-249 Emps.	250-499 Emps.	>500 Emps.	Non-Employer	Employ-ment
2017	2,890	1,932	1,430	285	28	9	1	0	1,564	8,140
2018	2,859	1,911	1,415	282	28	9	1	0	1,548	8,052
2019	2,845	1,902	1,408	280	28	9	1	0	1,540	8,013

3-Year Trend – Estimated Industry Sales ($Millions)

Year	Employee Size of Establishment									Total
	1-4 Emps.	5-9 Emps.	10-19 Emps.	20-49 Emps.	50-99 Emps.	100-249 Emps.	250-499 Emps.	>500 Emps.	Non-Employer	Employ-ment
2017	874.0	1,535.4	2,858.4	1,506.2	327.8	294.5	99.3	5.3	150.7	7,651.6
2018	901.4	1,583.5	2,947.8	1,553.3	338.1	303.7	102.4	5.5	155.4	7,891.0
2019	936.8	1,645.8	3,063.8	1,614.4	351.4	315.7	106.4	5.8	161.5	8,201.6

3-Year Trend – Estimated Number of Employees

Year	Employee Size of Establishment									Total
	1-4 Emps.	5-9 Emps.	10-19 Emps.	20-49 Emps.	50-99 Emps.	100-249 Emps.	250-499 Emps.	>500 Emps.	Non-Employer	Employ-ment
2017	7,226	11,205	19,449	8,570	1,674	1,185	273	17	1,564	51,164
2018	7,147	11,083	19,239	8,477	1,656	1,172	270	17	1,548	50,609
2019	7,113	11,030	19,146	8,436	1,648	1,166	269	17	1,540	50,364

© Barnes Reports: 2018 U.S. Industry & Market Outlook

Men's Clothing Stores Industry (NAICS 44811)

Sub-Industries – 2018 Estimated Industry Sales, Establishments & Employment

Sub-Industries	Category*	Establishments	Sales ($Mill)	Employment
Men's and boys' clothing stores	Major1	5,538	5,478.9	37,978
Clothing accessories: men's and boys'	Minor2	536	305.4	1,854
Clothing, male: everyday, except suits and sportswear	Minor2	296	101.1	2,494
Clothing, sportswear, men's and boys'	Minor2	895	233.4	4,778
Haberdashery stores	Minor2	30	11.4	76
Hats, men's and boys'	Minor2	142	31.2	266
Suits, men's	Minor2	547	1,716.1	2,916
Tie shops	Minor2	68	13.5	247

*Category-Major categories (Major1) are more general descriptions for companies that self-selected to capture the many functions they perform in the industry. Minor categories (Minor1, Minor2) are more specific for companies that have more detailed functions (Minor1 is a larger category than Minor2). Minor categories figures (sales, etc.) can be aggregated to larger minor categories (Minor2 sums to Minor1) and major categories overall figures.

Women's Clothing Stores Industry (NAICS 44812)

NAICS 44812: Women's Clothing Stores. This industry comprises establishments primarily engaged in retailing a general line of new women's, misses' and juniors' clothing, including maternity wear. These establishments may provide basic alterations, such as hemming, taking in or letting out seams, or lengthening or shortening sleeves.

Industry Establishments, Sales & Employment Trends

	Year					Percent Chg. Year-to-Year			
	2015	2016	2017	2018	2019	15-16	16-17	17-18	18-19
Establishments	43,668	44,106	45,449	46,277	47,405	1.0%	3.0%	1.8%	2.4%
Sales ($Millions)	42,643	44,340	47,253	49,845	53,016	4.0%	6.6%	5.5%	6.4%
Employment	347,561	351,050	361,737	368,323	377,303	1.0%	3.0%	1.8%	2.4%
Sales ($M)/Estab.	0.98	1.01	1.04	1.08	1.12	2.9%	3.4%	3.6%	3.8%
Sales ($)/Emp.	122,693	126,308	130,627	135,331	140,513	2.9%	3.4%	3.6%	3.8%

3-Year Trend – Estimated Number of Establishments

Year	Employee Size of Establishment									Total Employment
	1-4 Emps.	5-9 Emps.	10-19 Emps.	20-49 Emps.	50-99 Emps.	100-249 Emps.	250-499 Emps.	>500 Emps.	Non-Employer	
2017	13,085	11,118	9,433	2,514	404	138	17	7	8,734	45,449
2018	13,323	11,320	9,604	2,559	411	141	17	7	8,893	46,277
2019	13,648	11,596	9,839	2,622	421	144	17	8	9,110	47,405

3-Year Trend – Estimated Industry Sales ($Millions)

Year	Employee Size of Establishment									Total Employment
	1-4 Emps.	5-9 Emps.	10-19 Emps.	20-49 Emps.	50-99 Emps.	100-249 Emps.	250-499 Emps.	>500 Emps.	Non-Employer	
2017	3,205.7	7,159.0	15,274.4	10,773.2	3,804.8	3,515.1	1,425.3	1,379.8	715.3	47,252.5
2018	3,382.3	7,553.5	16,116.0	11,366.8	4,014.4	3,708.8	1,503.8	1,445.1	754.7	49,845.3
2019	3,598.5	8,036.2	17,146.0	12,093.2	4,271.0	3,945.8	1,599.9	1,522.5	803.0	53,016.1

3-Year Trend – Estimated Number of Employees

Year	Employee Size of Establishment									Total Employment
	1-4 Emps.	5-9 Emps.	10-19 Emps.	20-49 Emps.	50-99 Emps.	100-249 Emps.	250-499 Emps.	>500 Emps.	Non-Employer	
2017	32,712	64,483	128,284	75,656	23,987	17,455	4,844	5,581	8,734	361,737
2018	33,308	65,657	130,620	77,034	24,424	17,773	4,932	5,682	8,893	368,323
2019	34,120	67,257	133,804	78,912	25,019	18,206	5,053	5,821	9,110	377,303

© Barnes Reports: 2018 U.S. Industry & Market Outlook

WOMEN'S CLOTHING STORES INDUSTRY
(NAICS 44812)

SUB-INDUSTRIES — 2018 ESTIMATED INDUSTRY SALES, ESTABLISHMENTS & EMPLOYMENT

Sub-Industries	Category*	Establishments	Sales ($Mill)	Employment
Women's clothing stores	Major1	19,866	15,441.3	168,633
Women's specialty clothing stores	Minor1	767	267.6	6,484
Boutiques	Minor2	7,058	1,985.4	24,586
Bridal shops	Minor2	3,382	1,444.6	20,763
Dress shops	Minor2	443	193.4	3,280
Women's sportswear	Minor2	264	168.2	2,228
Maternity wear	Minor2	555	112.4	2,917
Ready-to-wear apparel, women's	Minor2	13,857	30,190.7	138,301
Teenage apparel	Minor2	84	41.9	1,132

*Category-Major categories (Major1) are more general descriptions for companies that self-selected to capture the many functions they perform in the industry. Minor categories (Minor1, Minor2) are more specific for companies that have more detailed functions (Minor1 is a larger category than Minor2). Minor categories figures (sales, etc.) can be aggregated to larger minor categories (Minor2 sums to Minor1) and major categories overall figures.

Family Clothing Stores Industry (NAICS 44814)

NAICS 44814: Family Clothing Stores. This industry comprises establishments primarily engaged in retailing a general line of new clothing for men, women, and children, without specializing in sales for an individual gender or age group. These establishments may provide basic alterations, such as hemming, taking in or letting out seams, or lengthening or shortening sleeves.

Industry Establishments, Sales & Employment Trends

	Year					Percent Chg. Year-to-Year			
	2015	2016	2017	2018	2019	15-16	16-17	17-18	18-19
Establishments	34,841	34,277	34,411	35,085	35,988	-1.6%	0.4%	2.0%	2.6%
Sales ($Millions)	102,410	103,467	107,189	112,961	120,056	1.0%	3.6%	5.4%	6.3%
Employment	676,729	665,769	668,382	681,459	699,005	-1.6%	0.4%	2.0%	2.6%
Sales ($M)/Estab.	2.94	3.02	3.11	3.22	3.34	2.7%	3.2%	3.4%	3.6%
Sales ($)/Emp.	151,332	155,410	160,370	165,764	171,753	2.7%	3.2%	3.4%	3.6%

3-Year Trend – Estimated Number of Establishments

Year	Employee Size of Establishment									Total Employment
	1-4 Emps.	5-9 Emps.	10-19 Emps.	20-49 Emps.	50-99 Emps.	100-249 Emps.	250-499 Emps.	>500 Emps.	Non-Employer	
2017	5,566	4,377	6,575	8,256	3,318	339	95	28	5,858	34,411
2018	5,675	4,463	6,704	8,417	3,382	345	97	28	5,972	35,085
2019	5,822	4,578	6,876	8,634	3,470	354	99	29	6,126	35,988

3-Year Trend – Estimated Industry Sales ($Millions)

Year	Employee Size of Establishment									Total Employment
	1-4 Emps.	5-9 Emps.	10-19 Emps.	20-49 Emps.	50-99 Emps.	100-249 Emps.	250-499 Emps.	>500 Emps.	Non-Employer	
2017	1,415.6	2,925.9	11,051.6	36,731.2	32,445.9	8,929.6	8,423.6	4,877.4	387.9	107,188.5
2018	1,492.1	3,083.9	11,648.6	38,715.5	34,198.6	9,412.0	8,878.6	5,122.9	408.8	112,961.0
2019	1,586.1	3,278.3	12,382.8	41,155.5	36,354.0	10,005.2	9,438.2	5,421.3	434.6	120,056.0

3-Year Trend – Estimated Number of Employees

Year	Employee Size of Establishment									Total Employment
	1-4 Emps.	5-9 Emps.	10-19 Emps.	20-49 Emps.	50-99 Emps.	100-249 Emps.	250-499 Emps.	>500 Emps.	Non-Employer	
2017	13,916	25,389	89,418	248,502	197,064	42,719	27,582	17,934	5,858	668,382
2018	14,188	25,885	91,168	253,364	200,919	43,555	28,122	18,285	5,972	681,459
2019	14,554	26,552	93,515	259,888	206,092	44,676	28,846	18,756	6,126	699,005

© Barnes Reports: 2018 U.S. Industry & Market Outlook

Family Clothing Stores Industry (NAICS 44814)

Sub-Industries — 2018 Estimated Industry Sales, Establishments & Employment

Sub-Industries	Category*	Establishments	Sales ($Mill)	Employment
Family clothing stores	Major1	28,941	111,793.3	617,544
Jeans stores	Minor2	541	325.1	10,732
Unisex clothing stores	Minor2	5,602	842.6	53,183

*Category-Major categories (Major1) are more general descriptions for companies that self-selected to capture the many functions they perform in the industry. Minor categories (Minor1, Minor2) are more specific for companies that have more detailed functions (Minor1 is a larger category than Minor2). Minor categories figures (sales, etc.) can be aggregated to larger minor categories (Minor2 sums to Minor1) and major categories overall figures.

BOOK STORES RETAILING INDUSTRY
(NAICS 451211)

NAICS 451211: Book Stores. This industry comprises establishments primarily engaged in the retail sale of new books and magazines. Establishments primarily engaged in the retail sale of used books are classified in 5932.

Industry Establishments, Sales & Employment Trends

	Year					Percent Chg. Year-to-Year			
	2015	2016	2017	2018	2019	15-16	16-17	17-18	18-19
Establishments	10,755	10,279	9,990	9,882	9,833	-4.4%	-2.8%	-1.1%	-0.5%
Sales ($Millions)	11,365	11,366	11,599	12,046	12,597	0.0%	2.0%	3.9%	4.6%
Employment	94,900	90,696	88,153	87,195	86,767	-4.4%	-2.8%	-1.1%	-0.5%
Sales ($M)/Estab.	1.06	1.11	1.16	1.22	1.28	4.7%	5.0%	5.0%	5.1%
Sales ($)/Emp.	119,754	125,323	131,578	138,147	145,178	4.7%	5.0%	5.0%	5.1%

3-Year Trend – Estimated Number of Establishments

Year	Employee Size of Establishment									Total Employ-ment
	1-4 Emps.	5-9 Emps.	10-19 Emps.	20-49 Emps.	50-99 Emps.	100-249 Emps.	250-499 Emps.	>500 Emps.	Non-Employer	
2017	2,453	1,416	1,120	1,126	223	38	3	3	3,609	9,990
2018	2,427	1,400	1,108	1,114	221	38	3	3	3,570	9,882
2019	2,415	1,393	1,103	1,108	219	37	3	3	3,552	9,833

3-Year Trend – Estimated Industry Sales ($Millions)

Year	Employee Size of Establishment									Total Employ-ment
	1-4 Emps.	5-9 Emps.	10-19 Emps.	20-49 Emps.	50-99 Emps.	100-249 Emps.	250-499 Emps.	>500 Emps.	Non-Employer	
2017	565.1	857.1	1,705.7	4,537.2	1,975.0	909.3	224.3	539.7	285.7	11,599.0
2018	586.7	889.9	1,770.9	4,710.7	2,050.5	944.1	232.8	563.4	296.6	12,045.7
2019	613.5	930.5	1,851.7	4,925.6	2,144.0	987.2	243.5	590.6	310.1	12,596.6

3-Year Trend – Estimated Number of Employees

Year	Employee Size of Establishment									Total Employ-ment
	1-4 Emps.	5-9 Emps.	10-19 Emps.	20-49 Emps.	50-99 Emps.	100-249 Emps.	250-499 Emps.	>500 Emps.	Non-Employer	
2017	6,133	8,211	15,236	33,888	13,242	4,803	811	2,222	3,609	88,153
2018	6,066	8,122	15,070	33,519	13,098	4,750	802	2,198	3,570	87,195
2019	6,037	8,082	14,996	33,354	13,034	4,727	798	2,187	3,552	86,767

© Barnes Reports: 2018 U.S. Industry & Market Outlook

Book Stores Retailing Industry
(NAICS 451211)

Sub-Industries – 2018 Estimated Industry Sales, Establishments & Employment

Sub-Industries	Category*	Establishments	Sales ($Mill)	Employment
Book stores	Major1	7,478	10,007.3	68,473
Books, foreign	Minor2	41	11.8	167
Books, religious	Minor2	943	838.4	6,846
Children's books	Minor2	147	41.0	463
College book stores	Minor2	606	1,019.1	9,687
Comic books	Minor2	666	128.0	1,558

*Category-Major categories (Major1) are more general descriptions for companies that self-selected to capture the many functions they perform in the industry. Minor categories (Minor1, Minor2) are more specific for companies that have more detailed functions (Minor1 is a larger category than Minor2). Minor categories figures (sales, etc.) can be aggregated to larger minor categories (Minor2 sums to Minor1) and major categories overall figures.

Department Stores Industry
(NAICS 45211)

NAICS 45211: Department Stores Industry. This industry comprises establishments known as department stores primarily engaged in retailing a wide range of the following new products with no one merchandise line predominating: apparel, furniture, appliances and home furnishings; and selected additional items, such as paint, hardware, toiletries, cosmetics, photographic equipment, jewelry, toys, and sporting goods. Merchandise lines are normally arranged in separate departments.

Industry Establishments, Sales & Employment Trends

	Year					Percent Chg. Year-to-Year			
	2015	2016	2017	2018	2019	15-16	16-17	17-18	18-19
Establishments	10,150	9,678	9,402	9,285	9,225	-4.6%	-2.9%	-1.2%	-0.6%
Sales ($Millions)	134,248	128,549	126,142	126,169	127,424	-4.2%	-1.9%	0.0%	1.0%
Employment	835,587	796,742	774,026	764,388	759,449	-4.6%	-2.9%	-1.2%	-0.6%
Sales ($M)/Estab.	13.23	13.28	13.42	13.59	13.81	0.4%	1.0%	1.3%	1.7%
Sales ($)/Emp.	160,663	161,343	162,969	165,059	167,785	0.4%	1.0%	1.3%	1.7%

3-Year Trend – Estimated Number of Establishments

Year	Employee Size of Establishment									Total Employment
	1-4 Emps.	5-9 Emps.	10-19 Emps.	20-49 Emps.	50-99 Emps.	100-249 Emps.	250-499 Emps.	>500 Emps.	Non-Employer	
2017	27	13	11	356	2,937	3,500	430	31	2,098	9,402
2018	27	13	11	351	2,901	3,456	424	30	2,072	9,285
2019	26	13	11	349	2,882	3,434	422	30	2,059	9,225

3-Year Trend – Estimated Industry Sales ($Millions)

Year	Employee Size of Establishment									Total Employment
	1-4 Emps.	5-9 Emps.	10-19 Emps.	20-49 Emps.	50-99 Emps.	100-249 Emps.	250-499 Emps.	>500 Emps.	Non-Employer	
2017	5.2	6.6	14.2	1,198.7	21,759.7	69,872.5	28,923.4	4,184.1	177.7	126,142.0
2018	5.2	6.6	14.2	1,198.9	21,762.4	69,881.1	28,927.0	4,195.9	177.8	126,168.9
2019	5.2	6.6	14.3	1,210.7	21,977.8	70,573.0	29,213.3	4,243.4	179.5	127,423.9

3-Year Trend – Estimated Number of Employees

Year	Employee Size of Establishment									Total Employment
	1-4 Emps.	5-9 Emps.	10-19 Emps.	20-49 Emps.	50-99 Emps.	100-249 Emps.	250-499 Emps.	>500 Emps.	Non-Employer	
2017	67	75	151	10,707	174,480	441,307	125,033	20,107	2,098	774,026
2018	66	74	149	10,574	172,308	435,812	123,476	19,856	2,072	764,388
2019	66	74	148	10,505	171,194	432,996	122,678	19,728	2,059	759,449

Department Stores Industry (NAICS 45211)

Sub-Industries — 2018 Estimated Industry Sales, Establishments & Employment

Sub-Industries	Category*	Establishments	Sales ($Mill)	Employment
Department stores	Major1	2,771	12,690.1	121,281
Department stores, discount	Minor2	5,119	100,055.0	520,319
Department stores, non-discount	Minor2	1,395	13,423.8	122,788

*Category-Major categories (Major1) are more general descriptions for companies that self-selected to capture the many functions they perform in the industry. Minor categories (Minor1, Minor2) are more specific for companies that have more detailed functions (Minor1 is a larger category than Minor2). Minor categories figures (sales, etc.) can be aggregated to larger minor categories (Minor2 sums to Minor1) and major categories overall figures.

WAREHOUSE CLUBS & SUPERSTORES INDUSTRY
(NAICS 45291)

NAICS 45291: Warehouse Clubs and Superstores This industry comprises establishments known as warehouse clubs, superstores or supercenters primarily engaged in retailing a general line of groceries in combination with general lines of new merchandise, such as apparel, furniture, and appliances.

INDUSTRY ESTABLISHMENTS, SALES & EMPLOYMENT TRENDS

	Year					Percent Chg. Year-to-Year			
	2015	2016	2017	2018	2019	15-16	16-17	17-18	18-19
Establishments	7,189	7,526	7,896	8,215	8,391	4.7%	4.9%	4.0%	2.1%
Sales ($Millions)	442,774	476,310	516,020	555,354	588,253	7.6%	8.3%	7.6%	5.9%
Employment	1,182,962	1,238,432	1,299,244	1,351,710	1,380,762	4.7%	4.9%	4.0%	2.1%
Sales ($M)/Estab.	61.59	63.28	65.35	67.60	70.10	2.8%	3.3%	3.4%	3.7%
Sales ($)/Emp.	374,292	384,608	397,169	410,853	426,035	2.8%	3.3%	3.4%	3.7%

3-YEAR TREND – ESTIMATED NUMBER OF ESTABLISHMENTS

Year	Employee Size of Establishment									Total Employment
	1-4 Emps.	5-9 Emps.	10-19 Emps.	20-49 Emps.	50-99 Emps.	100-249 Emps.	250-499 Emps.	>500 Emps.	Non-Employer	
2017	76	8	10	136	118	2,490	3,252	45	1,762	7,896
2018	79	8	10	142	122	2,590	3,383	47	1,833	8,215
2019	81	8	11	145	125	2,646	3,456	48	1,873	8,391

3-YEAR TREND – ESTIMATED INDUSTRY SALES ($MILLIONS)

Year	Employee Size of Establishment									Total Employment
	1-4 Emps.	5-9 Emps.	10-19 Emps.	20-49 Emps.	50-99 Emps.	100-249 Emps.	250-499 Emps.	>500 Emps.	Non-Employer	
2017	27.3	7.3	23.6	859.6	1,630.5	93,107.0	409,879.4	10,328.6	156.2	516,019.6
2018	29.4	7.8	25.4	925.1	1,754.8	100,204.3	441,123.5	11,115.8	168.1	555,354.3
2019	31.2	8.3	26.9	979.9	1,858.8	106,140.3	467,255.0	11,774.2	178.1	588,252.5

3-YEAR TREND – ESTIMATED NUMBER OF EMPLOYEES

Year	Employee Size of Establishment									Total Employment
	1-4 Emps.	5-9 Emps.	10-19 Emps.	20-49 Emps.	50-99 Emps.	100-249 Emps.	250-499 Emps.	>500 Emps.	Non-Employer	
2017	189	45	134	4,099	6,981	313,969	946,024	26,041	1,762	1,299,244
2018	197	46	140	4,265	7,262	326,647	984,226	27,093	1,833	1,351,710
2019	201	47	143	4,356	7,419	333,668	1,005,380	27,675	1,873	1,380,762

© Barnes Reports: 2018 U.S. Industry & Market Outlook

WAREHOUSE CLUBS & SUPERSTORES INDUSTRY
(NAICS 45291)

SUB-INDUSTRIES – 2018 ESTIMATED INDUSTRY SALES, ESTABLISHMENTS & EMPLOYMENT

Sub-Industries	Category*	Establishments	Sales ($Mill)	Employment
Department stores	Major1	1,635	37,238.5	142,979
Department stores, discount	Minor2	3,019	293,606.3	613,406
Department stores, non-discount	Minor2	823	39,391.3	144,755
Warehouse club stores	Minor2	2,738	185,118.1	450,570

*Category-Major categories (Major1) are more general descriptions for companies that self-selected to capture the many functions they perform in the industry. Minor categories (Minor1, Minor2) are more specific for companies that have more detailed functions (Minor1 is a larger category than Minor2). Minor categories figures (sales, etc.) can be aggregated to larger minor categories (Minor2 sums to Minor1) and major categories overall figures.

OFFICE SUPPLIES & STATIONERY STORES INDUSTRY
(NAICS 45321)

NAICS 45321: Office Supplies and Stationery Stores. This industry comprises establishments primarily engaged in one or more of the following: (1) retailing new stationery, school supplies, and office supplies; (2) selling a combination of new office equipment, furniture, and supplies; and (3) selling new office equipment, furniture, and supplies in combination with selling new computers.

Industry Establishments, Sales & Employment Trends

	Year					Percent Chg. Year-to-Year			
	2015	2016	2017	2018	2019	15-16	16-17	17-18	18-19
Establishments	8,341	7,925	7,669	7,415	7,213	-5.0%	-3.2%	-3.3%	-2.7%
Sales ($Millions)	15,039	14,171	13,682	13,238	12,939	-5.8%	-3.5%	-3.2%	-2.3%
Employment	88,072	83,678	80,977	78,293	76,157	-5.0%	-3.2%	-3.3%	-2.7%
Sales ($M)/Estab.	1.80	1.79	1.78	1.79	1.79	-0.8%	-0.2%	0.1%	0.5%
Sales ($)/Emp.	170,763	169,351	168,963	169,087	169,893	-0.8%	-0.2%	0.1%	0.5%

3-Year Trend – Estimated Number of Establishments

Year	Employee Size of Establishment									Total Employ-ment
	1-4 Emps.	5-9 Emps.	10-19 Emps.	20-49 Emps.	50-99 Emps.	100-249 Emps.	250-499 Emps.	>500 Emps.	Non-Employer	
2017	2,105	643	1,638	1,549	15	4	0	0	1,716	7,669
2018	2,035	621	1,584	1,498	14	4	0	0	1,659	7,415
2019	1,979	604	1,541	1,457	14	3	0	0	1,614	7,213

3-Year Trend – Estimated Industry Sales ($Millions)

Year	Employee Size of Establishment									Total Employ-ment
	1-4 Emps.	5-9 Emps.	10-19 Emps.	20-49 Emps.	50-99 Emps.	100-249 Emps.	250-499 Emps.	>500 Emps.	Non-Employer	
2017	666.4	534.8	3,428.8	8,581.6	179.1	120.7	1.0	5.5	164.1	13,682.1
2018	644.7	517.5	3,317.6	8,303.2	173.3	116.8	1.0	5.5	158.8	13,238.3
2019	630.1	505.8	3,242.4	8,115.1	169.4	114.1	1.0	5.5	155.2	12,938.5

3-Year Trend – Estimated Number of Employees

Year	Employee Size of Establishment									Total Employ-ment
	1-4 Emps.	5-9 Emps.	10-19 Emps.	20-49 Emps.	50-99 Emps.	100-249 Emps.	250-499 Emps.	>500 Emps.	Non-Employer	
2017	5,261	3,728	22,283	46,633	874	464	3	17	1,716	80,977
2018	5,087	3,604	21,544	45,087	845	448	3	16	1,659	78,293
2019	4,948	3,506	20,956	43,857	822	436	3	16	1,614	76,157

© Barnes Reports: 2018 U.S. Industry & Market Outlook

Office Supplies & Stationery Stores Industry (NAICS 45321)

Sub-Industries — 2018 Estimated Industry Sales, Establishments & Employment

Sub-Industries	Category*	Establishments	Sales ($Mill)	Employment
Stationery stores	Major1	1,291	4,056.1	19,984
Notary and corporate seals	Minor2	22	2.7	72
Office forms and supplies	Minor2	932	279.0	5,240
School supplies	Minor2	138	66.1	500
Writing supplies	Minor2	89	8.9	302
Stationery and office supplies	Major1	1,302	6,670.8	19,029
Writing instruments and supplies	Minor1	21	16.4	389
Marking devices	Minor2	21	27.9	361
Pens and/or pencils	Minor2	53	38.1	613
Writing ink	Minor2	14	6.8	101
Social stationery and greeting cards	Minor1	53	19.3	776
Greeting cards	Minor2	201	104.9	1,789
Stationery	Minor2	176	92.4	1,166
Albums, scrapbooks and binders	Minor1	48	12.8	230
Albums (photo) and scrapbooks	Minor2	84	46.8	1,347
Looseleaf binders	Minor2	21	6.6	75
Computer and photocopying supplies	Minor1	188	174.3	3,253
Computer paper	Minor2	48	72.7	398
Data processing supplies	Minor2	64	36.0	587
Mimeograph paper	Minor2	2	10.1	78
Photocopying supplies	Minor2	36	24.5	606
Laser printer supplies	Minor2	86	61.9	810
Office filing supplies	Minor1	86	32.9	518
File cards	Minor2	6	9.7	91
File folders	Minor2	9	6.7	70
Blank books	Minor2	4	2.9	45
Business forms	Minor2	1,422	669.7	9,133
Carbon paper	Minor2	3	5.8	21
Envelopes	Minor2	107	57.5	1,230
Inked ribbons	Minor2	25	11.3	128
Manifold business forms	Minor2	15	3.8	214
Office supplies, nec	Minor2	782	568.1	8,531
Sales and receipt books	Minor2	41	12.8	190
Stationers, commercial	Minor2	23	21.9	412
Tabulation cards	Minor2	2	0.3	4

*Category-Major categories (Major1) are more general descriptions for companies that self-selected to capture the many functions they perform in the industry. Minor categories (Minor1, Minor2) are more specific for companies that have more detailed functions (Minor1 is a larger category than Minor2). Minor categories figures (sales, etc.) can be aggregated to larger minor categories (Minor2 sums to Minor1) and major categories overall figures.

ELECTRONIC SHOPPING & MAIL ORDER HOUSES (NAICS 45411)

NAICS 45411: Electronic Shopping and Mail-Order Houses This industry comprises establishments primarily engaged in retailing all types of merchandise by means of mail or by electronic media, such as interactive television or computer. Included in this industry are establishments primarily engaged in retailing from catalogue showrooms of mail-order houses.

INDUSTRY ESTABLISHMENTS, SALES & EMPLOYMENT TRENDS

	Year					Percent Chg. Year-to-Year			
	2015	2016	2017	2018	2019	15-16	16-17	17-18	18-19
Establishments	83,097	89,317	94,745	100,219	105,165	7.5%	6.1%	5.8%	4.9%
Sales ($Millions)	366,148	413,278	462,232	515,432	570,711	12.9%	11.8%	11.5%	10.7%
Employment	439,027	471,887	500,569	529,488	555,616	7.5%	6.1%	5.8%	4.9%
Sales ($M)/Estab.	4.41	4.63	4.88	5.14	5.43	5.0%	5.4%	5.4%	5.5%
Sales ($)/Emp.	834,000	875,799	923,414	973,453	1,027,169	5.0%	5.4%	5.4%	5.5%

3-YEAR TREND – ESTIMATED NUMBER OF ESTABLISHMENTS

Year	Employee Size of Establishment									Total Employment
	1-4 Emps.	5-9 Emps.	10-19 Emps.	20-49 Emps.	50-99 Emps.	100-249 Emps.	250-499 Emps.	>500 Emps.	Non-Employer	
2017	27,511	5,392	3,098	1,965	673	462	185	125	55,335	94,745
2018	29,101	5,703	3,277	2,078	712	488	195	133	58,532	100,219
2019	30,537	5,985	3,439	2,181	747	513	205	139	61,420	105,165

3-YEAR TREND – ESTIMATED INDUSTRY SALES ($MILLIONS)

Year	Employee Size of Establishment									Total Employment
	1-4 Emps.	5-9 Emps.	10-19 Emps.	20-49 Emps.	50-99 Emps.	100-249 Emps.	250-499 Emps.	>500 Emps.	Non-Employer	
2017	38,565.3	19,866.0	28,702.7	48,178.5	36,265.1	67,093.4	90,453.8	127,686.9	5,420.6	462,232.2
2018	43,220.3	22,263.9	32,167.2	53,993.8	40,642.4	75,191.8	101,371.8	140,505.9	6,074.8	515,431.8
2019	48,052.4	24,753.0	35,763.6	60,030.4	45,186.3	83,598.4	112,705.4	153,868.0	6,754.0	570,711.5

3-YEAR TREND – ESTIMATED NUMBER OF EMPLOYEES

Year	Employee Size of Establishment									Total Employment
	1-4 Emps.	5-9 Emps.	10-19 Emps.	20-49 Emps.	50-99 Emps.	100-249 Emps.	250-499 Emps.	>500 Emps.	Non-Employer	
2017	68,778	31,273	42,131	59,132	39,959	58,230	53,732	91,999	55,335	500,569
2018	72,752	33,080	44,565	62,549	42,267	61,594	56,836	97,314	58,532	529,488
2019	76,342	34,712	46,764	65,635	44,353	64,633	59,641	102,116	61,420	555,616

© Barnes Reports: 2018 U.S. Industry & Market Outlook

Electronic Shopping & Mail Order Houses (NAICS 45411)

Sub-Industries – 2018 Estimated Industry Sales, Establishments & Employment

Sub-Industries	Category*	Establishments	Sales ($Mill)	Employment
Catalog and mail-order houses	Major1	22,629	39,202.3	115,565
Food, mail order	Minor1	1,196	703.6	7,050
Cheese, mail order	Minor2	85	25.0	4,203
Fruit, mail order	Minor2	1,002	257.0	4,601
Computer equipment and electronics, mail order	Minor1	2,769	10,493.7	8,777
Computer software, mail order	Minor2	2,192	53,392.9	14,535
Computers and peripheral equipment, mail order	Minor2	996	19,147.0	5,114
Electronic kits and parts, mail order	Minor2	449	240.1	1,953
Book and record clubs	Minor1	455	142,655.8	6,817
Book club, mail order	Minor2	522	215.7	6,554
Magazines, mail order	Minor2	595	264.6	3,012
Record and/or tape (music or video) club, mail order	Minor2	2,132	2,381.1	18,744
Stamps, coins, and other collectibles, mail order	Minor1	1,895	334.3	2,284
Coins, mail order	Minor2	346	385.5	1,717
Collectibles and antiques, mail order	Minor2	7,500	1,000.7	11,435
Stamps, mail order	Minor2	516	300.6	2,402
Catalog and mail-order houses, nec	Minor2	1,184	51,214.8	3,505
Arts and crafts equipment and supplies, mail order	Minor2	2,126	259.3	4,078
Automotive supplies and equipment, mail order	Minor2	1,913	2,484.0	7,539
Books, mail order (except book clubs)	Minor2	3,079	937.9	7,923
Cards, mail order	Minor2	571	283.2	4,368
Catalog sales	Minor2	6,948	9,985.5	57,794
Clothing, mail order (except women's)	Minor2	1,518	814.0	8,500
Cosmetics and perfumes, mail order	Minor2	1,555	696.0	2,631
Educational supplies and equipment, mail order	Minor2	1,834	1,056.5	5,498
Fishing, hunting and camping equipment and supplies: by	Minor2	814	15,529.2	15,024
Fitness and sporting goods, mail order	Minor2	1,828	1,107.7	9,370
Flowers, plants and bulbs: mail order	Minor2	947	368.1	2,827
Furniture and furnishings, mail order	Minor2	996	598.3	3,866
General merchandise, mail order	Minor2	8,575	8,123.1	21,011
Gift items, mail order	Minor2	4,148	1,558.3	13,364
Jewelry, mail order	Minor2	2,022	1,168.2	3,265
Mail order house, nec	Minor2	7,810	7,279.9	63,633
Misc. mail order items	Minor2	7,069	140,967.8	80,532

*Category-Major categories (Major1) are more general descriptions for companies that self-selected to capture the many functions they perform in the industry. Minor categories (Minor1, Minor2) are more specific for companies that have more detailed functions (Minor1 is a larger category than Minor2). Minor categories figures (sales, etc.) can be aggregated to larger minor categories (Minor2 sums to Minor1) and major categories overall figures.

Scheduled Air Transportation Industry (NAICS 48111)

NAICS 48111: Scheduled Air Transportation Industry. This industry comprises establishments primarily engaged in providing air transportation of passengers and/or cargo over regular routes and on regular schedules. Establishments in this industry operate flights even if partially loaded. Establishments primarily engaged in providing scheduled air transportation of mail on a contract basis are included in this industry.

Industry Establishments, Sales & Employment Trends

	Year					Percent Chg. Year-to-Year			
	2015	2016	2017	2018	2019	15-16	16-17	17-18	18-19
Establishments	5,954	5,775	5,716	5,592	5,472	-3.0%	-1.0%	-2.2%	-2.1%
Sales ($Millions)	133,760	142,577	153,554	163,757	174,252	6.6%	7.7%	6.6%	6.4%
Employment	201,838	195,763	193,760	189,545	185,470	-3.0%	-1.0%	-2.2%	-2.1%
Sales ($M)/Estab.	22.46	24.69	26.86	29.29	31.85	9.9%	8.8%	9.0%	8.7%
Sales ($)/Emp.	662,707	728,312	792,499	863,948	939,513	9.9%	8.8%	9.0%	8.7%

3-Year Trend – Estimated Number of Establishments

Year	Employee Size of Establishment									Total Employ-ment
	1-4 Emps.	5-9 Emps.	10-19 Emps.	20-49 Emps.	50-99 Emps.	100-249 Emps.	250-499 Emps.	>500 Emps.	Non-Employer	
2017	827	276	340	386	202	186	84	115	3,301	5,716
2018	809	270	332	378	197	182	82	113	3,229	5,592
2019	792	264	325	369	193	178	80	110	3,160	5,472

3-Year Trend – Estimated Industry Sales ($Millions)

Year	Employee Size of Establishment									Total Employ-ment
	1-4 Emps.	5-9 Emps.	10-19 Emps.	20-49 Emps.	50-99 Emps.	100-249 Emps.	250-499 Emps.	>500 Emps.	Non-Employer	
2017	709.3	620.7	1,925.2	5,786.7	6,644.9	16,544.8	25,007.2	95,886.0	429.6	153,554.4
2018	748.8	655.3	2,032.6	6,109.5	7,015.6	17,467.7	26,402.2	102,871.9	453.6	163,757.0
2019	788.8	690.3	2,141.2	6,436.0	7,390.6	18,401.3	27,813.3	110,112.3	477.8	174,251.7

3-Year Trend – Estimated Number of Employees

Year	Employee Size of Establishment									Total Employ-ment
	1-4 Emps.	5-9 Emps.	10-19 Emps.	20-49 Emps.	50-99 Emps.	100-249 Emps.	250-499 Emps.	>500 Emps.	Non-Employer	
2017	2,069	1,598	4,622	11,616	11,975	23,484	24,295	110,800	3,301	193,760
2018	2,024	1,563	4,521	11,363	11,714	22,973	23,767	108,390	3,229	189,545
2019	1,980	1,530	4,424	11,119	11,462	22,480	23,256	106,060	3,160	185,470

© Barnes Reports: 2018 U.S. Industry & Market Outlook

Scheduled Air Transportation Industry (NAICS 48111)

Sub-Industries — 2018 Estimated Industry Sales, Establishments & Employment

Sub-Industries	Category*	Establishments	Sales ($Mill)	Employment
Air transportation, scheduled	Major1	1,921	26,056.5	41,987
Air cargo carrier, scheduled	Minor2	982	1,782.4	17,953
Air passenger carrier, scheduled	Minor2	2,390	135,397.3	126,342
Helicopter carrier, scheduled	Minor2	299	520.8	3,263

*Category-Major categories (Major1) are more general descriptions for companies that self-selected to capture the many functions they perform in the industry. Minor categories (Minor1, Minor2) are more specific for companies that have more detailed functions (Minor1 is a larger category than Minor2). Minor categories figures (sales, etc.) can be aggregated to larger minor categories (Minor2 sums to Minor1) and major categories overall figures.

LOCAL FREIGHT TRUCKING INDUSTRY
(NAICS 48411)

NAICS 48411: Freight Trucking, Local. This industry comprises establishments primarily engaged in providing local general freight trucking. General freight establishments handle a wide variety of commodities, generally palletized and transported in a container or van trailer. Local general freight trucking establishments usually provide trucking within a metropolitan area which may cross state lines. Generally the trips are same-day return.

INDUSTRY ESTABLISHMENTS, SALES & EMPLOYMENT TRENDS

	Year					Percent Chg. Year-to-Year			
	2015	2016	2017	2018	2019	15-16	16-17	17-18	18-19
Establishments	59,166	60,579	60,934	62,098	63,328	2.4%	0.6%	1.9%	2.0%
Sales ($Millions)	22,884	23,104	23,060	23,385	23,828	1.0%	-0.2%	1.4%	1.9%
Employment	239,033	244,740	246,174	250,878	255,846	2.4%	0.6%	1.9%	2.0%
Sales ($M)/Estab.	0.39	0.38	0.38	0.38	0.38	-1.4%	-0.8%	-0.5%	-0.1%
Sales ($)/Emp.	95,734	94,403	93,675	93,214	93,135	-1.4%	-0.8%	-0.5%	-0.1%

3-YEAR TREND – ESTIMATED NUMBER OF ESTABLISHMENTS

Year	Employee Size of Establishment									Total Employment
	1-4 Emps.	5-9 Emps.	10-19 Emps.	20-49 Emps.	50-99 Emps.	100-249 Emps.	250-499 Emps.	>500 Emps.	Non-Employer	
2017	21,744	4,079	2,689	1,711	407	123	19	6	30,157	60,934
2018	22,159	4,157	2,740	1,743	415	125	19	6	30,733	62,098
2019	22,598	4,240	2,795	1,778	423	127	19	6	31,342	63,328

3-YEAR TREND – ESTIMATED INDUSTRY SALES ($MILLIONS)

Year	Employee Size of Establishment									Total Employment
	1-4 Emps.	5-9 Emps.	10-19 Emps.	20-49 Emps.	50-99 Emps.	100-249 Emps.	250-499 Emps.	>500 Emps.	Non-Employer	
2017	3,618.7	1,784.4	2,957.9	4,980.7	2,603.7	2,114.1	1,077.8	822.6	3,100.4	23,060.3
2018	3,670.9	1,810.1	3,000.6	5,052.4	2,641.2	2,144.5	1,093.3	827.1	3,145.1	23,385.3
2019	3,741.6	1,845.0	3,058.4	5,149.8	2,692.1	2,185.9	1,114.4	835.4	3,205.7	23,828.3

3-YEAR TREND – ESTIMATED NUMBER OF EMPLOYEES

Year	Employee Size of Establishment									Total Employment
	1-4 Emps.	5-9 Emps.	10-19 Emps.	20-49 Emps.	50-99 Emps.	100-249 Emps.	250-499 Emps.	>500 Emps.	Non-Employer	
2017	54,359	23,660	36,570	51,490	24,164	15,454	5,393	4,927	30,157	246,174
2018	55,398	24,112	37,269	52,473	24,626	15,749	5,496	5,021	30,733	250,878
2019	56,495	24,590	38,007	53,513	25,113	16,061	5,605	5,121	31,342	255,846

LOCAL FREIGHT TRUCKING INDUSTRY
(NAICS 48411)

SUB-INDUSTRIES – 2018 ESTIMATED INDUSTRY SALES, ESTABLISHMENTS & EMPLOYMENT

Sub-Industries	Category*	Establishments	Sales ($Mill)	Employment
Local trucking, without storage	Major1	45,210	14,716.2	156,111
Animal and farm product transportation services	Minor1	239	100.4	1,023
Animal transport	Minor2	281	93.1	975
Farm to market haulage, local	Minor2	267	137.6	1,297
Live poultry haulage	Minor2	20	16.5	172
Liquid transfer services	Minor1	90	102.4	978
Liquid haulage, local	Minor2	289	300.9	2,464
Petroleum haulage, local	Minor2	183	385.6	2,616
Lumber and timber trucking	Minor1	127	69.5	662
Lumber (log) trucking, local	Minor2	283	141.6	1,357
Timber trucking, local	Minor2	67	48.6	486
Moving services	Minor1	2,300	1,070.9	14,037
Furniture moving, local: without storage	Minor2	266	143.0	1,864
Safe moving, local	Minor2	20	11.7	103
Baggage transfer	Minor2	24	66.1	765
Coal haulage, local	Minor2	154	120.4	1,289
Delivery service, vehicular	Minor2	4,660	1,787.4	21,357
Draying, local: without storage	Minor2	42	38.5	432
Dump truck haulage	Minor2	2,346	1,258.4	12,050
Garbage collection and transport, no disposal	Minor2	945	674.9	11,791
Hazardous waste transport	Minor2	129	219.0	2,159
Heavy machinery transport, local	Minor2	202	145.6	1,335
Light haulage and cartage, local	Minor2	3,051	756.5	8,889
Mail carriers, contract	Minor2	495	432.4	4,284
Star routes, local	Minor2	6	11.2	83
Steel hauling, local	Minor2	88	44.0	422
Truck rental with drivers	Minor2	314	492.6	1,875

*Category-Major categories (Major1) are more general descriptions for companies that self-selected to capture the many functions they perform in the industry. Minor categories (Minor1, Minor2) are more specific for companies that have more detailed functions (Minor1 is a larger category than Minor2). Minor categories figures (sales, etc.) can be aggregated to larger minor categories (Minor2 sums to Minor1) and major categories overall figures.

FREIGHT TRUCKING LONG DISTANCE INDUSTRY
(NAICS 48412)

NAICS 48412: Freight Trucking, Long-Distance. This industry comprises establishments primarily engaged in providing long-distance general freight trucking. General freight establishments handle a wide variety of commodities, generally palletized and transported in a container or van trailer. Long-distance general freight trucking establishments usually provide trucking between metropolitan areas which may cross North American country borders. Included in this industry are establishments operating as truckload (TL) or less than truckload (LTL) carriers.

INDUSTRY ESTABLISHMENTS, SALES & EMPLOYMENT TRENDS

	Year					Percent Chg. Year-to-Year			
	2015	2016	2017	2018	2019	15-16	16-17	17-18	18-19
Establishments	73,888	74,050	75,877	79,626	84,378	0.2%	2.5%	4.9%	6.0%
Sales ($Millions)	132,786	138,874	148,815	163,141	180,725	4.6%	7.2%	9.6%	10.8%
Employment	715,747	717,314	735,014	771,331	817,362	0.2%	2.5%	4.9%	6.0%
Sales ($M)/Estab.	1.80	1.88	1.96	2.05	2.14	4.4%	4.6%	4.5%	4.5%
Sales ($)/Emp.	185,520	193,603	202,466	211,505	221,107	4.4%	4.6%	4.5%	4.5%

3-YEAR TREND – ESTIMATED NUMBER OF ESTABLISHMENTS

Year	Employee Size of Establishment									Total Employment
	1-4 Emps.	5-9 Emps.	10-19 Emps.	20-49 Emps.	50-99 Emps.	100-249 Emps.	250-499 Emps.	>500 Emps.	Non-Employer	
2017	29,687	4,890	3,743	3,766	1,738	1,148	290	143	30,473	75,877
2018	31,154	5,132	3,928	3,952	1,823	1,205	304	150	31,978	79,626
2019	33,013	5,438	4,162	4,188	1,932	1,277	322	159	33,887	84,378

3-YEAR TREND – ESTIMATED INDUSTRY SALES ($MILLIONS)

Year	Employee Size of Establishment									Total Employment
	1-4 Emps.	5-9 Emps.	10-19 Emps.	20-49 Emps.	50-99 Emps.	100-249 Emps.	250-499 Emps.	>500 Emps.	Non-Employer	
2017	8,115.5	3,513.6	6,763.3	18,009.7	18,266.9	32,530.7	27,655.9	29,536.4	4,423.4	148,815.5
2018	8,927.3	3,865.1	7,439.8	19,811.0	20,093.9	35,784.5	30,422.1	31,931.1	4,865.9	163,140.6
2019	9,928.3	4,298.5	8,274.0	22,032.5	22,347.1	39,797.1	33,833.4	34,802.3	5,411.5	180,724.6

3-YEAR TREND – ESTIMATED NUMBER OF EMPLOYEES

Year	Employee Size of Establishment									Total Employment
	1-4 Emps.	5-9 Emps.	10-19 Emps.	20-49 Emps.	50-99 Emps.	100-249 Emps.	250-499 Emps.	>500 Emps.	Non-Employer	
2017	74,218	28,363	50,906	113,348	103,210	144,775	84,242	105,479	30,473	735,014
2018	77,885	29,764	53,422	118,948	108,310	151,928	88,404	110,691	31,978	771,331
2019	82,533	31,541	56,610	126,047	114,774	160,995	93,680	117,296	33,887	817,362

© Barnes Reports: 2018 U.S. Industry & Market Outlook

FREIGHT TRUCKING LONG DISTANCE INDUSTRY (NAICS 48412)

SUB-INDUSTRIES – 2018 ESTIMATED INDUSTRY SALES, ESTABLISHMENTS & EMPLOYMENT

Sub-Industries	Category*	Establishments	Sales ($Mill)	Employment
Trucking, except local	Major1	54,569	113,158.1	500,565
Automobiles, transport and delivery	Minor2	2,932	2,449.6	16,394
Building materials transport	Minor2	499	536.0	7,646
Contract haulers	Minor2	9,079	17,026.0	125,482
Heavy hauling, nec	Minor2	5,131	3,966.6	28,956
Heavy machinery transport	Minor2	591	883.5	5,202
Household goods transport	Minor2	2,082	5,998.3	29,587
Less-than-truckload (LTL)	Minor2	435	10,591.4	17,613
Liquid petroleum transport, non-local	Minor2	628	2,494.5	13,719
Mobile homes transport	Minor2	1,784	618.3	5,146
Refrigerated products transport	Minor2	1,546	5,246.0	19,313
Trailer or container on flat car (TOFC/COFC)	Minor2	350	172.4	1,708

*Category-Major categories (Major1) are more general descriptions for companies that self-selected to capture the many functions they perform in the industry. Minor categories (Minor1, Minor2) are more specific for companies that have more detailed functions (Minor1 is a larger category than Minor2). Minor categories figures (sales, etc.) can be aggregated to larger minor categories (Minor2 sums to Minor1) and major categories overall figures.

General Warehousing & Storage Industry
(NAICS 49311)

NAICS 49311: General Warehousing and Storage. This industry comprises establishments primarily engaged in operating merchandise warehousing and storage facilities. These establishments generally handle goods in containers, such as boxes, barrels, and/or drums, using equipment, such as forklifts, pallets, and racks. They are not specialized in handling bulk products of any particular type, size, or quantity of goods or products.

Industry Establishments, Sales & Employment Trends

	Year					Percent Chg. Year-to-Year			
	2015	2016	2017	2018	2019	15-16	16-17	17-18	18-19
Establishments	13,893	13,495	13,412	13,572	13,867	-2.9%	-0.6%	1.2%	2.2%
Sales ($Millions)	48,057	48,793	50,758	53,696	57,379	1.5%	4.0%	5.8%	6.9%
Employment	582,920	566,258	562,764	569,458	581,869	-2.9%	-0.6%	1.2%	2.2%
Sales ($M)/Estab.	3.46	3.62	3.78	3.96	4.14	4.5%	4.7%	4.5%	4.6%
Sales ($)/Emp.	82,443	86,167	90,194	94,293	98,611	4.5%	4.7%	4.5%	4.6%

3-Year Trend – Estimated Number of Establishments

Year	Employee Size of Establishment									Total Employment
	1-4 Emps.	5-9 Emps.	10-19 Emps.	20-49 Emps.	50-99 Emps.	100-249 Emps.	250-499 Emps.	>500 Emps.	Non-Employer	
2017	3,004	1,606	1,653	1,689	950	789	369	304	2,968	13,412
2018	3,120	1,626	1,672	1,710	961	798	373	308	3,004	13,572
2019	3,188	1,661	1,709	1,747	982	816	381	314	3,069	13,867

3-Year Trend – Estimated Industry Sales ($Millions)

Year	Employee Size of Establishment									Total Employment
	1-4 Emps.	5-9 Emps.	10-19 Emps.	20-49 Emps.	50-99 Emps.	100-249 Emps.	250-499 Emps.	>500 Emps.	Non-Employer	
2017	302.5	414.2	1,071.6	2,899.4	3,583.8	8,019.6	12,638.1	21,542.6	286.3	50,758.2
2018	320.4	438.7	1,135.1	3,071.1	3,796.0	8,494.5	13,386.5	22,750.1	303.3	53,695.8
2019	343.2	469.9	1,215.7	3,289.3	4,065.6	9,097.9	14,337.4	24,235.1	324.8	57,378.8

3-Year Trend – Estimated Number of Employees

Year	Employee Size of Establishment									Total Employment
	1-4 Emps.	5-9 Emps.	10-19 Emps.	20-49 Emps.	50-99 Emps.	100-249 Emps.	250-499 Emps.	>500 Emps.	Non-Employer	
2017	7,709	9,317	22,478	50,854	56,429	99,461	107,281	206,266	2,968	562,764
2018	7,801	9,428	22,745	51,458	57,100	100,644	108,557	208,720	3,004	569,458
2019	7,971	9,634	23,241	52,580	58,344	102,838	110,923	213,269	3,069	581,869

GENERAL WAREHOUSING & STORAGE INDUSTRY (NAICS 49311)

SUB-INDUSTRIES — 2018 ESTIMATED INDUSTRY SALES, ESTABLISHMENTS & EMPLOYMENT

Sub-Industries	Category*	Establishments	Sales ($Mill)	Employment
General warehousing and storage	Major1	6,055	24,522.5	364,976
General warehousing	Minor2	2,550	20,329.8	128,671
Miniwarehouse, warehousing	Minor2	1,639	2,342.9	21,190
Warehousing, self storage	Minor2	3,328	6,500.6	54,621

*Category-Major categories (Major1) are more general descriptions for companies that self-selected to capture the many functions they perform in the industry. Minor categories (Minor1, Minor2) are more specific for companies that have more detailed functions (Minor1 is a larger category than Minor2). Minor categories figures (sales, etc.) can be aggregated to larger minor categories (Minor2 sums to Minor1) and major categories overall figures.

NEWSPAPER PUBLISHING INDUSTRY
(NAICS 51111)

NAICS 51111: Newspaper Publishers. Establishments primarily engaged in publishing newspapers, or in publishing and printing newspapers. These establishments carry on the various operations necessary for issuing newspapers, including the gathering of news and the preparation of editorials and advertisements, but may or may not perform their own printing.

INDUSTRY ESTABLISHMENTS, SALES & EMPLOYMENT TRENDS

	Year					Percent Chg. Year-to-Year			
	2015	2016	2017	2018	2019	15-16	16-17	17-18	18-19
Establishments	17,732	17,393	17,209	17,085	17,119	-1.9%	-1.1%	-0.7%	0.2%
Sales ($Millions)	31,163	30,743	30,753	30,946	31,519	-1.3%	0.0%	0.6%	1.9%
Employment	186,737	183,169	181,236	179,930	180,281	-1.9%	-1.1%	-0.7%	0.2%
Sales ($M)/Estab.	1.76	1.77	1.79	1.81	1.84	0.6%	1.1%	1.4%	1.7%
Sales ($)/Emp.	166,880	167,839	169,686	171,989	174,830	0.6%	1.1%	1.4%	1.7%

3-YEAR TREND – ESTIMATED NUMBER OF ESTABLISHMENTS

Year	Employee Size of Establishment									Total
	1-4 Emps.	5-9 Emps.	10-19 Emps.	20-49 Emps.	50-99 Emps.	100-249 Emps.	250-499 Emps.	>500 Emps.	Non-Employer	Employment
2017	2,520	1,514	1,175	984	388	242	86	44	10,255	17,209
2018	2,502	1,503	1,167	977	385	240	86	43	10,181	17,085
2019	2,507	1,506	1,169	979	386	240	86	43	10,201	17,119

3-YEAR TREND – ESTIMATED INDUSTRY SALES ($MILLIONS)

Year	Employee Size of Establishment									Total
	1-4 Emps.	5-9 Emps.	10-19 Emps.	20-49 Emps.	50-99 Emps.	100-249 Emps.	250-499 Emps.	>500 Emps.	Non-Employer	Employment
2017	562.4	888.0	1,733.5	3,841.9	3,331.5	5,589.4	6,733.5	7,410.9	662.2	30,753.1
2018	565.6	893.0	1,743.3	3,863.6	3,350.3	5,621.0	6,771.6	7,471.8	665.9	30,946.0
2019	576.2	909.7	1,775.8	3,935.8	3,412.9	5,725.9	6,898.0	7,606.0	678.3	31,518.6

3-YEAR TREND – ESTIMATED NUMBER OF EMPLOYEES

Year	Employee Size of Establishment									Total
	1-4 Emps.	5-9 Emps.	10-19 Emps.	20-49 Emps.	50-99 Emps.	100-249 Emps.	250-499 Emps.	>500 Emps.	Non-Employer	Employment
2017	6,301	8,781	15,984	29,622	23,060	30,474	25,127	31,630	10,255	181,236
2018	6,256	8,718	15,869	29,409	22,894	30,254	24,946	31,402	10,181	179,930
2019	6,268	8,735	15,900	29,466	22,939	30,313	24,995	31,463	10,201	180,281

© Barnes Reports: 2018 U.S. Industry & Market Outlook

Newspaper Publishing Industry (NAICS 51111)

Sub-Industries – 2018 Estimated Industry Sales, Establishments & Employment

Sub-Industries	Category*	Establishments	Sales ($Mill)	Employment
Newspapers	Major1	7,088	3,052.6	50,763
Newspapers, publishing and printing	Minor1	5,557	24,373.7	82,755
Commercial printing and newspaper publishing combined	Minor2	774	438.6	12,320
Job printing and newspaper publishing combined	Minor2	500	158.3	3,427
Newspapers: publishing only, not printed on site	Minor2	3,166	2,922.7	30,666

*Category-Major categories (Major1) are more general descriptions for companies that self-selected to capture the many functions they perform in the industry. Minor categories (Minor1, Minor2) are more specific for companies that have more detailed functions (Minor1 is a larger category than Minor2). Minor categories figures (sales, etc.) can be aggregated to larger minor categories (Minor2 sums to Minor1) and major categories overall figures.

PERIODICAL PUBLISHING INDUSTRY
(NAICS 51112)

NAICS 51112: Periodical Publishing. Establishments primarily engaged in publishing periodicals, or in publishing and printing periodicals. These establishments carry on the various operations necessary for issuing periodicals, but may or may not perform their own printing. Establishments not engaged in publishing periodicals, but which print periodicals for publishers, are classified in SIC 2752-2759.

INDUSTRY ESTABLISHMENTS, SALES & EMPLOYMENT TRENDS

	Year					Percent Chg. Year-to-Year			
	2015	2016	2017	2018	2019	15-16	16-17	17-18	18-19
Establishments	14,452	13,936	13,542	13,204	12,993	-3.6%	-2.8%	-2.5%	-1.6%
Sales ($Millions)	26,055	25,293	24,866	24,591	24,605	-2.9%	-1.7%	-1.1%	0.1%
Employment	100,426	96,841	94,097	91,750	90,287	-3.6%	-2.8%	-2.5%	-1.6%
Sales ($M)/Estab.	1.80	1.81	1.84	1.86	1.89	0.7%	1.2%	1.4%	1.7%
Sales ($)/Emp.	259,448	261,184	264,255	268,026	272,524	0.7%	1.2%	1.4%	1.7%

3-YEAR TREND – ESTIMATED NUMBER OF ESTABLISHMENTS

Year	Employee Size of Establishment									Total Employment
	1-4 Emps.	5-9 Emps.	10-19 Emps.	20-49 Emps.	50-99 Emps.	100-249 Emps.	250-499 Emps.	>500 Emps.	Non-Employer	
2017	2,960	968	740	461	179	117	29	18	8,070	13,542
2018	2,886	944	722	449	174	114	28	17	7,868	13,204
2019	2,840	929	710	442	172	112	28	17	7,743	12,993

3-YEAR TREND – ESTIMATED INDUSTRY SALES ($MILLIONS)

Year	Employee Size of Establishment									Total Employment
	1-4 Emps.	5-9 Emps.	10-19 Emps.	20-49 Emps.	50-99 Emps.	100-249 Emps.	250-499 Emps.	>500 Emps.	Non-Employer	
2017	1,135.2	975.7	1,876.5	3,093.2	2,639.7	4,656.0	3,891.8	6,078.8	518.5	24,865.6
2018	1,118.6	961.4	1,849.0	3,048.0	2,601.0	4,587.9	3,834.9	6,079.7	510.9	24,591.4
2019	1,116.6	959.7	1,845.7	3,042.5	2,596.3	4,579.6	3,827.9	6,127.1	510.0	24,605.4

3-YEAR TREND – ESTIMATED NUMBER OF EMPLOYEES

Year	Employee Size of Establishment									Total Employment
	1-4 Emps.	5-9 Emps.	10-19 Emps.	20-49 Emps.	50-99 Emps.	100-249 Emps.	250-499 Emps.	>500 Emps.	Non-Employer	
2017	7,400	5,614	10,067	13,876	10,630	14,769	8,450	15,222	8,070	94,097
2018	7,215	5,474	9,816	13,530	10,365	14,401	8,239	14,842	7,868	91,750
2019	7,100	5,386	9,659	13,314	10,200	14,171	8,107	14,606	7,743	90,287

© Barnes Reports: 2018 U.S. Industry & Market Outlook

Periodical Publishing Industry
(NAICS 51112)

Sub-Industries – 2018 Estimated Industry Sales, Establishments & Employment

Sub-Industries	Category*	Establishments	Sales ($Mill)	Employment
Periodicals	Major1	5,510	2,517.6	23,247
Periodicals, publishing only	Minor1	1,009	1,222.0	7,824
Comic books: publishing only, not printed on site	Minor2	68	41.9	252
Magazines: publishing only, not printed on site	Minor2	2,886	4,695.3	28,736
Statistical reports (periodicals): publishing only	Minor2	92	990.3	2,460
Television schedules: publishing only, not printed on site	Minor2	9	4.1	110
Trade journals: publishing only, not printed on site	Minor2	561	10,040.0	6,505
Periodicals, publishing and printing	Minor1	300	423.1	4,137
Comic books: publishing and printing	Minor2	96	18.9	161
Magazines: publishing and printing	Minor2	2,300	4,063.4	14,864
Statistical reports (periodicals): publishing and printing	Minor2	74	25.7	983
Television schedules: publishing and printing	Minor2	15	52.6	368
Trade journals: publishing and printing	Minor2	284	496.4	2,102

*Category-Major categories (Major1) are more general descriptions for companies that self-selected to capture the many functions they perform in the industry. Minor categories (Minor1, Minor2) are more specific for companies that have more detailed functions (Minor1 is a larger category than Minor2). Minor categories figures (sales, etc.) can be aggregated to larger minor categories (Minor2 sums to Minor1) and major categories overall figures.

Book Publishing Industry (NAICS 51113)

NAICS 51113: Book Publishers. This U.S. industry comprises establishments known as book publishers. Establishments in this industry carry out design, editing, and marketing activities necessary for producing and distributing books. These establishments may publish books in print, electronic, or audio form.

Industry Establishments, Sales & Employment Trends

	Year					Percent Chg. Year-to-Year			
	2015	2016	2017	2018	2019	15-16	16-17	17-18	18-19
Establishments	6,323	6,076	5,881	5,771	5,717	-3.9%	-3.2%	-1.9%	-1.0%
Sales ($Millions)	20,084	19,918	19,978	20,304	20,843	-0.8%	0.3%	1.6%	2.7%
Employment	58,565	56,274	54,469	53,457	52,949	-3.9%	-3.2%	-1.9%	-1.0%
Sales ($M)/Estab.	3.18	3.28	3.40	3.52	3.65	3.2%	3.6%	3.6%	3.6%
Sales ($)/Emp.	342,929	353,951	366,774	379,816	393,652	3.2%	3.6%	3.6%	3.6%

3-Year Trend – Estimated Number of Establishments

Year	Employee Size of Establishment									Total Employment
	1-4 Emps.	5-9 Emps.	10-19 Emps.	20-49 Emps.	50-99 Emps.	100-249 Emps.	250-499 Emps.	>500 Emps.	Non-Employer	
2017	1,414	304	233	206	95	87	21	16	3,504	5,881
2018	1,387	298	229	202	93	86	21	16	3,439	5,771
2019	1,374	296	227	200	92	85	21	15	3,407	5,717

3-Year Trend – Estimated Industry Sales ($Millions)

Year	Employee Size of Establishment									Total Employment
	1-4 Emps.	5-9 Emps.	10-19 Emps.	20-49 Emps.	50-99 Emps.	100-249 Emps.	250-499 Emps.	>500 Emps.	Non-Employer	
2017	671.2	379.5	732.6	1,707.3	1,732.1	4,302.2	3,548.0	6,669.4	235.4	19,977.7
2018	679.7	384.3	741.8	1,728.8	1,754.0	4,356.6	3,592.8	6,827.6	238.3	20,303.9
2019	696.4	393.8	760.1	1,771.4	1,797.2	4,463.9	3,681.3	7,035.1	244.2	20,843.5

3-Year Trend – Estimated Number of Employees

Year	Employee Size of Establishment									Total Employment
	1-4 Emps.	5-9 Emps.	10-19 Emps.	20-49 Emps.	50-99 Emps.	100-249 Emps.	250-499 Emps.	>500 Emps.	Non-Employer	
2017	3,534	1,764	3,175	6,187	5,635	11,024	6,223	13,422	3,504	54,469
2018	3,469	1,731	3,116	6,072	5,530	10,820	6,107	13,173	3,439	53,457
2019	3,436	1,715	3,086	6,014	5,478	10,717	6,049	13,048	3,407	52,949

© Barnes Reports: 2018 U.S. Industry & Market Outlook

Book Publishing Industry
(NAICS 51113)

Sub-Industries – 2018 Estimated Industry Sales, Establishments & Employment

Sub-Industries	Category*	Establishments	Sales ($Mill)	Employment
Book publishing	Major1	3,576	2,475.2	19,582
Books, publishing only	Minor1	1,205	14,474.3	17,953
Book clubs: publishing only, not printed on site	Minor2	33	27.3	140
Book music: publishing only, not printed on site	Minor2	46	24.1	145
Pamphlets: publishing only, not printed on site	Minor2	71	79.4	476
Textbooks: publishing only, not printed on site	Minor2	149	2,407.5	2,263
Books, publishing and printing	Minor1	385	457.9	8,359
Book clubs: publishing and printing	Minor2	59	93.7	370
Book music: publishing and printing	Minor2	82	23.8	240
Pamphlets: publishing and printing	Minor2	86	162.0	1,092
Textbooks: publishing and printing	Minor2	80	78.7	2,838

*Category-Major categories (Major1) are more general descriptions for companies that self-selected to capture the many functions they perform in the industry. Minor categories (Minor1, Minor2) are more specific for companies that have more detailed functions (Minor1 is a larger category than Minor2). Minor categories figures (sales, etc.) can be aggregated to larger minor categories (Minor2 sums to Minor1) and major categories overall figures.

DATABASE & DIRECTORY PUBLISHING INDUSTRY (NAICS 51114)

NAICS 51114: Database and Directory Publishers . This U.S. industry comprises establishments primarily engaged in publishing compilations and collections of information or facts that are logically organized to facilitate their use. These collections may be published in print or electronic form. Electronic versions may be provided directly to customers by the establishment or offered through on-line services or third-party vendors.

INDUSTRY ESTABLISHMENTS, SALES & EMPLOYMENT TRENDS

	Year					Percent Chg. Year-to-Year			
	2015	2016	2017	2018	2019	15-16	16-17	17-18	18-19
Establishments	2,193	2,077	1,979	1,838	1,723	-5.3%	-4.7%	-7.1%	-6.3%
Sales ($Millions)	5,805	5,582	5,427	5,180	5,003	-3.8%	-2.8%	-4.6%	-3.4%
Employment	21,570	20,435	19,473	18,084	16,949	-5.3%	-4.7%	-7.1%	-6.3%
Sales ($M)/Estab.	2.65	2.69	2.74	2.82	2.90	1.5%	2.0%	2.8%	3.1%
Sales ($)/Emp.	269,102	273,135	278,707	286,443	295,194	1.5%	2.0%	2.8%	3.1%

3-YEAR TREND – ESTIMATED NUMBER OF ESTABLISHMENTS

Year	Employee Size of Establishment									Total Employ-ment
	1-4 Emps.	5-9 Emps.	10-19 Emps.	20-49 Emps.	50-99 Emps.	100-249 Emps.	250-499 Emps.	>500 Emps.	Non-Employer	
2017	383	124	136	88	32	22	9	6	1,180	1,979
2018	355	115	127	81	30	20	8	6	1,095	1,838
2019	333	108	119	76	28	19	8	6	1,027	1,723

3-YEAR TREND – ESTIMATED INDUSTRY SALES ($MILLIONS)

Year	Employee Size of Establishment									Total Employ-ment
	1-4 Emps.	5-9 Emps.	10-19 Emps.	20-49 Emps.	50-99 Emps.	100-249 Emps.	250-499 Emps.	>500 Emps.	Non-Employer	
2017	136.7	116.1	321.8	547.1	446.3	801.9	1,126.2	1,854.6	76.6	5,427.3
2018	128.9	109.5	303.5	516.1	421.0	756.5	1,062.4	1,809.7	72.3	5,180.1
2019	123.2	104.6	290.0	493.1	402.3	722.8	1,015.1	1,783.0	69.1	5,003.3

3-YEAR TREND – ESTIMATED NUMBER OF EMPLOYEES

Year	Employee Size of Establishment									Total Employ-ment
	1-4 Emps.	5-9 Emps.	10-19 Emps.	20-49 Emps.	50-99 Emps.	100-249 Emps.	250-499 Emps.	>500 Emps.	Non-Employer	
2017	957	717	1,854	2,636	1,930	2,732	2,626	4,841	1,180	19,473
2018	889	666	1,722	2,448	1,793	2,537	2,439	4,495	1,095	18,084
2019	833	624	1,614	2,294	1,680	2,378	2,286	4,213	1,027	16,949

© Barnes Reports: 2018 U.S. Industry & Market Outlook

Database & Directory Publishing Industry (NAICS 51114)

Sub-Industries – 2018 Estimated Industry Sales, Establishments & Employment

Sub-Industries	Category*	Establishments	Sales ($Mill)	Employment
Telephone and other directory publishing	Minor1	623	1,439.8	2,767
Directories, nec: publishing and printing	Minor2	157	1,757.9	1,624
Directories, nec: publishing only, not printed on site	Minor2	259	109.6	3,631
Directories, telephone: publishing and printing	Minor2	61	53.4	892
Directories, telephone: publishing only, not printed on site	Minor2	126	92.6	3,142
Mailing list compilers	Minor2	55	112.6	372
Mailing service	Minor2	513	1,394.3	5,288
Mailing list management	Minor2	10	73.9	104
Mailing list brokers	Minor2	34	145.9	265

*Category-Major categories (Major1) are more general descriptions for companies that self-selected to capture the many functions they perform in the industry. Minor categories (Minor1, Minor2) are more specific for companies that have more detailed functions (Minor1 is a larger category than Minor2). Minor categories figures (sales, etc.) can be aggregated to larger minor categories (Minor2 sums to Minor1) and major categories overall figures.

Software Publishing Industry (NAICS 51121)

NAICS 51121: Software Publishers. This industry comprises establishments primarily engaged in computer software publishing or publishing and reproduction. Establishments in this industry carry out operations necessary for producing and distributing computer software, such as designing, providing documentation, assisting in installation, and providing support services to software purchasers. These establishments may design, develop, and publish, or publish only.

Industry Establishments, Sales & Employment Trends

	Year					Percent Chg. Year-to-Year			
	2015	2016	2017	2018	2019	15-16	16-17	17-18	18-19
Establishments	23,755	23,182	22,815	23,434	24,292	-2.4%	-1.6%	2.7%	3.7%
Sales ($Millions)	188,481	204,163	221,744	247,523	277,087	8.3%	8.6%	11.6%	11.9%
Employment	373,854	364,838	359,054	368,800	382,306	-2.4%	-1.6%	2.7%	3.7%
Sales ($M)/Estab.	7.93	8.81	9.72	10.56	11.41	11.0%	10.4%	8.7%	8.0%
Sales ($)/Emp.	504,157	559,600	617,578	671,158	724,779	11.0%	10.4%	8.7%	8.0%

3-Year Trend – Estimated Number of Establishments

Year	Employee Size of Establishment									Total Employment
	1-4 Emps.	5-9 Emps.	10-19 Emps.	20-49 Emps.	50-99 Emps.	100-249 Emps.	250-499 Emps.	>500 Emps.	Non-Employer	
2017	4,111	1,262	1,185	1,250	687	482	183	153	13,596	22,815
2018	4,222	1,296	1,217	1,290	603	495	188	157	13,965	23,434
2019	4,377	1,344	1,262	1,338	625	513	195	163	14,476	24,292

3-Year Trend – Estimated Industry Sales ($Millions)

Year	Employee Size of Establishment									Total Employment
	1-4 Emps.	5-9 Emps.	10-19 Emps.	20-49 Emps.	50-99 Emps.	100-249 Emps.	250-499 Emps.	>500 Emps.	Non-Employer	
2017	2,994.7	2,416.5	5,706.9	16,011.3	16,441.0	36,406.6	46,687.1	94,028.6	1,050.9	221,743.7
2018	3,362.5	2,713.3	6,407.9	17,978.0	18,460.5	40,878.4	52,421.7	104,120.7	1,180.0	247,523.0
2019	3,793.2	3,060.9	7,228.6	20,280.7	20,825.0	46,114.4	59,136.1	115,317.2	1,331.1	277,087.3

3-Year Trend – Estimated Number of Employees

Year	Employee Size of Establishment									Total Employment
	1-4 Emps.	5-9 Emps.	10-19 Emps.	20-49 Emps.	50-99 Emps.	100-249 Emps.	250-499 Emps.	>500 Emps.	Non-Employer	
2017	10,276	7,319	16,118	37,812	34,857	60,796	53,362	124,917	13,596	359,054
2018	10,555	7,518	16,556	38,839	35,803	62,446	54,811	128,308	13,965	368,800
2019	10,942	7,793	17,162	40,261	37,114	64,733	56,818	133,007	14,476	382,306

© Barnes Reports: 2018 U.S. Industry & Market Outlook

Software Publishing Industry (NAICS 51121)

Sub-Industries – 2018 Estimated Industry Sales, Establishments & Employment

Sub-Industries	Category*	Establishments	Sales ($Mill)	Employment
Prepackaged software	Major1	19,502	192,205.4	257,203
Application computer software	Minor2	1,054	22,495.2	41,043
Business oriented computer software	Minor2	1,282	18,822.6	48,206
Educational computer software	Minor2	597	2,505.6	10,127
Home entertainment computer software	Minor2	136	9,402.0	2,121
Operating systems computer software	Minor2	255	1,621.4	3,653
Publisher's computer software	Minor2	444	318.0	4,248
Utility computer software	Minor2	109	136.1	2,011
Word processing computer software	Minor2	55	16.9	188

*Category-Major categories (Major1) are more general descriptions for companies that self-selected to capture the many functions they perform in the industry. Minor categories (Minor1, Minor2) are more specific for companies that have more detailed functions (Minor1 is a larger category than Minor2). Minor categories figures (sales, etc.) can be aggregated to larger minor categories (Minor2 sums to Minor1) and major categories overall figures.

MOTION PICTURES & VIDEO PRODUCTION INDUSTRY
(NAICS 51211)

NAICS 51211: Motion Picture and Video Production Industry. This industry comprises establishments primarily engaged in producing, or producing and distributing motion pictures, videos, television programs, or television and video commercials.

INDUSTRY ESTABLISHMENTS, SALES & EMPLOYMENT TRENDS

	Year					Percent Chg. Year-to-Year			
	2015	2016	2017	2018	2019	15-16	16-17	17-18	18-19
Establishments	35,138	35,391	35,973	37,012	38,433	0.7%	1.6%	2.9%	3.8%
Sales ($Millions)	57,042	60,469	64,703	69,827	75,905	6.0%	7.0%	7.9%	8.7%
Employment	140,242	141,253	143,576	147,724	153,394	0.7%	1.6%	2.9%	3.8%
Sales ($M)/Estab.	1.62	1.71	1.80	1.89	1.98	5.2%	5.3%	4.9%	4.7%
Sales ($)/Emp.	406,744	428,088	450,652	472,686	494,837	5.2%	5.3%	4.9%	4.7%

3-YEAR TREND – ESTIMATED NUMBER OF ESTABLISHMENTS

Year	Employee Size of Establishment									Total Employment
	1-4 Emps.	5-9 Emps.	10-19 Emps.	20-49 Emps.	50-99 Emps.	100-249 Emps.	250-499 Emps.	>500 Emps.	Non-Employer	
2017	12,187	1,238	605	388	136	88	33	38	21,260	35,973
2018	12,539	1,273	623	399	140	91	34	39	21,874	37,012
2019	13,020	1,322	646	415	145	94	35	40	22,714	38,433

3-YEAR TREND – ESTIMATED INDUSTRY SALES ($MILLIONS)

Year	Employee Size of Establishment									Total Employment
	1-4 Emps.	5-9 Emps.	10-19 Emps.	20-49 Emps.	50-99 Emps.	100-249 Emps.	250-499 Emps.	>500 Emps.	Non-Employer	
2017	8,833.7	2,358.1	2,898.8	4,920.4	3,795.6	6,614.8	8,295.7	25,239.6	1,745.9	64,702.6
2018	9,607.1	2,564.5	3,152.6	5,351.2	4,127.9	7,193.9	9,022.0	26,908.9	1,898.8	69,826.9
2019	10,547.8	2,815.6	3,461.2	5,875.1	4,532.1	7,898.3	9,905.4	28,784.7	2,084.7	75,904.9

3-YEAR TREND – ESTIMATED NUMBER OF EMPLOYEES

Year	Employee Size of Establishment									Total Employment
	1-4 Emps.	5-9 Emps.	10-19 Emps.	20-49 Emps.	50-99 Emps.	100-249 Emps.	250-499 Emps.	>500 Emps.	Non-Employer	
2017	30,467	7,179	8,229	11,679	8,088	11,102	9,530	36,041	21,260	143,576
2018	31,348	7,386	8,466	12,016	8,322	11,423	9,805	37,082	21,874	147,724
2019	32,551	7,670	8,791	12,478	8,641	11,862	10,182	38,505	22,714	153,394

© Barnes Reports: 2018 U.S. Industry & Market Outlook

MOTION PICTURES & VIDEO PRODUCTION INDUSTRY (NAICS 51211)

SUB-INDUSTRIES – 2018 ESTIMATED INDUSTRY SALES, ESTABLISHMENTS & EMPLOYMENT

Sub-Industries	Category*	Establishments	Sales ($Mill)	Employment
Motion picture and video production	Major1	20,320	58,313.8	58,810
Motion picture production	Minor1	1,187	872.2	6,958
Cartoon motion picture production	Minor2	137	1,313.7	759
Educational motion picture production	Minor2	177	128.4	1,221
Educational motion picture production, television	Minor2	99	143.7	786
Industrial motion picture production	Minor2	63	47.6	457
Motion picture production and distribution	Minor2	426	313.2	17,136
Motion picture production and distribution, television	Minor2	195	169.3	3,215
Non-theatrical motion picture production	Minor2	43	17.0	117
Non-theatrical motion picture production, television	Minor2	55	26.5	242
Religious motion picture production	Minor2	19	5.2	99
Television film production	Minor2	2,396	2,912.1	17,288
Training motion picture production	Minor2	56	45.8	280
Video production	Minor1	6,916	2,057.9	17,242
Music video production	Minor2	731	259.9	2,263
Video tape production	Minor2	1,524	1,305.3	8,707
Audio-visual program production	Minor2	1,977	1,238.4	8,064
Cartoon production, television	Minor2	87	27.6	880
Commercials, television: tape or film	Minor2	606	629.2	3,199

*Category-Major categories (Major1) are more general descriptions for companies that self-selected to capture the many functions they perform in the industry. Minor categories (Minor1, Minor2) are more specific for companies that have more detailed functions (Minor1 is a larger category than Minor2). Minor categories figures (sales, etc.) can be aggregated to larger minor categories (Minor2 sums to Minor1) and major categories overall figures.

MUSIC PUBLISHING INDUSTRY
(NAICS 51223)

NAICS 51223: Music Publishers. This U.S. industry comprises establishments known as music publishers. Establishments in this industry carry out design, editing, and marketing activities necessary for producing and distributing music books. These establishments may publish books in print, electronic, or audio form.

INDUSTRY ESTABLISHMENTS, SALES & EMPLOYMENT TRENDS

	Year					Percent Chg. Year-to-Year			
	2015	2016	2017	2018	2019	15-16	16-17	17-18	18-19
Establishments	3,009	3,156	3,334	3,403	3,505	4.9%	5.7%	2.1%	3.0%
Sales ($Millions)	2,941	3,143	3,401	3,563	3,779	6.9%	8.2%	4.8%	6.1%
Employment	8,452	8,866	9,367	9,559	9,845	4.9%	5.7%	2.1%	3.0%
Sales ($M)/Estab.	0.98	1.00	1.02	1.05	1.08	1.9%	2.4%	2.7%	3.0%
Sales ($)/Emp.	347,972	354,499	363,107	372,788	383,852	1.9%	2.4%	2.7%	3.0%

3-YEAR TREND – ESTIMATED NUMBER OF ESTABLISHMENTS

Year	Employee Size of Establishment									Total Employment
	1-4 Emps.	5-9 Emps.	10-19 Emps.	20-49 Emps.	50-99 Emps.	100-249 Emps.	250-499 Emps.	>500 Emps.	Non-Employer	
2017	596	82	58	24	10	9	3	1	2,551	3,334
2018	608	84	59	25	10	9	3	1	2,603	3,403
2019	627	86	61	26	10	9	3	1	2,681	3,505

3-YEAR TREND – ESTIMATED INDUSTRY SALES ($MILLIONS)

Year	Employee Size of Establishment									Total Employment
	1-4 Emps.	5-9 Emps.	10-19 Emps.	20-49 Emps.	50-99 Emps.	100-249 Emps.	250-499 Emps.	>500 Emps.	Non-Employer	
2017	404.5	146.2	258.4	289.4	260.2	623.5	788.0	485.7	145.1	3,401.0
2018	423.8	153.2	270.8	303.2	272.7	653.3	825.7	508.8	152.0	3,563.4
2019	449.5	162.5	287.2	321.6	289.2	692.8	875.7	539.3	161.2	3,779.0

3-YEAR TREND – ESTIMATED NUMBER OF EMPLOYEES

Year	Employee Size of Establishment									Total Employment
	1-4 Emps.	5-9 Emps.	10-19 Emps.	20-49 Emps.	50-99 Emps.	100-249 Emps.	250-499 Emps.	>500 Emps.	Non-Employer	
2017	1,491	476	784	734	592	1,118	967	654	2,551	9,367
2018	1,521	485	800	749	605	1,141	987	668	2,603	9,559
2019	1,567	500	824	771	623	1,175	1,017	688	2,681	9,845

© Barnes Reports: 2018 U.S. Industry & Market Outlook

MUSIC PUBLISHING INDUSTRY
(NAICS 51223)

Sub-Industries — 2018 Estimated Industry Sales, Establishments & Employment

Sub-Industries	Category*	Establishments	Sales ($Mill)	Employment
Book music: publishing only, not printed on site	Minor2	36	11.4	25
Book music: publishing and printing	Minor2	64	11.3	41
Song writings	Minor1	601	719.4	1,610
Music arranging and composing	Minor2	2,701	2,821.3	7,883

*Category-Major categories (Major1) are more general descriptions for companies that self-selected to capture the many functions they perform in the industry. Minor categories (Minor1, Minor2) are more specific for companies that have more detailed functions (Minor1 is a larger category than Minor2). Minor categories figures (sales, etc.) can be aggregated to larger minor categories (Minor2 sums to Minor1) and major categories overall figures.

Radio Broadcasting Industry
(NAICS 51511)

NAICS 51511: Radio Broadcasting . This industry comprises establishments primarily engaged in broadcasting audio signals. These establishments operate radio broadcasting studios and facilities for the transmission of aural programming by radio to the public, to affiliates, or to subscribers. The radio programs may include entertainment, news, talk shows, business data, or religious services.

Industry Establishments, Sales & Employment Trends

	Year					Percent Chg. Year-to-Year			
	2015	2016	2017	2018	2019	15-16	16-17	17-18	18-19
Establishments	11,041	11,363	11,794	11,670	11,653	2.9%	3.8%	-1.1%	-0.1%
Sales ($Millions)	13,452	14,132	15,050	15,327	15,794	5.1%	6.5%	1.8%	3.0%
Employment	88,826	91,418	94,884	93,884	93,752	2.9%	3.8%	-1.1%	-0.1%
Sales ($M)/Estab.	1.22	1.24	1.28	1.31	1.36	2.1%	2.6%	2.9%	3.2%
Sales ($)/Emp.	151,438	154,589	158,619	163,256	168,469	2.1%	2.6%	2.9%	3.2%

3-Year Trend – Estimated Number of Establishments

Year	Employee Size of Establishment									Total Employment
	1-4 Emps.	5-9 Emps.	10-19 Emps.	20-49 Emps.	50-99 Emps.	100-249 Emps.	250-499 Emps.	>500 Emps.	Non-Employer	
2017	2,222	1,271	1,172	933	245	75	11	7	5,859	11,794
2018	2,198	1,258	1,159	923	242	74	11	7	5,797	11,670
2019	2,195	1,256	1,158	921	242	74	11	7	5,789	11,653

3-Year Trend – Estimated Industry Sales ($Millions)

Year	Employee Size of Establishment									Total Employment
	1-4 Emps.	5-9 Emps.	10-19 Emps.	20-49 Emps.	50-99 Emps.	100-249 Emps.	250-499 Emps.	>500 Emps.	Non-Employer	
2017	582.6	876.1	2,030.9	4,278.0	2,466.8	2,032.2	978.5	1,372.8	432.5	15,050.4
2018	593.2	892.0	2,067.8	4,355.7	2,511.6	2,069.2	996.3	1,401.1	440.3	15,327.1
2019	611.3	919.2	2,130.8	4,488.3	2,588.0	2,132.2	1,026.6	1,444.2	453.7	15,794.3

3-Year Trend – Estimated Number of Employees

Year	Employee Size of Establishment									Total Employment
	1-4 Emps.	5-9 Emps.	10-19 Emps.	20-49 Emps.	50-99 Emps.	100-249 Emps.	250-499 Emps.	>500 Emps.	Non-Employer	
2017	5,555	7,373	15,937	28,069	14,530	9,429	3,107	5,025	5,859	94,884
2018	5,496	7,295	15,769	27,774	14,377	9,330	3,075	4,972	5,797	93,884
2019	5,488	7,285	15,747	27,734	14,357	9,316	3,070	4,965	5,789	93,752

© Barnes Reports: 2018 U.S. Industry & Market Outlook

RADIO BROADCASTING INDUSTRY
(NAICS 51511)

SUB-INDUSTRIES – 2018 ESTIMATED INDUSTRY SALES, ESTABLISHMENTS & EMPLOYMENT

Sub-Industries	Category*	Establishments	Sales ($Mill)	Employment
Radio broadcasting stations	Major1	9,701	14,837.9	85,649
Radio broadcasting stations, music format	Minor1	179	61.8	1,916
Big band	Minor2	53	7.2	109
Classical	Minor2	20	13.1	116
Contemporary	Minor2	28	13.1	504
Country	Minor2	43	56.6	432
Easy listening	Minor2	16	11.9	214
Gospel	Minor2	107	9.7	144
Jazz	Minor2	22	4.7	33
Rhythm and blues	Minor2	4	0.3	3
Rock	Minor2	136	14.6	259
Radio broadcasting stations, except music format	Minor1	52	12.6	190
Educational	Minor2	356	78.5	1,182
News	Minor2	104	20.9	612
Religious	Minor2	333	84.1	769
Sports	Minor2	416	83.0	1,353
Talk	Minor2	76	12.0	212
Ethnic programming	Minor2	24	5.3	185

*Category-Major categories (Major1) are more general descriptions for companies that self-selected to capture the many functions they perform in the industry. Minor categories (Minor1, Minor2) are more specific for companies that have more detailed functions (Minor1 is a larger category than Minor2). Minor categories figures (sales, etc.) can be aggregated to larger minor categories (Minor2 sums to Minor1) and major categories overall figures.

TELEVISION BROADCASTING SERVICES INDUSTRY
(NAICS 51512)

NAICS 51512: Television Broadcasting. This industry comprises establishments primarily engaged in broadcasting images together with sound. These establishments operate television broadcasting studios and facilities for the programming and transmission of programs to the public. These establishments also produce or transmit visual programming to affiliated broadcast television stations, which in turn broadcast the programs to the public on a predetermined schedule. Programming may originate in their own studios, from an affiliated network, or from external sources.

INDUSTRY ESTABLISHMENTS, SALES & EMPLOYMENT TRENDS

	Year					Percent Chg. Year-to-Year			
	2015	2016	2017	2018	2019	15-16	16-17	17-18	18-19
Establishments	4,310	4,238	4,204	4,228	4,291	-1.7%	-0.8%	0.6%	1.5%
Sales ($Millions)	37,920	36,732	36,080	35,990	36,350	-3.1%	-1.8%	-0.3%	1.0%
Employment	101,320	99,631	98,834	99,384	100,859	-1.7%	-0.8%	0.6%	1.5%
Sales ($M)/Estab.	8.80	8.67	8.58	8.51	8.47	-1.5%	-1.0%	-0.8%	-0.5%
Sales ($)/Emp.	374,260	368,681	365,060	362,126	360,406	-1.5%	-1.0%	-0.8%	-0.5%

3-YEAR TREND – ESTIMATED NUMBER OF ESTABLISHMENTS

Year	Employee Size of Establishment									Total
	1-4 Emps.	5-9 Emps.	10-19 Emps.	20-49 Emps.	50-99 Emps.	100-249 Emps.	250-499 Emps.	>500 Emps.	Non-Employer	Employment
2017	714	206	219	281	330	312	40	14	2,089	4,204
2018	718	207	221	282	332	314	40	14	2,100	4,228
2019	729	210	224	287	336	319	41	14	2,132	4,291

3-YEAR TREND – ESTIMATED INDUSTRY SALES ($MILLIONS)

Year	Employee Size of Establishment									Total
	1-4 Emps.	5-9 Emps.	10-19 Emps.	20-49 Emps.	50-99 Emps.	100-249 Emps.	250-499 Emps.	>500 Emps.	Non-Employer	Employment
2017	326.6	247.5	663.6	2,248.3	5,800.3	14,800.4	6,391.4	5,459.1	143.1	36,080.4
2018	326.0	247.0	662.3	2,243.8	5,788.6	14,770.4	6,378.4	5,430.4	142.8	35,989.6
2019	329.7	249.8	669.8	2,269.2	5,854.1	14,937.7	6,450.7	5,445.1	144.4	36,350.3

3-YEAR TREND – ESTIMATED NUMBER OF EMPLOYEES

Year	Employee Size of Establishment									Total
	1-4 Emps.	5-9 Emps.	10-19 Emps.	20-49 Emps.	50-99 Emps.	100-249 Emps.	250-499 Emps.	>500 Emps.	Non-Employer	Employment
2017	1,785	1,194	2,985	8,456	19,585	39,362	11,634	11,745	2,089	98,834
2018	1,795	1,200	3,002	8,503	19,694	39,581	11,699	11,810	2,100	99,384
2019	1,822	1,218	3,046	8,629	19,986	40,169	11,873	11,985	2,132	100,859

© Barnes Reports: 2018 U.S. Industry & Market Outlook

TELEVISION BROADCASTING SERVICES INDUSTRY (NAICS 51512)

Sub-Industries – 2018 Estimated Industry Sales, Establishments & Employment

Sub-Industries	Category*	Establishments	Sales ($Mill)	Employment
Television broadcasting stations	Major1	4,045	35,916.2	97,208
Television translator station	Minor2	182	73.4	2,176

*Category-Major categories (Major1) are more general descriptions for companies that self-selected to capture the many functions they perform in the industry. Minor categories (Minor1, Minor2) are more specific for companies that have more detailed functions (Minor1 is a larger category than Minor2). Minor categories figures (sales, etc.) can be aggregated to larger minor categories (Minor2 sums to Minor1) and major categories overall figures.

Cable Television Networks Industry (NAICS 51521)

NAICS 51521: Cable Networks. This industry comprises establishments primarily engaged in operating studios and facilities for the broadcasting of programs on a subscription or fee basis. The broadcast programming is typically narrowcast in nature (e.g., limited format, such as news, sports, education, or youth-oriented). These establishments produce programming in their own facilities or acquire programming from external sources. The programming material is usually delivered to a third party, such as cable systems or direct-to-home satellite systems, for transmission to viewers.

Industry Establishments, Sales & Employment Trends

	Year					Percent Chg. Year-to-Year			
	2015	2016	2017	2018	2019	15-16	16-17	17-18	18-19
Establishments	1,419	1,493	1,583	1,630	1,695	5.3%	6.0%	3.0%	4.0%
Sales ($Millions)	60,810	66,832	74,005	80,258	87,621	9.9%	10.7%	8.4%	9.2%
Employment	42,341	44,564	47,226	48,648	50,575	5.3%	6.0%	3.0%	4.0%
Sales ($M)/Estab.	42.86	44.75	46.76	49.23	51.70	4.4%	4.5%	5.3%	5.0%
Sales ($)/Emp.	1,436,200	1,499,679	1,567,050	1,649,766	1,732,475	4.4%	4.5%	5.3%	5.0%

3-Year Trend – Estimated Number of Establishments

Year	Employee Size of Establishment									Total Employment
	1-4 Emps.	5-9 Emps.	10-19 Emps.	20-49 Emps.	50-99 Emps.	100-249 Emps.	250-499 Emps.	>500 Emps.	Non-Employer	
2017	292	125	104	112	54	61	22	27	786	1,583
2018	301	129	107	115	55	63	23	28	810	1,630
2019	313	134	111	119	57	66	24	29	842	1,695

3-Year Trend – Estimated Industry Sales ($Millions)

Year	Employee Size of Establishment									Total Employment
	1-4 Emps.	5-9 Emps.	10-19 Emps.	20-49 Emps.	50-99 Emps.	100-249 Emps.	250-499 Emps.	>500 Emps.	Non-Employer	
2017	526.8	591.9	1,236.0	3,517.9	3,711.8	11,463.0	14,049.2	38,846.2	62.3	74,005.2
2018	576.1	647.3	1,351.6	3,846.9	4,059.0	12,535.3	15,363.4	41,810.0	68.2	80,257.9
2019	635.7	714.2	1,491.4	4,244.7	4,478.7	13,831.3	16,951.9	45,197.5	75.2	87,620.7

3-Year Trend – Estimated Number of Employees

Year	Employee Size of Establishment									Total Employment
	1-4 Emps.	5-9 Emps.	10-19 Emps.	20-49 Emps.	50-99 Emps.	100-249 Emps.	250-499 Emps.	>500 Emps.	Non-Employer	
2017	731	725	1,411	3,357	3,180	7,736	6,489	22,812	786	47,226
2018	753	746	1,453	3,458	3,276	7,969	6,685	23,499	810	48,648
2019	782	776	1,511	3,595	3,406	8,284	6,949	24,430	842	50,575

© Barnes Reports: 2018 U.S. Industry & Market Outlook

CABLE TELEVISION NETWORKS INDUSTRY
(NAICS 51521)

SUB-INDUSTRIES — 2018 ESTIMATED INDUSTRY SALES, ESTABLISHMENTS & EMPLOYMENT

Sub-Industries	Category*	Establishments	Sales ($Mill)	Employment
Cable and other pay television services	Major1	460	39,122.7	16,609
Cable television services	Minor2	983	27,935.5	27,551
Closed circuit television services	Minor2	10	25.1	253
Direct broadcast satellite services (DBS)	Minor2	78	12,620.5	2,680
Multipoint distribution systems services (MDS)	Minor2	9	11.6	64
Satellite master antenna systems services (SMATV)	Minor2	77	267.0	785
Subscription television services	Minor2	13	275.4	706

*Category-Major categories (Major1) are more general descriptions for companies that self-selected to capture the many functions they perform in the industry. Minor categories (Minor1, Minor2) are more specific for companies that have more detailed functions (Minor1 is a larger category than Minor2). Minor categories figures (sales, etc.) can be aggregated to larger minor categories (Minor2 sums to Minor1) and major categories overall figures.

Wired Telecommunications Carriers Industry (NAICS 51711)

NAICS 51711: Wired Telecommunications Carriers. This industry comprises establishments engaged in (1) operating and maintaining switching and transmission facilities to provide direct communications via landlines, microwave, or a combination of landlines and satellite linkups or (2) furnishing telegraph and other nonvocal communications using their own facilities.

Industry Establishments, Sales & Employment Trends

	Year					Percent Chg. Year-to-Year			
	2015	2016	2017	2018	2019	15-16	16-17	17-18	18-19
Establishments	42,532	42,148	42,145	42,837	43,942	-0.9%	0.0%	1.6%	2.6%
Sales ($Millions)	366,844	362,311	362,992	370,291	382,459	-1.2%	0.2%	2.0%	3.3%
Employment	675,623	669,515	669,476	680,467	698,020	-0.9%	0.0%	1.6%	2.6%
Sales ($M)/Estab.	8.63	8.60	8.61	8.64	8.70	-0.3%	0.2%	0.4%	0.7%
Sales ($)/Emp.	542,972	541,154	542,203	544,171	547,920	-0.3%	0.2%	0.4%	0.7%

3-Year Trend – Estimated Number of Establishments

Year	Employee Size of Establishment									Total Employment
	1-4 Emps.	5-9 Emps.	10-19 Emps.	20-49 Emps.	50-99 Emps.	100-249 Emps.	250-499 Emps.	>500 Emps.	Non-Employer	
2017	19,113	5,173	3,978	3,283	1,543	941	314	183	7,618	42,145
2018	19,426	5,257	4,044	3,337	1,568	957	319	186	7,743	42,837
2019	19,927	5,393	4,148	3,423	1,609	981	328	191	7,942	43,942

3-Year Trend – Estimated Industry Sales ($Millions)

Year	Employee Size of Establishment									Total Employment
	1-4 Emps.	5-9 Emps.	10-19 Emps.	20-49 Emps.	50-99 Emps.	100-249 Emps.	250-499 Emps.	>500 Emps.	Non-Employer	
2017	13,350.0	9,496.2	18,367.8	40,116.8	41,444.1	68,153.1	76,649.3	94,768.9	645.6	362,991.9
2018	13,636.2	9,699.7	18,761.5	40,976.8	42,332.5	69,614.0	78,292.3	96,318.1	659.5	370,290.5
2019	14,112.5	10,038.5	19,416.8	42,408.0	43,811.0	72,045.5	81,026.9	98,917.7	682.5	382,459.4

3-Year Trend – Estimated Number of Employees

Year	Employee Size of Establishment									Total Employment
	1-4 Emps.	5-9 Emps.	10-19 Emps.	20-49 Emps.	50-99 Emps.	100-249 Emps.	250-499 Emps.	>500 Emps.	Non-Employer	
2017	47,781	30,001	54,107	98,814	91,644	118,705	91,376	129,430	7,618	669,476
2018	48,566	30,493	54,995	100,436	93,149	120,654	92,876	131,554	7,743	680,467
2019	49,819	31,280	56,414	103,027	95,552	123,766	95,272	134,948	7,942	698,020

© Barnes Reports: 2018 U.S. Industry & Market Outlook

WIRED TELECOMMUNICATIONS CARRIERS INDUSTRY (NAICS 51711)

SUB-INDUSTRIES – 2018 ESTIMATED INDUSTRY SALES, ESTABLISHMENTS & EMPLOYMENT

Sub-Industries	Category*	Establishments	Sales ($Mill)	Employment
Telephone communication, except radio	Major1	10,837	104,475.3	279,994
Local and long distance telephone communications	Minor1	3,214	194,115.6	103,175
Data telephone communications	Minor2	602	1,806.7	14,821
Local telephone communications	Minor2	1,897	38,183.4	96,078
Long distance telephone communications	Minor2	1,664	4,503.3	32,170
Voice telephone communications	Minor2	637	5,495.1	9,770
Online service providers	Minor1	6,528	7,249.9	42,223
Internet connectivity services	Minor2	6,503	6,421.3	33,673
Internet host services	Minor2	8,418	5,179.2	47,298
Proprietary online service networks	Minor2	1,118	438.9	6,996
Telephone cable service, land or submarine	Minor2	206	409.1	1,622
Wire telephone	Minor2	154	111.8	2,008
Telephone/video communications	Minor2	287	530.1	5,822
Telephone communications broker	Minor2	772	1,370.9	4,818

*Category-Major categories (Major1) are more general descriptions for companies that self-selected to capture the many functions they perform in the industry. Minor categories (Minor1, Minor2) are more specific for companies that have more detailed functions (Minor1 is a larger category than Minor2). Minor categories figures (sales, etc.) can be aggregated to larger minor categories (Minor2 sums to Minor1) and major categories overall figures.

WIRELESS TELECOMMUNICATIONS CARRIERS
(NAICS 51721)

NAICS 51721: Wireless Telecommunications Carriers. This industry comprises establishments primarily engaged in providing two-way radiotelephone communications services, such as cellular telephone services. This business also includes establishments primarily engaged in providing telephone paging and beeper services and those engaged in leasing telephone lines or other methods of telephone transmission, such as optical fiber lines and microwave or satellite facilities, and reselling the use of such methods to others.

INDUSTRY ESTABLISHMENTS, SALES & EMPLOYMENT TRENDS

	Year					Percent Chg. Year-to-Year			
	2015	2016	2017	2018	2019	15-16	16-17	17-18	18-19
Establishments	14,488	14,693	15,037	15,626	16,389	1.4%	2.3%	3.9%	4.9%
Sales ($Millions)	130,652	140,891	153,431	169,215	188,111	7.8%	8.9%	10.3%	11.2%
Employment	221,430	224,575	229,825	238,834	250,486	1.4%	2.3%	3.9%	4.9%
Sales ($M)/Estab.	9.02	9.59	10.20	10.83	11.48	6.3%	6.4%	6.1%	6.0%
Sales ($)/Emp.	590,038	627,366	667,600	708,507	750,982	6.3%	6.4%	6.1%	6.0%

3-YEAR TREND – ESTIMATED NUMBER OF ESTABLISHMENTS

Year	Employee Size of Establishment									Total Employment
	1-4 Emps.	5-9 Emps.	10-19 Emps.	20-49 Emps.	50-99 Emps.	100-249 Emps.	250-499 Emps.	>500 Emps.	Non-Employer	
2017	4,433	2,209	3,690	1,516	168	144	75	84	2,718	15,037
2018	4,607	2,295	3,834	1,576	175	150	78	87	2,824	15,626
2019	4,831	2,407	4,021	1,653	183	157	81	92	2,962	16,389

3-YEAR TREND – ESTIMATED INDUSTRY SALES ($MILLIONS)

Year	Employee Size of Establishment									Total Employment
	1-4 Emps.	5-9 Emps.	10-19 Emps.	20-49 Emps.	50-99 Emps.	100-249 Emps.	250-499 Emps.	>500 Emps.	Non-Employer	
2017	4,026.1	5,272.4	22,149.9	24,094.4	5,872.9	13,581.2	23,710.6	54,461.1	262.1	153,430.8
2018	4,455.3	5,834.5	24,511.3	26,663.2	6,499.0	15,029.1	26,238.4	59,694.4	290.0	169,215.4
2019	4,972.8	6,512.2	27,358.3	29,760.1	7,253.8	16,774.7	29,286.0	65,869.0	323.7	188,110.6

3-YEAR TREND – ESTIMATED NUMBER OF EMPLOYEES

Year	Employee Size of Establishment									Total Employment
	1-4 Emps.	5-9 Emps.	10-19 Emps.	20-49 Emps.	50-99 Emps.	100-249 Emps.	250-499 Emps.	>500 Emps.	Non-Employer	
2017	11,082	12,810	50,181	45,643	9,988	18,192	21,739	57,471	2,718	229,825
2018	11,517	13,312	52,148	47,432	10,379	18,906	22,591	59,724	2,824	238,834
2019	12,079	13,962	54,692	49,747	10,886	19,828	23,693	62,638	2,962	250,486

© Barnes Reports: 2018 U.S. Industry & Market Outlook

Wireless Telecommunications Carriers (NAICS 51721)

Sub-Industries – 2018 Estimated Industry Sales, Establishments & Employment

Sub-Industries	Category*	Establishments	Sales ($Mill)	Employment
Radiotelephone communication	Major1	2,381	1,195.4	97,384
Cellular telephone services	Minor2	12,546	167,463.0	133,263
Paging services	Minor2	550	430.0	6,669
Radio pager (beeper) communication services	Minor2	150	126.9	1,517

*Category-Major categories (Major1) are more general descriptions for companies that self-selected to capture the many functions they perform in the industry. Minor categories (Minor1, Minor2) are more specific for companies that have more detailed functions (Minor1 is a larger category than Minor2). Minor categories figures (sales, etc.) can be aggregated to larger minor categories (Minor2 sums to Minor1) and major categories overall figures.

DATA PROCESSING SERVICES INDUSTRY
(NAICS 51821)

NAICS 51821: Data Processing Services. This industry comprises establishments primarily engaged in providing computer processing and data preparation services. The service may consist of complete processing and preparation of reports from data supplied by the customer or a specialized service, such as data entry or making data processing equipment available on an hourly or time-sharing basis.

INDUSTRY ESTABLISHMENTS, SALES & EMPLOYMENT TRENDS

	Year					Percent Chg. Year-to-Year			
	2015	2016	2017	2018	2019	15-16	16-17	17-18	18-19
Establishments	36,708	38,283	40,230	41,599	43,412	4.3%	5.1%	3.4%	4.4%
Sales ($Millions)	95,260	97,157	100,346	102,574	106,124	2.0%	3.3%	2.2%	3.5%
Employment	463,534	483,420	508,010	525,300	548,191	4.3%	5.1%	3.4%	4.4%
Sales ($M)/Estab.	2.60	2.54	2.49	2.47	2.44	-2.2%	-1.7%	-1.1%	-0.9%
Sales ($)/Emp.	205,508	200,979	197,528	195,267	193,589	-2.2%	-1.7%	-1.1%	-0.9%

3-YEAR TREND – ESTIMATED NUMBER OF ESTABLISHMENTS

Year	Employee Size of Establishment									Total Employment
	1-4 Emps.	5-9 Emps.	10-19 Emps.	20-49 Emps.	50-99 Emps.	100-249 Emps.	250-499 Emps.	>500 Emps.	Non-Employer	
2017	6,949	2,135	1,803	1,905	903	764	266	179	25,326	40,230
2018	7,186	2,208	1,864	1,970	934	790	275	185	26,188	41,599
2019	7,499	2,304	1,945	2,055	974	824	287	193	27,330	43,412

3-YEAR TREND – ESTIMATED INDUSTRY SALES ($MILLIONS)

Year	Employee Size of Establishment									Total Employment
	1-4 Emps.	5-9 Emps.	10-19 Emps.	20-49 Emps.	50-99 Emps.	100-249 Emps.	250-499 Emps.	>500 Emps.	Non-Employer	
2017	1,695.2	1,368.8	2,906.8	8,129.0	8,471.9	19,314.1	22,695.3	34,058.7	1,706.4	100,346.3
2018	1,742.0	1,406.5	2,986.9	8,352.9	8,705.3	19,846.2	23,320.6	34,459.9	1,753.5	102,573.8
2019	1,813.9	1,464.6	3,110.2	8,697.9	9,064.8	20,665.8	24,283.6	35,196.9	1,825.9	106,123.6

3-YEAR TREND – ESTIMATED NUMBER OF EMPLOYEES

Year	Employee Size of Establishment									Total Employment
	1-4 Emps.	5-9 Emps.	10-19 Emps.	20-49 Emps.	50-99 Emps.	100-249 Emps.	250-499 Emps.	>500 Emps.	Non-Employer	
2017	17,374	12,382	24,519	57,333	53,642	96,325	77,471	143,638	25,326	508,010
2018	17,965	12,804	25,353	59,285	55,468	99,603	80,108	148,526	26,188	525,300
2019	18,748	13,362	26,458	61,868	57,885	103,944	83,599	154,998	27,330	548,191

© Barnes Reports: 2018 U.S. Industry & Market Outlook

Data Processing Services Industry (NAICS 51821)

Sub-Industries – 2018 Estimated Industry Sales, Establishments & Employment

Sub-Industries	Category*	Establishments	Sales ($Mill)	Employment
Data processing and preparation	Major1	7,997	30,884.1	141,932
Computer processing services	Minor1	656	445.5	25,309
Calculating service (computer)	Minor2	94	58.5	1,236
Computer graphics service	Minor2	26,314	7,215.5	91,099
Computer time-sharing	Minor2	137	73.4	2,246
Service bureau, computer	Minor2	403	228.1	7,343
Data entry service	Minor2	1,017	3,644.2	17,691
Data processing service	Minor2	4,345	59,365.8	230,527
Data verification service	Minor2	202	351.8	2,733
Keypunch service	Minor2	40	35.4	568
Optical scanning data service	Minor2	373	227.5	3,859
Tabulating service	Minor2	22	44.1	758

*Category-Major categories (Major1) are more general descriptions for companies that self-selected to capture the many functions they perform in the industry. Minor categories (Minor1, Minor2) are more specific for companies that have more detailed functions (Minor1 is a larger category than Minor2). Minor categories figures (sales, etc.) can be aggregated to larger minor categories (Minor2 sums to Minor1) and major categories overall figures.

COMMERCIAL BANKING INDUSTRY
(NAICS 52211)

NAICS 52211: Commercial Banking. This industry comprises commercial banks and trust companies (accepting deposits) chartered under the National Bank Act. Trust companies engaged in fiduciary business, but not regularly engaged in deposit banking, are classified in 6091.

INDUSTRY ESTABLISHMENTS, SALES & EMPLOYMENT TRENDS

	Year					Percent Chg. Year-to-Year			
	2015	2016	2017	2018	2019	15-16	16-17	17-18	18-19
Establishments	93,949	94,491	95,650	96,563	98,408	0.6%	1.2%	1.0%	1.9%
Sales ($Millions)	469,400	479,263	494,716	510,738	533,143	2.1%	3.2%	3.2%	4.4%
Employment	1,383,826	1,391,808	1,408,871	1,422,319	1,449,502	0.6%	1.2%	1.0%	1.9%
Sales ($M)/Estab.	5.00	5.07	5.17	5.29	5.42	1.5%	2.0%	2.3%	2.4%
Sales ($)/Emp.	339,205	344,346	351,144	359,088	367,811	1.5%	2.0%	2.3%	2.4%

3-YEAR TREND – ESTIMATED NUMBER OF ESTABLISHMENTS

Year	Employee Size of Establishment									Total Employment
	1-4 Emps.	5-9 Emps.	10-19 Emps.	20-49 Emps.	50-99 Emps.	100-249 Emps.	250-499 Emps.	>500 Emps.	Non-Employer	
2016	23,482	30,363	20,612	7,624	1,799	893	363	346	2,167	95,650
2017	23,707	38,729	20,809	7,696	1,816	901	367	349	2,188	96,563
2018	24,160	39,469	21,207	7,843	1,851	919	374	356	2,230	98,408

3-YEAR TREND – ESTIMATED INDUSTRY SALES ($MILLIONS)

Year	Employee Size of Establishment									Total Employment
	1-4 Emps.	5-9 Emps.	10-19 Emps.	20-49 Emps.	50-99 Emps.	100-249 Emps.	250-499 Emps.	>500 Emps.	Non-Employer	
2016	11,946.2	51,295.7	69,309.1	67,850.2	35,195.8	47,080.6	64,594.8	147,308.3	135.5	494,716.1
2017	12,351.9	53,037.8	71,663.0	70,154.6	36,391.1	48,679.6	66,788.6	151,530.8	140.1	510,737.5
2018	12,932.6	55,531.2	75,032.0	73,452.7	38,101.9	50,968.1	69,928.4	157,049.0	146.7	533,142.6

3-YEAR TREND – ESTIMATED NUMBER OF EMPLOYEES

Year	Employee Size of Establishment									Total Employment
	1-4 Emps.	5-9 Emps.	10-19 Emps.	20-49 Emps.	50-99 Emps.	100-249 Emps.	250-499 Emps.	>500 Emps.	Non-Employer	
2016	58,706	222,505	280,329	229,468	106,859	112,591	105,731	290,514	2,167	1,408,871
2017	59,266	224,629	283,005	231,658	107,879	113,666	106,740	293,287	2,188	1,422,319
2018	60,399	228,922	288,413	236,086	109,941	115,838	108,780	298,893	2,230	1,449,502

COMMERCIAL BANKING INDUSTRY
(NAICS 52211)

SUB-INDUSTRIES – 2018 ESTIMATED INDUSTRY SALES, ESTABLISHMENTS & EMPLOYMENT

Sub-Industries	Category*	Establishments	Sales ($Mill)	Employment
National commercial banks	Major1	30,663	168,541.8	445,245
National trust companies with deposits, commercial	Minor2	1,524	1,704.0	28,862
State commercial banks	Major1	58,775	319,852.0	845,422
State trust companies accepting deposits, commercial	Minor2	5,600	20,639.7	102,791

*Category-Major categories (Major1) are more general descriptions for companies that self-selected to capture the many functions they perform in the industry. Minor categories (Minor1, Minor2) are more specific for companies that have more detailed functions (Minor1 is a larger category than Minor2). Minor categories figures (sales, etc.) can be aggregated to larger minor categories (Minor2 sums to Minor1) and major categories overall figures.

Mortgage & Non-Mortgage Loan Brokers
(NAICS 52231)

NAICS 52231: Mortgage & Non-Mortgage Loan Brokers. This industry comprises establishments primarily engaged in arranging loans for others. These establishments operate mostly on a commission or fee basis and do not ordinarily have any continuing relationship with either borrower or lender.

Industry Establishments, Sales & Employment Trends

	Year					Percent Chg. Year-to-Year			
	2015	2016	2017	2018	2019	15-16	16-17	17-18	18-19
Establishments	8,853	8,271	7,565	7,430	7,367	-6.6%	-8.5%	-1.8%	-0.9%
Sales ($Millions)	9,650	8,868	8,045	7,804	7,665	-8.1%	-9.3%	-3.0%	-1.8%
Employment	44,458	41,534	37,989	37,313	36,996	-6.6%	-8.5%	-1.8%	-0.9%
Sales ($M)/Estab.	1.09	1.07	1.06	1.05	1.04	-1.6%	-0.8%	-1.2%	-0.9%
Sales ($)/Emp.	217,066	213,506	211,765	209,144	207,193	-1.6%	-0.8%	-1.2%	-0.9%

3-Year Trend – Estimated Number of Establishments

Year	Employee Size of Establishment									Total Employment
	1-4 Emps.	5-9 Emps.	10-19 Emps.	20-49 Emps.	50-99 Emps.	100-249 Emps.	250-499 Emps.	>500 Emps.	Non-Employer	
2016	4,807	793	305	160	46	29	7	3	1,416	7,565
2017	4,721	779	300	157	45	29	7	3	1,391	7,430
2018	4,681	772	297	156	45	28	7	2	1,379	7,367

3-Year Trend – Estimated Industry Sales ($Millions)

Year	Employee Size of Establishment									Total Employment
	1-4 Emps.	5-9 Emps.	10-19 Emps.	20-49 Emps.	50-99 Emps.	100-249 Emps.	250-499 Emps.	>500 Emps.	Non-Employer	
2016	1,754.5	760.8	736.0	1,020.4	647.8	1,099.2	871.7	1,046.9	107.5	8,044.8
2017	1,698.7	736.6	712.6	988.0	627.1	1,064.2	844.0	1,028.4	104.1	7,803.8
2018	1,667.0	722.8	699.3	969.5	615.4	1,044.4	828.2	1,016.3	102.1	7,665.2

3-Year Trend – Estimated Number of Employees

Year	Employee Size of Establishment									Total Employment
	1-4 Emps.	5-9 Emps.	10-19 Emps.	20-49 Emps.	50-99 Emps.	100-249 Emps.	250-499 Emps.	>500 Emps.	Non-Employer	
2016	12,016	4,599	4,149	4,810	2,741	3,664	1,989	2,606	1,416	37,989
2017	11,802	4,517	4,075	4,724	2,692	3,598	1,953	2,560	1,391	37,313
2018	11,702	4,479	4,040	4,684	2,669	3,568	1,937	2,538	1,379	36,996

© Barnes Reports: 2018 U.S. Industry & Market Outlook

MORTGAGE & NON-MORTGAGE LOAN BROKERS (NAICS 52231)

Sub-Industries — 2018 Estimated Industry Sales, Establishments & Employment

Sub-Industries	Category*	Establishments	Sales ($Mill)	Employment
Loan brokers	Major1	1,844	2,188.8	7,994
Agents, farm or business loan	Minor2	31	257.1	117
Brokers, farm or business loan	Minor2	61	23.0	323
Loan agents	Minor2	594	239.0	2,198
Mortgage brokers arranging for loans, using money of oth	Minor2	4,901	5,095.9	26,680

*Category-Major categories (Major1) are more general descriptions for companies that self-selected to capture the many functions they perform in the industry. Minor categories (Minor1, Minor2) are more specific for companies that have more detailed functions (Minor1 is a larger category than Minor2). Minor categories figures (sales, etc.) can be aggregated to larger minor categories (Minor2 sums to Minor1) and major categories overall figures.

INVESTMENT BANKING & SECURITIES DEALING (NAICS 52311)

NAICS 52311: Investment Banking & Securities Dealing. This industry compromises establishments primarily engaged in the purchase, sale, and brokerage of securities; and those, generally known as investment bankers, primarily engaged in originating, underwriting, and distributing issues of securities. Establishments primarily engaged in issuing shares of mutual and money market funds, unit investment trusts, and face amount certificates are classified in 6722 or 6726.

Industry Establishments, Sales & Employment Trends

	Year					Percent Chg. Year-to-Year			
	2015	2016	2017	2018	2019	15-16	16-17	17-18	18-19
Establishments	5,532	5,313	5,123	4,997	4,921	-4.0%	-3.6%	-2.4%	-1.5%
Sales ($Millions)	97,518	106,967	116,752	127,272	138,632	9.7%	9.1%	9.0%	8.9%
Employment	70,717	67,918	65,486	63,884	62,912	-4.0%	-3.6%	-2.4%	-1.5%
Sales ($M)/Estab.	17.63	20.13	22.79	25.47	28.17	14.2%	13.2%	11.7%	10.6%
Sales ($)/Emp.	1,378,985	1,574,955	1,782,844	1,992,230	2,203,603	14.2%	13.2%	11.7%	10.6%

3-Year Trend – Estimated Number of Establishments

Year	Employee Size of Establishment									Total Employment
	1-4 Emps.	5-9 Emps.	10-19 Emps.	20-49 Emps.	50-99 Emps.	100-249 Emps.	250-499 Emps.	>500 Emps.	Non-Employer	
2016	2,207	503	275	169	70	66	28	27	1,778	5,123
2017	2,153	491	268	165	69	64	27	26	1,734	4,997
2018	2,120	483	264	163	68	63	27	26	1,708	4,921

3-Year Trend – Estimated Industry Sales ($Millions)

Year	Employee Size of Establishment									Total Employment
	1-4 Emps.	5-9 Emps.	10-19 Emps.	20-49 Emps.	50-99 Emps.	100-249 Emps.	250-499 Emps.	>500 Emps.	Non-Employer	
2016	4,720.2	2,827.0	3,888.4	6,341.6	5,789.4	14,576.9	20,759.5	57,374.8	473.8	116,751.7
2017	5,099.3	3,054.0	4,200.6	6,850.9	6,254.3	15,747.4	22,426.4	63,127.0	511.9	127,271.7
2018	5,523.0	3,307.8	4,549.7	7,420.2	6,774.0	17,056.1	24,290.1	69,156.8	554.4	138,632.1

3-Year Trend – Estimated Number of Employees

Year	Employee Size of Establishment									Total Employment
	1-4 Emps.	5-9 Emps.	10-19 Emps.	20-49 Emps.	50-99 Emps.	100-249 Emps.	250-499 Emps.	>500 Emps.	Non-Employer	
2016	5,517	2,916	3,740	5,101	4,180	8,291	8,081	25,881	1,778	65,486
2017	5,382	2,845	3,649	4,976	4,078	8,088	7,884	25,248	1,734	63,884
2018	5,300	2,802	3,593	4,900	4,016	7,965	7,764	24,863	1,708	62,912

© Barnes Reports: 2018 U.S. Industry & Market Outlook

INVESTMENT BANKING & SECURITIES DEALING (NAICS 52311)

SUB-INDUSTRIES – 2018 ESTIMATED INDUSTRY SALES, ESTABLISHMENTS & EMPLOYMENT

Sub-Industries	Category*	Establishments	Sales ($Mill)	Employment
Flotation companies	Minor1	20	234.8	222
Distributors, security	Minor2	75	451.0	532
Investment bankers	Minor2	967	54,925.9	18,736
Investment certificate sales	Minor2	24	206.3	158
Investment firm, general brokerage	Minor2	1,558	24,689.1	21,854
Securities flotation companies	Minor2	309	780.0	1,465
Syndicate shares (real estate, entertainment, equip.) sale	Minor2	34	117.4	360
Underwriters, security	Minor2	149	29,230.7	1,797
Mineral, oil, and gas leasing and royalty dealers	Minor1	45	383.6	417
Mineral leasing dealers	Minor2	16	73.2	73
Mineral royalties dealers	Minor2	8	1,367.6	43
Oil and gas lease brokers	Minor2	184	1,418.7	1,130
Oil royalties dealers	Minor2	48	187.7	170
Mortgages, buying and selling	Minor2	1,257	7,842.8	9,669
Mutual funds, selling by independent salesperson	Minor2	303	5,362.8	7,257

*Category-Major categories (Major1) are more general descriptions for companies that self-selected to capture the many functions they perform in the industry. Minor categories (Minor1, Minor2) are more specific for companies that have more detailed functions (Minor1 is a larger category than Minor2). Minor categories figures (sales, etc.) can be aggregated to larger minor categories (Minor2 sums to Minor1) and major categories overall figures.

Securities Brokerage Industry
(NAICS 52312)

NAICS 52312: Securities Brokerage Industry. This industry comprises establishments primarily engaged in the purchase, sale, and brokerage of securities; and those, generally known as investment bankers, primarily engaged in originating, underwriting, and distributing issues of securities. Establishments primarily engaged in issuing shares of mutual and money market funds, unit investment trusts, and face amount certificates are classified in 6722 or 6726.

Industry Establishments, Sales & Employment Trends

	Year					Percent Chg. Year-to-Year			
	2015	2016	2017	2018	2019	15-16	16-17	17-18	18-19
Establishments	40,470	42,521	44,736	46,039	47,829	5.1%	5.2%	2.9%	3.9%
Sales ($Millions)	140,647	154,395	170,241	184,139	200,957	9.8%	10.3%	8.2%	9.1%
Employment	303,446	318,826	335,432	345,203	358,624	5.1%	5.2%	2.9%	3.9%
Sales ($M)/Estab.	3.48	3.63	3.81	4.00	4.20	4.5%	4.8%	5.1%	5.0%
Sales ($)/Emp.	463,499	484,261	507,526	533,423	560,357	4.5%	4.8%	5.1%	5.0%

3-Year Trend – Estimated Number of Establishments

Year	Employee Size of Establishment									Total Employment
	1-4 Emps.	5-9 Emps.	10-19 Emps.	20-49 Emps.	50-99 Emps.	100-249 Emps.	250-499 Emps.	>500 Emps.	Non-Employer	
2016	32,625	3,429	2,273	1,635	631	270	83	64	3,726	44,736
2017	33,575	3,529	2,339	1,683	650	278	85	66	3,835	46,039
2018	34,881	3,666	2,430	1,748	675	288	89	69	3,984	47,829

3-Year Trend – Estimated Industry Sales ($Millions)

Year	Employee Size of Establishment									Total Employment
	1-4 Emps.	5-9 Emps.	10-19 Emps.	20-49 Emps.	50-99 Emps.	100-249 Emps.	250-499 Emps.	>500 Emps.	Non-Employer	
2016	25,342.4	7,000.7	11,668.6	22,217.6	18,855.3	21,715.8	22,497.5	40,223.6	719.0	170,240.7
2017	27,510.5	7,599.7	12,666.9	24,118.4	20,468.5	23,573.7	24,422.2	42,999.0	780.6	184,139.3
2018	30,163.3	8,332.5	13,888.3	26,444.1	22,442.2	25,846.8	26,777.2	46,207.3	855.8	200,957.4

3-Year Trend – Estimated Number of Employees

Year	Employee Size of Establishment									Total Employment
	1-4 Emps.	5-9 Emps.	10-19 Emps.	20-49 Emps.	50-99 Emps.	100-249 Emps.	250-499 Emps.	>500 Emps.	Non-Employer	
2016	81,563	19,888	30,909	49,211	37,493	34,012	24,117	54,514	3,726	335,432
2017	83,938	20,467	31,809	50,644	38,585	35,002	24,820	56,102	3,835	345,203
2018	87,202	21,263	33,046	52,613	40,085	36,363	25,785	58,283	3,984	358,624

© Barnes Reports: 2018 U.S. Industry & Market Outlook

SECURITIES BROKERAGE INDUSTRY
(NAICS 52312)

SUB-INDUSTRIES – 2018 ESTIMATED INDUSTRY SALES, ESTABLISHMENTS & EMPLOYMENT

Sub-Industries	Category*	Establishments	Sales ($Mill)	Employment
Security brokers and dealers	Major1	25,219	102,150.5	152,500
Security brokers and dealers	Minor1	7,299	19,655.3	64,568
Bond dealers and brokers	Minor2	640	4,851.8	6,257
Brokers, security	Minor2	6,978	40,346.0	65,420
Dealers, security	Minor2	595	5,615.7	16,707
Floor traders, security	Minor2	47	144.6	389
Note brokers	Minor2	445	108.4	573
Stock brokers and dealers	Minor2	4,261	10,891.4	33,996
Stock option dealers	Minor2	109	90.8	1,237
Tax certificate dealers	Minor2	56	65.4	416
Traders, security	Minor2	391	219.4	3,141

*Category-Major categories (Major1) are more general descriptions for companies that self-selected to capture the many functions they perform in the industry. Minor categories (Minor1, Minor2) are more specific for companies that have more detailed functions (Minor1 is a larger category than Minor2). Minor categories figures (sales, etc.) can be aggregated to larger minor categories (Minor2 sums to Minor1) and major categories overall figures.

LIFE INSURANCE CARRIERS INDUSTRY
(NAICS 524113)

NAICS 524113: Life Insurance Carriers. This industry comprises establishments primarily engaged in underwriting life insurance. These establishments are operated by enterprises that may be owned by stockholders, policyholders, or other carriers.

INDUSTRY ESTABLISHMENTS, SALES & EMPLOYMENT TRENDS

	Year					Percent Chg. Year-to-Year			
	2015	2016	2017	2018	2019	15-16	16-17	17-18	18-19
Establishments	8,550	9,075	9,654	9,824	10,092	6.1%	6.4%	1.8%	2.7%
Sales ($Millions)	544,071	577,177	617,084	640,883	672,210	6.1%	6.9%	3.9%	4.9%
Employment	281,957	299,287	318,379	323,990	332,814	6.1%	6.4%	1.8%	2.7%
Sales ($M)/Estab.	63.64	63.60	63.92	65.24	66.61	-0.1%	0.5%	2.1%	2.1%
Sales ($)/Emp.	1,929,623	1,928,507	1,938,205	1,978,095	2,019,779	-0.1%	0.5%	2.1%	2.1%

3-YEAR TREND – ESTIMATED NUMBER OF ESTABLISHMENTS

Year	Employee Size of Establishment									Total Employment
	1-4 Emps.	5-9 Emps.	10-19 Emps.	20-49 Emps.	50-99 Emps.	100-249 Emps.	250-499 Emps.	>500 Emps.	Non-Employer	
2016	5,307	1,135	1,013	1,023	437	316	159	160	103	9,654
2017	5,401	1,155	1,031	1,041	445	322	162	163	105	9,824
2018	5,548	1,186	1,059	1,069	457	331	166	168	108	10,092

3-YEAR TREND – ESTIMATED INDUSTRY SALES ($MILLIONS)

Year	Employee Size of Establishment									Total Employment
	1-4 Emps.	5-9 Emps.	10-19 Emps.	20-49 Emps.	50-99 Emps.	100-249 Emps.	250-499 Emps.	>500 Emps.	Non-Employer	
2016	12,159.1	6,833.6	15,338.1	41,005.5	38,502.9	75,080.8	127,431.5	300,720.7	11.5	617,083.7
2017	12,690.7	7,132.4	16,008.6	42,798.1	40,186.1	78,363.1	133,002.4	310,690.0	12.0	640,883.4
2018	13,411.0	7,537.2	16,917.3	45,227.4	42,467.2	82,811.1	140,551.9	323,274.5	12.7	672,210.3

3-YEAR TREND – ESTIMATED NUMBER OF EMPLOYEES

Year	Employee Size of Establishment									Total Employment
	1-4 Emps.	5-9 Emps.	10-19 Emps.	20-49 Emps.	50-99 Emps.	100-249 Emps.	250-499 Emps.	>500 Emps.	Non-Employer	
2016	13,268	6,582	13,775	30,793	25,957	39,869	46,315	141,716	103	318,379
2017	13,502	6,698	14,018	31,336	26,415	40,572	47,132	144,214	105	323,990
2018	13,869	6,880	14,400	32,189	27,134	41,677	48,415	148,141	108	332,814

© Barnes Reports: 2018 U.S. Industry & Market Outlook

LIFE INSURANCE CARRIERS INDUSTRY
(NAICS 524113)

SUB-INDUSTRIES – 2018 ESTIMATED INDUSTRY SALES, ESTABLISHMENTS & EMPLOYMENT

Sub-Industries	Category*	Establishments	Sales ($Mill)	Employment
Life insurance	Major1	7,370	137,807.7	152,786
Mutual association life insurance	Minor1	199	11,660.5	10,247
Cooperative life insurance organizations	Minor2	53	20,021.7	1,873
Fraternal life insurance organizations	Minor2	274	15,603.0	5,216
Fraternal protective associations	Minor2	20	11.5	94
Assessment life insurance agents	Minor2	131	138.2	1,166
Benevolent insurance associations	Minor2	22	196.1	310
Burial insurance societies	Minor2	18	13.5	110
Funeral insurance	Minor2	41	65.0	598
Legal reserve life insurance	Minor2	84	1,140.5	699
Life insurance carriers	Minor2	1,505	443,320.6	145,064
Life insurance funds, savings bank	Minor2	22	6,865.9	192
Life reinsurance carriers	Minor2	87	4,039.1	5,635

*Category-Major categories (Major1) are more general descriptions for companies that self-selected to capture the many functions they perform in the industry. Minor categories (Minor1, Minor2) are more specific for companies that have more detailed functions (Minor1 is a larger category than Minor2). Minor categories figures (sales, etc.) can be aggregated to larger minor categories (Minor2 sums to Minor1) and major categories overall figures.

HEALTH & MEDICAL INSURANCE CARRIERS (NAICS 524114)

NAICS 524114: Health & Medical Insurance Carrier. This industry comprises establishments primarily engaged in providing hospital, medical, and other health services to subscribers or members in accordance with prearranged agreements or service plans, generally in return for specified subscription charges. The plans may be through a contract with a participating hospital or physician. Other plans provide for partial indemnity and service benefits. Includes separate establishments of HMOs which provide insurance.

INDUSTRY ESTABLISHMENTS, SALES & EMPLOYMENT TRENDS

	Year					Percent Chg. Year-to-Year			
	2015	2016	2017	2018	2019	15-16	16-17	17-18	18-19
Establishments	5,437	5,423	5,445	5,605	5,826	-0.3%	0.4%	3.0%	3.9%
Sales ($Millions)	557,286	592,678	634,137	689,431	754,147	6.4%	7.0%	8.7%	9.4%
Employment	387,191	386,186	387,717	399,171	414,844	-0.3%	0.4%	3.0%	3.9%
Sales ($M)/Estab.	102.49	109.29	116.47	122.99	129.45	6.6%	6.6%	5.6%	5.3%
Sales ($)/Emp.	1,439,302	1,534,697	1,635,566	1,727,159	1,817,908	6.6%	6.6%	5.6%	5.3%

3-YEAR TREND – ESTIMATED NUMBER OF ESTABLISHMENTS

Year	Employee Size of Establishment									Total Employ-ment
	1-4 Emps.	5-9 Emps.	10-19 Emps.	20-49 Emps.	50-99 Emps.	100-249 Emps.	250-499 Emps.	>500 Emps.	Non-Employer	
2016	2,523	626	499	521	338	382	229	268	58	5,445
2017	2,598	644	513	536	348	393	236	276	60	5,605
2018	2,700	670	534	557	362	408	245	287	62	5,826

3-YEAR TREND – ESTIMATED INDUSTRY SALES ($MILLIONS)

Year	Employee Size of Establishment									Total Employ-ment
	1-4 Emps.	5-9 Emps.	10-19 Emps.	20-49 Emps.	50-99 Emps.	100-249 Emps.	250-499 Emps.	>500 Emps.	Non-Employer	
2016	4,303.1	2,805.1	5,620.6	15,534.3	22,196.0	67,432.8	136,605.6	379,632.6	7.1	634,137.3
2017	4,720.2	3,077.0	6,165.5	17,040.2	24,347.6	73,969.4	149,847.6	410,256.1	7.7	689,431.3
2018	5,223.1	3,404.8	6,822.4	18,855.7	26,941.7	81,850.7	165,813.4	445,226.8	8.6	754,147.3

3-YEAR TREND – ESTIMATED NUMBER OF EMPLOYEES

Year	Employee Size of Establishment									Total Employ-ment
	1-4 Emps.	5-9 Emps.	10-19 Emps.	20-49 Emps.	50-99 Emps.	100-249 Emps.	250-499 Emps.	>500 Emps.	Non-Employer	
2016	6,309	3,630	6,782	15,673	20,104	48,109	66,707	220,345	58	387,717
2017	6,495	3,737	6,982	16,136	20,698	49,531	68,677	226,854	60	399,171
2018	6,750	3,884	7,256	16,770	21,511	51,475	71,374	235,761	62	414,844

© Barnes Reports: 2018 U.S. Industry & Market Outlook

Health & Medical Insurance Carriers (NAICS 524114)

Sub-Industries – 2018 Estimated Industry Sales, Establishments & Employment

Sub-Industries	Category*	Establishments	Sales ($Mill)	Employment
Hospital and medical service plans	Major1	3,031	384,778.4	232,894
Dental insurance	Minor2	440	7,889.8	18,738
Group hospitalization plans	Minor2	526	81,664.8	47,894
Health Maintenance Organization (HMO), insurance only	Minor2	1,608	215,098.3	99,644

*Category-Major categories (Major1) are more general descriptions for companies that self-selected to capture the many functions they perform in the industry. Minor categories (Minor1, Minor2) are more specific for companies that have more detailed functions (Minor1 is a larger category than Minor2). Minor categories figures (sales, etc.) can be aggregated to larger minor categories (Minor2 sums to Minor1) and major categories overall figures.

Property & Casualty Insurance Carriers (NAICS 524126)

NAICS 524126: Property & Casualty Insurance Carriers. This industry comprises establishments primarily engaged in underwriting fire, marine, and casualty insurance. These establishments are operated by enterprises that may be owned by stockholders, policyholders, or other carriers.

Industry Establishments, Sales & Employment Trends

	Year					Percent Chg. Year-to-Year			
	2015	2016	2017	2018	2019	15-16	16-17	17-18	18-19
Establishments	14,151	13,229	12,451	12,171	12,008	-6.5%	-5.9%	-2.3%	-1.3%
Sales ($Millions)	459,609	463,629	471,370	492,093	517,095	0.9%	1.7%	4.4%	5.1%
Employment	422,675	395,158	371,917	363,535	358,677	-6.5%	-5.9%	-2.3%	-1.3%
Sales ($M)/Estab.	32.48	35.05	37.86	40.43	43.06	7.9%	8.0%	6.8%	6.5%
Sales ($)/Emp.	1,087,382	1,173,277	1,267,408	1,353,633	1,441,672	7.9%	8.0%	6.8%	6.5%

3-Year Trend – Estimated Number of Establishments

Year	Employee Size of Establishment									Total Employment
	1-4 Emps.	5-9 Emps.	10-19 Emps.	20-49 Emps.	50-99 Emps.	100-249 Emps.	250-499 Emps.	>500 Emps.	Non-Employer	
2016	7,162	1,423	1,239	1,136	543	452	184	180	133	12,451
2017	7,000	1,391	1,211	1,110	531	442	180	175	130	12,171
2018	6,907	1,372	1,195	1,096	524	436	177	173	129	12,008

3-Year Trend – Estimated Industry Sales ($Millions)

Year	Employee Size of Establishment									Total Employment
	1-4 Emps.	5-9 Emps.	10-19 Emps.	20-49 Emps.	50-99 Emps.	100-249 Emps.	250-499 Emps.	>500 Emps.	Non-Employer	
2016	10,073.3	5,260.1	11,518.1	27,953.7	29,367.5	65,937.5	90,365.5	230,878.2	16.0	471,369.9
2017	10,446.9	5,455.2	11,945.2	28,990.2	30,456.4	68,382.5	93,716.3	242,684.1	16.6	492,093.3
2018	10,934.3	5,709.7	12,502.6	30,342.9	31,877.5	71,573.2	98,089.1	256,048.7	17.4	517,095.4

3-Year Trend – Estimated Number of Employees

Year	Employee Size of Establishment									Total Employment
	1-4 Emps.	5-9 Emps.	10-19 Emps.	20-49 Emps.	50-99 Emps.	100-249 Emps.	250-499 Emps.	>500 Emps.	Non-Employer	
2016	17,904	8,252	16,849	34,193	32,249	57,032	53,497	151,808	133	371,917
2017	17,501	8,066	16,470	33,422	31,522	55,747	52,291	148,387	130	363,535
2018	17,267	7,959	16,249	32,975	31,101	55,002	51,593	146,404	129	358,677

© Barnes Reports: 2018 U.S. Industry & Market Outlook

PROPERTY & CASUALTY INSURANCE CARRIERS (NAICS 524126)

SUB-INDUSTRIES — 2018 ESTIMATED INDUSTRY SALES, ESTABLISHMENTS & EMPLOYMENT

Sub-Industries	Category*	Establishments	Sales ($Mill)	Employment
Fire, marine, and casualty insurance	Major1	4,032	154,901.9	135,726
Agricultural insurance	Minor1	136	1,220.5	1,731
Federal Crop Insurance Corporation	Minor2	79	11.3	321
Fire, marine and casualty insurance and carriers	Minor1	911	48,636.7	49,951
Associated factory mutuals, fire and marine insurance	Minor2	17	5.0	69
Fire, marine, and casualty insurance: mutual	Minor2	544	10,889.0	20,512
Fire, marine, and casualty insurance: stock	Minor2	79	26,217.8	12,262
Assessment associations: fire, marine and casualty insura	Minor2	74	23.0	3,689
Automobile insurance	Minor2	2,081	49,080.4	37,348
Boiler insurance	Minor2	14	518.3	374
Burglary and theft insurance	Minor2	10	9.7	218
Contact lens insurance	Minor2	3	0.9	14
Plate glass insurance	Minor2	5	0.9	36
Property damage insurance	Minor2	3,448	187,076.1	66,980
Reciprocal interinsurance exchanges: fire, marine, casual	Minor2	34	4,311.0	4,294
Workers' compensation insurance	Minor2	701	9,190.9	30,008

*Category-Major categories (Major1) are more general descriptions for companies that self-selected to capture the many functions they perform in the industry. Minor categories (Minor1, Minor2) are more specific for companies that have more detailed functions (Minor1 is a larger category than Minor2). Minor categories figures (sales, etc.) can be aggregated to larger minor categories (Minor2 sums to Minor1) and major categories overall figures.

INSURANCE AGENCIES & BROKERAGES INDUSTRY
(NAICS 52421)

NAICS 52421: Insurance Agencies & Brokerages. This industry comprises establishments primarily representing one or more insurance carriers, or brokers not representing any particular carriers primarily engaged as independent contractors in the sale or placement of insurance contracts with carriers, but not employees of the insurance carriers they represent. This business also includes independent organizations concerned with insurance services.

INDUSTRY ESTABLISHMENTS, SALES & EMPLOYMENT TRENDS

	Year					Percent Chg. Year-to-Year			
	2015	2016	2017	2018	2019	15-16	16-17	17-18	18-19
Establishments	235,579	231,744	229,486	231,007	234,741	-1.6%	-1.0%	0.7%	1.6%
Sales ($Millions)	129,178	130,865	134,084	139,832	147,518	1.3%	2.5%	4.3%	5.5%
Employment	824,515	811,091	803,191	808,512	821,581	-1.6%	-1.0%	0.7%	1.6%
Sales ($M)/Estab.	0.55	0.56	0.58	0.61	0.63	3.0%	3.5%	3.6%	3.8%
Sales ($)/Emp.	156,671	161,344	166,939	172,950	179,553	3.0%	3.5%	3.6%	3.8%

3-YEAR TREND – ESTIMATED NUMBER OF ESTABLISHMENTS

Year	Employee Size of Establishment									Total Employment
	1-4 Emps.	5-9 Emps.	10-19 Emps.	20-49 Emps.	50-99 Emps.	100-249 Emps.	250-499 Emps.	>500 Emps.	Non-Employer	
2016	97,037	21,967	7,050	3,248	858	378	73	28	98,848	229,486
2017	97,680	22,112	7,097	3,269	864	380	74	28	99,503	231,007
2018	99,259	22,470	7,211	3,322	878	387	75	29	101,111	234,741

3-YEAR TREND – ESTIMATED INDUSTRY SALES ($MILLIONS)

Year	Employee Size of Establishment									Total Employment
	1-4 Emps.	5-9 Emps.	10-19 Emps.	20-49 Emps.	50-99 Emps.	100-249 Emps.	250-499 Emps.	>500 Emps.	Non-Employer	
2016	32,036.3	19,061.4	15,383.7	18,758.6	10,896.3	12,933.7	8,426.4	7,182.8	9,404.9	134,084.1
2017	33,414.1	19,881.2	16,045.3	19,565.4	11,365.0	13,490.0	8,788.8	7,473.3	9,809.4	139,832.5
2018	35,261.7	20,980.5	16,932.5	20,647.3	11,993.4	14,235.9	9,274.8	7,839.8	10,351.8	147,517.7

3-YEAR TREND – ESTIMATED NUMBER OF EMPLOYEES

Year	Employee Size of Establishment									Total Employment
	1-4 Emps.	5-9 Emps.	10-19 Emps.	20-49 Emps.	50-99 Emps.	100-249 Emps.	250-499 Emps.	>500 Emps.	Non-Employer	
2016	242,592	127,407	95,878	97,758	50,978	47,661	21,253	20,815	98,848	803,191
2017	244,199	128,252	96,513	98,406	51,316	47,977	21,394	20,953	99,503	808,512
2018	248,146	130,325	98,073	99,996	52,145	48,753	21,740	21,292	101,111	821,581

© Barnes Reports: 2018 U.S. Industry & Market Outlook

INSURANCE AGENCIES & BROKERAGES INDUSTRY (NAICS 52421)

Sub-Industries – 2018 Estimated Industry Sales, Establishments & Employment

Sub-Industries	Category*	Establishments	Sales ($Mill)	Employment
Insurance agents, brokers, and service	Major1	154,987	61,110.7	417,661
Insurance information and consulting services	Minor1	3,574	6,014.4	17,952
Advisory services, insurance	Minor2	681	419.9	3,687
Education services, insurance	Minor2	147	106.3	943
Information bureaus, insurance	Minor2	109	84.9	1,658
Pension and retirement plan consultants	Minor2	2,007	2,533.0	10,894
Policyholders' consulting service	Minor2	97	41.5	3,154
Insurance adjusters	Minor1	2,446	682.5	12,241
Insurance claim adjusters, not employed by insurance co	Minor2	2,921	1,015.7	14,125
Insurance agents and brokers	Minor1	23,657	8,994.6	88,973
Insurance agents, nec	Minor2	26,567	18,733.3	127,310
Insurance brokers, nec	Minor2	4,950	18,841.0	45,462
Life insurance agents	Minor2	2,498	1,156.9	13,453
Real estate insurance agents	Minor2	1,069	247.3	2,547
Property and casualty insurance agent	Minor2	1,849	17,438.8	16,737
Title insurance agents	Minor2	367	168.0	2,026
Fire loss appraisal	Minor2	70	40.9	302
Fire Insurance Underwriters' Laboratories	Minor2	39	77.4	160
Inspection and investigation services, insurance	Minor2	927	353.7	4,190
Insurance claim processing, except medical	Minor2	711	519.0	6,975
Loss prevention services, insurance	Minor2	113	80.6	1,786
Medical insurance claim processing, contract or fee basis	Minor2	789	897.8	10,731
Patrol services, insurance	Minor2	18	32.6	2,497
Professional standards services, insurance	Minor2	118	70.9	729
Ratemaking organizations, insurance	Minor2	31	44.0	594
Reporting services, insurance	Minor2	71	52.4	559
Research services, insurance	Minor2	195	74.1	1,167

*Category-Major categories (Major1) are more general descriptions for companies that self-selected to capture the many functions they perform in the industry. Minor categories (Minor1, Minor2) are more specific for companies that have more detailed functions (Minor1 is a larger category than Minor2). Minor categories figures (sales, etc.) can be aggregated to larger minor categories (Minor2 sums to Minor1) and major categories overall figures.

OFFICES OF REAL ESTATE AGENTS & BROKERS (NAICS 53121)

NAICS 53121: Real Estate Agents & Brokers. This industry comprises establishments primarily engaged in renting, buying, selling, managing, and appraising real estate for others.

INDUSTRY ESTABLISHMENTS, SALES & EMPLOYMENT TRENDS

	Year					Percent Chg. Year-to-Year			
	2015	2016	2017	2018	2019	15-16	16-17	17-18	18-19
Establishments	279,518	280,859	284,974	297,225	311,442	0.5%	1.5%	4.3%	4.8%
Sales ($Millions)	87,958	87,469	88,353	91,983	96,595	-0.6%	1.0%	4.1%	5.0%
Employment	563,651	566,356	574,654	599,358	628,027	0.5%	1.5%	4.3%	4.8%
Sales ($M)/Estab.	0.31	0.31	0.31	0.31	0.31	-1.0%	-0.4%	-0.2%	0.2%
Sales ($)/Emp.	156,050	154,441	153,749	153,469	153,808	-1.0%	-0.4%	-0.2%	0.2%

3-YEAR TREND – ESTIMATED NUMBER OF ESTABLISHMENTS

Year	Employee Size of Establishment									Total Employ-ment
	1-4 Emps.	5-9 Emps.	10-19 Emps.	20-49 Emps.	50-99 Emps.	100-249 Emps.	250-499 Emps.	>500 Emps.	Non-Employer	
2016	92,928	7,620	2,644	1,141	275	117	25	12	180,211	284,974
2017	96,923	7,947	2,757	1,190	287	122	27	13	187,958	297,225
2018	101,559	8,328	2,889	1,247	301	128	28	13	196,949	311,442

3-YEAR TREND – ESTIMATED INDUSTRY SALES ($MILLIONS)

Year	Employee Size of Establishment									Total Employ-ment
	1-4 Emps.	5-9 Emps.	10-19 Emps.	20-49 Emps.	50-99 Emps.	100-249 Emps.	250-499 Emps.	>500 Emps.	Non-Employer	
2016	32,053.9	6,908.2	6,027.1	6,884.4	3,651.5	4,191.7	3,071.3	3,214.2	22,350.1	88,352.5
2017	33,389.8	7,196.1	6,278.3	7,171.4	3,803.7	4,366.4	3,199.3	3,296.5	23,281.6	91,983.0
2018	35,085.0	7,561.4	6,597.0	7,535.4	3,996.8	4,588.1	3,361.7	3,406.3	24,463.6	96,595.4

3-YEAR TREND – ESTIMATED NUMBER OF EMPLOYEES

Year	Employee Size of Establishment									Total Employ-ment
	1-4 Emps.	5-9 Emps.	10-19 Emps.	20-49 Emps.	50-99 Emps.	100-249 Emps.	250-499 Emps.	>500 Emps.	Non-Employer	
2016	232,321	44,195	35,953	34,339	16,351	14,785	7,414	9,084	180,211	574,654
2017	242,308	46,095	37,499	35,816	17,054	15,420	7,733	9,474	187,958	599,358
2018	253,898	48,300	39,292	37,529	17,870	16,158	8,103	9,928	196,949	628,027

© Barnes Reports: 2018 U.S. Industry & Market Outlook

Offices of Real Estate Agents & Brokers (NAICS 53121)

Sub-Industries – 2018 Estimated Industry Sales, Establishments & Employment

Sub-Industries	Category*	Establishments	Sales ($Mill)	Employment
Real estate agents and managers	Major1	114,364	35,653.8	244,271
Real estate brokers and agents	Minor1	141,584	31,302.2	227,989
Broker of manufactured homes, on site	Minor2	440	229.7	1,155
Buying agent, real estate	Minor2	2,193	687.8	3,381
Escrow agent, real estate	Minor2	899	288.3	2,719
Real estate agent, commercial	Minor2	11,734	11,286.2	31,481
Real estate agent, residential	Minor2	24,004	11,868.5	82,876
Selling agent, real estate	Minor2	2,007	666.6	5,485

*Category-Major categories (Major1) are more general descriptions for companies that self-selected to capture the many functions they perform in the industry. Minor categories (Minor1, Minor2) are more specific for companies that have more detailed functions (Minor1 is a larger category than Minor2). Minor categories figures (sales, etc.) can be aggregated to larger minor categories (Minor2 sums to Minor1) and major categories overall figures.

REAL ESTATE PROPERTY MANAGERS INDUSTRY (NAICS 53131)

NAICS 53131: Real Estate Property Managers. This industry comprises establishments primarily engaged in renting, buying, selling, managing, and appraising real estate for others.

Industry Establishments, Sales & Employment Trends

	Year					Percent Chg. Year-to-Year			
	2015	2016	2017	2018	2019	15-16	16-17	17-18	18-19
Establishments	111,795	116,187	122,825	127,528	133,026	3.9%	5.7%	3.8%	4.3%
Sales ($Millions)	46,604	47,495	49,496	50,849	52,692	1.9%	4.2%	2.7%	3.6%
Employment	609,003	632,930	669,088	694,708	724,659	3.9%	5.7%	3.8%	4.3%
Sales ($M)/Estab.	0.42	0.41	0.40	0.40	0.40	-1.9%	-1.4%	-1.1%	-0.7%
Sales ($)/Emp.	76,525	75,040	73,975	73,194	72,713	-1.9%	-1.4%	-1.1%	-0.7%

3-Year Trend – Estimated Number of Establishments

Year	Employee Size of Establishment									Total Employment
	1-4 Emps.	5-9 Emps.	10-19 Emps.	20-49 Emps.	50-99 Emps.	100-249 Emps.	250-499 Emps.	>500 Emps.	Non-Employer	
2016	45,123	13,646	6,697	3,585	1,159	603	134	57	51,819	122,825
2017	46,851	14,169	6,954	3,722	1,203	626	139	59	53,804	127,528
2018	48,871	14,780	7,254	3,883	1,255	653	145	62	56,123	133,026

3-Year Trend – Estimated Industry Sales ($Millions)

Year	Employee Size of Establishment									Total Employment
	1-4 Emps.	5-9 Emps.	10-19 Emps.	20-49 Emps.	50-99 Emps.	100-249 Emps.	250-499 Emps.	>500 Emps.	Non-Employer	
2016	5,252.6	4,175.2	5,153.0	7,300.8	5,188.9	7,277.5	5,450.7	4,928.8	4,767.9	49,495.6
2017	5,403.3	4,295.0	5,300.9	7,510.2	5,337.7	7,486.3	5,607.1	5,003.5	4,904.7	50,848.8
2018	5,607.1	4,457.0	5,500.8	7,793.5	5,539.1	7,768.6	5,818.6	5,117.5	5,089.7	52,691.9

3-Year Trend – Estimated Number of Employees

Year	Employee Size of Establishment									Total Employment
	1-4 Emps.	5-9 Emps.	10-19 Emps.	20-49 Emps.	50-99 Emps.	100-249 Emps.	250-499 Emps.	>500 Emps.	Non-Employer	
2016	112,808	79,150	91,085	107,906	68,850	76,059	38,991	42,419	51,819	669,088
2017	117,127	82,180	94,573	112,038	71,486	78,972	40,484	44,044	53,804	694,708
2018	122,177	85,723	98,650	116,869	74,568	82,376	42,230	45,942	56,123	724,659

© Barnes Reports: 2018 U.S. Industry & Market Outlook

REAL ESTATE PROPERTY MANAGERS INDUSTRY (NAICS 53131)

SUB-INDUSTRIES – 2018 ESTIMATED INDUSTRY SALES, ESTABLISHMENTS & EMPLOYMENT

Sub-Industries	Category*	Establishments	Sales ($Mill)	Employment
Real estate managers	Minor1	106,766	43,645.8	587,068
Cemetery management service	Minor2	988	261.0	6,753
Condominium manager	Minor2	16,967	5,651.0	81,329
Cooperative apartment manager	Minor2	2,807	1,291.0	19,558

*Category-Major categories (Major1) are more general descriptions for companies that self-selected to capture the many functions they perform in the industry. Minor categories (Minor1, Minor2) are more specific for companies that have more detailed functions (Minor1 is a larger category than Minor2). Minor categories figures (sales, etc.) can be aggregated to larger minor categories (Minor2 sums to Minor1) and major categories overall figures.

Offices of Lawyers Industry
(NAICS 54111)

NAICS 54111: Offices of Lawyers. This industry comprises offices of legal practitioners known as lawyers or attorneys (i.e., counselors-at-law) primarily engaged in the practice of law. Establishments in this industry may provide expertise in a range or in specific areas of law, such as criminal law, corporate law, family and estate law, patent law, real estate law, or tax law.

Industry Establishments, Sales & Employment Trends

	Year					Percent Chg. Year-to-Year			
	2015	2016	2017	2018	2019	15-16	16-17	17-18	18-19
Establishments	249,520	253,618	255,676	258,658	262,623	1.6%	0.8%	1.2%	1.5%
Sales ($Millions)	193,118	205,655	217,977	231,881	247,767	6.5%	6.0%	6.4%	6.9%
Employment	1,182,210	1,201,626	1,211,379	1,225,506	1,244,291	1.6%	0.8%	1.2%	1.5%
Sales ($M)/Estab.	0.77	0.81	0.85	0.90	0.94	4.8%	5.1%	5.2%	5.2%
Sales ($)/Emp.	163,353	171,148	179,941	189,213	199,123	4.8%	5.1%	5.2%	5.2%

3-Year Trend – Estimated Number of Establishments

Year	Employee Size of Establishment									Total Employment
	1-4 Emps.	5-9 Emps.	10-19 Emps.	20-49 Emps.	50-99 Emps.	100-249 Emps.	250-499 Emps.	>500 Emps.	Non-Employer	
2017	130,777	25,585	11,755	6,040	1,797	838	204	66	78,614	255,676
2018	132,302	25,883	11,892	6,111	1,818	848	206	66	79,531	258,658
2019	134,330	26,280	12,074	6,205	1,846	861	209	67	80,750	262,623

3-Year Trend – Estimated Industry Sales ($Millions)

Year	Employee Size of Establishment									Total Employment
	1-4 Emps.	5-9 Emps.	10-19 Emps.	20-49 Emps.	50-99 Emps.	100-249 Emps.	250-499 Emps.	>500 Emps.	Non-Employer	
2017	41,792.4	21,489.9	24,829.4	33,771.1	22,088.2	27,763.3	22,764.5	14,788.7	8,689.6	217,977.0
2018	44,466.1	22,864.8	26,417.9	35,931.6	23,501.3	29,539.5	24,220.9	15,693.8	9,245.5	231,881.2
2019	47,523.3	24,436.8	28,234.2	38,402.0	25,117.1	31,570.4	25,886.1	16,716.1	9,881.1	247,767.1

3-Year Trend – Estimated Number of Employees

Year	Employee Size of Establishment									Total Employment
	1-4 Emps.	5-9 Emps.	10-19 Emps.	20-49 Emps.	50-99 Emps.	100-249 Emps.	250-499 Emps.	>500 Emps.	Non-Employer	
2017	326,942	148,393	159,869	181,817	106,758	105,695	59,317	43,973	78,614	1,211,379
2018	330,755	150,124	161,733	183,938	108,003	106,927	60,009	44,486	79,531	1,225,506
2019	335,825	152,425	164,212	186,757	109,659	108,566	60,929	45,168	80,750	1,244,291

Offices of Lawyers Industry (NAICS 54111)

Sub-Industries – 2018 Estimated Industry Sales, Establishments & Employment

Sub-Industries	Category*	Establishments	Sales ($Mill)	Employment
Legal services	Major1	87,236	60,298.3	321,179
Specialized legal services	Minor1	1,370	1,848.9	8,156
Bankruptcy referee	Minor2	193	401.6	1,443
Patent solicitor	Minor2	100	180.2	1,199
Specialized law offices, attorneys	Minor1	8,382	8,062.9	40,991
Administrative and government law	Minor2	441	1,483.1	4,042
Antitrust and trade regulation law	Minor2	32	41.4	904
Bankrupcy law	Minor2	1,358	1,031.4	5,106
Corporate, partnership and business law	Minor2	1,286	2,897.9	15,118
Criminal law	Minor2	2,786	1,652.3	8,244
Debt collection law	Minor2	192	350.3	1,550
Divorce and family law	Minor2	2,317	1,406.2	7,000
Environmental law	Minor2	157	211.4	856
Immigration and naturalization law	Minor2	1,164	806.7	3,925
Labor and employment law	Minor2	1,113	1,017.9	5,021
Malpractice and negligence law	Minor2	553	803.2	4,057
Patent, trademark and copyright law	Minor2	765	966.1	4,653
Product liability law	Minor2	48	45.1	324
Real estate law	Minor2	2,063	2,015.4	9,038
Securities law	Minor2	99	122.5	735
Taxation law	Minor2	406	504.0	1,551
Will, estate and trust law	Minor2	1,476	942.9	4,426
General practice attorney, lawyer	Minor2	107,558	83,841.1	440,116
General practice law office	Minor2	36,481	57,868.7	325,415
Legal aid service	Minor2	1,084	3,081.9	10,458

*Category-Major categories (Major1) are more general descriptions for companies that self-selected to capture the many functions they perform in the industry. Minor categories (Minor1, Minor2) are more specific for companies that have more detailed functions (Minor1 is a larger category than Minor2). Minor categories figures (sales, etc.) can be aggregated to larger minor categories (Minor2 sums to Minor1) and major categories overall figures.

OFFICES OF CERTIFIED PUBLIC ACCOUNTANTS (NAICS 541211)

NAICS 541211: Offices of Certified Public Accountants This U.S. industry comprises establishments of accountants that are certified to audit the accounting records of public and private organizations and to attest to compliance with generally accepted accounting practices. Offices of certified public accountants (CPAs) may provide one or more of the following accounting services: (1) auditing financial statements; (2) designing accounting systems; (3) preparing financial statements; (4) developing budgets; and (5) providing advice on matters related to accounting.

INDUSTRY ESTABLISHMENTS, SALES & EMPLOYMENT TRENDS

	Year					Percent Chg. Year-to-Year			
	2015	2016	2017	2018	2019	15-16	16-17	17-18	18-19
Establishments	68,263	69,333	69,922	70,722	71,782	1.6%	0.8%	1.1%	1.5%
Sales ($Millions)	65,376	70,318	75,315	80,794	86,919	7.6%	7.1%	7.3%	7.6%
Employment	471,746	479,142	483,208	488,736	496,066	1.6%	0.8%	1.1%	1.5%
Sales ($M)/Estab.	0.96	1.01	1.08	1.14	1.21	5.9%	6.2%	6.1%	6.0%
Sales ($)/Emp.	138,583	146,758	155,865	165,313	175,216	5.9%	6.2%	6.1%	6.0%

3-YEAR TREND – ESTIMATED NUMBER OF ESTABLISHMENTS

Year	Employee Size of Establishment									Total Employment
	1-4 Emps.	5-9 Emps.	10-19 Emps.	20-49 Emps.	50-99 Emps.	100-249 Emps.	250-499 Emps.	>500 Emps.	Non-Employer	
2017	38,426	11,134	4,990	2,162	665	372	97	73	12,003	69,922
2018	38,865	11,261	5,047	2,187	672	376	98	74	12,140	70,722
2019	39,448	11,430	5,123	2,220	682	382	100	75	12,322	71,782

3-YEAR TREND – ESTIMATED INDUSTRY SALES ($MILLIONS)

Year	Employee Size of Establishment									Total Employment
	1-4 Emps.	5-9 Emps.	10-19 Emps.	20-49 Emps.	50-99 Emps.	100-249 Emps.	250-499 Emps.	>500 Emps.	Non-Employer	
2017	9,535.2	7,261.9	8,185.1	9,387.2	6,344.0	9,563.4	8,435.6	15,403.3	1,199.8	75,315.4
2018	10,242.6	7,800.7	8,792.3	10,083.6	6,814.6	10,272.9	9,061.4	16,437.3	1,288.8	80,794.2
2019	11,038.2	8,406.6	9,475.2	10,866.9	7,344.0	11,070.8	9,765.3	17,562.9	1,388.9	86,918.8

3-YEAR TREND – ESTIMATED NUMBER OF EMPLOYEES

Year	Employee Size of Establishment									Total Employment
	1-4 Emps.	5-9 Emps.	10-19 Emps.	20-49 Emps.	50-99 Emps.	100-249 Emps.	250-499 Emps.	>500 Emps.	Non-Employer	
2017	96,064	64,578	67,869	65,085	39,487	46,887	28,307	62,929	12,003	483,208
2018	97,163	65,317	68,646	65,830	39,939	47,423	28,631	63,649	12,140	488,736
2019	98,620	66,296	69,675	66,817	40,538	48,134	29,060	64,603	12,322	496,066

© Barnes Reports: 2018 U.S. Industry & Market Outlook

Offices of Certified Public Accountants (NAICS 541211)

Sub-Industries – 2018 Estimated Industry Sales, Establishments & Employment

Sub-Industries	Category*	Establishments	Sales ($Mill)	Employment
Accounting, auditing, and bookkeeping	Major1	21,951	12,983.3	128,057
Auditing services	Minor1	776	918.7	10,464
Certified public accountant	Minor2	34,141	50,538.7	220,959
Accounting services, except auditing	Minor1	4,305	3,030.1	44,293
Calculating and statistical service	Minor2	79	52.3	408
Payroll accounting service	Minor2	1,095	8,053.1	28,817
Billing and bookkeeping service	Minor2	8,375	5,218.0	55,739

*Category-Major categories (Major1) are more general descriptions for companies that self-selected to capture the many functions they perform in the industry. Minor categories (Minor1, Minor2) are more specific for companies that have more detailed functions (Minor1 is a larger category than Minor2). Minor categories figures (sales, etc.) can be aggregated to larger minor categories (Minor2 sums to Minor1) and major categories overall figures.

Architectural Services Industry
(NAICS 54131)

NAICS 54131: Architectural Services. This industry comprises establishments primarily engaged in planning and designing residential, institutional, leisure, commercial, and industrial buildings and structures by applying knowledge of design, construction procedures, zoning regulations, building codes, and building materials.

Industry Establishments, Sales & Employment Trends

	Year					Percent Chg. Year-to-Year			
	2015	2016	2017	2018	2019	15-16	16-17	17-18	18-19
Establishments	37,395	35,467	33,741	33,325	33,033	-5.2%	-4.9%	-1.2%	-0.9%
Sales ($Millions)	27,295	27,499	27,841	29,230	30,788	0.7%	1.2%	5.0%	5.3%
Employment	183,502	174,042	165,571	163,529	162,098	-5.2%	-4.9%	-1.2%	-0.9%
Sales ($M)/Estab.	0.73	0.78	0.83	0.88	0.93	6.2%	6.4%	6.3%	6.3%
Sales ($)/Emp.	148,745	158,002	168,151	178,746	189,936	6.2%	6.4%	6.3%	6.3%

3-Year Trend – Estimated Number of Establishments

Year	Employee Size of Establishment									Total Employment
	1-4 Emps.	5-9 Emps.	10-19 Emps.	20-49 Emps.	50-99 Emps.	100-249 Emps.	250-499 Emps.	>500 Emps.	Non-Employer	
2017	12,563	3,432	1,942	1,029	310	129	18	5	14,314	33,741
2018	12,408	3,390	1,918	1,016	307	127	18	4	14,137	33,325
2019	12,299	3,360	1,901	1,007	304	126	18	4	14,014	33,033

3-Year Trend – Estimated Industry Sales ($Millions)

Year	Employee Size of Establishment									Total Employment
	1-4 Emps.	5-9 Emps.	10-19 Emps.	20-49 Emps.	50-99 Emps.	100-249 Emps.	250-499 Emps.	>500 Emps.	Non-Employer	
2017	3,834.4	2,753.5	3,917.2	5,492.6	3,643.3	4,081.9	1,924.2	878.6	1,315.3	27,841.0
2018	4,025.7	2,890.9	4,112.7	5,766.6	3,825.1	4,285.6	2,020.2	922.5	1,380.9	29,230.2
2019	4,240.3	3,045.0	4,331.9	6,074.0	4,029.0	4,514.0	2,127.9	971.7	1,454.5	30,788.2

3-Year Trend – Estimated Number of Employees

Year	Employee Size of Establishment									Total Employment
	1-4 Emps.	5-9 Emps.	10-19 Emps.	20-49 Emps.	50-99 Emps.	100-249 Emps.	250-499 Emps.	>500 Emps.	Non-Employer	
2017	31,406	19,907	26,407	30,961	18,437	16,270	5,249	2,619	14,314	165,571
2018	31,019	19,662	26,082	30,579	18,210	16,070	5,185	2,586	14,137	163,529
2019	30,747	19,490	25,853	30,312	18,050	15,929	5,139	2,564	14,014	162,098

© Barnes Reports: 2018 U.S. Industry & Market Outlook

Architectural Services Industry (NAICS 54131)

Sub-Industries – 2018 Estimated Industry Sales, Establishments & Employment

Sub-Industries	Category*	Establishments	Sales ($Mill)	Employment
Architectural services	Major1	29,474	20,105.0	133,270
Architectural engineering	Minor1	479	487.8	3,818
Architectural engineering	Minor2	2,115	8,312.3	23,549
House designer	Minor2	1,257	325.1	2,893

*Category-Major categories (Major1) are more general descriptions for companies that self-selected to capture the many functions they perform in the industry. Minor categories (Minor1, Minor2) are more specific for companies that have more detailed functions (Minor1 is a larger category than Minor2). Minor categories figures (sales, etc.) can be aggregated to larger minor categories (Minor2 sums to Minor1) and major categories overall figures.

ENGINEERING SERVICES INDUSTRY
(NAICS 54133)

NAICS 54133: Engineering Services. This industry comprises establishments primarily engaged in applying physical laws and principles of engineering in the design, development, and utilization of machines, materials, instruments, structures, processes, and systems. The assignments undertaken by these establishments may involve any of the following activities: provision of advice, preparation of feasibility studies, preparation of preliminary and final plans and designs, provision of technical services during the construction or installation phase, inspection and evaluation of engineering projects, and related services.

INDUSTRY ESTABLISHMENTS, SALES & EMPLOYMENT TRENDS

	Year					Percent Chg. Year-to-Year			
	2015	2016	2017	2018	2019	15-16	16-17	17-18	18-19
Establishments	91,313	88,912	88,908	89,911	91,255	-2.6%	0.0%	1.1%	1.5%
Sales ($Millions)	199,528	206,024	218,375	233,650	250,819	3.3%	6.0%	7.0%	7.3%
Employment	950,925	925,919	925,875	936,323	950,319	-2.6%	0.0%	1.1%	1.5%
Sales ($M)/Estab.	2.19	2.32	2.46	2.60	2.75	6.0%	6.0%	5.8%	5.8%
Sales ($)/Emp.	209,826	222,507	235,858	249,540	263,931	6.0%	6.0%	5.8%	5.8%

3-YEAR TREND – ESTIMATED NUMBER OF ESTABLISHMENTS

Year	Employee Size of Establishment									Total Employment
	1-4 Emps.	5-9 Emps.	10-19 Emps.	20-49 Emps.	50-99 Emps.	100-249 Emps.	250-499 Emps.	>500 Emps.	Non-Employer	
2017	33,198	9,056	7,434	5,883	2,126	1,184	291	145	29,590	88,908
2018	33,572	9,158	7,518	5,949	2,150	1,197	294	147	29,924	89,911
2019	34,074	9,295	7,630	6,038	2,183	1,215	299	149	30,372	91,255

3-YEAR TREND – ESTIMATED INDUSTRY SALES ($MILLIONS)

Year	Employee Size of Establishment									Total Employment
	1-4 Emps.	5-9 Emps.	10-19 Emps.	20-49 Emps.	50-99 Emps.	100-249 Emps.	250-499 Emps.	>500 Emps.	Non-Employer	
2017	11,163.3	8,003.9	16,522.4	34,608.3	27,499.2	41,265.8	34,199.1	41,971.0	3,142.2	218,375.2
2018	11,958.5	8,574.0	17,699.3	37,073.5	29,458.0	44,205.2	36,635.1	44,680.3	3,366.0	233,649.9
2019	12,857.3	9,218.5	19,029.7	39,860.1	31,672.3	47,527.8	39,388.8	47,645.3	3,619.0	250,818.8

3-YEAR TREND – ESTIMATED NUMBER OF EMPLOYEES

Year	Employee Size of Establishment									Total Employment
	1-4 Emps.	5-9 Emps.	10-19 Emps.	20-49 Emps.	50-99 Emps.	100-249 Emps.	250-499 Emps.	>500 Emps.	Non-Employer	
2017	82,995	52,525	101,101	177,073	126,312	149,298	84,688	122,293	29,590	925,875
2018	83,931	53,117	102,241	179,071	127,737	150,983	85,643	123,673	29,924	936,323
2019	85,186	53,911	103,770	181,748	129,647	153,240	86,924	125,522	30,372	950,319

© Barnes Reports: 2018 U.S. Industry & Market Outlook

ENGINEERING SERVICES INDUSTRY
(NAICS 54133)

SUB-INDUSTRIES – 2018 ESTIMATED INDUSTRY SALES, ESTABLISHMENTS & EMPLOYMENT

Sub-Industries	Category*	Establishments	Sales ($Mill)	Employment
Engineering services	Major1	46,530	139,671.4	492,154
Sanitary engineers	Minor1	156	629.1	1,866
Pollution control engineering	Minor2	219	592.5	3,009
Industrial engineers	Minor1	567	10,400.9	7,849
Machine tool design	Minor2	428	396.9	2,308
Mechanical engineering	Minor2	1,995	2,363.2	16,895
Petroleum, mining, and chemical engineers	Minor1	128	688.8	1,365
Chemical engineering	Minor2	313	450.0	3,769
Mining engineer	Minor2	124	80.0	969
Petroleum engineering	Minor2	311	860.6	2,855
Construction and civil engineering	Minor1	1,379	2,129.5	16,993
Building construction consultant	Minor2	2,455	1,700.8	10,935
Civil engineering	Minor2	5,568	16,609.7	82,252
Heating and ventilation engineering	Minor2	333	478.0	2,425
Structural engineering	Minor2	2,257	1,762.0	14,326
Acoustical engineering	Minor2	296	233.4	2,314
Aviation and/or aeronautical engineering	Minor2	1,070	7,222.9	16,101
Consulting engineer	Minor2	18,279	35,142.9	194,057
Designing: ship, boat, machine, and product	Minor2	896	1,131.2	11,054
Electrical or electronic engineering	Minor2	2,688	5,031.4	28,006
Energy conservation engineering	Minor2	659	1,149.7	6,260
Fire protection engineering	Minor2	303	396.0	2,546
Marine engineering	Minor2	362	1,130.7	3,739
Professional engineer	Minor2	2,596	3,398.4	12,277

*Category-Major categories (Major1) are more general descriptions for companies that self-selected to capture the many functions they perform in the industry. Minor categories (Minor1, Minor2) are more specific for companies that have more detailed functions (Minor1 is a larger category than Minor2). Minor categories figures (sales, etc.) can be aggregated to larger minor categories (Minor2 sums to Minor1) and major categories overall figures.

INTERIOR DESIGN SERVICES INDUSTRY
(NAICS 54141)

NAICS 54141: Interior Design Services. This industry comprises establishments primarily engaged in planning, designing, and administering projects in interior spaces to meet the physical and aesthetic needs of people using them, taking into consideration building codes, health and safety regulations, traffic patterns and floor planning, mechanical and electrical needs, and interior fittings and furniture. Interior designers and interior design consultants work in areas, such as hospitality design, health care design, institutional design, commercial and corporate design, and residential design.

INDUSTRY ESTABLISHMENTS, SALES & EMPLOYMENT TRENDS

	Year					Percent Chg. Year-to-Year			
	2015	2016	2017	2018	2019	15-16	16-17	17-18	18-19
Establishments	52,548	50,229	48,651	48,126	47,779	-4.4%	-3.1%	-1.1%	-0.7%
Sales ($Millions)	9,872	9,678	9,663	9,872	10,147	-2.0%	-0.2%	2.2%	2.8%
Employment	90,975	86,960	84,229	83,319	82,718	-4.4%	-3.1%	-1.1%	-0.7%
Sales ($M)/Estab.	0.19	0.19	0.20	0.21	0.21	2.6%	3.1%	3.3%	3.5%
Sales ($)/Emp.	108,514	111,295	114,727	118,483	122,674	2.6%	3.1%	3.3%	3.5%

3-YEAR TREND – ESTIMATED NUMBER OF ESTABLISHMENTS

Year	Employee Size of Establishment									Total Employment
	1-4 Emps.	5-9 Emps.	10-19 Emps.	20-49 Emps.	50-99 Emps.	100-249 Emps.	250-499 Emps.	>500 Emps.	Non-Employer	
2017	9,553	1,255	440	198	37	11	1	0	37,150	48,651
2018	9,450	1,241	441	196	37	11	1	0	36,749	48,126
2019	9,382	1,232	438	195	36	11	1	0	36,484	47,779

3-YEAR TREND – ESTIMATED INDUSTRY SALES ($MILLIONS)

Year	Employee Size of Establishment									Total Employment
	1-4 Emps.	5-9 Emps.	10-19 Emps.	20-49 Emps.	50-99 Emps.	100-249 Emps.	250-499 Emps.	>500 Emps.	Non-Employer	
2017	3,029.9	1,045.8	935.5	1,099.4	451.7	365.2	102.6	5.6	2,627.6	9,663.3
2018	3,095.3	1,068.4	955.7	1,123.1	461.5	373.1	104.8	5.7	2,684.3	9,871.9
2019	3,181.6	1,098.2	982.4	1,154.5	474.3	383.5	107.7	5.9	2,759.2	10,147.4

3-YEAR TREND – ESTIMATED NUMBER OF EMPLOYEES

Year	Employee Size of Establishment									Total Employment
	1-4 Emps.	5-9 Emps.	10-19 Emps.	20-49 Emps.	50-99 Emps.	100-249 Emps.	250-499 Emps.	>500 Emps.	Non-Employer	
2017	23,882	7,276	6,069	5,964	2,200	1,401	269	17	37,150	84,229
2018	23,624	7,198	6,004	5,899	2,176	1,386	266	17	36,749	83,319
2019	23,454	7,146	5,960	5,857	2,160	1,376	264	16	36,484	82,718

© Barnes Reports: 2018 U.S. Industry & Market Outlook

INTERIOR DESIGN SERVICES INDUSTRY
(NAICS 54141)

Sub-Industries — 2018 Estimated Industry Sales, Establishments & Employment

Sub-Industries	Category*	Establishments	Sales ($Mill)	Employment
Interior design services	Minor1	30,100	5,302.3	48,524
Decoration service for special events	Minor2	1,354	436.5	4,308
Interior designer	Minor2	9,515	2,596.6	18,491
Interior decorating	Minor2	7,157	1,536.6	11,997

*Category-Major categories (Major1) are more general descriptions for companies that self-selected to capture the many functions they perform in the industry. Minor categories (Minor1, Minor2) are more specific for companies that have more detailed functions (Minor1 is a larger category than Minor2). Minor categories figures (sales, etc.) can be aggregated to larger minor categories (Minor2 sums to Minor1) and major categories overall figures.

GRAPHIC DESIGNS SERVICES INDUSTRY
(NAICS 54143)

NAICS 54143: Graphic Design Services. This industry comprises establishments primarily engaged in planning, designing, and managing the production of visual communication in order to convey specific messages or concepts, clarify complex information, or project visual identities. These services can include the design of printed materials, packaging, advertising, signage systems, and corporate identification (logos). This industry also includes commercial artists engaged exclusively in generating drawings and illustrations requiring technical accuracy or interpretative skills.

INDUSTRY ESTABLISHMENTS, SALES & EMPLOYMENT TRENDS

	Year					Percent Chg. Year-to-Year			
	2015	2016	2017	2018	2019	15-16	16-17	17-18	18-19
Establishments	64,837	63,856	62,787	62,829	63,099	-1.5%	-1.7%	0.1%	0.4%
Sales ($Millions)	10,561	10,303	10,095	10,097	10,176	-2.4%	-2.0%	0.0%	0.8%
Employment	115,334	113,589	111,688	111,762	112,242	-1.5%	-1.7%	0.1%	0.4%
Sales ($M)/Estab.	0.16	0.16	0.16	0.16	0.16	-0.9%	-0.4%	0.0%	0.4%
Sales ($)/Emp.	91,570	90,702	90,384	90,339	90,661	-0.9%	-0.4%	0.0%	0.4%

3-YEAR TREND – ESTIMATED NUMBER OF ESTABLISHMENTS

Year	Employee Size of Establishment									Total
	1-4 Emps.	5-9 Emps.	10-19 Emps.	20-49 Emps.	50-99 Emps.	100-249 Emps.	250-499 Emps.	>500 Emps.	Non-Employer	Employment
2017	12,220	1,563	692	295	53	16	2	0	47,945	62,787
2018	12,228	1,564	693	296	53	16	2	0	47,977	62,829
2019	12,281	1,571	696	297	54	17	2	0	48,182	63,099

3-YEAR TREND – ESTIMATED INDUSTRY SALES ($MILLIONS)

Year	Employee Size of Establishment									Total
	1-4 Emps.	5-9 Emps.	10-19 Emps.	20-49 Emps.	50-99 Emps.	100-249 Emps.	250-499 Emps.	>500 Emps.	Non-Employer	Employment
2017	2,774.2	932.6	1,038.9	1,173.1	465.0	387.4	153.6	4.0	3,165.9	10,094.7
2018	2,774.7	932.8	1,039.1	1,173.3	465.1	387.4	153.6	4.0	3,166.5	10,096.5
2019	2,796.5	940.1	1,047.3	1,182.5	468.7	390.5	154.8	4.1	3,191.4	10,176.0

3-YEAR TREND – ESTIMATED NUMBER OF EMPLOYEES

Year	Employee Size of Establishment									Total
	1-4 Emps.	5-9 Emps.	10-19 Emps.	20-49 Emps.	50-99 Emps.	100-249 Emps.	250-499 Emps.	>500 Emps.	Non-Employer	Employment
2017	30,550	9,065	9,417	8,890	3,164	2,076	563	18	47,945	111,688
2018	30,571	9,071	9,423	8,896	3,166	2,077	564	18	47,977	111,762
2019	30,702	9,110	9,463	8,934	3,179	2,086	566	18	48,182	112,242

© Barnes Reports: 2018 U.S. Industry & Market Outlook

Graphic Designs Services Industry (NAICS 54143)

Sub-Industries – 2018 Estimated Industry Sales, Establishments & Employment

Sub-Industries	Category*	Establishments	Sales ($Mill)	Employment
Commercial art and graphic design	Major1	34,932	4,783.5	52,233
Art design services	Minor1	2,896	461.8	5,135
Chart and graph design	Minor2	912	82.9	1,318
Creative services to advertisers, except writers	Minor2	992	240.0	2,453
Graphic arts and related design	Minor2	17,289	3,275.7	36,318
Package design	Minor2	485	271.6	2,246
Silk screen design	Minor2	1,758	592.9	6,902
Film strip, slide, and still film production	Minor1	625	106.2	1,316
Film strip and slide producer	Minor2	129	19.5	263
Still film producer	Minor2	73	17.5	150
Commercial art and illustration	Minor2	2,738	245.0	3,430

*Category-Major categories (Major1) are more general descriptions for companies that self-selected to capture the many functions they perform in the industry. Minor categories (Minor1, Minor2) are more specific for companies that have more detailed functions (Minor1 is a larger category than Minor2). Minor categories figures (sales, etc.) can be aggregated to larger minor categories (Minor2 sums to Minor1) and major categories overall figures.

COMPUTER SYSTEMS DESIGNS SERVICES INDUSTRY (NAICS 54151)

NAICS 54151: Computer Systems Design and Related Services.
This industry comprises establishments primarily engaged in providing expertise in the field of information technologies through one or more of the following activities: (1) writing, modifying, testing, and supporting software to meet the needs of a particular customer; (2) planning and designing computer systems that integrate computer hardware, software, and communication technologies; (3) on-site management and operation of clients' computer systems and/or data processing facilities; and (4) other professional and technical computer-related advice and services.

INDUSTRY ESTABLISHMENTS, SALES & EMPLOYMENT TRENDS

	Year					Percent Chg. Year-to-Year			
	2015	2016	2017	2018	2019	15-16	16-17	17-18	18-19
Establishments	268,682	275,238	286,948	296,914	308,340	2.4%	4.3%	3.5%	3.8%
Sales ($Millions)	318,971	339,882	369,341	398,953	432,951	6.6%	8.7%	8.0%	8.5%
Employment	1,701,340	1,742,857	1,817,002	1,880,111	1,952,461	2.4%	4.3%	3.5%	3.8%
Sales ($M)/Estab.	1.19	1.23	1.29	1.34	1.40	4.0%	4.2%	4.4%	4.5%
Sales ($)/Emp.	187,482	195,014	203,269	212,197	221,746	4.0%	4.2%	4.4%	4.5%

3-YEAR TREND – ESTIMATED NUMBER OF ESTABLISHMENTS

Year	Employee Size of Establishment									Total Employment
	1-4 Emps.	5-9 Emps.	10-19 Emps.	20-49 Emps.	50-99 Emps.	100-249 Emps.	250-499 Emps.	>500 Emps.	Non-Employer	
2017	107,971	15,270	10,474	8,138	3,259	2,108	613	376	138,738	286,948
2018	111,721	15,800	10,837	8,421	3,373	2,181	634	389	143,557	296,914
2019	116,020	16,408	11,255	8,745	3,502	2,265	659	404	149,081	308,340

3-YEAR TREND – ESTIMATED INDUSTRY SALES ($MILLIONS)

Year	Employee Size of Establishment									Total Employment
	1-4 Emps.	5-9 Emps.	10-19 Emps.	20-49 Emps.	50-99 Emps.	100-249 Emps.	250-499 Emps.	>500 Emps.	Non-Employer	
2017	31,826.2	11,830.4	20,405.8	41,966.9	36,949.2	64,410.4	63,126.0	86,105.0	12,721.0	369,341.0
2018	34,496.0	12,822.9	22,117.6	45,487.5	40,048.9	69,813.7	68,421.5	91,956.9	13,788.2	398,953.2
2019	37,573.5	13,966.8	24,090.8	49,545.4	43,621.6	76,041.9	74,525.4	98,567.0	15,018.2	432,950.7

3-YEAR TREND – ESTIMATED NUMBER OF EMPLOYEES

Year	Employee Size of Establishment									Total Employment
	1-4 Emps.	5-9 Emps.	10-19 Emps.	20-49 Emps.	50-99 Emps.	100-249 Emps.	250-499 Emps.	>500 Emps.	Non-Employer	
2017	269,927	88,566	142,442	244,955	193,613	265,844	178,328	294,588	138,738	1,817,002
2018	279,302	91,642	147,390	253,462	200,338	275,077	184,522	304,820	143,557	1,880,111
2019	290,051	95,169	153,062	263,216	208,047	285,663	191,623	316,550	149,081	1,952,461

Computer Systems Designs Services Industry (NAICS 54151)

Sub-Industries – 2018 Estimated Industry Sales, Establishments & Employment

Sub-Industries	Category*	Establishments	Sales ($Mill)	Employment
Custom computer programming services	Major1	101,838	70,225.1	489,633
Custom computer programming services	Minor1	9,126	12,867.5	61,332
Computer software systems analysis and design, custom	Minor2	42,891	39,147.0	198,999
Computer software writing services	Minor1	3,489	2,314.5	15,092
Computer code authors	Minor2	429	134.2	1,690
Computer software writers, freelance	Minor2	2,161	508.6	5,632
Computer software development and applications	Minor1	29,111	116,271.2	242,575
Computer software development	Minor2	97,311	146,846.2	802,631
Software programming applications	Minor2	10,557	10,638.9	62,525

*Category-Major categories (Major1) are more general descriptions for companies that self-selected to capture the many functions they perform in the industry. Minor categories (Minor1, Minor2) are more specific for companies that have more detailed functions (Minor1 is a larger category than Minor2). Minor categories figures (sales, etc.) can be aggregated to larger minor categories (Minor2 sums to Minor1) and major categories overall figures.

MANAGEMENT CONSULTING SERVICES INDUSTRY (NAICS 54161)

NAICS 54161: Management Consulting Services. This industry comprises establishments primarily engaged in providing advice and assistance to businesses and other organizations on management issues, such as strategic and organizational planning; financial planning and budgeting; marketing objectives and policies; human resource policies, practices, and planning; production scheduling; and control planning.

INDUSTRY ESTABLISHMENTS, SALES & EMPLOYMENT TRENDS

	Year					Percent Chg. Year-to-Year			
	2015	2016	2017	2018	2019	15-16	16-17	17-18	18-19
Establishments	354,508	366,739	386,579	403,913	423,554	3.5%	5.4%	4.5%	4.9%
Sales ($Millions)	144,247	152,225	164,260	176,220	190,213	5.5%	7.9%	7.3%	7.9%
Employment	1,213,538	1,255,405	1,323,321	1,382,660	1,449,895	3.5%	5.4%	4.5%	4.9%
Sales ($M)/Estab.	0.41	0.42	0.42	0.44	0.45	2.0%	2.4%	2.7%	2.9%
Sales ($)/Emp.	118,865	121,256	124,127	127,450	131,191	2.0%	2.4%	2.7%	2.9%

3-YEAR TREND – ESTIMATED NUMBER OF ESTABLISHMENTS

Year	Employee Size of Establishment									Total Employ-ment
	1-4 Emps.	5-9 Emps.	10-19 Emps.	20-49 Emps.	50-99 Emps.	100-249 Emps.	250-499 Emps.	>500 Emps.	Non-Employer	
2017	119,950	11,575	6,762	4,594	1,764	1,090	294	190	240,358	386,579
2018	125,329	12,094	7,065	4,800	1,843	1,139	308	198	251,136	403,913
2019	131,423	12,682	7,409	5,034	1,933	1,195	323	208	263,348	423,554

3-YEAR TREND – ESTIMATED INDUSTRY SALES ($MILLIONS)

Year	Employee Size of Establishment									Total Employ-ment
	1-4 Emps.	5-9 Emps.	10-19 Emps.	20-49 Emps.	50-99 Emps.	100-249 Emps.	250-499 Emps.	>500 Emps.	Non-Employer	
2017	24,003.8	6,088.3	8,943.9	16,083.9	13,578.4	22,618.2	20,583.0	30,423.8	21,936.6	164,259.8
2018	25,856.8	6,558.3	9,634.4	17,325.6	14,626.6	24,364.3	22,172.0	32,052.0	23,630.1	176,219.9
2019	28,028.5	7,109.1	10,443.6	18,780.7	15,855.1	26,410.6	24,034.2	33,936.3	25,614.7	190,212.8

3-YEAR TREND – ESTIMATED NUMBER OF EMPLOYEES

Year	Employee Size of Establishment									Total Employ-ment
	1-4 Emps.	5-9 Emps.	10-19 Emps.	20-49 Emps.	50-99 Emps.	100-249 Emps.	250-499 Emps.	>500 Emps.	Non-Employer	
2017	299,875	67,137	91,963	138,283	104,804	137,508	85,648	157,745	240,358	1,323,321
2018	313,322	70,147	96,087	144,484	109,503	143,674	89,489	164,818	251,136	1,382,660
2019	328,558	73,558	100,759	151,510	114,828	150,660	93,841	172,833	263,348	1,449,895

© Barnes Reports: 2018 U.S. Industry & Market Outlook

Management Consulting Services Industry (NAICS 54161)

Sub-Industries – 2018 Estimated Industry Sales, Establishments & Employment

Sub-Industries	Category*	Establishments	Sales ($Mill)	Employment
Management consulting services	Major1	123,075	69,896.4	426,184
Industrial and labor consulting services	Minor1	1,245	455.1	5,019
Automation and robotics consultant	Minor2	1,383	425.2	4,711
Industrial consultant	Minor2	2,008	534.4	5,390
Industrial hygiene consultant	Minor2	363	109.2	1,169
Maintenance management consultant	Minor2	1,229	515.5	7,776
Management engineering	Minor2	546	579.7	3,002
Manufacturing management consultant	Minor2	3,847	2,009.0	10,784
Quality assurance consultant	Minor2	1,343	684.9	8,639
Human resource consulting services	Minor1	8,112	3,506.8	67,805
Compensation and benefits planning consultant	Minor2	2,389	4,492.9	19,225
Incentive or award program consultant	Minor2	718	1,613.3	5,676
Labor and union relations consultant	Minor2	479	140.3	1,142
Personnel management consultant	Minor2	2,192	727.1	9,920
Programmed instruction service	Minor2	578	112.8	1,932
Training and development consultant	Minor2	10,123	3,982.8	30,700
Marketing consulting services	Minor1	85,816	20,363.1	211,318
Distribution channels consultant	Minor2	570	221.3	2,296
Franchising consultant	Minor2	404	90.7	963
Merchandising consultant	Minor2	781	388.9	5,572
New products and services consultants	Minor2	868	286.0	3,494
Sales (including sales management) consultant	Minor2	5,670	1,374.3	14,034
Industry specialist consultants	Minor1	53,280	33,007.0	254,813
Business planning and organizing services	Minor1	27,065	4,927.9	57,463
Administrative services consultant	Minor2	3,376	1,489.0	18,224
Business management consultant	Minor2	14,060	6,460.1	55,735
Foreign trade consultant	Minor2	1,841	626.5	4,140
General management consultant	Minor2	6,061	3,233.2	19,222
Management information systems consultant	Minor2	2,300	1,213.6	15,106
Productivity improvement consultant	Minor2	491	121.4	1,472
Site location consultant	Minor2	414	135.2	1,480
Financial consultant	Minor2	41,283	12,496.3	108,255

*Category-Major categories (Major1) are more general descriptions for companies that self-selected to capture the many functions they perform in the industry. Minor categories (Minor1, Minor2) are more specific for companies that have more detailed functions (Minor1 is a larger category than Minor2). Minor categories figures (sales, etc.) can be aggregated to larger minor categories (Minor2 sums to Minor1) and major categories overall figures.

ADVERTISING AGENCIES INDUSTRY
(NAICS 54181)

NAICS 54181: Advertising Agencies. This industry comprises establishments primarily engaged in designing and implementing public relations campaigns. These campaigns are designed to promote the interests and image of their clients. Establishments providing lobbying, political consulting, or public relations consulting are included in this industry.

INDUSTRY ESTABLISHMENTS, SALES & EMPLOYMENT TRENDS

	Year					Percent Chg. Year-to-Year			
	2015	2016	2017	2018	2019	15-16	16-17	17-18	18-19
Establishments	33,876	33,196	32,508	32,506	32,623	-2.0%	-2.1%	0.0%	0.4%
Sales ($Millions)	66,780	67,829	69,158	72,008	75,372	1.6%	2.0%	4.1%	4.7%
Employment	197,436	193,470	189,461	189,453	190,133	-2.0%	-2.1%	0.0%	0.4%
Sales ($M)/Estab.	1.97	2.04	2.13	2.22	2.31	3.7%	4.1%	4.1%	4.3%
Sales ($)/Emp.	338,236	350,590	365,025	380,082	396,418	3.7%	4.1%	4.1%	4.3%

3-YEAR TREND – ESTIMATED NUMBER OF ESTABLISHMENTS

Year	Employee Size of Establishment									Total Employment
	1-4 Emps.	5-9 Emps.	10-19 Emps.	20-49 Emps.	50-99 Emps.	100-249 Emps.	250-499 Emps.	>500 Emps.	Non-Employer	
2017	8,098	1,868	1,256	915	364	209	65	40	19,691	32,508
2018	8,098	1,868	1,256	915	364	209	65	40	19,690	32,506
2019	8,127	1,875	1,261	919	365	210	65	40	19,761	32,623

3-YEAR TREND – ESTIMATED INDUSTRY SALES ($MILLIONS)

Year	Employee Size of Establishment									Total Employment
	1-4 Emps.	5-9 Emps.	10-19 Emps.	20-49 Emps.	50-99 Emps.	100-249 Emps.	250-499 Emps.	>500 Emps.	Non-Employer	
2017	4,360.2	2,644.0	4,470.2	8,623.3	7,530.6	11,674.5	12,273.7	15,575.6	2,005.8	69,157.9
2018	4,539.8	2,753.0	4,654.4	8,978.6	7,840.9	12,155.5	12,779.5	16,217.6	2,088.5	72,007.9
2019	4,752.9	2,882.1	4,872.8	9,399.9	8,208.9	12,725.9	13,379.1	16,963.9	2,186.5	75,371.9

3-YEAR TREND – ESTIMATED NUMBER OF EMPLOYEES

Year	Employee Size of Establishment									Total Employment
	1-4 Emps.	5-9 Emps.	10-19 Emps.	20-49 Emps.	50-99 Emps.	100-249 Emps.	250-499 Emps.	>500 Emps.	Non-Employer	
2017	20,245	10,836	17,083	27,556	21,603	26,379	18,982	27,084	19,691	189,461
2018	20,245	10,836	17,083	27,554	21,602	26,378	18,981	27,083	19,690	189,453
2019	20,317	10,875	17,144	27,653	21,680	26,473	19,050	27,180	19,761	190,133

© Barnes Reports: 2018 U.S. Industry & Market Outlook

ADVERTISING AGENCIES INDUSTRY
(NAICS 54181)

SUB-INDUSTRIES – 2018 ESTIMATED INDUSTRY SALES, ESTABLISHMENTS & EMPLOYMENT

Sub-Industries	Category*	Establishments	Sales ($Mill)	Employment
Advertising agencies	Major1	26,398	67,165.3	167,835
Advertising consultant	Minor2	6,108	4,842.6	21,619

*Category-Major categories (Major1) are more general descriptions for companies that self-selected to capture the many functions they perform in the industry. Minor categories (Minor1, Minor2) are more specific for companies that have more detailed functions (Minor1 is a larger category than Minor2). Minor categories figures (sales, etc.) can be aggregated to larger minor categories (Minor2 sums to Minor1) and major categories overall figures.

PUBLIC RELATIONS AGENCIES INDUSTRY (NAICS 54182)

NAICS 54182: Public Relations Agencies. This industry comprises establishments primarily engaged in designing and implementing public relations campaigns. These campaigns are designed to promote the interests and image of their clients. Establishments providing lobbying, political consulting, or public relations consulting are included in this industry.

INDUSTRY ESTABLISHMENTS, SALES & EMPLOYMENT TRENDS

	Year					Percent Chg. Year-to-Year			
	2015	2016	2017	2018	2019	15-16	16-17	17-18	18-19
Establishments	21,483	21,647	22,101	22,528	23,047	0.8%	2.1%	1.9%	2.3%
Sales ($Millions)	11,148	11,869	12,830	13,839	14,981	6.5%	8.1%	7.9%	8.3%
Employment	71,340	71,883	73,392	74,811	76,534	0.8%	2.1%	1.9%	2.3%
Sales ($M)/Estab.	0.52	0.55	0.58	0.61	0.65	5.7%	5.9%	5.8%	5.8%
Sales ($)/Emp.	156,271	165,108	174,811	184,980	195,745	5.7%	5.9%	5.8%	5.8%

3-YEAR TREND – ESTIMATED NUMBER OF ESTABLISHMENTS

Year	Employee Size of Establishment									Total Employment
	1-4 Emps.	5-9 Emps.	10-19 Emps.	20-49 Emps.	50-99 Emps.	100-249 Emps.	250-499 Emps.	>500 Emps.	Non-Employer	
2017	6,428	1,145	634	329	109	57	9	3	13,387	22,101
2018	6,552	1,167	646	336	111	58	9	3	13,646	22,528
2019	6,703	1,194	661	343	114	59	10	3	13,961	23,047

3-YEAR TREND – ESTIMATED INDUSTRY SALES ($MILLIONS)

Year	Employee Size of Establishment									Total Employment
	1-4 Emps.	5-9 Emps.	10-19 Emps.	20-49 Emps.	50-99 Emps.	100-249 Emps.	250-499 Emps.	>500 Emps.	Non-Employer	
2017	2,086.9	977.1	1,360.0	1,869.9	1,361.6	1,904.1	1,050.2	802.0	1,417.8	12,829.6
2018	2,252.3	1,054.5	1,467.7	2,018.1	1,469.5	2,055.0	1,133.4	857.8	1,530.2	13,838.6
2019	2,439.9	1,142.4	1,589.9	2,186.2	1,591.9	2,226.1	1,227.8	919.5	1,657.6	14,981.2

3-YEAR TREND – ESTIMATED NUMBER OF EMPLOYEES

Year	Employee Size of Establishment									Total Employment
	1-4 Emps.	5-9 Emps.	10-19 Emps.	20-49 Emps.	50-99 Emps.	100-249 Emps.	250-499 Emps.	>500 Emps.	Non-Employer	
2017	16,069	6,641	8,618	9,909	6,477	7,135	2,693	2,461	13,387	73,392
2018	16,380	6,769	8,785	10,101	6,603	7,273	2,745	2,508	13,646	74,811
2019	16,757	6,925	8,988	10,333	6,755	7,440	2,809	2,566	13,961	76,534

© Barnes Reports: 2018 U.S. Industry & Market Outlook

Public Relations Agencies Industry (NAICS 54182)

Sub-Industries – 2018 Estimated Industry Sales, Establishments & Employment

Sub-Industries	Category*	Establishments	Sales ($Mill)	Employment
Public relations services	Major1	8,909	5,410.1	32,720
Lobbyist	Minor2	1,404	891.0	4,147
Promotion service	Minor2	5,991	3,557.5	14,080
Public relations and publicity	Minor2	2,863	1,939.6	14,113
Sales promotion	Minor2	3,362	2,040.5	9,751

*Category-Major categories (Major1) are more general descriptions for companies that self-selected to capture the many functions they perform in the industry. Minor categories (Minor1, Minor2) are more specific for companies that have more detailed functions (Minor1 is a larger category than Minor2). Minor categories figures (sales, etc.) can be aggregated to larger minor categories (Minor2 sums to Minor1) and major categories overall figures.

DIRECT MAIL ADVERTISING INDUSTRY
(NAICS 54186)

NAICS 54186: Direct Mail Advertising. This industry comprises establishments primarily engaged in (1) creating and designing advertising campaigns for the purpose of distributing advertising materials (e.g., coupons, flyers, samples) or specialties (e.g., key chains, magnets, pens with customized messages imprinted) by mail or other direct distribution; and/or (2) preparing advertising materials or specialties for mailing or other direct distribution. These establishments may also compile, maintain, sell, and rent mailing lists.

INDUSTRY ESTABLISHMENTS, SALES & EMPLOYMENT TRENDS

	Year					Percent Chg. Year-to-Year			
	2015	2016	2017	2018	2019	15-16	16-17	17-18	18-19
Establishments	6,716	6,608	6,348	6,203	6,083	-1.6%	-3.9%	-2.3%	-1.9%
Sales ($Millions)	7,122	7,246	7,237	7,358	7,522	1.7%	-0.1%	1.7%	2.2%
Employment	46,763	46,010	44,199	43,189	42,355	-1.6%	-3.9%	-2.3%	-1.9%
Sales ($M)/Estab.	1.06	1.10	1.14	1.19	1.24	3.4%	4.0%	4.0%	4.2%
Sales ($)/Emp.	152,307	157,493	163,749	170,377	177,607	3.4%	4.0%	4.0%	4.2%

3-YEAR TREND – ESTIMATED NUMBER OF ESTABLISHMENTS

Year	Employee Size of Establishment									Total Employment
	1-4 Emps.	5-9 Emps.	10-19 Emps.	20-49 Emps.	50-99 Emps.	100-249 Emps.	250-499 Emps.	>500 Emps.	Non-Employer	
2017	1,375	383	297	256	105	69	10	8	3,845	6,348
2018	1,344	374	290	250	103	67	10	7	3,757	6,203
2019	1,318	367	284	245	101	66	10	7	3,685	6,083

3-YEAR TREND – ESTIMATED INDUSTRY SALES ($MILLIONS)

Year	Employee Size of Establishment									Total Employment
	1-4 Emps.	5-9 Emps.	10-19 Emps.	20-49 Emps.	50-99 Emps.	100-249 Emps.	250-499 Emps.	>500 Emps.	Non-Employer	
2017	324.6	237.5	463.0	1,057.7	952.3	1,688.0	857.3	1,266.8	390.3	7,237.5
2018	329.7	241.2	470.3	1,074.4	967.4	1,714.7	870.8	1,293.3	396.4	7,358.4
2019	336.8	246.4	480.4	1,097.5	988.2	1,751.6	889.6	1,326.9	405.0	7,522.5

3-YEAR TREND – ESTIMATED NUMBER OF EMPLOYEES

Year	Employee Size of Establishment									Total Employment
	1-4 Emps.	5-9 Emps.	10-19 Emps.	20-49 Emps.	50-99 Emps.	100-249 Emps.	250-499 Emps.	>500 Emps.	Non-Employer	
2017	3,438	2,220	4,036	7,710	6,232	8,701	3,024	4,992	3,845	44,199
2018	3,359	2,169	3,944	7,534	6,089	8,502	2,955	4,878	3,757	43,189
2019	3,295	2,128	3,868	7,388	5,972	8,338	2,898	4,784	3,685	42,355

© Barnes Reports: 2018 U.S. Industry & Market Outlook

Direct Mail Advertising Industry
(NAICS 54186)

Sub-Industries – 2018 Estimated Industry Sales, Establishments & Employment

Sub-Industries	Category*	Establishments	Sales ($Mill)	Employment
Direct mail advertising services	Major1	3,173	4,195.7	22,966
Addressing service	Minor2	88	54.9	1,006
Addressographing service	Minor2	2	1.4	6
Mailing list compilers	Minor2	266	202.6	1,185
Mailing service	Minor2	2,463	2,508.4	16,853
Mailing list management	Minor2	48	132.9	331
Mailing list brokers	Minor2	164	262.4	844

*Category-Major categories (Major1) are more general descriptions for companies that self-selected to capture the many functions they perform in the industry. Minor categories (Minor1, Minor2) are more specific for companies that have more detailed functions (Minor1 is a larger category than Minor2). Minor categories figures (sales, etc.) can be aggregated to larger minor categories (Minor2 sums to Minor1) and major categories overall figures.

MARKETING RESEARCH & PUBLIC OPINION POLLING
(NAICS 54191)

NAICS 54191: Marketing Research & Public Opinion Polling. This industry comprises establishments primarily engaged in systematically gathering, recording, tabulating, and presenting marketing and public opinion data.

Industry Establishments, Sales & Employment Trends

	Year					Percent Chg. Year-to-Year			
	2015	2016	2017	2018	2019	15-16	16-17	17-18	18-19
Establishments	23,523	24,516	24,312	24,271	24,317	4.2%	-0.8%	-0.2%	0.2%
Sales ($Millions)	16,800	17,962	18,444	19,084	19,856	6.9%	2.7%	3.5%	4.0%
Employment	109,030	113,630	112,689	112,495	112,709	4.2%	-0.8%	-0.2%	0.2%
Sales ($M)/Estab.	0.71	0.73	0.76	0.79	0.82	2.6%	3.5%	3.6%	3.8%
Sales ($)/Emp.	154,082	158,071	163,672	169,643	176,174	2.6%	3.5%	3.6%	3.8%

3-Year Trend – Estimated Number of Establishments

Year	Employee Size of Establishment									Total Employment
	1-4 Emps.	5-9 Emps.	10-19 Emps.	20-49 Emps.	50-99 Emps.	100-249 Emps.	250-499 Emps.	>500 Emps.	Non-Employer	
2017	3,076	682	588	530	195	129	40	25	19,046	24,312
2018	3,071	681	587	529	195	129	40	25	19,014	24,271
2019	3,076	682	588	530	195	129	40	25	19,050	24,317

3-Year Trend – Estimated Industry Sales ($Millions)

Year	Employee Size of Establishment									Total Employment
	1-4 Emps.	5-9 Emps.	10-19 Emps.	20-49 Emps.	50-99 Emps.	100-249 Emps.	250-499 Emps.	>500 Emps.	Non-Employer	
2017	720.9	420.2	911.1	2,174.2	1,760.8	3,138.7	3,300.6	4,405.9	1,611.6	18,444.0
2018	745.9	434.8	942.6	2,249.3	1,821.6	3,247.1	3,414.6	4,561.0	1,667.3	19,084.0
2019	776.2	452.4	980.9	2,340.7	1,895.7	3,379.1	3,553.4	4,743.0	1,735.0	19,856.4

3-Year Trend – Estimated Number of Employees

Year	Employee Size of Establishment									Total Employment
	1-4 Emps.	5-9 Emps.	10-19 Emps.	20-49 Emps.	50-99 Emps.	100-249 Emps.	250-499 Emps.	>500 Emps.	Non-Employer	
2017	7,690	3,956	7,998	15,959	11,603	16,291	11,726	18,418	19,046	112,689
2018	7,676	3,950	7,984	15,932	11,583	16,263	11,706	18,386	19,014	112,495
2019	7,691	3,957	7,999	15,962	11,605	16,294	11,728	18,421	19,050	112,709

© Barnes Reports: 2018 U.S. Industry & Market Outlook

Marketing Research & Public Opinion Polling (NAICS 54191)

Sub-Industries – 2018 Estimated Industry Sales, Establishments & Employment

Sub-Industries	Category*	Establishments	Sales ($Mill)	Employment
Commercial nonphysical research	Major1	4,598	5,636.3	15,070
Market analysis, business, and economic research	Minor1	2,576	1,239.9	9,278
Business analysis	Minor2	558	176.5	1,780
Business economic service	Minor2	904	382.0	2,852
Business research service	Minor2	1,504	941.0	5,396
Economic research	Minor2	830	437.0	2,598
Market analysis or research	Minor2	6,572	5,737.4	41,743
Merger, acquisition, and reorganization research	Minor2	609	287.8	1,704
Opinion research	Minor2	169	70.9	1,437
Research services, except laboratory	Minor2	3,125	2,070.1	16,051
Survey service: marketing, location, etc.	Minor2	740	235.5	3,785
Commercial sociological and educational research	Minor1	179	65.7	673
Educational research	Minor2	1,681	1,618.3	9,173
Sociological research	Minor2	226	185.4	955

*Category-Major categories (Major1) are more general descriptions for companies that self-selected to capture the many functions they perform in the industry. Minor categories (Minor1, Minor2) are more specific for companies that have more detailed functions (Minor1 is a larger category than Minor2). Minor categories figures (sales, etc.) can be aggregated to larger minor categories (Minor2 sums to Minor1) and major categories overall figures.

VETERINARY SERVICES INDUSTRY
(NAICS 54194)

NAICS 54194: Veterinary Services. This industry comprises establishments of licensed veterinary practitioners primarily engaged in the practice of veterinary medicine, dentistry, or surgery for animals; and establishments primarily engaged in providing testing services for licensed veterinary practitioners.

INDUSTRY ESTABLISHMENTS, SALES & EMPLOYMENT TRENDS

	Year					Percent Chg. Year-to-Year			
	2015	2016	2017	2018	2019	15-16	16-17	17-18	18-19
Establishments	38,213	39,066	40,182	41,166	42,327	2.2%	2.9%	2.4%	2.8%
Sales ($Millions)	26,114	28,275	30,869	33,540	36,570	8.3%	9.2%	8.7%	9.0%
Employment	347,651	355,410	365,561	374,516	385,082	2.2%	2.9%	2.4%	2.8%
Sales ($M)/Estab.	0.68	0.72	0.77	0.81	0.86	5.9%	6.1%	6.1%	6.0%
Sales ($)/Emp.	75,115	79,556	84,443	89,556	94,966	5.9%	6.1%	6.1%	6.0%

3-YEAR TREND – ESTIMATED NUMBER OF ESTABLISHMENTS

Year	Employee Size of Establishment									Total Employment
	1-4 Emps.	5-9 Emps.	10-19 Emps.	20-49 Emps.	50-99 Emps.	100-249 Emps.	250-499 Emps.	>500 Emps.	Non-Employer	
2017	9,808	9,023	9,479	3,825	341	91	9	3	7,601	40,182
2018	10,048	9,244	9,712	3,919	349	94	10	3	7,788	41,166
2019	10,331	9,505	9,986	4,030	359	96	10	3	8,007	42,327

3-YEAR TREND – ESTIMATED INDUSTRY SALES ($MILLIONS)

Year	Employee Size of Establishment									Total Employment
	1-4 Emps.	5-9 Emps.	10-19 Emps.	20-49 Emps.	50-99 Emps.	100-249 Emps.	250-499 Emps.	>500 Emps.	Non-Employer	
2017	1,544.0	3,733.6	9,864.0	10,536.2	2,062.7	1,492.8	520.5	393.4	721.8	30,869.0
2018	1,677.9	4,057.3	10,719.1	11,449.6	2,241.5	1,622.2	565.6	422.8	784.3	33,540.2
2019	1,829.7	4,424.5	11,689.2	12,485.8	2,444.4	1,769.0	616.8	455.2	855.3	36,569.8

3-YEAR TREND – ESTIMATED NUMBER OF EMPLOYEES

Year	Employee Size of Establishment									Total Employment
	1-4 Emps.	5-9 Emps.	10-19 Emps.	20-49 Emps.	50-99 Emps.	100-249 Emps.	250-499 Emps.	>500 Emps.	Non-Employer	
2017	24,519	52,334	128,920	115,145	20,237	11,536	2,753	2,515	7,601	365,561
2018	25,119	53,616	132,079	117,966	20,733	11,818	2,820	2,577	7,788	374,516
2019	25,828	55,128	135,805	121,294	21,318	12,152	2,900	2,650	8,007	385,082

© Barnes Reports: 2018 U.S. Industry & Market Outlook

Veterinary Services Industry (NAICS 54194)

Sub-Industries – 2018 Estimated Industry Sales, Establishments & Employment

Sub-Industries	Category*	Establishments	Sales ($Mill)	Employment
Veterinary services, specialties	Major1	13,605	10,960.9	106,798
Animal hospital services, pets and other animal specialtie	Minor2	16,272	15,395.4	171,442
Veterinarian, animal specialties	Minor2	11,288	7,183.9	96,276

*Category-Major categories (Major1) are more general descriptions for companies that self-selected to capture the many functions they perform in the industry. Minor categories (Minor1, Minor2) are more specific for companies that have more detailed functions (Minor1 is a larger category than Minor2). Minor categories figures (sales, etc.) can be aggregated to larger minor categories (Minor2 sums to Minor1) and major categories overall figures.

TELEMARKETING SERVICES INDUSTRY
(NAICS 561422)

NAICS 561422: Telemarketing Services. This industry comprises establishments primarily engaged in providing telemarketing services on a contract or fee basis for others, such as: (1) promoting clients' products or services by telephone, (2) taking orders for clients by telephone, and (3) soliciting contributions or providing information for clients by telephone. These establishments never own the product or provide the services they are representing and generally can originate and/or receive calls for others.

INDUSTRY ESTABLISHMENTS, SALES & EMPLOYMENT TRENDS

	Year					Percent Chg. Year-to-Year			
	2015	2016	2017	2018	2019	15-16	16-17	17-18	18-19
Establishments	12,588	12,718	12,947	13,156	13,451	1.0%	1.8%	1.6%	2.2%
Sales ($Millions)	30,179	31,533	33,294	35,144	37,350	4.5%	5.6%	5.6%	6.3%
Employment	351,313	354,939	361,333	367,169	375,413	1.0%	1.8%	1.6%	2.2%
Sales ($M)/Estab.	2.40	2.48	2.57	2.67	2.78	3.4%	3.7%	3.9%	3.9%
Sales ($)/Emp.	85,904	88,841	92,143	95,715	99,490	3.4%	3.7%	3.9%	3.9%

3-YEAR TREND – ESTIMATED NUMBER OF ESTABLISHMENTS

Year	Employee Size of Establishment									Total Employment
	1-4 Emps.	5-9 Emps.	10-19 Emps.	20-49 Emps.	50-99 Emps.	100-249 Emps.	250-499 Emps.	>500 Emps.	Non-Employer	
2017	1,199	371	482	580	380	426	244	237	9,028	12,947
2018	1,219	377	490	589	386	433	248	240	9,174	13,156
2019	1,246	386	501	603	394	442	253	246	9,380	13,451

3-YEAR TREND – ESTIMATED INDUSTRY SALES ($MILLIONS)

Year	Employee Size of Establishment									Total Employment
	1-4 Emps.	5-9 Emps.	10-19 Emps.	20-49 Emps.	50-99 Emps.	100-249 Emps.	250-499 Emps.	>500 Emps.	Non-Employer	
2017	116.4	94.7	309.5	985.2	1,416.9	4,284.5	8,266.8	17,459.0	361.2	33,294.4
2018	123.3	100.3	327.7	1,043.2	1,500.3	4,536.7	8,753.4	18,376.4	382.4	35,143.7
2019	131.6	107.1	349.8	1,113.4	1,601.3	4,842.1	9,342.7	19,453.7	408.2	37,349.8

3-YEAR TREND – ESTIMATED NUMBER OF EMPLOYEES

Year	Employee Size of Establishment									Total Employment
	1-4 Emps.	5-9 Emps.	10-19 Emps.	20-49 Emps.	50-99 Emps.	100-249 Emps.	250-499 Emps.	>500 Emps.	Non-Employer	
2017	2,998	2,154	6,560	17,461	22,544	53,694	70,910	175,984	9,028	361,333
2018	3,047	2,188	6,666	17,743	22,908	54,562	72,055	178,827	9,174	367,169
2019	3,115	2,237	6,816	18,141	23,422	55,787	73,673	182,842	9,380	375,413

© Barnes Reports: 2018 U.S. Industry & Market Outlook

TELEMARKETING SERVICES INDUSTRY
(NAICS 561422)

Sub-Industries – 2018 Estimated Industry Sales, Establishments & Employment

Sub-Industries	Category*	Establishments	Sales ($Mill)	Employment
Telemarketing services	Minor2	13,156	35,143.7	367,169

*Category-Major categories (Major1) are more general descriptions for companies that self-selected to capture the many functions they perform in the industry. Minor categories (Minor1, Minor2) are more specific for companies that have more detailed functions (Minor1 is a larger category than Minor2). Minor categories figures (sales, etc.) can be aggregated to larger minor categories (Minor2 sums to Minor1) and major categories overall figures.

SECURITY GUARDS & PATROL SERVICES INDUSTRY
(NAICS 561612)

NAICS 561612: Security Guards & Patrol Services. This industry comprises establishments primarily engaged in providing detective, guard, and armored car services. Establishments primarily engaged in monitoring and maintaining security systems devices, such as burglar and fire alarms, are classified in 7382.

Industry Establishments, Sales & Employment Trends

	Year					Percent Chg. Year-to-Year			
	2015	2016	2017	2018	2019	15-16	16-17	17-18	18-19
Establishments	35,508	37,171	39,208	40,896	42,942	4.7%	5.5%	4.3%	5.0%
Sales ($Millions)	43,700	45,386	47,741	49,898	52,669	3.9%	5.2%	4.5%	5.6%
Employment	612,428	641,123	676,253	705,363	740,656	4.7%	5.5%	4.3%	5.0%
Sales ($M)/Estab.	1.23	1.22	1.22	1.22	1.23	-0.8%	-0.3%	0.2%	0.5%
Sales ($)/Emp.	71,356	70,791	70,597	70,741	71,112	-0.8%	-0.3%	0.2%	0.5%

3-Year Trend – Estimated Number of Establishments

Year	Employee Size of Establishment									Total Employment
	1-4 Emps.	5-9 Emps.	10-19 Emps.	20-49 Emps.	50-99 Emps.	100-249 Emps.	250-499 Emps.	>500 Emps.	Non-Employer	
2017	3,085	1,371	1,494	1,687	1,149	1,186	443	282	28,511	39,208
2018	3,218	1,430	1,558	1,760	1,199	1,237	462	294	29,738	40,896
2019	3,379	1,502	1,636	1,848	1,259	1,299	485	308	31,226	42,942

3-Year Trend – Estimated Industry Sales ($Millions)

Year	Employee Size of Establishment									Total Employment
	1-4 Emps.	5-9 Emps.	10-19 Emps.	20-49 Emps.	50-99 Emps.	100-249 Emps.	250-499 Emps.	>500 Emps.	Non-Employer	
2017	247.7	289.4	792.9	2,370.1	3,549.5	9,869.8	12,420.4	16,994.2	1,207.4	47,741.4
2018	260.4	304.2	833.5	2,491.4	3,731.2	10,375.0	13,056.2	17,576.7	1,269.2	49,897.8
2019	276.6	323.2	885.4	2,646.7	3,963.7	11,021.6	13,869.9	18,334.0	1,348.3	52,669.4

3-Year Trend – Estimated Number of Employees

Year	Employee Size of Establishment									Total Employment
	1-4 Emps.	5-9 Emps.	10-19 Emps.	20-49 Emps.	50-99 Emps.	100-249 Emps.	250-499 Emps.	>500 Emps.	Non-Employer	
2017	7,713	7,954	20,318	50,786	68,280	149,546	128,808	214,337	28,511	676,253
2018	8,045	8,297	21,193	52,972	71,219	155,983	134,353	223,564	29,738	705,363
2019	8,448	8,712	22,254	55,623	74,782	163,788	141,075	234,750	31,226	740,656

© Barnes Reports: 2018 U.S. Industry & Market Outlook

Security Guards & Patrol Services Industry (NAICS 561612)

Sub-Industries — 2018 Estimated Industry Sales, Establishments & Employment

Sub-Industries	Category*	Establishments	Sales ($Mill)	Employment
Detective and armored car services	Major1	5,127	3,211.0	101,547
Guard services	Minor1	11,929	9,164.8	77,709
Armored car services	Minor2	770	1,643.7	29,335
Burglary protection service	Minor2	50	35.5	737
Guard dog rental	Minor2	58	32.5	818
Protective services, guard	Minor2	1,505	11,171.1	53,122
Security guard service	Minor2	6,175	20,000.2	336,376
Detective services	Minor1	2,340	976.7	22,636
Detective agency	Minor2	1,620	767.1	21,470
Fingerprint service	Minor2	188	48.7	1,446
Lie detection service	Minor2	333	68.5	1,584
Private investigator	Minor2	10,801	2,777.9	58,584

*Category-Major categories (Major1) are more general descriptions for companies that self-selected to capture the many functions they perform in the industry. Minor categories (Minor1, Minor2) are more specific for companies that have more detailed functions (Minor1 is a larger category than Minor2). Minor categories figures (sales, etc.) can be aggregated to larger minor categories (Minor2 sums to Minor1) and major categories overall figures.

COLLEGES & UNIVERSITIES INDUSTRY
(NAICS 61131)

NAICS 61131: Colleges & Universities. This industry comprises establishments primarily furnishing academic courses and granting academic degrees. The requirement for admission is at least a high school diploma or equivalent general academic training.

INDUSTRY ESTABLISHMENTS, SALES & EMPLOYMENT TRENDS

	Year					Percent Chg. Year-to-Year			
	2015	2016	2017	2018	2019	15-16	16-17	17-18	18-19
Establishments	24,746	25,064	25,443	26,229	27,108	1.3%	1.5%	3.1%	3.3%
Sales ($Millions)	212,621	219,934	228,850	240,229	253,118	3.4%	4.1%	5.0%	5.4%
Employment	969,176	981,660	996,485	1,027,290	1,061,687	1.3%	1.5%	3.1%	3.3%
Sales ($M)/Estab.	8.59	8.77	8.99	9.16	9.34	2.1%	2.5%	1.8%	2.0%
Sales ($)/Emp.	219,383	224,043	229,657	233,847	238,411	2.1%	2.5%	1.8%	2.0%

3-YEAR TREND – ESTIMATED NUMBER OF ESTABLISHMENTS

Year	Employee Size of Establishment									Total
	1-4 Emps.	5-9 Emps.	10-19 Emps.	20-49 Emps.	50-99 Emps.	100-249 Emps.	250-499 Emps.	>500 Emps.	Non-Employer	Employment
2017	1,226	455	476	741	470	419	329	806	20,520	25,443
2018	1,263	470	491	764	484	432	339	831	21,154	26,229
2019	1,306	485	507	790	501	447	351	859	21,863	27,108

3-YEAR TREND – ESTIMATED INDUSTRY SALES ($MILLIONS)

Year	Employee Size of Establishment									Total
	1-4 Emps.	5-9 Emps.	10-19 Emps.	20-49 Emps.	50-99 Emps.	100-249 Emps.	250-499 Emps.	>500 Emps.	Non-Employer	Employment
2017	299.6	292.7	769.3	3,170.9	4,418.1	10,630.8	28,102.3	180,254.6	911.2	228,849.6
2018	319.8	312.4	821.1	3,384.3	4,715.4	11,346.1	29,993.3	188,363.9	972.6	240,228.8
2019	343.0	335.0	880.6	3,629.5	5,057.1	12,168.3	32,166.8	197,494.9	1,043.0	253,118.3

3-YEAR TREND – ESTIMATED NUMBER OF EMPLOYEES

Year	Employee Size of Establishment									Total
	1-4 Emps.	5-9 Emps.	10-19 Emps.	20-49 Emps.	50-99 Emps.	100-249 Emps.	250-499 Emps.	>500 Emps.	Non-Employer	Employment
2017	3,064	2,642	6,474	22,314	27,911	52,898	95,711	764,951	20,520	996,485
2018	3,159	2,723	6,674	23,003	28,773	54,534	98,670	788,598	21,154	1,027,290
2019	3,264	2,815	6,898	23,774	29,737	56,360	101,973	815,003	21,863	1,061,687

© Barnes Reports: 2018 U.S. Industry & Market Outlook

Colleges & Universities Industry (NAICS 61131)

Sub-Industries – 2018 Estimated Industry Sales, Establishments & Employment

Sub-Industries	Category*	Establishments	Sales ($Mill)	Employment
Colleges and universities	Major1	8,051	35,725.2	234,035
Colleges and universities	Minor1	1,212	3,546.5	39,889
College, except junior	Minor2	1,773	36,289.6	106,902
University	Minor2	13,754	158,744.9	627,083
Professional schools	Minor1	969	4,802.4	11,007
Service academy	Minor2	87	151.6	1,712
Theological seminary	Minor2	383	968.6	6,663

*Category-Major categories (Major1) are more general descriptions for companies that self-selected to capture the many functions they perform in the industry. Minor categories (Minor1, Minor2) are more specific for companies that have more detailed functions (Minor1 is a larger category than Minor2). Minor categories figures (sales, etc.) can be aggregated to larger minor categories (Minor2 sums to Minor1) and major categories overall figures.

Exam Preparation & Tutoring Industry
(NAICS 611691)

NAICS 6111691: Exam Preparation & Tutoring. This industry comprises establishments primarily engaged in offering educational courses and services, not elsewhere classified. Includes music schools, drama schools, language schools, short-term examination preparatory schools, student exchange programs, curriculum development, and vocational counseling, except rehabilitation counseling. Dance schools are classified in 7911, and rehabilitation counseling is classified in 8331.

Industry Establishments, Sales & Employment Trends

	Year					Percent Chg. Year-to-Year			
	2015	2016	2017	2018	2019	15-16	16-17	17-18	18-19
Establishments	47,992	50,397	52,928	55,211	57,725	5.0%	5.0%	4.3%	4.6%
Sales ($Millions)	6,764	7,387	8,101	8,832	9,665	9.2%	9.7%	9.0%	9.4%
Employment	144,056	151,275	158,873	165,724	173,271	5.0%	5.0%	4.3%	4.6%
Sales ($M)/Estab.	0.14	0.15	0.15	0.16	0.17	4.0%	4.4%	4.5%	4.7%
Sales ($)/Emp.	46,953	48,831	50,988	53,292	55,777	4.0%	4.4%	4.5%	4.7%

3-Year Trend – Estimated Number of Establishments

Year	Employee Size of Establishment									Total Employment
	1-4 Emps.	5-9 Emps.	10-19 Emps.	20-49 Emps.	50-99 Emps.	100-249 Emps.	250-499 Emps.	>500 Emps.	Non-Employer	
2017	4,806	2,143	1,990	982	217	76	17	11	42,687	52,928
2018	5,014	2,235	2,075	1,024	227	79	17	12	44,528	55,211
2019	5,242	2,337	2,170	1,070	237	83	18	12	46,556	57,725

3-Year Trend – Estimated Industry Sales ($Millions)

Year	Employee Size of Establishment									Total Employment
	1-4 Emps.	5-9 Emps.	10-19 Emps.	20-49 Emps.	50-99 Emps.	100-249 Emps.	250-499 Emps.	>500 Emps.	Non-Employer	
2017	418.6	490.6	1,145.4	1,495.7	727.7	687.0	503.4	690.8	1,941.5	8,100.6
2018	456.9	535.4	1,250.0	1,632.3	794.2	749.8	549.4	744.8	2,118.9	8,831.8
2019	500.5	586.5	1,369.3	1,788.1	870.0	821.3	601.8	805.8	2,321.2	9,664.6

3-Year Trend – Estimated Number of Employees

Year	Employee Size of Establishment									Total Employment
	1-4 Emps.	5-9 Emps.	10-19 Emps.	20-49 Emps.	50-99 Emps.	100-249 Emps.	250-499 Emps.	>500 Emps.	Non-Employer	
2017	12,016	12,428	27,058	29,544	12,905	9,596	4,812	7,826	42,687	158,873
2018	12,534	12,964	28,225	30,818	13,462	10,010	5,020	8,163	44,528	165,724
2019	13,104	13,555	29,510	32,222	14,075	10,465	5,248	8,535	46,556	173,271

© Barnes Reports: 2018 U.S. Industry & Market Outlook

Exam Preparation & Tutoring Industry (NAICS 611691)

Sub-Industries — 2018 Estimated Industry Sales, Establishments & Employment

Sub-Industries	Category*	Establishments	Sales ($Mill)	Employment
Educational services	Minor1	41,588	7,593.0	136,844
Educational service, nondegree granting: continuing educ	Minor2	3,578	900.3	15,540
Tutoring school	Minor2	10,045	338.4	13,340

*Category-Major categories (Major1) are more general descriptions for companies that self-selected to capture the many functions they perform in the industry. Minor categories (Minor1, Minor2) are more specific for companies that have more detailed functions (Minor1 is a larger category than Minor2). Minor categories figures (sales, etc.) can be aggregated to larger minor categories (Minor2 sums to Minor1) and major categories overall figures.

EDUCATIONAL SUPPORT SERVICES INDUSTRY
(NAICS 61171)

NAICS 61171: Educational Support Services. This industry comprises establishments primarily engaged in offering educational courses and services, not elsewhere classified. Includes music schools, drama schools, language schools, short-term examination preparatory schools, student exchange programs, curriculum development, and vocational counseling, except rehabilitation counseling. Dance schools are classified in 7911, and rehabilitation counseling is classified in 8331.

INDUSTRY ESTABLISHMENTS, SALES & EMPLOYMENT TRENDS

	Year					Percent Chg. Year-to-Year			
	2015	2016	2017	2018	2019	15-16	16-17	17-18	18-19
Establishments	42,834	42,609	42,482	43,645	44,952	-0.5%	-0.3%	2.7%	3.0%
Sales ($Millions)	14,108	14,261	14,528	15,258	16,114	1.1%	1.9%	5.0%	5.6%
Employment	127,396	126,726	126,348	129,808	133,694	-0.5%	-0.3%	2.7%	3.0%
Sales ($M)/Estab.	0.33	0.33	0.34	0.35	0.36	1.6%	2.2%	2.2%	2.5%
Sales ($)/Emp.	110,739	112,537	114,984	117,545	120,525	1.6%	2.2%	2.2%	2.5%

3-YEAR TREND – ESTIMATED NUMBER OF ESTABLISHMENTS

Year	Employee Size of Establishment									Total
	1-4 Emps.	5-9 Emps.	10-19 Emps.	20-49 Emps.	50-99 Emps.	100-249 Emps.	250-499 Emps.	>500 Emps.	Non-Employer	Employment
2017	5,528	1,176	740	450	160	110	36	20	34,262	42,482
2018	5,680	1,208	760	463	164	113	37	20	35,200	43,645
2019	5,850	1,245	783	476	169	116	38	21	36,254	44,952

3-YEAR TREND – ESTIMATED INDUSTRY SALES ($MILLIONS)

Year	Employee Size of Establishment									Total
	1-4 Emps.	5-9 Emps.	10-19 Emps.	20-49 Emps.	50-99 Emps.	100-249 Emps.	250-499 Emps.	>500 Emps.	Non-Employer	Employment
2017	1,090.0	609.6	964.3	1,553.3	1,210.8	2,249.9	2,459.4	2,905.3	1,485.4	14,528.0
2018	1,146.8	641.3	1,014.4	1,634.1	1,273.8	2,367.0	2,587.4	3,030.7	1,562.7	15,258.2
2019	1,213.2	678.5	1,073.2	1,728.8	1,347.6	2,504.2	2,737.3	3,177.5	1,653.2	16,113.6

3-YEAR TREND – ESTIMATED NUMBER OF EMPLOYEES

Year	Employee Size of Establishment									Total
	1-4 Emps.	5-9 Emps.	10-19 Emps.	20-49 Emps.	50-99 Emps.	100-249 Emps.	250-499 Emps.	>500 Emps.	Non-Employer	Employment
2017	13,820	6,822	10,062	13,553	9,485	13,882	10,386	14,075	34,262	126,348
2018	14,199	7,009	10,338	13,924	9,744	14,262	10,671	14,461	35,200	129,808
2019	14,624	7,219	10,647	14,341	10,036	14,689	10,990	14,894	36,254	133,694

© Barnes Reports: 2018 U.S. Industry & Market Outlook

Educational Support Services Industry (NAICS 61171)

Sub-Industries – 2018 Estimated Industry Sales, Establishments & Employment

Sub-Industries	Category*	Establishments	Sales ($Mill)	Employment
Schools and educational services, nec	Major1	9,806	1,239.9	18,690
Arts and crafts schools	Minor1	574	1,326.6	1,890
Art school, except commercial	Minor2	557	248.8	2,610
Ceramic school	Minor2	124	21.6	361
Floral arrangement instruction	Minor2	272	12.7	185
Educational services	Minor1	14,302	8,631.9	63,098
Educational service, nondegree granting: continuing educ	Minor2	1,230	1,023.5	7,166
Tutoring school	Minor2	3,454	384.7	6,151
Music and drama schools	Minor1	605	69.3	1,139
Dramatic school	Minor2	141	39.6	390
Music school	Minor2	1,275	289.2	3,917
Musical instrument lessons	Minor2	1,871	118.1	1,877
Voice lessons	Minor2	310	16.8	241
Vehicle driving school	Minor1	2,368	216.0	3,515
Automobile driving instruction	Minor2	572	76.7	1,243
Truck driving training	Minor2	195	37.4	590
Reading and speaking schools	Minor1	479	49.1	846
Diction school	Minor2	12	1.3	18
Language school	Minor2	1,132	221.8	3,364
Public speaking school	Minor2	267	29.3	896
Reading school, including speed reading	Minor2	164	32.7	463
Airline training	Minor2	181	107.0	767
Bartending school	Minor2	189	10.8	166
Baton instruction	Minor2	55	4.8	123
Bible school	Minor2	227	79.9	770
Cooking school	Minor2	254	59.4	794
Dressmaking school	Minor2	5	0.6	8
Finishing school, charm and modeling	Minor2	114	14.0	361
Flying instruction	Minor2	335	70.1	721
Hypnosis school	Minor2	35	5.9	71
Meditation therapy	Minor2	502	43.0	651
Personal development school	Minor2	505	98.2	1,269
Prenatal instruction	Minor2	34	5.4	89
Misc. schools	Minor2	1,499	672.1	5,367

*Category-Major categories (Major1) are more general descriptions for companies that self-selected to capture the many functions they perform in the industry. Minor categories (Minor1, Minor2) are more specific for companies that have more detailed functions (Minor1 is a larger category than Minor2). Minor categories figures (sales, etc.) can be aggregated to larger minor categories (Minor2 sums to Minor1) and major categories overall figures.

OFFICES OF PHYSICIANS INDUSTRY
(NAICS 62111)

NAICS 62111: Offices of Physicians. This industry comprises establishments primarily of licensed practitioners having the degree of M.D. and engaged in the practice of general or specialized medicine and surgery. Establishments operating as clinics of physicians are included in this business. Osteopathic physicians are classified in 8031.

INDUSTRY ESTABLISHMENTS, SALES & EMPLOYMENT TRENDS

	Year					Percent Chg. Year-to-Year			
	2015	2016	2017	2018	2019	15-16	16-17	17-18	18-19
Establishments	276,634	276,181	277,696	281,374	285,173	-0.2%	0.5%	1.3%	1.4%
Sales ($Millions)	331,261	344,187	361,463	382,675	405,822	3.9%	5.0%	5.9%	6.0%
Employment	2,424,351	2,420,383	2,433,655	2,465,894	2,499,185	-0.2%	0.5%	1.3%	1.4%
Sales ($M)/Estab.	1.20	1.25	1.30	1.36	1.42	4.1%	4.4%	4.5%	4.6%
Sales ($)/Emp.	136,639	142,203	148,527	155,187	162,382	4.1%	4.4%	4.5%	4.6%

3-YEAR TREND – ESTIMATED NUMBER OF ESTABLISHMENTS

Year	Employee Size of Establishment									Total Employment
	1-4 Emps.	5-9 Emps.	10-19 Emps.	20-49 Emps.	50-99 Emps.	100-249 Emps.	250-499 Emps.	>500 Emps.	Non-Employer	
2017	119,515	48,699	31,723	19,157	4,452	1,762	419	232	51,737	277,696
2018	121,098	49,344	32,144	19,411	4,511	1,785	424	235	52,422	281,374
2019	122,733	50,010	32,577	19,673	4,572	1,809	430	238	53,130	285,173

3-YEAR TREND – ESTIMATED INDUSTRY SALES ($MILLIONS)

Year	Employee Size of Establishment									Total Employment
	1-4 Emps.	5-9 Emps.	10-19 Emps.	20-49 Emps.	50-99 Emps.	100-249 Emps.	250-499 Emps.	>500 Emps.	Non-Employer	
2017	28,587.2	30,616.4	50,153.8	80,166.6	40,953.0	43,677.5	34,978.7	44,783.0	7,547.0	361,463.3
2018	30,288.0	32,437.9	53,137.6	84,935.9	43,389.4	46,276.0	37,059.7	47,154.5	7,996.0	382,675.0
2019	32,144.8	34,426.5	56,395.2	90,142.8	46,049.4	49,112.9	39,331.6	49,732.9	8,486.2	405,822.2

3-YEAR TREND – ESTIMATED NUMBER OF EMPLOYEES

Year	Employee Size of Establishment									Total Employment
	1-4 Emps.	5-9 Emps.	10-19 Emps.	20-49 Emps.	50-99 Emps.	100-249 Emps.	250-499 Emps.	>500 Emps.	Non-Employer	
2017	298,787	282,455	431,437	576,633	264,450	222,155	121,771	184,230	51,737	2,433,655
2018	302,745	286,197	437,152	584,272	267,953	225,098	123,384	186,671	52,422	2,465,894
2019	306,833	290,061	443,054	592,160	271,571	228,137	125,050	189,191	53,130	2,499,185

© Barnes Reports: 2018 U.S. Industry & Market Outlook

Offices of Physicians Industry (NAICS 62111)

Sub-Industries – 2018 Estimated Industry Sales, Establishments & Employment

Sub-Industries	Category*	Establishments	Sales ($Mill)	Employment
Offices and clinics of medical doctors	Major1	183,718	192,038.0	1,277,390
Internal medicine practitioners	Minor1	5,081	5,545.8	41,836
Cardiologist and cardio-vascular specialist	Minor2	10,426	15,327.4	137,352
Endocrinologist	Minor2	1,698	1,497.7	11,487
Gastronomist	Minor2	3,300	3,909.8	30,228
Hematologist	Minor2	1,247	1,948.5	20,197
Internal medicine, physician/surgeon	Minor2	22,536	16,918.6	140,873
Nephrologist	Minor2	2,125	1,670.2	14,894
Neurologist	Minor2	6,450	5,479.7	44,444
Oncologist	Minor2	4,049	6,196.6	44,727
Pulmonary specialist, physician/surgeon	Minor2	1,957	3,002.1	18,991
Neurosurgeon	Minor2	1,199	2,234.9	9,748
Medical centers	Minor1	14,785	56,836.4	306,123
Ambulatory surgical center	Minor2	1,226	6,663.6	26,719
Clinic, operated by physicians	Minor2	16,758	49,601.6	274,971
Dispensery, operated by physicians	Minor2	160	232.1	6,481
Freestanding emergency medical center	Minor2	940	1,687.0	13,413
Primary care medical clinic	Minor2	3,721	11,885.0	46,021

*Category-Major categories (Major1) are more general descriptions for companies that self-selected to capture the many functions they perform in the industry. Minor categories (Minor1, Minor2) are more specific for companies that have more detailed functions (Minor1 is a larger category than Minor2). Minor categories figures (sales, etc.) can be aggregated to larger minor categories (Minor2 sums to Minor1) and major categories overall figures.

OFFICES OF DENTISTS INDUSTRY
(NAICS 62121)

NAICS 62121: Offices of Dentists. This industry comprises establishments primarily of licensed practitioners having the degree of D.M.D. or D.D.S. (or D.D.Sc.) and engaged in the practice of general or specialized dentistry, including dental surgery. Establishments operating as clinics of dentists are included in this business.

INDUSTRY ESTABLISHMENTS, SALES & EMPLOYMENT TRENDS

	Year					Percent Chg. Year-to-Year			
	2015	2016	2017	2018	2019	15-16	16-17	17-18	18-19
Establishments	149,410	151,173	154,022	157,075	160,229	1.2%	1.9%	2.0%	2.0%
Sales ($Millions)	98,168	103,131	109,559	116,613	124,355	5.1%	6.2%	6.4%	6.6%
Employment	924,066	934,969	952,590	971,473	990,978	1.2%	1.9%	2.0%	2.0%
Sales ($M)/Estab.	0.66	0.68	0.71	0.74	0.78	3.8%	4.3%	4.4%	4.5%
Sales ($)/Emp.	106,235	110,304	115,011	120,037	125,487	3.8%	4.3%	4.4%	4.5%

3-YEAR TREND – ESTIMATED NUMBER OF ESTABLISHMENTS

Year	Employee Size of Establishment									Total Employment
	1-4 Emps.	5-9 Emps.	10-19 Emps.	20-49 Emps.	50-99 Emps.	100-249 Emps.	250-499 Emps.	>500 Emps.	Non-Employer	
2017	55,630	54,245	24,300	4,298	255	55	4	1	15,235	154,022
2018	56,732	55,321	24,781	4,383	260	56	4	1	15,537	157,075
2019	57,872	56,431	25,279	4,471	265	57	4	1	15,849	160,229

3-YEAR TREND – ESTIMATED INDUSTRY SALES ($MILLIONS)

Year	Employee Size of Establishment									Total Employment
	1-4 Emps.	5-9 Emps.	10-19 Emps.	20-49 Emps.	50-99 Emps.	100-249 Emps.	250-499 Emps.	>500 Emps.	Non-Employer	
2017	13,249.6	33,957.9	38,253.5	17,907.8	2,332.2	1,348.8	343.1	158.8	2,006.9	109,558.6
2018	14,102.7	36,144.3	40,716.5	19,060.8	2,482.4	1,435.6	365.2	169.0	2,136.1	116,612.6
2019	15,039.1	38,544.2	43,419.9	20,326.3	2,647.2	1,530.9	389.4	180.1	2,278.0	124,355.2

3-YEAR TREND – ESTIMATED NUMBER OF EMPLOYEES

Year	Employee Size of Establishment									Total Employment
	1-4 Emps.	5-9 Emps.	10-19 Emps.	20-49 Emps.	50-99 Emps.	100-249 Emps.	250-499 Emps.	>500 Emps.	Non-Employer	
2017	139,074	314,623	330,475	129,360	15,125	6,890	1,200	609	15,235	952,590
2018	141,831	320,859	337,026	131,925	15,425	7,026	1,223	621	15,537	971,473
2019	144,679	327,302	343,792	134,573	15,734	7,167	1,248	633	15,849	990,978

© Barnes Reports: 2018 U.S. Industry & Market Outlook

Offices of Dentists Industry (NAICS 62121)

Sub-Industries – 2018 Estimated Industry Sales, Establishments & Employment

Sub-Industries	Category*	Establishments	Sales ($Mill)	Employment
Offices and clinics of dentists	Major1	85,672	59,169.8	493,404
Specialized dental practitioners	Minor1	1,137	988.0	8,124
Dental surgeon	Minor2	6,389	4,667.9	38,996
Endodontist	Minor2	1,779	1,208.1	10,508
Maxillofacial specialist	Minor2	805	677.4	6,001
Oral pathologist	Minor2	594	472.5	4,030
Orthodontist	Minor2	6,965	5,112.2	49,352
Pedodontist	Minor2	577	592.2	5,044
Periodontist	Minor2	1,872	1,558.0	12,908
Prosthodontist	Minor2	811	592.8	4,838
Dental clinics and offices	Minor1	3,265	2,755.4	22,981
Dental clinic	Minor2	5,019	3,753.9	33,450
Dentists' office	Minor2	41,619	34,002.3	275,802
Dental insurance plan	Minor2	181	671.4	2,735
Group and corporate practice, dentist	Minor2	391	390.8	3,302

*Category-Major categories (Major1) are more general descriptions for companies that self-selected to capture the many functions they perform in the industry. Minor categories (Minor1, Minor2) are more specific for companies that have more detailed functions (Minor1 is a larger category than Minor2). Minor categories figures (sales, etc.) can be aggregated to larger minor categories (Minor2 sums to Minor1) and major categories overall figures.

Medical Laboratories Industry
(NAICS 621511)

NAICS 621511: Medical Laboratories. This industry comprises establishments primarily engaged in providing professional analytic or diagnostic services to the medical profession, or to the patient on prescription of a physician.

Industry Establishments, Sales & Employment Trends

	Year					Percent Chg. Year-to-Year			
	2015	2016	2017	2018	2019	15-16	16-17	17-18	18-19
Establishments	15,348	15,759	16,294	16,959	17,653	2.7%	3.4%	4.1%	4.1%
Sales ($Millions)	26,165	27,668	29,577	31,851	34,377	5.7%	6.9%	7.7%	7.9%
Employment	177,108	181,850	188,031	195,705	203,712	2.7%	3.4%	4.1%	4.1%
Sales ($M)/Estab.	1.70	1.76	1.82	1.88	1.95	3.0%	3.4%	3.5%	3.7%
Sales ($)/Emp.	147,737	152,148	157,299	162,749	168,754	3.0%	3.4%	3.5%	3.7%

3-Year Trend – Estimated Number of Establishments

Year	Employee Size of Establishment									Total Employment
	1-4 Emps.	5-9 Emps.	10-19 Emps.	20-49 Emps.	50-99 Emps.	100-249 Emps.	250-499 Emps.	>500 Emps.	Non-Employer	
2017	7,113	1,743	996	757	335	248	64	68	4,969	16,294
2018	7,404	1,814	1,036	788	349	259	66	71	5,172	16,959
2019	7,706	1,889	1,079	820	363	269	69	74	5,384	17,653

3-Year Trend – Estimated Industry Sales ($Millions)

Year	Employee Size of Establishment									Total Employment
	1-4 Emps.	5-9 Emps.	10-19 Emps.	20-49 Emps.	50-99 Emps.	100-249 Emps.	250-499 Emps.	>500 Emps.	Non-Employer	
2017	1,448.9	933.3	1,340.8	2,697.6	2,628.1	5,245.1	4,532.9	10,186.5	563.9	29,577.0
2018	1,567.2	1,009.5	1,450.2	2,917.8	2,842.6	5,673.2	4,902.9	10,877.4	609.9	31,850.7
2019	1,698.7	1,094.2	1,571.9	3,162.6	3,081.2	6,149.4	5,314.4	11,643.6	661.1	34,377.1

3-Year Trend – Estimated Number of Employees

Year	Employee Size of Establishment									Total Employment
	1-4 Emps.	5-9 Emps.	10-19 Emps.	20-49 Emps.	50-99 Emps.	100-249 Emps.	250-499 Emps.	>500 Emps.	Non-Employer	
2017	17,783	10,111	13,544	22,785	19,928	31,327	18,530	49,054	4,969	188,031
2018	18,509	10,524	14,096	23,715	20,741	32,606	19,287	51,056	5,172	195,705
2019	19,266	10,954	14,673	24,685	21,590	33,940	20,076	53,144	5,384	203,712

© Barnes Reports: 2018 U.S. Industry & Market Outlook

MEDICAL LABORATORIES INDUSTRY
(NAICS 621511)

SUB-INDUSTRIES – 2018 ESTIMATED INDUSTRY SALES, ESTABLISHMENTS & EMPLOYMENT

Sub-Industries	Category*	Establishments	Sales ($Mill)	Employment
Medical laboratories	Major1	12,054	10,375.2	119,858
Testing laboratories	Minor1	1,506	18,609.5	33,978
Bacteriological laboratory	Minor2	30	27.4	292
Biological laboratory	Minor2	292	523.3	5,312
Blood analysis laboratory	Minor2	274	253.8	4,117
Pathological laboratory	Minor2	831	921.9	14,833
Urinalysis laboratory	Minor2	33	28.0	215
Neurological laboratory	Minor2	116	50.1	1,052
Ultrasound laboratory	Minor2	543	233.8	3,579
X-ray laboratory, including dental	Minor2	1,280	827.8	12,469

*Category-Major categories (Major1) are more general descriptions for companies that self-selected to capture the many functions they perform in the industry. Minor categories (Minor1, Minor2) are more specific for companies that have more detailed functions (Minor1 is a larger category than Minor2). Minor categories figures (sales, etc.) can be aggregated to larger minor categories (Minor2 sums to Minor1) and major categories overall figures.

Home Health Care Services Industry (NAICS 62161)

NAICS 62161: Home Health Care Services. This industry comprises establishments primarily engaged in providing skilled nursing or medical care in the home, under supervision of a physician. Registered or practical nurses engaged in the independent practice of their profession are classified in 8049, and nurses' registries are classified in 7361. Selling health care products for personal or household consumption is classified in retail trade and renting or leasing products for health care is classified in 7352.

Industry Establishments, Sales & Employment Trends

	Year					Percent Chg. Year-to-Year			
	2015	2016	2017	2018	2019	15-16	16-17	17-18	18-19
Establishments	182,524	188,935	196,614	203,622	210,933	3.5%	4.1%	3.6%	3.6%
Sales ($Millions)	99,099	105,459	113,313	121,414	130,416	6.4%	7.4%	7.1%	7.4%
Employment	1,335,473	1,382,377	1,438,563	1,489,840	1,543,332	3.5%	4.1%	3.6%	3.6%
Sales ($M)/Estab.	0.54	0.56	0.58	0.60	0.62	2.8%	3.3%	3.5%	3.7%
Sales ($)/Emp.	74,205	76,288	78,768	81,495	84,503	2.8%	3.3%	3.5%	3.7%

3-Year Trend – Estimated Number of Establishments

Year	Employee Size of Establishment									Total Employment
	1-4 Emps.	5-9 Emps.	10-19 Emps.	20-49 Emps.	50-99 Emps.	100-249 Emps.	250-499 Emps.	>500 Emps.	Non-Employer	
2017	9,780	3,583	5,312	7,508	3,870	2,474	552	294	163,241	196,614
2018	10,128	3,710	5,501	7,776	4,008	2,563	571	305	169,060	203,622
2019	10,492	3,844	5,698	8,055	4,152	2,655	592	315	175,130	210,933

3-Year Trend – Estimated Industry Sales ($Millions)

Year	Employee Size of Establishment									Total Employment
	1-4 Emps.	5-9 Emps.	10-19 Emps.	20-49 Emps.	50-99 Emps.	100-249 Emps.	250-499 Emps.	>500 Emps.	Non-Employer	
2017	1,045.5	1,006.7	3,753.2	14,042.1	15,912.1	27,416.9	20,597.5	24,270.0	5,269.3	113,313.2
2018	1,123.8	1,082.1	4,034.3	15,093.9	17,103.9	29,470.5	22,140.3	25,701.7	5,663.9	121,414.4
2019	1,210.9	1,165.9	4,346.9	16,263.3	18,429.0	31,753.6	23,855.5	27,288.2	6,102.7	130,416.0

3-Year Trend – Estimated Number of Employees

Year	Employee Size of Establishment									Total Employment
	1-4 Emps.	5-9 Emps.	10-19 Emps.	20-49 Emps.	50-99 Emps.	100-249 Emps.	250-499 Emps.	>500 Emps.	Non-Employer	
2017	24,450	20,780	72,238	225,992	229,899	312,011	160,438	229,513	163,241	1,438,563
2018	25,321	21,521	74,813	234,048	238,094	323,133	166,157	237,694	169,060	1,489,840
2019	26,230	22,293	77,499	242,451	246,643	334,734	172,123	246,229	175,130	1,543,332

© Barnes Reports: 2018 U.S. Industry & Market Outlook

Home Health Care Services Industry (NAICS 62161)

Sub-Industries — 2018 Estimated Industry Sales, Establishments & Employment

Sub-Industries	Category*	Establishments	Sales ($Mill)	Employment
Home health care services	Major1	195,961	114,892.8	1,375,712
Oxygen tent service	Minor2	665	54.7	1,321
Visiting nurse service	Minor2	6,996	6,467.0	112,807

*Category-Major categories (Major1) are more general descriptions for companies that self-selected to capture the many functions they perform in the industry. Minor categories (Minor1, Minor2) are more specific for companies that have more detailed functions (Minor1 is a larger category than Minor2). Minor categories figures (sales, etc.) can be aggregated to larger minor categories (Minor2 sums to Minor1) and major categories overall figures.

MEDICAL & SURGICAL HOSPITALS INDUSTRY
(NAICS 62211)

NAICS 62211: Medical & Surgical Hospital. This industry comprises establishments primarily engaged in providing general medical and surgical services and other hospital services. Specialty hospitals are classified in 8063 and 8069.

INDUSTRY ESTABLISHMENTS, SALES & EMPLOYMENT TRENDS

	Year					Percent Chg. Year-to-Year			
	2015	2016	2017	2018	2019	15-16	16-17	17-18	18-19
Establishments	5,623	5,596	5,608	5,664	5,723	-0.5%	0.2%	1.0%	1.0%
Sales ($Millions)	825,480	883,778	949,275	1,020,327	1,095,345	7.1%	7.4%	7.5%	7.4%
Employment	2,990,019	2,975,311	2,981,750	3,011,878	3,043,072	-0.5%	0.2%	1.0%	1.0%
Sales ($M)/Estab.	146.80	157.94	169.28	180.13	191.39	7.6%	7.2%	6.4%	6.3%
Sales ($)/Emp.	276,078	297,037	318,362	338,768	359,947	7.6%	7.2%	6.4%	6.3%

3-YEAR TREND – ESTIMATED NUMBER OF ESTABLISHMENTS

Year	Employee Size of Establishment									Total Employment
	1-4 Emps.	5-9 Emps.	10-19 Emps.	20-49 Emps.	50-99 Emps.	100-249 Emps.	250-499 Emps.	>500 Emps.	Non-Employer	
2017	158	52	55	113	334	1,133	906	2,596	262	5,608
2018	159	52	55	114	337	1,144	916	2,622	264	5,664
2019	161	53	56	115	341	1,156	925	2,649	267	5,723

3-YEAR TREND – ESTIMATED INDUSTRY SALES ($MILLIONS)

Year	Employee Size of Establishment									Total Employment
	1-4 Emps.	5-9 Emps.	10-19 Emps.	20-49 Emps.	50-99 Emps.	100-249 Emps.	250-499 Emps.	>500 Emps.	Non-Employer	
2017	50.8	43.9	116.8	635.4	4,141.0	37,846.8	102,071.0	804,352.1	16.9	949,274.9
2018	54.9	47.5	126.4	687.3	4,479.3	40,938.2	110,408.3	863,566.3	18.3	1,020,326.6
2019	59.4	51.3	136.6	742.7	4,839.8	44,233.5	119,295.3	925,967.1	19.8	1,095,345.4

3-YEAR TREND – ESTIMATED NUMBER OF EMPLOYEES

Year	Employee Size of Establishment									Total Employment
	1-4 Emps.	5-9 Emps.	10-19 Emps.	20-49 Emps.	50-99 Emps.	100-249 Emps.	250-499 Emps.	>500 Emps.	Non-Employer	
2017	394	301	746	3,392	19,844	142,853	263,697	2,550,261	262	2,981,750
2018	398	304	753	3,426	20,044	144,297	266,361	2,576,030	264	3,011,878
2019	402	307	761	3,462	20,252	145,791	269,120	2,602,710	267	3,043,072

Medical & Surgical Hospitals Industry (NAICS 62211)

Sub-Industries – 2018 Estimated Industry Sales, Establishments & Employment

Sub-Industries	Category*	Establishments	Sales ($Mill)	Employment
General medical and surgical hospitals	Major1	5,236	886,320.8	2,647,291
Hospital, affiliated with AMA residency	Minor2	117	25,042.6	77,119
Hospital, med school affiliated with nursing and residency	Minor2	42	13,043.1	52,147
Hospital, medical school affiliated with residency	Minor2	42	14,431.5	48,216
Hospital, medical school affiliation	Minor2	118	17,911.6	86,756
Hospital, professional nursing school	Minor2	37	5,975.0	23,409
Hospital, professional nursing school with AMA residency	Minor2	17	5,356.9	12,238
Hospital, AMA approved residency	Minor2	57	52,245.1	64,703

*Category-Major categories (Major1) are more general descriptions for companies that self-selected to capture the many functions they perform in the industry. Minor categories (Minor1, Minor2) are more specific for companies that have more detailed functions (Minor1 is a larger category than Minor2). Minor categories figures (sales, etc.) can be aggregated to larger minor categories (Minor2 sums to Minor1) and major categories overall figures.

NURSING CARE FACILITIES INDUSTRY
(NAICS 62311)

NAICS 62311: Nursing Care Facilities. This industry comprises establishments primarily engaged in providing inpatient nursing and rehabilitative services, but not on a continuous basis. Staffing must include 24-hour per day personnel with a licensed nurse on duty full-time during each day shift. At least once a week, consultation from a registered nurse on the delivery of care is required. Included are facilities certified to deliver intermediate care under the Medicaid program.

INDUSTRY ESTABLISHMENTS, SALES & EMPLOYMENT TRENDS

	Year					Percent Chg. Year-to-Year			
	2015	2016	2017	2018	2019	15-16	16-17	17-18	18-19
Establishments	22,723	22,576	22,589	22,838	23,095	-0.6%	0.1%	1.1%	1.1%
Sales ($Millions)	130,140	135,272	142,098	150,865	160,375	3.9%	5.0%	6.2%	6.3%
Employment	1,429,642	1,420,404	1,421,250	1,436,900	1,453,086	-0.6%	0.1%	1.1%	1.1%
Sales ($M)/Estab.	5.73	5.99	6.29	6.61	6.94	4.6%	5.0%	5.0%	5.1%
Sales ($)/Emp.	91,030	95,235	99,981	104,993	110,369	4.6%	5.0%	5.0%	5.1%

3-YEAR TREND – ESTIMATED NUMBER OF ESTABLISHMENTS

Year	Employee Size of Establishment									Total Employment
	1-4 Emps.	5-9 Emps.	10-19 Emps.	20-49 Emps.	50-99 Emps.	100-249 Emps.	250-499 Emps.	>500 Emps.	Non-Employer	
2017	1,011	608	762	1,626	4,626	6,796	604	62	5,604	22,589
2018	1,831	706	770	1,644	4,677	6,871	611	62	5,666	22,838
2019	1,852	714	779	1,663	4,729	6,948	618	63	5,730	23,095

3-YEAR TREND – ESTIMATED INDUSTRY SALES ($MILLIONS)

Year	Employee Size of Establishment									Total Employment
	1-4 Emps.	5-9 Emps.	10-19 Emps.	20-49 Emps.	50-99 Emps.	100-249 Emps.	250-499 Emps.	>500 Emps.	Non-Employer	
2017	218.8	221.6	608.1	3,437.5	21,491.4	85,098.4	25,510.0	5,180.9	331.7	142,098.4
2018	232.3	235.3	645.6	3,649.9	22,819.0	90,355.3	27,085.8	5,489.6	352.2	150,865.0
2019	247.0	250.1	686.4	3,880.2	24,259.3	96,058.4	28,795.4	5,823.9	374.4	160,375.2

3-YEAR TREND – ESTIMATED NUMBER OF EMPLOYEES

Year	Employee Size of Establishment									Total Employment
	1-4 Emps.	5-9 Emps.	10-19 Emps.	20-49 Emps.	50-99 Emps.	100-249 Emps.	250-499 Emps.	>500 Emps.	Non-Employer	
2017	4,528	4,048	10,356	48,955	274,766	856,959	175,829	40,205	5,604	1,421,250
2018	4,578	4,092	10,470	49,494	277,791	866,396	177,765	40,647	5,666	1,436,900
2019	4,630	4,138	10,588	50,051	280,921	876,155	179,768	41,105	5,730	1,453,086

© Barnes Reports: 2018 U.S. Industry & Market Outlook

NURSING CARE FACILITIES INDUSTRY
(NAICS 62311)

SUB-INDUSTRIES — 2018 ESTIMATED INDUSTRY SALES, ESTABLISHMENTS & EMPLOYMENT

Sub-Industries	Category*	Establishments	Sales ($Mill)	Employment
Intermediate care facilities	Major1	11,651	112,068.4	1,060,855
Home for the mentally retarded, with health care	Minor2	4,093	6,386.7	201,433
Personal care facility	Minor2	7,094	32,409.9	174,612

*Category-Major categories (Major1) are more general descriptions for companies that self-selected to capture the many functions they perform in the industry. Minor categories (Minor1, Minor2) are more specific for companies that have more detailed functions (Minor1 is a larger category than Minor2). Minor categories figures (sales, etc.) can be aggregated to larger minor categories (Minor2 sums to Minor1) and major categories overall figures.

COMMUNITY CARE FACILITIES FOR THE ELDERLY
(NAICS 62331)

NAICS 62331: Community Care Facilities for the Elderly. This industry comprises establishments primarily engaged in the provision of residential social and personal care for children, the aged, and special categories of persons with some limits on ability for self-care, but where medical care is not a major element. Included are establishments providing 24-hour year-round care for children. Boarding schools providing elementary and secondary education are classified in 8211.

INDUSTRY ESTABLISHMENTS, SALES & EMPLOYMENT TRENDS

	Year					Percent Chg. Year-to-Year			
	2015	2016	2017	2018	2019	15-16	16-17	17-18	18-19
Establishments	31,825	32,591	33,593	34,685	35,822	2.4%	3.1%	3.3%	3.3%
Sales ($Millions)	68,370	72,783	78,298	84,447	91,240	6.5%	7.6%	7.9%	8.0%
Employment	810,022	829,524	855,034	882,827	911,751	2.4%	3.1%	3.3%	3.3%
Sales ($M)/Estab.	2.15	2.23	2.33	2.43	2.55	4.0%	4.4%	4.5%	4.6%
Sales ($)/Emp.	84,405	87,741	91,573	95,655	100,071	4.0%	4.4%	4.5%	4.6%

3-YEAR TREND – ESTIMATED NUMBER OF ESTABLISHMENTS

Year	Employee Size of Establishment									Total Employment
	1-4 Emps.	5-9 Emps.	10-19 Emps.	20-49 Emps.	50-99 Emps.	100-249 Emps.	250-499 Emps.	>500 Emps.	Non-Employer	
2017	7,178	3,374	3,575	5,531	3,347	1,720	471	63	8,335	33,593
2018	7,411	3,483	3,691	5,711	3,456	1,775	486	65	8,606	34,685
2019	7,654	3,597	3,812	5,898	3,569	1,834	502	68	8,888	35,822

3-YEAR TREND – ESTIMATED INDUSTRY SALES ($MILLIONS)

Year	Employee Size of Establishment									Total Employment
	1-4 Emps.	5-9 Emps.	10-19 Emps.	20-49 Emps.	50-99 Emps.	100-249 Emps.	250-499 Emps.	>500 Emps.	Non-Employer	
2017	857.2	1,058.9	2,822.1	11,556.3	15,372.8	21,284.6	19,641.1	5,217.6	487.6	78,298.1
2018	924.9	1,142.5	3,044.9	12,468.6	16,586.4	22,964.9	21,191.7	5,596.6	526.1	84,446.5
2019	999.7	1,234.9	3,291.1	13,476.8	17,927.6	24,821.8	22,905.2	6,014.3	568.6	91,240.0

3-YEAR TREND – ESTIMATED NUMBER OF EMPLOYEES

Year	Employee Size of Establishment									Total Employment
	1-4 Emps.	5-9 Emps.	10-19 Emps.	20-49 Emps.	50-99 Emps.	100-249 Emps.	250-499 Emps.	>500 Emps.	Non-Employer	
2017	17,945	19,567	48,623	166,489	198,824	216,832	136,951	41,469	8,335	855,034
2018	18,528	20,203	50,203	171,900	205,287	223,880	141,403	42,817	8,606	882,827
2019	19,135	20,865	51,848	177,532	212,013	231,215	146,035	44,220	8,888	911,751

© Barnes Reports: 2018 U.S. Industry & Market Outlook

COMMUNITY CARE FACILITIES FOR THE ELDERLY (NAICS 62331)

Sub-Industries – 2018 Estimated Industry Sales, Establishments & Employment

Sub-Industries	Category*	Establishments	Sales ($Mill)	Employment
Geriatric residential care	Minor1	12,101	15,977.7	231,613
Aged home	Minor2	17,922	51,834.4	474,145
Old soldiers' home	Minor2	116	124.1	7,905
Rest home, with health care incidental	Minor2	4,546	16,510.3	169,164

*Category-Major categories (Major1) are more general descriptions for companies that self-selected to capture the many functions they perform in the industry. Minor categories (Minor1, Minor2) are more specific for companies that have more detailed functions (Minor1 is a larger category than Minor2). Minor categories figures (sales, etc.) can be aggregated to larger minor categories (Minor2 sums to Minor1) and major categories overall figures.

Musical Groups & Artists Industry (NAICS 71113)

NAICS 71113: Musical Groups and Artists. This industry comprises (1) groups primarily engaged in producing live musical entertainment (except theatrical musical or opera productions) and (2) independent (i.e., freelance) artists primarily engaged in providing live musical entertainment. Musical groups and artists may perform in front of a live audience or in a studio, and may or may not operate their own facilities for staging their shows.

Industry Establishments, Sales & Employment Trends

	Year					Percent Chg. Year-to-Year			
	2015	2016	2017	2018	2019	15-16	16-17	17-18	18-19
Establishments	31,133	30,570	30,099	29,905	29,936	-1.8%	-1.5%	-0.6%	0.1%
Sales ($Millions)	5,325	5,508	5,728	6,010	6,356	3.4%	4.0%	4.9%	5.8%
Employment	64,927	63,754	62,771	62,367	62,432	-1.8%	-1.5%	-0.6%	0.1%
Sales ($M)/Estab.	0.17	0.18	0.19	0.20	0.21	5.3%	5.6%	5.6%	5.6%
Sales ($)/Emp.	82,021	86,393	91,257	96,367	101,805	5.3%	5.6%	5.6%	5.6%

5-Year Trend – Estimated Number of Establishments

Year	Employee Size of Establishment									Total Employment
	1-4 Emps.	5-9 Emps.	10-19 Emps.	20-49 Emps.	50-99 Emps.	100-249 Emps.	250-499 Emps.	>500 Emps.	Non-Employer	
2017	3,264	540	283	126	83	59	14	3	25,727	30,099
2018	3,243	536	281	125	83	58	14	3	25,562	29,905
2019	3,247	537	281	125	83	58	14	3	25,588	29,936

5-Year Trend – Estimated Industry Sales ($Millions)

Year	Employee Size of Establishment									Total Employment
	1-4 Emps.	5-9 Emps.	10-19 Emps.	20-49 Emps.	50-99 Emps.	100-249 Emps.	250-499 Emps.	>500 Emps.	Non-Employer	
2017	544.8	236.8	312.0	368.0	535.1	1,012.9	810.1	317.7	1,590.9	5,728.3
2018	571.6	248.5	327.4	386.1	561.4	1,062.7	849.9	333.4	1,669.2	6,010.2
2019	604.5	262.8	346.2	408.3	593.7	1,123.9	898.8	352.5	1,765.2	6,355.9

5-Year Trend – Estimated Number of Employees

Year	Employee Size of Establishment									Total Employment
	1-4 Emps.	5-9 Emps.	10-19 Emps.	20-49 Emps.	50-99 Emps.	100-249 Emps.	250-499 Emps.	>500 Emps.	Non-Employer	
2017	8,161	3,131	3,847	3,794	4,952	7,384	4,042	1,733	25,727	62,771
2018	8,108	3,111	3,822	3,770	4,920	7,336	4,016	1,722	25,562	62,367
2019	8,117	3,115	3,826	3,773	4,925	7,344	4,020	1,724	25,588	62,432

© Barnes Reports: 2018 U.S. Industry & Market Outlook

Musical Groups & Artists Industry (NAICS 71113)

Sub-Industries — 2018 Estimated Industry Sales, Establishments & Employment

Sub-Industries	Category*	Establishments	Sales ($Mill)	Employment
Entertainers and entertainment groups	Major1	15,669	1,918.6	23,064
Musical entertainers	Minor1	1,193	338.0	3,108
Chamber music groups or artists	Minor2	87	22.9	302
Classical music groups or artists	Minor2	82	45.5	339
Country music groups or artists	Minor2	46	14.7	236
Dance band	Minor2	122	21.7	368
Drum and bugle corps (drill teams)	Minor2	27	28.4	107
Gospel singers	Minor2	144	25.5	356
Jazz music group or artist	Minor2	77	19.2	215
Musician	Minor2	1,804	191.5	2,410
Orchestras or bands, nec	Minor2	983	321.8	3,623
Popular music groups or artists	Minor2	125	44.2	350
Symphony orchestra	Minor2	395	673.5	3,867
Actor	Minor2	184	25.0	271
Actress	Minor2	59	7.5	63
Disc jockey service	Minor2	2,549	288.7	4,062
Entertainers	Minor2	1,862	295.5	3,458
Entertainment group	Minor2	440	109.4	1,552
Entertainment service	Minor2	3,593	1,572.9	14,056
Magician	Minor2	425	40.2	487
Singing telegram service	Minor2	39	5.4	72

*Category-Major categories (Major1) are more general descriptions for companies that self-selected to capture the many functions they perform in the industry. Minor categories (Minor1, Minor2) are more specific for companies that have more detailed functions (Minor1 is a larger category than Minor2). Minor categories figures (sales, etc.) can be aggregated to larger minor categories (Minor2 sums to Minor1) and major categories overall figures.

Spectator Sports Industry
(NAICS 71121)

NAICS 71121: Spectator Sports. This industry comprises (1) sports teams or clubs primarily participating in live sporting events before a paying audience; (2) establishments primarily engaged in operating racetracks; (3) independent athletes engaged in participating in live sporting or racing events before a paying audience; (4) owners of racing participants, such as cars, dogs, and horses, primarily engaged in entering them in racing events or other spectator sports events; and (5) establishments, such as sports trainers, primarily engaged in providing specialized services to support participants in sports events or competitions.

Industry Establishments, Sales & Employment Trends

	Year					Percent Chg. Year-to-Year			
	2015	2016	2017	2018	2019	15-16	16-17	17-18	18-19
Establishments	127,216	124,146	121,449	119,844	119,149	-2.4%	-2.2%	-1.3%	-0.6%
Sales ($Millions)	33,353	35,107	37,045	39,288	41,871	5.3%	5.5%	6.1%	6.6%
Employment	237,870	232,131	227,088	224,087	222,786	-2.4%	-2.2%	-1.3%	-0.6%
Sales ($M)/Estab.	0.26	0.28	0.31	0.33	0.35	7.9%	7.9%	7.5%	7.2%
Sales ($)/Emp.	140,215	151,238	163,132	175,325	187,943	7.9%	7.9%	7.5%	7.2%

5-Year Trend – Estimated Number of Establishments

Year	Employee Size of Establishment									Total Employment
	1-4 Emps.	5-9 Emps.	10-19 Emps.	20-49 Emps.	50-99 Emps.	100-249 Emps.	250-499 Emps.	>500 Emps.	Non-Employer	
2017	2,636	483	338	308	108	103	88	55	117,330	121,449
2018	2,601	477	334	304	106	102	86	55	115,779	119,844
2019	2,586	474	332	302	106	101	86	54	115,107	119,149

5-Year Trend – Estimated Industry Sales ($Millions)

Year	Employee Size of Establishment									Total Employment
	1-4 Emps.	5-9 Emps.	10-19 Emps.	20-49 Emps.	50-99 Emps.	100-249 Emps.	250-499 Emps.	>500 Emps.	Non-Employer	
2017	731.6	352.5	620.7	1,496.6	1,152.0	2,965.0	8,484.9	12,042.9	9,199.0	37,045.3
2018	774.5	373.2	657.2	1,584.5	1,219.6	3,139.0	8,982.9	12,818.3	9,738.9	39,288.0
2019	824.8	397.4	699.8	1,687.4	1,298.8	3,342.8	9,566.1	13,682.8	10,371.2	41,871.1

5-Year Trend – Estimated Number of Employees

Year	Employee Size of Establishment									Total Employment
	1-4 Emps.	5-9 Emps.	10-19 Emps.	20-49 Emps.	50-99 Emps.	100-249 Emps.	250-499 Emps.	>500 Emps.	Non-Employer	
2017	6,589	2,803	4,601	9,277	6,410	12,996	25,454	41,628	117,330	227,088
2018	6,502	2,766	4,541	9,154	6,326	12,824	25,118	41,078	115,779	224,087
2019	6,465	2,750	4,514	9,101	6,289	12,749	24,972	40,839	115,107	222,786

© Barnes Reports: 2018 U.S. Industry & Market Outlook

Spectator Sports Industry (NAICS 71121)

Sub-Industries – 2018 Estimated Industry Sales, Establishments & Employment

Sub-Industries	Category*	Establishments	Sales ($Mill)	Employment
Sports clubs, managers, and promoters	Major1	28,730	15,016.2	46,226
Professional and semi-professional sports clubs	Minor1	3,256	473.7	4,338
Baseball club, professional and semi-professional	Minor2	7,565	5,360.8	37,727
Basketball club	Minor2	4,825	2,146.9	11,758
Football club	Minor2	25,017	3,225.2	22,928
Ice hockey club	Minor2	2,561	825.4	7,202
Soccer club	Minor2	13,859	1,647.5	9,972
Stadium event operator services	Minor1	4,110	1,637.1	32,564
Boxing and wrestling arena	Minor2	2,363	181.5	1,417
Sports field or stadium operator, promoting sports events	Minor2	8,418	2,939.3	31,281
Manager of individual professional athletes	Minor2	2,144	1,385.0	3,657
Sports promotion	Minor2	16,996	4,449.6	15,018

*Category-Major categories (Major1) are more general descriptions for companies that self-selected to capture the many functions they perform in the industry. Minor categories (Minor1, Minor2) are more specific for companies that have more detailed functions (Minor1 is a larger category than Minor2). Minor categories figures (sales, etc.) can be aggregated to larger minor categories (Minor2 sums to Minor1) and major categories overall figures.

Agents/Managers for Artists & Athletes (NAICS 71141)

NAICS 71141: Agents and Managers for Artists. This industry comprises establishments of agents and managers primarily engaged in representing and/or managing creative and performing artists, sports figures, entertainers, and other public figures. The representation and management includes activities, such as representing clients in contract negotiations; managing or organizing client's financial affairs; and generally promoting the careers of their clients.

Industry Establishments, Sales & Employment Trends

	Year					Percent Chg. Year-to-Year			
	2015	2016	2017	2018	2019	15-16	16-17	17-18	18-19
Establishments	23,978	23,638	23,369	23,628	24,069	-1.4%	-1.1%	1.1%	1.9%
Sales ($Millions)	8,265	8,507	8,813	9,343	9,991	2.9%	3.6%	6.0%	6.9%
Employment	43,857	43,237	42,744	43,218	44,025	-1.4%	-1.1%	1.1%	1.9%
Sales ($M)/Estab.	0.34	0.36	0.38	0.40	0.42	4.4%	4.8%	4.9%	5.0%
Sales ($)/Emp.	188,446	196,753	206,192	216,192	226,945	4.4%	4.8%	4.9%	5.0%

5-Year Trend – Estimated Number of Establishments

Year	Employee Size of Establishment									Total Employment
	1-4 Emps.	5-9 Emps.	10-19 Emps.	20-49 Emps.	50-99 Emps.	100-249 Emps.	250-499 Emps.	>500 Emps.	Non-Employer	
2017	3,322	422	194	115	24	19	5	2	19,265	23,369
2018	3,359	426	197	116	25	19	5	2	19,479	23,628
2019	3,422	434	200	119	25	20	5	2	19,842	24,069

5-Year Trend – Estimated Industry Sales ($Millions)

Year	Employee Size of Establishment									Total Employment
	1-4 Emps.	5-9 Emps.	10-19 Emps.	20-49 Emps.	50-99 Emps.	100-249 Emps.	250-499 Emps.	>500 Emps.	Non-Employer	
2017	1,708.3	570.0	661.0	1,036.5	480.8	1,014.1	949.4	696.8	1,696.5	8,813.5
2018	1,811.1	604.3	700.8	1,098.8	509.7	1,075.1	1,006.5	738.6	1,798.5	9,343.3
2019	1,936.7	646.2	749.4	1,175.0	545.0	1,149.6	1,076.3	789.8	1,923.2	9,991.2

5-Year Trend – Estimated Number of Employees

Year	Employee Size of Establishment									Total Employment
	1-4 Emps.	5-9 Emps.	10-19 Emps.	20-49 Emps.	50-99 Emps.	100-249 Emps.	250-499 Emps.	>500 Emps.	Non-Employer	
2017	8,305	2,446	2,645	3,468	1,444	2,399	1,537	1,235	19,265	42,744
2018	8,397	2,473	2,674	3,506	1,460	2,426	1,554	1,249	19,479	43,218
2019	8,554	2,519	2,724	3,572	1,487	2,471	1,583	1,272	19,842	44,025

© Barnes Reports: 2018 U.S. Industry & Market Outlook

Agents/Managers for Artists & Athletes (NAICS 71141)

Sub-Industries – 2018 Estimated Industry Sales, Establishments & Employment

Sub-Industries	Category*	Establishments	Sales ($Mill)	Employment
Theatrical producers and services	Major1	12,247	5,833.4	25,242
Theatrical talent and booking agencies	Minor1	2,219	566.7	2,951
Agent or manager for entertainers	Minor2	1,864	563.4	3,173
Booking agency, theatrical	Minor2	648	201.3	997
Casting bureau, theatrical	Minor2	293	49.9	247
Employment agency: theatrical, radio, and television	Minor2	245	240.7	592
Entertainment promotion	Minor2	4,721	1,538.5	7,037
Talent agent, theatrical	Minor2	1,391	349.5	2,978

*Category-Major categories (Major1) are more general descriptions for companies that self-selected to capture the many functions they perform in the industry. Minor categories (Minor1, Minor2) are more specific for companies that have more detailed functions (Minor1 is a larger category than Minor2). Minor categories figures (sales, etc.) can be aggregated to larger minor categories (Minor2 sums to Minor1) and major categories overall figures.

GOLF COURSES & COUNTRY CLUBS INDUSTRY (NAICS 71391)

NAICS 71391: Golf Courses and Country Clubs. This industry comprises (1) establishments primarily engaged in operating golf courses (except miniature) and (2) establishments primarily engaged in operating golf courses, along with dining facilities and other recreational facilities that are known as country clubs. These establishments often provide food and beverage services, equipment rental services, and golf instruction services.

Industry Establishments, Sales & Employment Trends

	Year					Percent Chg. Year-to-Year			
	2015	2016	2017	2018	2019	15-16	16-17	17-18	18-19
Establishments	23,675	23,576	23,545	23,293	23,216	-0.4%	-0.1%	-1.1%	-0.3%
Sales ($Millions)	22,530	23,245	24,158	24,898	25,901	3.2%	3.9%	3.1%	4.0%
Employment	279,385	278,209	277,844	274,867	273,965	-0.4%	-0.1%	-1.1%	-0.3%
Sales ($M)/Estab.	0.95	0.99	1.03	1.07	1.12	3.6%	4.1%	4.2%	4.4%
Sales ($)/Emp.	80,643	83,553	86,947	90,583	94,542	3.6%	4.1%	4.2%	4.4%

5-Year Trend – Estimated Number of Establishments

Year	Employee Size of Establishment									Total Employment
	1-4 Emps.	5-9 Emps.	10-19 Emps.	20-49 Emps.	50-99 Emps.	100-249 Emps.	250-499 Emps.	>500 Emps.	Non-Employer	
2017	4,062	1,520	1,528	2,208	1,323	536	35	5	12,327	23,545
2018	4,019	1,504	1,512	2,184	1,309	530	35	5	12,195	23,293
2019	4,006	1,499	1,507	2,177	1,304	528	35	5	12,155	23,216

5-Year Trend – Estimated Industry Sales ($Millions)

Year	Employee Size of Establishment									Total Employment
	1-4 Emps.	5-9 Emps.	10-19 Emps.	20-49 Emps.	50-99 Emps.	100-249 Emps.	250-499 Emps.	>500 Emps.	Non-Employer	
2017	525.6	517.0	1,306.9	4,997.3	6,581.2	7,187.4	1,600.2	405.8	1,036.4	24,157.7
2018	541.7	532.9	1,346.9	5,150.5	6,783.0	7,407.7	1,649.2	418.3	1,068.2	24,898.4
2019	563.5	554.3	1,401.2	5,357.9	7,056.2	7,706.1	1,715.6	435.1	1,111.2	25,901.2

5-Year Trend – Estimated Number of Employees

Year	Employee Size of Establishment									Total Employment
	1-4 Emps.	5-9 Emps.	10-19 Emps.	20-49 Emps.	50-99 Emps.	100-249 Emps.	250-499 Emps.	>500 Emps.	Non-Employer	
2017	10,156	8,818	20,784	66,454	78,568	67,584	10,299	2,854	12,327	277,844
2018	10,047	8,724	20,561	65,742	77,726	66,860	10,188	2,824	12,195	274,867
2019	10,014	8,695	20,494	65,526	77,471	66,641	10,155	2,814	12,155	273,965

© Barnes Reports: 2018 U.S. Industry & Market Outlook

GOLF COURSES & COUNTRY CLUBS INDUSTRY
(NAICS 71391)

SUB-INDUSTRIES – 2018 ESTIMATED INDUSTRY SALES, ESTABLISHMENTS & EMPLOYMENT

Sub-Industries	Category*	Establishments	Sales ($Mill)	Employment
Public golf courses	Major1	11,646	12,449.2	137,434
Country club, membership	Minor2	6,111	7,935.7	84,348
Golf club, membership	Minor2	5,535	4,513.4	53,085

*Category-Major categories (Major1) are more general descriptions for companies that self-selected to capture the many functions they perform in the industry. Minor categories (Minor1, Minor2) are more specific for companies that have more detailed functions (Minor1 is a larger category than Minor2). Minor categories figures (sales, etc.) can be aggregated to larger minor categories (Minor2 sums to Minor1) and major categories overall figures.

Fitness & Recreational Sports Centers (NAICS 71394)

NAICS 71394: Fitness and Recreational Sports Centers. This industry comprises establishments primarily engaged in operating fitness and recreational sports facilities featuring exercise and other active physical fitness conditioning or recreational sports activities, such as swimming, skating, or racquet sports.

Industry Establishments, Sales & Employment Trends

	Year					Percent Chg. Year-to-Year			
	2015	2016	2017	2018	2019	15-16	16-17	17-18	18-19
Establishments	68,659	70,490	72,549	75,442	79,039	2.7%	2.9%	4.0%	4.8%
Sales ($Millions)	27,512	28,792	30,369	32,435	35,004	4.7%	5.5%	6.8%	7.9%
Employment	635,721	652,674	671,744	698,526	731,832	2.7%	2.9%	4.0%	4.8%
Sales ($M)/Estab.	0.40	0.41	0.42	0.43	0.44	1.9%	2.5%	2.7%	3.0%
Sales ($)/Emp.	43,277	44,113	45,209	46,434	47,830	1.9%	2.5%	2.7%	3.0%

5-Year Trend – Estimated Number of Establishments

Year	1-4 Emps.	5-9 Emps.	10-19 Emps.	20-49 Emps.	50-99 Emps.	100-249 Emps.	250-499 Emps.	>500 Emps.	Non-Employer	Total Employment
2017	16,116	5,258	4,660	4,867	2,179	1,296	174	15	37,984	72,549
2018	16,759	5,467	4,846	5,061	2,266	1,348	181	16	39,498	75,442
2019	17,558	5,728	5,077	5,303	2,374	1,412	190	17	41,381	79,039

5-Year Trend – Estimated Industry Sales ($Millions)

Year	1-4 Emps.	5-9 Emps.	10-19 Emps.	20-49 Emps.	50-99 Emps.	100-249 Emps.	250-499 Emps.	>500 Emps.	Non-Employer	Total Employment
2017	1,010.3	866.3	1,931.0	5,338.1	5,252.3	8,420.0	3,818.9	637.3	3,094.7	30,368.9
2018	1,079.1	925.3	2,062.5	5,701.9	5,610.2	8,993.7	4,079.1	677.8	3,305.6	32,435.0
2019	1,164.7	998.7	2,226.1	6,154.1	6,055.1	9,706.9	4,402.6	727.8	3,567.7	35,003.7

5-Year Trend – Estimated Number of Employees

Year	1-4 Emps.	5-9 Emps.	10-19 Emps.	20-49 Emps.	50-99 Emps.	100-249 Emps.	250-499 Emps.	>500 Emps.	Non-Employer	Total Employment
2017	40,290	30,494	63,381	146,509	129,413	163,409	50,727	9,536	37,984	671,744
2018	41,897	31,710	65,907	152,350	134,573	169,924	52,750	9,917	39,498	698,526
2019	43,894	33,222	69,050	159,615	140,989	178,026	55,265	10,390	41,381	731,832

© Barnes Reports: 2018 U.S. Industry & Market Outlook

FITNESS & RECREATIONAL SPORTS CENTERS
(NAICS 71394)

SUB-INDUSTRIES – 2018 ESTIMATED INDUSTRY SALES, ESTABLISHMENTS & EMPLOYMENT

Sub-Industries	Category*	Establishments	Sales ($Mill)	Employment
Physical fitness facilities	Major1	16,257	6,976.8	132,116
Physical fitness clubs with training equipment	Minor1	2,105	1,095.2	22,759
Athletic club and gymnasiums, membership	Minor2	3,007	2,253.1	53,421
Health club	Minor2	5,775	5,031.3	111,317
Spas	Minor2	16,104	4,388.2	101,648
Weight reducing clubs	Minor1	318	158.6	2,176
Reducing facility	Minor2	19	7.6	162
Slenderizing salon	Minor2	118	24.2	564
Exercise facilities	Minor1	1,163	330.9	7,480
Aerobic dance and exercise classes	Minor2	1,511	450.3	10,663
Exercise salon	Minor2	3,917	907.1	23,378
Membership sports and recreation clubs	Major1	25,147	10,811.7	232,842

*Category-Major categories (Major1) are more general descriptions for companies that self-selected to capture the many functions they perform in the industry. Minor categories (Minor1, Minor2) are more specific for companies that have more detailed functions (Minor1 is a larger category than Minor2). Minor categories figures (sales, etc.) can be aggregated to larger minor categories (Minor2 sums to Minor1) and major categories overall figures.

Hotels & Motels Industry
(NAICS 72111)

NAICS 72111: Hotels (except Casino Hotels) and Motels. This industry comprises establishments primarily engaged in providing short-term lodging in facilities known as hotels, motor hotels, resort hotels, and motels. The establishments in this industry may offer services, such as food and beverage services, recreational services, conference rooms and convention services, laundry services, parking, and other services.

Industry Establishments, Sales & Employment Trends

	Year					Percent Chg. Year-to-Year			
	2015	2016	2017	2018	2019	15-16	16-17	17-18	18-19
Establishments	61,927	60,957	60,172	59,855	59,685	-1.6%	-1.3%	-0.5%	-0.3%
Sales ($Millions)	149,130	152,343	156,712	162,529	169,241	2.2%	2.9%	3.7%	4.1%
Employment	1,399,539	1,377,603	1,359,869	1,352,702	1,348,861	-1.6%	-1.3%	-0.5%	-0.3%
Sales ($M)/Estab.	2.41	2.50	2.60	2.72	2.84	3.8%	4.2%	4.3%	4.4%
Sales ($)/Emp.	106,556	110,585	115,240	120,152	125,470	3.8%	4.2%	4.3%	4.4%

5-Year Trend – Estimated Number of Establishments

Year	Employee Size of Establishment									Total Employment
	1-4 Emps.	5-9 Emps.	10-19 Emps.	20-49 Emps.	50-99 Emps.	100-249 Emps.	250-499 Emps.	>500 Emps.	Non-Employer	
2017	15,116	6,997	11,924	10,947	2,442	1,951	534	322	9,940	60,172
2018	15,036	6,960	11,861	10,889	2,429	1,941	531	320	9,888	59,855
2019	14,993	6,940	11,827	10,858	2,422	1,936	529	319	9,860	59,685

5-Year Trend – Estimated Industry Sales ($Millions)

Year	Employee Size of Establishment									Total Employment
	1-4 Emps.	5-9 Emps.	10-19 Emps.	20-49 Emps.	50-99 Emps.	100-249 Emps.	250-499 Emps.	>500 Emps.	Non-Employer	
2017	2,283.4	2,778.1	11,905.1	28,928.9	14,183.9	30,554.7	28,162.2	36,770.3	1,145.4	156,712.0
2018	2,367.1	2,879.9	12,341.7	29,989.8	14,704.1	31,675.2	29,195.0	38,189.2	1,187.4	162,529.3
2019	2,464.3	2,998.2	12,848.4	31,220.9	15,307.7	32,975.5	30,393.5	39,796.5	1,236.1	169,241.0

5-Year Trend – Estimated Number of Employees

Year	Employee Size of Establishment									Total Employment
	1-4 Emps.	5-9 Emps.	10-19 Emps.	20-49 Emps.	50-99 Emps.	100-249 Emps.	250-499 Emps.	>500 Emps.	Non-Employer	
2017	37,790	40,583	162,163	329,490	145,030	246,082	155,243	233,548	9,940	1,359,869
2018	37,590	40,369	161,308	327,754	144,266	244,785	154,424	232,317	9,888	1,352,702
2019	37,484	40,254	160,850	326,823	143,856	244,090	153,986	231,658	9,860	1,348,861

© Barnes Reports: 2018 U.S. Industry & Market Outlook

HOTELS & MOTELS INDUSTRY
(NAICS 72111)

SUB-INDUSTRIES — 2018 ESTIMATED INDUSTRY SALES, ESTABLISHMENTS & EMPLOYMENT

Sub-Industries	Category*	Establishments	Sales ($Mill)	Employment
Hotels and motels	Major1	23,701	69,069.8	656,600
Motels	Minor1	12,066	5,880.6	82,251
Motel, franchised	Minor2	596	562.8	10,942
Vacation lodges	Minor1	1,158	645.5	8,982
Ski lodge	Minor2	244	1,800.9	10,963
Tourist camps, cabins, cottages, and courts	Minor2	949	357.8	5,183
Hotels	Minor1	6,462	16,005.5	228,510
Casino hotel	Minor2	661	45,568.8	133,729
Hotel, franchised	Minor2	1,202	12,340.9	35,066
Resort hotel	Minor2	2,546	5,936.8	115,825
Resort hotel, franchised	Minor2	60	395.3	4,898
Seasonal hotel	Minor2	67	122.7	1,482
YMCA/YMHA hotel	Minor2	18	41.4	1,210
YWCA/YWHA hotel	Minor2	1	7.9	69
Inns	Minor1	4,159	2,203.0	35,184
Bed and breakfast inn	Minor2	5,561	1,252.6	17,141
Motor inn	Minor2	255	183.6	2,661
Hostels	Minor2	149	153.3	2,006

*Category-Major categories (Major1) are more general descriptions for companies that self-selected to capture the many functions they perform in the industry. Minor categories (Minor1, Minor2) are more specific for companies that have more detailed functions (Minor1 is a larger category than Minor2). Minor categories figures (sales, etc.) can be aggregated to larger minor categories (Minor2 sums to Minor1) and major categories overall figures.

FULL-SERVICE RESTAURANTS INDUSTRY
(NAICS 722511)

NAICS 722511: Full-Service Restaurants -- This industry comprises establishments primarily engaged in providing food services to patrons who order and are served while seated (i.e. waiter/waitress service) and pay after eating. These establishments may provide this type of food services to patrons in combination with selling alcoholic beverages, providing takeout services, or presenting live nontheatrical entertainment.

INDUSTRY ESTABLISHMENTS, SALES & EMPLOYMENT TRENDS

	Year					Percent Chg. Year-to-Year			
	2015	2016	2017	2018	2019	15-16	16-17	17-18	18-19
Establishments	257,934	261,418	265,694	270,768	276,606	1.4%	1.6%	1.9%	2.2%
Sales ($Millions)	240,429	248,836	259,633	272,203	286,877	3.5%	4.3%	4.8%	5.4%
Employment	4,901,277	4,967,483	5,048,736	5,145,159	5,256,093	1.4%	1.6%	1.9%	2.2%
Sales ($M)/Estab.	0.93	0.95	0.98	1.01	1.04	2.1%	2.7%	2.9%	3.2%
Sales ($)/Emp.	49,054	50,093	51,425	52,905	54,580	2.1%	2.7%	2.9%	3.2%

5-YEAR TREND – ESTIMATED NUMBER OF ESTABLISHMENTS

Year	Employee Size of Establishment									Total Employment
	1-4 Emps.	5-9 Emps.	10-19 Emps.	20-49 Emps.	50-99 Emps.	100-249 Emps.	250-499 Emps.	>500 Emps.	Non-Employer	
2017	70,060	42,563	49,879	57,899	24,513	5,296	192	13	15,280	265,694
2018	71,398	43,376	50,832	59,005	24,981	5,397	195	13	15,572	270,768
2019	72,937	44,311	51,928	60,277	25,519	5,513	200	13	15,908	276,606

5-YEAR TREND – ESTIMATED INDUSTRY SALES ($MILLIONS)

Year	Employee Size of Establishment									Total Employment
	1-4 Emps.	5-9 Emps.	10-19 Emps.	20-49 Emps.	50-99 Emps.	100-249 Emps.	250-499 Emps.	>500 Emps.	Non-Employer	
2017	5,876.0	9,382.8	27,650.8	84,956.2	79,064.4	46,036.3	5,618.3	878.4	169.9	259,633.1
2018	6,160.7	9,837.4	28,990.5	89,072.4	82,895.2	48,266.8	5,890.5	911.4	178.1	272,202.9
2019	6,493.1	10,368.1	30,554.5	93,877.8	87,367.3	50,870.7	6,208.3	949.4	187.7	286,876.8

5-YEAR TREND – ESTIMATED NUMBER OF EMPLOYEES

Year	Employee Size of Establishment									Total Employment
	1-4 Emps.	5-9 Emps.	10-19 Emps.	20-49 Emps.	50-99 Emps.	100-249 Emps.	250-499 Emps.	>500 Emps.	Non-Employer	
2017	175,150	246,867	678,355	1,742,761	1,456,046	667,782	55,780	10,715	15,280	5,048,736
2018	178,495	251,582	691,311	1,776,045	1,483,854	680,535	56,845	10,920	15,572	5,145,159
2019	182,344	257,006	706,216	1,814,338	1,515,847	695,208	58,071	11,155	15,908	5,256,093

© Barnes Reports: 2018 U.S. Industry & Market Outlook

Full-Service Restaurants Industry
(NAICS 722511)

Sub-Industries — 2018 Estimated Industry Sales, Establishments & Employment

Sub-Industries	Category*	Establishments	Sales ($Mill)	Employment
Eating places	Major1	62,970	44,134.3	824,432
Ethnic food restaurants	Minor1	3,507	2,259.7	39,325
American restaurant	Minor2	9,522	14,551.8	355,995
Cajun restaurant	Minor2	361	473.4	9,069
Chinese restaurant	Minor2	20,111	13,304.4	171,646
French restaurant	Minor2	756	1,162.9	19,635
German restaurant	Minor2	214	227.2	4,157
Greek restaurant	Minor2	798	730.7	13,313
Indian/Pakistan restaurant	Minor2	1,325	704.2	10,615
Italian restaurant	Minor2	8,741	10,781.6	238,171
Japanese restaurant	Minor2	3,929	3,259.9	47,680
Korean restaurant	Minor2	491	239.1	3,478
Lebanese restaurant	Minor2	81	73.7	843
Mexican restaurant	Minor2	16,816	10,239.6	236,072
Spanish restaurant	Minor2	414	408.2	6,135
Sushi bar	Minor2	1,840	646.6	11,012
Thai restaurant	Minor2	3,035	1,155.5	18,391
Vietnamese restaurant	Minor2	759	273.7	4,502
Pakistani restaurant	Minor2	32	11.5	144
Lunchrooms and cafeterias	Minor1	1,354	642.8	16,034
Automat (eating places)	Minor2	18	21.2	427
Cafeteria	Minor2	1,324	1,817.8	47,585
Luncheonette	Minor2	991	313.9	5,441
Lunchroom	Minor2	35	16.1	424
Restaurant, lunch counter	Minor2	351	273.1	5,664
Family restaurants	Minor1	24,334	54,662.7	994,409
Pizza restaurants	Minor1	41,577	29,204.1	687,352
Seafood restaurants	Minor1	6,256	24,252.9	268,410
Steak and barbecue restaurants	Minor1	13,097	22,730.0	346,005
Buffet (eating places)	Minor2	2,027	830.3	33,375
Cafe	Minor2	19,321	11,836.3	185,572
Caterers	Minor2	16,066	12,306.1	216,516
Chicken restaurant	Minor2	3,410	4,099.0	41,916
Misc. full-service restaurants	Minor2	4,904	4,558.5	281,414

*Category-Major categories (Major1) are more general descriptions for companies that self-selected to capture the many functions they perform in the industry. Minor categories (Minor1, Minor2) are more specific for companies that have more detailed functions (Minor1 is a larger category than Minor2). Minor categories figures (sales, etc.) can be aggregated to larger minor categories (Minor2 sums to Minor1) and major categories overall figures.

Fast Food Restaurants Industry
(NAICS 722513)

NAICS 722513: Fast Food Restaurants. This industry comprises establishments primarily engaged in the retail sale of prepared food and drinks for on-premise or immediate consumption. Caterers and industrial and institutional food service establishments are also included in this business.

Industry Establishments, Sales & Employment Trends

	Year					Percent Chg. Year-to-Year			
	2015	2016	2017	2018	2019	15-16	16-17	17-18	18-19
Establishments	242,329	245,856	250,131	255,107	260,811	1.5%	1.7%	2.0%	2.2%
Sales ($Millions)	202,291	209,701	219,140	230,046	242,750	3.7%	4.5%	5.0%	5.5%
Employment	3,949,147	4,006,638	4,076,296	4,157,394	4,250,350	1.5%	1.7%	2.0%	2.2%
Sales ($M)/Estab.	0.83	0.85	0.88	0.90	0.93	2.2%	2.7%	2.9%	3.2%
Sales ($)/Emp.	51,224	52,338	53,760	55,334	57,113	2.2%	2.7%	2.9%	3.2%

5-Year Trend – Estimated Number of Establishments

Year	Employee Size of Establishment									Total Employment
	1-4 Emps.	5-9 Emps.	10-19 Emps.	20-49 Emps.	50-99 Emps.	100-249 Emps.	250-499 Emps.	>500 Emps.	Non-Employer	
2017	65,670	36,980	56,735	68,307	12,324	839	38	15	9,224	250,131
2018	66,976	37,716	57,864	69,665	12,569	855	39	15	9,408	255,107
2019	68,474	38,559	59,158	71,223	12,850	874	40	15	9,618	260,811

5-Year Trend – Estimated Industry Sales ($Millions)

Year	Employee Size of Establishment									Total Employment
	1-4 Emps.	5-9 Emps.	10-19 Emps.	20-49 Emps.	50-99 Emps.	100-249 Emps.	250-499 Emps.	>500 Emps.	Non-Employer	
2017	6,203.3	9,181.5	35,423.2	112,884.0	44,768.9	8,210.4	1,251.5	1,118.2	99.0	219,140.1
2018	6,512.4	9,638.9	37,187.8	118,507.5	46,999.1	8,619.4	1,313.9	1,162.7	104.0	230,045.6
2019	6,872.4	10,171.7	39,243.7	125,059.0	49,597.4	9,096.0	1,386.5	1,213.9	109.7	242,750.3

5-Year Trend – Estimated Number of Employees

Year	Employee Size of Establishment									Total Employment
	1-4 Emps.	5-9 Emps.	10-19 Emps.	20-49 Emps.	50-99 Emps.	100-249 Emps.	250-499 Emps.	>500 Emps.	Non-Employer	
2017	164,174	214,486	771,597	2,056,026	732,022	105,744	11,032	11,991	9,224	4,076,296
2018	167,440	218,753	786,948	2,096,931	746,585	107,847	11,252	12,229	9,408	4,157,394
2019	171,184	223,644	804,544	2,143,816	763,278	110,259	11,504	12,503	9,618	4,250,350

© Barnes Reports: 2018 U.S. Industry & Market Outlook

Fast Food Restaurants Industry (NAICS 722513)

Sub-Industries – 2018 Estimated Industry Sales, Establishments & Employment

Sub-Industries	Category*	Establishments	Sales ($Mill)	Employment
Eating places	Major1	91,326	33,481.3	1,078,677
Ice cream, soft drink and soda fountain stands	Minor1	1,861	448.3	15,825
Concessionaire	Minor2	1,652	5,523.2	30,035
Frozen yogurt stand	Minor2	807	236.2	7,139
Ice cream stands or dairy bars	Minor2	12,477	4,077.6	151,000
Snow cone stand	Minor2	285	34.5	991
Soda fountain	Minor2	130	26.9	852
Soft drink stand	Minor2	653	466.1	13,783
Fast food restaurants and stands	Minor1	3,625	1,175.1	43,549
Box lunch stand	Minor2	99	21.7	1,004
Carry-out only (except pizza) restaurant	Minor2	4,387	1,203.8	42,776
Chili stand	Minor2	129	54.9	1,822
Coffee shop	Minor2	17,709	19,930.4	221,588
Delicatessen (eating places)	Minor2	9,614	3,225.3	63,401
Drive-in restaurant	Minor2	5,933	3,491.9	131,649
Fast-food restaurant, chain	Minor2	53,933	138,526.9	1,775,366
Fast-food restaurant, independent	Minor2	3,358	1,183.5	43,557
Food bars	Minor2	341	259.1	13,578
Grills (eating places)	Minor2	14,727	8,178.6	229,672
Hamburger stand	Minor2	2,040	475.9	23,603
Hot dog stand	Minor2	1,584	218.0	8,419
Sandwiches and submarines shop	Minor2	26,996	7,529.7	246,794
Snack bar	Minor2	1,033	206.4	10,377
Snack shop	Minor2	406	70.6	1,939

*Category-Major categories (Major1) are more general descriptions for companies that self-selected to capture the many functions they perform in the industry. Minor categories (Minor1, Minor2) are more specific for companies that have more detailed functions (Minor1 is a larger category than Minor2). Minor categories figures (sales, etc.) can be aggregated to larger minor categories (Minor2 sums to Minor1) and major categories overall figures.

Drinking Places & Bars Industry
(NAICS 72241)

NAICS 72241: Drinking Places (Alcoholic Beverages). This industry comprises establishments known as bars, taverns, nightclubs or drinking places primarily engaged in preparing and serving alcoholic beverages for immediate consumption. These establishments may also provide limited food services.

Industry Establishments, Sales & Employment Trends

	Year					Percent Chg. Year-to-Year			
	2015	2016	2017	2018	2019	15-16	16-17	17-18	18-19
Establishments	49,193	47,470	45,918	44,675	43,572	-3.5%	-3.3%	-2.7%	-2.5%
Sales ($Millions)	21,225	21,144	21,213	21,437	21,761	-0.4%	0.3%	1.1%	1.5%
Employment	366,467	353,628	342,069	332,811	324,595	-3.5%	-3.3%	-2.7%	-2.5%
Sales ($M)/Estab.	0.43	0.45	0.46	0.48	0.50	3.2%	3.7%	3.9%	4.1%
Sales ($)/Emp.	57,917	59,792	62,015	64,411	67,040	3.2%	3.7%	3.9%	4.1%

5-Year Trend — Estimated Number of Establishments

Year	Employee Size of Establishment									Total Employment
	1-4 Emps.	5-9 Emps.	10-19 Emps.	20-49 Emps.	50-99 Emps.	100-249 Emps.	250-499 Emps.	>500 Emps.	Non-Employer	
2017	18,828	9,696	5,319	3,322	687	112	10	1	7,943	45,918
2018	18,318	9,433	5,175	3,232	669	109	10	1	7,728	44,675
2019	17,866	9,200	5,047	3,153	652	106	10	1	7,537	43,572

5-Year Trend — Estimated Industry Sales ($Millions)

Year	Employee Size of Establishment									Total Employment
	1-4 Emps.	5-9 Emps.	10-19 Emps.	20-49 Emps.	50-99 Emps.	100-249 Emps.	250-499 Emps.	>500 Emps.	Non-Employer	
2017	2,217.6	3,001.5	4,140.8	6,846.0	3,113.9	1,368.6	419.3	70.7	35.0	21,213.4
2018	2,241.0	3,033.1	4,184.4	6,918.1	3,146.7	1,383.0	423.8	71.5	35.4	21,436.8
2019	2,274.8	3,078.9	4,247.6	7,022.6	3,194.2	1,403.9	430.2	72.6	35.9	21,760.7

5-Year Trend — Estimated Number of Employees

Year	Employee Size of Establishment									Total Employment
	1-4 Emps.	5-9 Emps.	10-19 Emps.	20-49 Emps.	50-99 Emps.	100-249 Emps.	250-499 Emps.	>500 Emps.	Non-Employer	
2017	47,070	56,234	72,337	100,003	40,834	14,136	2,965	547	7,943	342,069
2018	45,796	54,712	70,379	97,296	39,729	13,754	2,884	532	7,728	332,811
2019	44,665	53,362	68,642	94,894	38,748	13,414	2,813	519	7,537	324,595

© Barnes Reports: 2018 U.S. Industry & Market Outlook

DRINKING PLACES & BARS INDUSTRY
(NAICS 72241)

SUB-INDUSTRIES – 2018 ESTIMATED INDUSTRY SALES, ESTABLISHMENTS & EMPLOYMENT

Sub-Industries	Category*	Establishments	Sales ($Mill)	Employment
Drinking places	Major1	9,355	5,737.2	62,132
Bars and lounges	Minor1	3,190	1,286.4	21,669
Bar (drinking places)	Minor2	9,501	4,315.1	87,575
Beer garden (drinking places)	Minor2	92	57.8	930
Cocktail lounge	Minor2	5,430	2,256.6	37,027
Saloon	Minor2	935	308.9	5,538
Tavern (drinking places)	Minor2	12,078	4,840.4	75,692
Wine bar	Minor2	313	111.2	1,850
Night clubs	Minor1	3,557	2,372.3	37,412
Cabaret	Minor2	177	107.7	2,392
Discotheque	Minor2	46	43.2	594

*Category-Major categories (Major1) are more general descriptions for companies that self-selected to capture the many functions they perform in the industry. Minor categories (Minor1, Minor2) are more specific for companies that have more detailed functions (Minor1 is a larger category than Minor2). Minor categories figures (sales, etc.) can be aggregated to larger minor categories (Minor2 sums to Minor1) and major categories overall figures.

2018 U.S. Industry & Market Outlook

Definitions and Terms

Number of Establishments

General Definition

An establishment is a single physical location at which business is conducted and/or services are provided. It is not necessarily identical with a company or enterprise, which may consist of one establishment or more. Economic census figures represent a summary of reports for individual establishments rather than companies. For cases where a census report was received, separate information was obtained for each location where business was conducted. When administrative records of other Federal agencies were used instead of a census report, no information was available on the number of locations operated. Each economic census establishment was tabulated according to the physical location at which the business was conducted.

When two activities or more were carried on at a single location under a single ownership, all activities generally were grouped together as a single establishment. The entire establishment was classified on the basis of its major activity and all data for it were included in that classification. However, when distinct and separate economic activities (for which different industry classification codes were appropriate) were conducted at a single location under a single ownership, separate establishment reports for each of the different activities were obtained in the census.

Sector-Specific Information

Construction sector. Establishments are defined as a relatively permanent office or other place of business where the usual business activities related to construction are conducted. Establishments do not represent each project or construction site. Includes all establishments that were in business at any time during the year. It covers all full-year and part-year operations. Construction establishments which were inactive or idle for the entire year were not included. Establishments are based on a survey which included all large employers and a sample of the smaller ones.

Information; Professional, Scientific, and Technical Services; Administrative and Support and Waste Management and Remediation Services; Educational Services; Health Care and Social Assistance; Arts, Entertainment, and Recreation; and Other Services (Except Public Administration) sectors. An establishment is included in the census if it is an employer, the establishment has $1,000 in payroll, and was in operation at any time during 2012. Leased service departments (separately owned businesses operated as departments or concessions of other service establishments or of retail businesses, such as a separately owned shoeshine parlor in a barber shop, or a beauty shop in a department store) are treated as separate service establishments for census purposes. Leased retail departments located in service establishments (e.g., a gift shop located in a hotel) are considered separate retail establishments.

Manufacturing sector. Includes all manufacturing establishments (plants) with one employee or more and establishments in operation at any time during the year.

Mining sector. Includes all mineral establishments with one employee or more and establishments in operation at any time during the year. Establishments in the crude petroleum and natural gas and support activities for mining represent statewide operations rather than those at a single physical location.

Real Estate and Rental and Leasing sector. Data for individual properties leased or managed by property lessors or property managers are not normally considered separate establishments, but rather the permanent offices from which the properties are leased or managed are considered establishments. Data for separate automotive rental offices or concessions (e.g., airport locations) in the same metropolitan area for which a common fleet of cars is maintained are merged together and not considered as separate establishments.

Retail Trade sector. Leased departments are treated as separate establishments and are classified according to the kind of business they conduct. For example, a leased department selling shoes within a department store would be considered a separate retail establishment under the "shoe stores" classification.

Accommodation and Foodservices sector. Leased departments are treated as separate establishments and are classified according to the kind of business they conduct. For example, a leased department selling gifts/souvenirs within a hotel would be considered a separate retail establishment under the "gift, novelty, and souvenir stores" classification.

Auxiliaries sector. In the Standard Industrial Classification (SIC) system, auxiliary establishments (i.e., those establishments primarily serving other establishments of the same enterprise) were classified in the industry of the establishments served. In the North American Industry Classification System (NAICS), auxiliary establishments are classified according to the services performed rather than the industry served.

Sales, Shipments, Receipts, Revenue, or Business Done
General Definition
Includes the total sales, shipments, receipts, revenue, or business done by establishments within the scope of the economic census. The definition of each of these items is included in the information provided below.
Sector-Specific Information
Construction sector - Includes the value of construction work and other business receipts for work done by establishments during the year. Included is new construction, additions and alterations or reconstruction, and maintenance and repair construction work. Also included is the value of any construction work done by the reporting establishments for themselves.
Speculative builders were instructed to include the value of buildings and other structures built or being built for sale in the current year but not sold. They were to include the costs of such construction plus normal profit. Also included is the cost of construction work done on buildings for rent or lease.
Establishments engaged in the sale and installation of such construction components as plumbing, heating, and central air-conditioning supplies and equipment; lumber and building materials; paint, glass, and wallpaper; electrical and wiring supplies; and elevators or escalators were instructed to include both the value for the installation and the receipts covering the price of the items installed.
Excluded was the cost of industrial and other specialized machinery and equipment, which are not an integral part of a structure.
Finance and Insurance sector - Includes revenue from all business activities whether or not payment was received in the census year, including commissions and fees from all sources, rents, net investment income, interest, dividends, royalties, and net insurance premiums earned. Revenue from leasing property marketed under operating leases is included, as well as interest earned from property marketed in the census year under capital, finance, or full payout leases. Revenue also includes the total value of service contracts and amounts received for work subcontracted to others.
Revenue does not include sales and other taxes collected from customers and remitted directly by the firm to a local, state, or Federal tax agency.
Information sector - Includes receipts from customers or clients for services rendered, from the use of facilities, and from merchandise sold, whether or not payment was received. Receipts include royalties, license fees, and other payments from the marketing of intangible products (e.g., licensing the use of or granting reproduction rights for software, musical compositions, and other intellectual property). Receipts also include the rental and leasing of vehicles, equipment, instruments, tools, etc.; total value of service contracts; market value of compensation received in lieu of cash; amounts received for work subcontracted to others; dues and assessments for members

2018 U.S. Industry & Market Outlook

and affiliates; this establishment's share of receipts from departments, concessions, and vending and amusement machines operated by others. Receipts from services provided to foreign customers from U.S. locations, including services preformed for foreign parent firms, subsidiaries, and branches are included. For public broadcast stations and libraries, include receipts from contributions, gifts, grants, and income from interest, rental of real estate, and dividends.

Receipts DO NOT include sales and other taxes collected directly from customers or clients and paid directly to a local, state, or Federal tax agency. Also excluded are gross receipts collected on behalf of others; gross receipts or departments or concessions operated by others; sales of used equipment previously rented or leased to customers; proceeds from the sale of real estate (land and buildings), investments, or other assets (except inventory held for resale); contributions, gifts, grants, and income from interest, rental of real estate, and dividends EXCEPT for public broadcast stations and libraries; domestic intracompany transfers; receipts of foreign subsidiaries; and other nonoperating income.

Management of Companies and Enterprises sector- For holding companies, revenue includes revenue of only the holding company establishment, including net investment income, interest, and dividends.

Manufacturing sector - Covers the received or receivable net selling values, f.o.b. plant (exclusive of freight and taxes), of all products shipped, both primary and secondary, as well as all miscellaneous receipts, such as receipts for contract work performed for others, installation and repair, sales of scrap, and sales of products bought and resold without further processing. Included are all items made by or for the establishments from materials owned by it, whether sold, transferred to other plants of the same company, or shipped on consignment. The net selling value of products made in one plant on a contract basis from materials owned by another was reported by the plant providing the materials.

In the case of multiunit companies, the manufacturer was requested to report the value of products transferred to other establishments of the same company at full economic or commercial value, including not only the direct cost of production but also a reasonable proportion of "all other costs" (including company overhead) and profit.

Mining sector - Includes the net selling values, f.o.b. mine or plant after discounts and allowances, excluding freight charges and excise taxes. Shipments includes all products physically shipped from the establishment during the year, including material withdrawn from stockpiles and products shipped on consignment, whether or not sold in the current year. Prepared material or concentrates includes preparation from ores mined at the same establishment, purchased, received from other operations of the same company, or received for milling on a custom or toll basis. For products transferred to other establishments of the same company or prepared on a custom basis, companies were requested to report the estimated value, not merely the cost of producing the items. Multiestablishment companies were asked to report value information for each establishment as if it were a separate economic unit. They were instructed to report the value of all products transferred to other plants of the company at their full economic value; to include, in addition to direct cost of production, a reasonable proportion of company overhead and profits. For all establishments classified in an industry, value of shipments and receipts includes (1) the value of all primary products of the industry; (2) the value of secondary products which are primary to other industries; (3) the receipts for contract work done for others, except custom milling; and (4) the value of products purchased and resold without further processing. Receipts for custom milling are not included to avoid duplication with the value of custom milled ores included in an industry's primary and secondary products. Some duplication exists in industry and industry group totals because of the inclusion of materials transferred from one establishment to another for mineral preparation or resale.

Professional, Scientific, and Technical Services; Administrative and Support and Waste Management and Remediation Services; Educational Services; Health Care and Social Assistance; Arts, Entertainment, and Recreation; and Other Services (Except Public Administration) sectors - TAXABLE ESTABLISHMENTS: Includes receipts from customers or clients for services rendered, from the use of facilities, and from merchandise sold whether or not payment was received. For advertising agencies, travel industries, and

2018 U.S. Industry & Market Outlook

other service establishments operating on a commission basis, receipts include commissions, fees, and other operating income, NOT gross billings and sales. Excise taxes on gasoline, liquor, tobacco, etc., which are paid by the manufacturer or wholesaler and passed on in the cost of goods purchased by the service establishment are also included. The establishments share of receipts from departments, concessions, and vending and amusement machines operated by others are included as part of receipts. Receipts also include the total value of service contracts, market value of compensation received in lieu of cash, amounts received for work subcontracted to others, and dues and assessments from members and affiliates. Receipts from services provided to foreign customers from U.S. locations, including services preformed for foreign parent firms, subsidiaries, and branches are included.

Receipts are net after deductions for refunds and allowances for merchandise returned by customers. Receipts DO NOT include sales, occupancy, admissions, or other taxes collected from customers and remitted directly by the firm to a local, state, or Federal tax agency, nor do they include income from such sources as contributions, gifts, and grants; dividends, interest, and investments; or sale or rental of real estate. Also excluded are receipts (gross) of departments and concessions which are operated by others; sales of used equipment rented or leased to customers; domestic intracompany transfers; receipts of foreign subsidiaries; and other nonoperating income, such as royalties, franchise fees, etc. Receipts DO NOT include service receipts of manufacturers, wholesalers, retail establishments, or other businesses whose primary activity is other than service. They do, however, include receipts other than from services rendered (e.g., sale of merchandise to individuals or other businesses) by establishments primarily engaged in performing services and classified in the service industries.

TAX EXEMPT ESTABLISHMENTS: Includes revenue from customers or clients for services rendered and merchandise, whether or not payment was received, and gross sales of merchandise, minus returns and allowances. Also included are income from interest, dividends, gross rents (including display space rentals and share of receipts from departments operated by other companies), gross contributions, gifts, grants (whether or not restricted for use in operations), royalties, dues and assessments from members and affiliates, commissions earned from the sale of merchandise owned by others (including commissions from vending machine operators), and gross receipts from fundraising activities. Receipts from taxable business activities of firms exempt from Federal income tax (unrelated business income) are also included in revenue. Revenue DOES NOT include sales, admissions, or other taxes collected by the organization from customers or clients and paid directly to a local, state, or Federal tax agency; income from the sale of real estate, investments, or other assets (except inventory held for resale); gross receipts of departments, concessions, etc., that are operated by others; and amounts transferred to operating funds from capital or reserve funds.

Real Estate and Rental and Leasing sector - Includes revenue from all business activities whether or not payment was received in the census year, including commissions and fees from all sources, rents, net investment income, interest, dividends, and royalties. Revenue from leasing property marketed under operating leases is included. Revenue also includes the total value of service contracts, amounts received for work subcontracted to others, and rents from real property sublet to others.

Revenue does not include sales and other taxes collected from customers and remitted directly by the firm to a local, state, or Federal tax agency.

Retail Trade sector - Includes merchandise sold for cash or credit at retail and wholesale by establishments primarily engaged in retail trade; amounts received from customers for layaway purchases; receipts from rental of vehicles, equipment, instruments, tools, etc.; receipts for delivery, installation, maintenance, repair, alteration, storage, and other services; the total value of service contracts; and gasoline, liquor, tobacco, and other excise taxes which are paid by the manufacturer or wholesaler and passed on to the retailer. Sales are net after deductions for refunds and allowances for merchandise returned by customers. Trade-in allowances are not deducted from sales. Sales do not include carrying or other credit charges; sales (or other) taxes collected from customers and forwarded to taxing authorities; gross sales and receipts of

2018 U.S. Industry & Market Outlook

departments or concessions operated by other companies; and commissions or receipts from the sale of government lottery tickets.

Sales do not include retail sales made by manufacturers, wholesalers, service establishments, or other businesses whose primary activity is other than retail trade. They do include receipts other than from the sale of merchandise at retail, e.g., service receipts, sales to industrial users, and sales to other retailers, by establishments primarily engaged in retail trade.

Transportation and Warehousing sector - Includes revenue from all business activities whether or not payment was received in the census year, including commissions and fees for arranging the transportation of freight. Revenue does not include sales and other taxes collected from customers and remitted directly by the firm to a local, state, or Federal tax agency.

Utilities sector - Includes revenue from all business activities whether or not payment was received in the census year.

Revenue does not include sales and other taxes collected from customers and remitted directly by the firm to a local, state, or Federal tax agency.

Accommodation and Foodservices sector - Includes sales from customers for services rendered, from the use of facilities, and from merchandise sold. Also includes dues and assessments from members and affiliates. Sales do not include carrying or other credit charges; sales (or other) taxes collected from customers and forwarded to taxing authorities; gross sales and receipts of departments or concessions operated by other companies; and commissions or receipts from the sale of government lottery tickets.

Excludes sales from civic and social organizations, amusement and recreation parks, theaters, and other recreation or entertainment facilities providing food and beverage services.

Number of Employees

General Definition

Paid employees consists of full-time and part-time employees, including salaried officers and executives of corporations. Included are employees on paid sick leave, paid holidays, and paid vacations; not included are proprietors and partners of unincorporated businesses. The definition of paid employees is the same as that used on IRS Form 941.

Sector-Specific Information

Construction and Manufacturing sectors. Comprises all full-time and part-time employees on the payrolls of establishments who worked or received pay for any part of the pay period including the 12th of March, May, August, and November, divided by 4.

Finance and Insurance sector. Includes all employees who were on the payroll during the pay period including March 12. Excludes independent (nonemployee) agents.

Information; Professional, Scientific, and Technical Services; Administrative and Support and Waste Management and Remediation Services; Educational Services; Health Care and Social Assistance; Arts, Entertainment, and Recreation; and Other Services (Except Public Administration) sectors - Includes all employees who were on the payroll during the pay period including March 12. Includes members of a professional service organization or association which operates under state professional corporation statutes and files a corporate Federal income tax return. Excludes employees of departments or concessions operated by other companies at the establishment.

Management of Companies and Enterprises sector. Includes all employees who were on the payroll during the pay period including March 12.

Mining sector. Also included are employees working for miners paid on a per ton, car, or yard basis. Excluded are employees at the mine but on the payroll of another employer (such as employees of contractors) and employees at company stores, boardinghouses, bunkhouses, and recreational centers.

2018 U.S. Industry & Market Outlook

Also excluded are members of the Armed Forces and pensioners carried on the active rolls but not working during the period. Includes all employees who were on the payroll during the pay period including March 12.

Real Estate and Rental and Leasing sector. Includes all employees who were on the payroll during the pay period including March 12. Excludes independent (nonemployee) agents.

Retail Trade and Accommodation and Foodservices sectors. Includes all employees on the payroll during the pay period including March 12. Excludes employees of departments or concessions operated by other companies at the establishment.

Transportation and Warehousing sector. Includes all employees who were on the payroll during the pay period including March 12.

Utilities sector. Includes all employees who were on the payroll during the pay period including March 12.

www.ingramcontent.com/pod-product-compliance
Lightning Source LLC
Chambersburg PA
CBHW082322220526
45470CB00008B/2379